GW00535644

04301320

THE UNEXPECTED STORY OF NATHANIEL ROTHSCHILD

THE UNEXPECTED STORY OF NATHANIEL ROTHSCHILD

John Cooper

BLOOMSBURY

LONDON · OXFORD · NEW YORK · NEW DELHI · SYDNEY

Bloomsbury Continuum
An imprint of Bloomsbury Publishing Plc

50 Bedford Square
London
WC1B 3DP
UK

1385 Broadway
New York
NY 10018
USA

www.bloomsbury.com

Bloomsbury, Continuum and the Diana logo are trademarks of
Bloomsbury Publishing Plc

First published 2015

British Library Cataloguing-in-Publication Data
A catalogue record for this book is available from the British Library.

Library of Congress Cataloguing-in-Publication data has been applied for.

ISBN: HB: 9781472917065
ePub: 9781472917072
ePdf: 9781472917089

2 4 6 8 10 9 7 5 3 1

Typeset by Fakenham Prepress Solutions, Fakenham, Norfolk NR21 8NN

Printed and bound in Great Britain by CPI Group (UK) Ltd, Croydon CR0 4YY

CONTENTS

LIST OF ILLUSTRATIONS

1   Portrait of Nathaniel, 1st Lord Rothschild (1840–1915), by Herbert Horowitz. Private Collection. Reproduced with the permission of the Trustees of the Rothschild Archive Trust Limited.

2   'Pillars of the City – A Scene on Change', sketch by Lockhart Bogle from *The Graphic*, 9 May 1891, showing Nathaniel Rothschild standing in front of a pillar, his son Walter and between them Carl Meyer. Reproduced by permission of the British Library.

3   'The Anti-Budget Pageant', cartoon from the *Westminster Gazette*, 16 June 1909, showing Nathaniel Rothschild standing between Arthur Balfour and Austen Chamberlain, the Opposition leaders. Reproduced by permission of the British Library.

4   'The City Penguins', cartoon from the *Westminster Gazette*, 28 June 1909, showing Lord Avebury, Sir Felix Schuster and Nathaniel Rothschild confronting Asquith and Lloyd George. Reproduced by permission of the British Library.

5   Tring Park, country estate of Nathaniel Rothschild. Main entrance, 1889. Reproduced with the permission of the Trustees of the Rothschild Archive Trust Limited.

ACKNOWLEDGEMENTS

Letters from the Royal Archives are reproduced by gracious permission of Her Majesty the Queen. I also acknowledge the permission to quote material from the following archives: Bodleian Libraries, Oxford; the British Library, London; the Central Archives for the History of the Jewish People, Jerusalem; Central Zionist Archives, Jerusalem; Hatfield House, the correspondence of the 3rd Marquess of Salisbury; Industrial Dwellings Society, London; London Metropolitan Archives; National Achives, London; National Maritime Museum, Greenwich; Rhodes House, Oxford; Rothschild Archive, London; School of Slavonic and East European Studies, London; Southampton University, Anglo-Jewish Archives; Yivo Archives, Lucien Wolf-David Mowshowitch Collection, New York. Dr Tessa Murdoch kindly granted me permission to quote from the Carl Meyer correspondence. It has not always been possible to trace copyright holders, and I beg the indulgence of any I may have missed.

I owe a special debt of gratitude to Melanie Aspey and her assistants Justin Cavernelis-Frost and Natalie Broad at the Rothschild Archive. I should also like to record my gratitude for the invaluable assistance of Pamela Clark at the Royal Archives; Professor Aubrey Newman; Paul Westbrook of the Industrial Dwellings Society; Vicki Perry at Hatfield House; Reneé Vincent, who checked some Alliance Israélite records in Paris; Dr Gerry Black for permission to quote from his books; and my brother Rabbi Dr Martin Cooper for his hospitality and unstinted help in New York; and the archivists and librarians at all the above mentioned institutions plus my local library at Swiss Cottage.

All who write about the English Rothschilds owe a great debt to Richard Davis and Niall Ferguson for their magnificent pioneering research.

I would also like to thank my son Zaki for his introduction to Robin Baird-Smith of Bloomsbury and the splendid editorial team he has around him of Jamie Birkett and Kim Storry, Jill Morris and Josephine Bacon.

I dedicate this book to my wife Judy without whose unflagging encouragement I might have started this book but would not have finished it.

INTRODUCTION

Nathaniel Mayer ('Natty'), the first Lord Rothschild, ordered that his papers were to be destroyed after his death. For the most part, his wishes were carried out. Little of his vast correspondence survives, save for a journal kept by his mother, Baroness Charlotte de Rothschild, chronicling his development during his childhood, some letters to his parents while he was studying at Cambridge, some business and general correspondence with his French cousins in the Edwardian era and a small batch of miscellaneous letters. Chapter 1 shows how Natty developed into a sensitive and secretive young man so as to avoid the prying eyes of his hyper-critical mother, whom he loved very much, although he found it hard to win her praise. His penchant for revealing very little about himself, his private thoughts and inner passions, was reinforced when Disraeli chose him to be the junior executor of his estate. After the death of Lord Rowton (Montagu Corry), Disraeli's literary executor, it became the duty of Sir Philip Rose to trawl through Natty's hero's extensive correspondence to vet it before unwelcome items were disclosed in an authorized biography of the Prime Minister by Monypenny and Buckle. To protect his reputation, the executors burnt Disraeli's somewhat chaotic financial correspondence with the Rothschild family and kept hidden the fact that Disraeli had fathered two children, Ralph Nevill and Catherine Donovan, outside marriage. His co-executor had reminded Natty in the past that Disraeli's will did not provide for an 'infant beneficiary', but that this child would have a good claim against the estate if an action were brought to claim an allowance.[1]

Nor was this the end of Natty's troubles as an executor of Disraeli's estate. On 8 October 1907, Francis Knollys, King Edward VII's private secretary, wrote to him that 'The King understands it is very probable that letters of a very confidential and family nature may have been written by the late Queen to Lord Beaconsfield between 1874 and 1880', and requested that all such letters in Mr Monypenny's possession should be sent to the King for him to look over. Highly embarrassed by the royal involvement in this affair, Natty related that after Disraeli's death Sir Philip Rose

> took charge of all Lord Beaconsfield's papers and letters, examined them thoroughly and had them arranged in a somewhat perfunctory manner by his head clerk, Mr Scanes. This was absolutely necessary, as a good many legal documents had to be found and accounted for, and there were also a good many letters referring to incidents in the lives of Lord Lyndhurst, Colonel Stanley and others, which had to be separated from the mass of papers ... I am writing this at full length to you so that both you and His Majesty should be aware that the various documents which I have in my possession were seen, and probably carefully examined, by many people before they were entrusted to me at New Court ... [Monypenny] has just been here and has told me in which box the letters from Her Majesty the Queen to Lord Beaconsfield were carefully collected and put together, and I send them to you for His Majesty's perusal. I am afraid it will take a very long time to read them and I shall be much obliged, when they have been read, if you will return them to me at New Court (as I only hold them as trustee of the Hughenden Estate), retaining those that do not refer to political affairs, if His Majesty should so think best to keep the strictly private letters.[2]

Knollys informed Natty that the King was 'horrified to hear that these confidential & also some secret Family Papers should have been seen by Sir Philip Rose's Head Clerk's Brother, by Mr Moberley Bell and Mr Monypenny'. A few weeks later, he stated that the King 'has kept, &

1   Stanley Weintraub, *Disraeli: A Biography* (New York, 1993), pp. 427–36. *Dictionary of National Biography*, Vol. 47 (Oxford, 2004), p. 767, Sir Philip Frederick Rose.
2   RA,VIC MAIN/W/41/5 Lord Knollys to Natty 8 October 1907; VIC MAIN/X/33/336 Natty to Lord Knollys 31 October 1907.

proposes to destroy, the letters relating to Family matters' and thought it 'incredible that the late Queen could have been aware that the most sacred letters & papers relating to the Royal Family had been examined & in some instances annotated by Mr Scanes & his Brother, two men who were utterly unknown to her either personally or by repute'.[3] Natty did his best to contain the King's ire, denying that Moberley Bell had seen the correspondence. In a later letter, he thanked Knollys for returning the tin box which had contained the correspondence, continuing that he 'had nothing to do with the Beaconsfield papers until they were brought here, arranged as you see them by Mr Skanes and his brother. Lord Rowton positively assured me that he had Her Majesty's – the late Queen's – permission for what took place and that he had, on various occasions, taken Mr Skanes down to Windsor to copy various letters'. He could give the King an assurance that he had never employed Scanes and had not even looked at the papers for more than two years.[4] With this final flourish, Natty extracted himself from a situation fraught with snares, hoping that he had kept his long-standing friendship with Edward intact. Meanwhile he was even more determined than ever that none of the secrets of his own life should be exposed after his death, that neither his family, business nor his diplomatic secrets, would become the subject of everyday gossip. Hence, after these experiences and being secretive by nature, he arranged for the destruction of the bulk of his own correspondence.

Niall Ferguson, in his masterly study of the Rothschild Bank, has gone into great detail concerning Natty's participation in general diplomacy, particularly his attempts to stop the Boer War and the outbreak of the First World War. So this biography, while not ignoring this past research, will shift its focus to Natty's diplomatic moves to ameliorate the condition of Russian Jewry and to assess how successful he was. Before proceeding further, however, it became necessary in Chapter 2 to outline his training as a banker, his emergence as a country gentleman and an M.P., and his ennoblement as the first Jewish peer. Chapter 3 describes how the British government stabilized political and economic conditions in Egypt, following its purchase of shares in the Suez Canal Company with the

3   4 and 24 November 1907.
4   RA, VIC/MAIN/x/33/342 Natty to Knollys 25 November 1907.

assistance of the Bank and Baron Lionel de Rothschild, this also being an affair in which Natty was deeply involved; this in turn led to the British occupation of Egypt and the recruitment of British civil servants to sort out its finances due to the scale of British investment, thereby paving the way for a series of profitable Egyptian loans issued by the Rothschild Bank under Natty's leadership. Natty and his brothers, growing more confident in their role as bankers, were persuaded to invest in the diamond and gold mines of South Africa. Thus, the sustained growth of the Rothschild Bank in the 1880s and 1890s coincided with a renewed period of expansion of the British Empire. At the time, Natty cooperated closely with British civil servants in the colonies, of whom the most outstanding was Alfred Milner. The British branch of the Bank reached a peak of prosperity at the end of the nineteenth century, when Baron Alphonse of the Paris house induced Natty to invest in the Rio Tinto copper mines in Spain; the British house made further gains in this sector, by securing a stake in a huge copper mine in Montana.

Without the prosperity of the British house of Rothschild, it would be difficult to explain Natty's growing prestige as a diplomat, particularly insofar as the plight of the Jews in Russia was concerned. In a series of chapters, starting with Chapter 4, his role as a *shtadlan* (intercessor) is examined in great detail. His response to the first wave of pogroms in 1881 was uncertain, as none of the remedies he suggested seemed to work. A memorial presented to the Tsar was rejected, while other European leaders rebuffed his proposal for an international Jewish delegation to appeal personally to the Russian ruler. Much against his will, Natty, who preferred secret diplomacy through back-door channels, was forced to agree to a large public protest meeting. Meanwhile, his brother-in-law, Baron Alphonse, introduced a new strategy of boycotting state loans to Russia until concessions were wrung out of a recalcitrant government. When the Jews were expelled from Moscow and Kiev in 1890 and a fresh exodus of Jews began from Russia, the Lord Mayor of London summoned a public protest meeting. This was boycotted by Natty and the Paris house refused to go ahead with a new state loan to Russia. A key role in this refusal was attributed to Natty's pressure on Alphonse, but whatever the truth of the matter he now ennobled as Lord Rothschild emerged from the scene with enhanced prestige and was now a significant player on the international scene. Chapter 5 describes the persistence with which Theodor Herzl sought Natty's help in the establishment of a Jewish colony in Palestine or close to its borders or even way beyond its borders in Uganda, since Natty enjoyed such excellent relations with the Imperial wing of the British government.

Because a Jewish colony in Palestine was seen as an alternative to the United States and Argentina as a destination for emigrant Russian Jewry, Herzl gave evidence before the Royal Commission on Alien Immigration; this leads, in the chapter, to a discussion of Natty's role as a member of the Commission and the implementation of the Aliens Act.

Chapter 6 continues to discuss Natty's policy towards the Tsarist regime, preceded by his activities on behalf of Jewish communities in Persia, Morocco and Romania, in order to assess the success of such interventions. This is followed by a more detailed account of Natty's role at the time of the Kishinev pogrom and the widespread violence against the Jews in Eastern Europe in 1905–6 which caused casualties on a much larger scale than the earlier pogroms of the 1880s. Even if Natty had become the titular head of world Jewry at the time of these disturbances in Russia and assisted the relief operations, the question has to be asked as to how effective his leadership was then and in the aftermath of the Russian Revolution of 1905.

In Chapter 7, Natty's role as a philanthropist is examined in an attempt made to assess the scale of his beneficence and also to focus on the charities on which he lavished his time and energy. Proud of his role as a model benefactor, Natty believed that the state should play a minimal role in the provision of social services, though he gradually became aware that the Liberal government was moving in the opposite direction. As a leader of City opinion, he led the opposition to the Licensing Bill which he saw as an attack on the property-owning classes and to the 1909 Budget, emerging from the campaign which is dealt with in the following chapter, in which he is shown as a national, if somewhat reviled figure. Chapter 9 is a discussion of how Natty's role as an intercessor lost much of its significance when a final effort on behalf of Russian Jewry failed in 1908. Control of the Anglo-Jewry's 'foreign policy' was wrested by Lucien Wolf both from the Conjoint Committee of the Anglo-Jewish Association and the Board of Deputies as well as from Lord Rothschild himself. The final chapter reveals why Natty's popularity remained at a low ebb before 1914, but experienced a dramatic recovery at the onset of the Great War when he cast aside personal interests and, as Chairman of the Council of the British Red Cross, collected over half a million pounds on behalf of the wounded soldiers and became an advocate of higher taxation that impacted heavily on the wealthy.

1

THE EDUCATION OF AN ENGLISH GENTLEMAN

Hannah Rothschild, travelling on the Continent to attend her son Lionel's wedding to his cousin wrote a note to her younger son, Nat, who had been left in charge of the family bank in London. She asked him to order some choice items from Gunter's, the famous pastrycooks, and to ship them with some grapes for the wedding in Frankfurt. Mrs Rothschild journeyed at a slow pace because her husband, Nathan Mayer Rothschild, a financial genius who had forged the pre-eminence of the Rothschild Bank in London, had fallen ill with a painful abscess on his buttocks.[1]

On 13 June 1836, two days after her seventeenth birthday, Charlotte married her cousin Lionel, some ten years her senior, and moved from Frankfurt to a new life in England. Although she was brought up for the first eight years or more of her life in Naples, where her father Carl von Rothschild was based, Charlotte and her three younger brothers, Mayer Carl, Adolph and Wilhelm Carl, were educated in Germany at the insistence of her father.[2] Shortly after their wedding, Nathan Mayer Rothschild died and Lionel, with his mother and brothers, sat *shivah* – the traditional

---

1 George Ireland, *Plutocrats. A Rothschild Inheritance* (London, 2007), pp. 5–7.
2 Stanley Weintraub, *Charlotte and Lionel: A Rothschild Love Story* (New York, 2003), pp. 21–2.

week-long Jewish mourning period – for his father. It was a depressing start to a marriage.

The mourning was to continue for a year, with lesser restrictions. Quickly, Lionel and his brothers became preoccupied with reviving the fortunes of the Rothschild Bank in London, leaving Charlotte isolated for long, tedious parts of the day, without the company of her family and friends in Germany. 'I felt my life to be gloomy because it was spent in England in the land & city of fogs', Charlotte remembered,

> because I missed the bright skies of other climes, the more exhilarating air of other countries, because I allowed the dense atmosphere of the metropolis to weigh down my spirits, which had been buoyant, because I was far away from my [adoring] parents, [affectionate] brothers and friends, because I knew no one in this large metropolis save those who seem so much engrossed by their own painful feelings & regrets [meaning her mother-in-law Hannah and family] to bestow indulgent thoughts on the stranger.[3]

Although the young couple were in love, 'with many a fond look and kiss from dimpled lips and brilliant eye', Lionel had little time to spare for his beautiful wife. Sexually experienced at the time of his marriage, he had had a brief liaison with a Spanish lady friend.[4] His marriage was, therefore, as much dynastic as a love match. He and his brothers busied themselves at the family bank, N. M. Rothschild & Sons, dealing with the falling price of British government securities and the stock crisis in the American market, which led the bank to register a loss at the end of the year. He 'was never with me between the hours of ten in the morning & 6 in the evening. Oh! Why did I waste those hours in vain regrets, in tears?' Charlotte recalled. 'Why did I not then ardently and assiduously apply [myself] to study? Possibly that would have dried my tears and made my thoughts flow into pleasant and profitable channels. I could have accomplished much in those days, when if I had no joys, I also had few cares, and domestic duties to fulfil'.[5] Charlotte, who had received a thorough grounding in English and French – besides the German which she already spoke – to prepare her for

---

3   RAL 000/1067 Leonora p. 2.
4   Weintraub, *Charlotte and Lionel*, p. 55; Ireland, *Plutocrats*, p. 161.
5   RAL OOO/1067 Leonora pp. 3 and 4; Ireland, *Plutocrats*, pp. 166–7.

marriage to a kinsman from another branch of the family, enjoyed intellectual stimulation and was later to correspond with Gladstone on matters of theology.

From this welter of gloom and depression, Charlotte was lifted by the birth of her first child, her eldest daughter Leonora (Laury) on 25 August 1837. Her arrival was greeted by Charlotte in ecstatic terms: 'My eldest child one whose birth was happiness so exquisite to me, felicity so perfect, bliss so unexpectedly great that the moments which followed her appearance in this world of joys and cares, sweep away at once all recollection of past sufferings, of moral anxiety & anguish, of physical pain & fatigue.' Her bliss was punctured a month later, when Hannah Mayer Rothschild tactlessly described the baby as looking 'like a frog or a toad', causing a fresh flow of tears on Charlotte's part.[6]

Towards the end of 1836, Lionel and Charlotte began living in their new home at 148 Piccadilly; here she filled her hours with a house to manage and a baby to nurse and probably felt more contented.[7] However, when Charlotte gave birth to a second daughter, Evelina, in 1839, she admitted that though the birth was 'less painful', it was 'followed by less intense joy than Laury's arrival. Perhaps I was disappointed in not having a son'. But

> Her father [Lionel] was not in the room at the time she made her appearance in this world ... He was neither glad nor sore to hear of her arrival, and thought her rather plain than otherwise when he condescended to look at her tiny face. As she was my second child and only a girl, no one thought much of her, and she passed through the earlier months & years of infancy unnoticed except by me.[8]

Then, on 8 November 1840, Charlotte gave birth to a son, Nathaniel Mayer Rothschild, followed by two more sons, Alfred born in 1842 and Leopold in 1845. To his mother Charlotte, a bookish, tall, beautiful woman with pronounced feminist opinions and confident in the merits of her own sex, Natty's birth was welcomed with reservations. Despite being born a Rothschild, she could not quite share her husband's dynastic concerns, and

6   RAL 000/1067 Leonora p. 1; Ireland, *Plutocrats*, p. 167.
7   Weintraub, *Charlotte and Lionel*, p. 52.
8   RAL 000/1067 Leonora p. 9 and Evelina p. 2.

as a feminist resented her own neglect by Lionel and his lack of enthusiasm for their daughters. In contrast to her effusive welcome for Leonora, she greeted Natty's arrival in a niggardly and somewhat mean manner, directing some of her pent-up resentment and frustration at her young son. Charlotte reluctantly admitted:

> My eldest son Nathaniel was ... a thin ugly baby but that did not signify, he was a boy and as such most welcome to his father & the whole family. I never could prefer him to his sisters. I nursed him not so well as he ought to have been nursed for he was a ugly child, and I was not a robust mother, could not give him nourishment enough. During his infancy he remained most delicate, and at times gave me great uneasiness. The nursing process fatigued him, and later he caught measles, the chickenpox and other infantine fevers which weakened him very much and kept him back in every respect. Now he is eight years & half old, tall and slight for his age being handsome & distinguished looking in repose but not graceful walking, reclining or dancing and also less good looking when speaking than when sitting.[9]

Charlotte was, perhaps, too objective, too clinical in her assessment, lacking in maternal warmth. Exposed to a lack of warmth from his mother, Natty was a shy child, who withdrew into himself, and quickly learnt to conceal his inner thoughts and feelings from others. Although inept in company, Charlotte conceded in 1849 that Natty

> is really amiable, that is to say mild, gentle, kind to all around him & most affectionately devoted to his father and brothers & sisters but he lacks cordiality & frankness, he is reserved & shy and not generous; in fact, he is the only one of my children fond of money for the sake of hoarding it.[10]

His redeeming feature was his devotion to his father and his excellent relations with his siblings which gradually gave him the confidence, as the eldest son, to assume, in the course of time, the leadership of the family. On the other hand, Charlotte complained that although her two daughters

> share[d] the same rooms, the same studies, the same pleasures, have

9   Ibid., Natty pp. 1–3.
10   RAL 000/1067 Natty p. 3. Richard Davis, *The English Rothschilds* (London, 1983), p. 111.

the same teachers, are even dressed alike, they do not experience those feelings of deep & devoted sisterly affection which would add so much to their happiness throughout life ... It but seldom happens that Laury consents to share the amusements of her brothers & sister.

As for Natty, Charlotte's catalogue of criticisms continued. He was 'constitutionally indolent and does not learn with great rapidity or facility', even though she admitted that he had an excellent memory for 'names, facts, events & even dates'. Nevertheless, he was 'extremely fond of reading', which would give him the basis for becoming a cultured gentleman.[11]

A year later Charlotte quoted an assessment of Natty's character and accomplishments by his tutor which was similar to her own.

Master N. Is very kindhearted & benevolent ... [He] venerates what is great & good and is gentlemanly in his feelings. He has not much self-esteem but he is fond of praise. A little vain, a little peevish but not often violent – Generally acts up to the dictates of conscience but he must avoid the temptations of bad companions – No fighter he can conceal his thoughts & feelings and is rather sly ... He has a great deal of imagination and is fond of the sublime & beautiful in nature and in fiction – Fond of order. Not mathematical but he must practise arithmetic! Fine talents for history and miscellaneous information. He has a good memory ... [no] talent for music. Not mechanical – Fine taste for drama & for astronomy. He has good talents for learning languages and can appreciate their beauties – this remark applies *more* to foreign languages than to the classics ... The reflective faculties are, at present, only moderate. Everything must be adapted by a sensible teacher to bring out' how he judges the matter.[12]

Charlotte noted that her eldest son was making some progress. Natty 'certainly writes German better than he did ... he speaks it more fluently and I can say the same with respect to his French and English'. At the close of 1850 she added that Natty 'is thought handsome and gentlemanlike looking but remains less prepossessing than Alfred owing to his shyness & reserve. His memory remains very good and his teachers are satisfied with him ... He writes English, German & Hebrew with great difficulty

11   RAL 000/1067, Leonora pp. 10–11; Natty, p. 4.
12   Ibid., pp. 5–6.

and very slowly indeed'. Next year, at the age of ten, he was 'to begin Mathematics & Greek'. As always with Charlotte, there was some positive comment counter-balanced by a cutting assessment of Natty's character and prospects. 'I find him more talkative & ambitious than he was,' Charlotte confided to her notebook, 'he also expresses himself better than he did and speaks both French & German more fluently. I do not think he will ever be a clever man, but I hope he will become a cultivated well-informed one, a useful member of society.' On 3 September 1851, she regretfully noted that 'I wish I could say that much improvement has taken place [since last December]. I will not, must not give way to illusions.' Charlotte was not satisfied that their tutor had 'brought the children sufficiently forward and ... [she was] determined to give them to a new one.'[13]

When he was twelve, Natty started to mature and grow in confidence, basking in the warmth and appreciation of his father and the wider family and, at the same time, realizing that as the eldest son and heir he had opportunities as well as responsibilities. At the end of 1853, Natty would celebrate his Bar Mitzvah, that is, he would become an adult in Jewish law. This goal allowed him to focus his efforts more carefully and utilize his talents to achieve more creditable educational results. On 4 January 1854, Charlotte happily declared that

> A whole year has elapsed since last I opened this little book and I have thank God nothing to chronicle but what is satisfactory. Natty being shy & nervous is not appreciated in Society ... [But he] succeeded in rousing his dormant ambition, & overcoming his constitutional indolence. His confirmation for which he laboured & studied most conscientiously proved the sincerity of his zeal and by application to his German lessons he made rapid progress. This autumn I trust he may improve in the French language and that he will ere long be able to express himself better in English, both verbally and pen in hand.[14]

In 1853, Dr Marcus Moritz Kalisch (1828–85), having studied at Berlin University and a rabbinical college, joined Baron Lionel's household at Gunnersbury, in order to tutor the Rothschild children in Hebrew; and here, where he became a much loved member of the family, he enjoyed

13   Ibid., Natty pp. 9, 11, 12.
14   Ibid., Natty pp. 22–3.

the leisure to produce his acclaimed commentaries on the Bible. Natty on one occasion 'informed us', his cousin Annie noted, 'that Dr Kalisch was at home so we three set out in the dark, well cloaked and bonneted to see him. We found him in his funny little low room in his dressing-gown. We all went in and Evy and Natty began to talk the most absurd nonsense ...', which shows another side to Natty than the solemn little boy portrayed by his mother.[15] In all probability Dr Kalisch was engaged to coach Natty for his *Bar Mitzvah* and the sudden improvement in his German may perhaps be attributed to his new tutor's influence. Under the heading 'Confirmation at the Great Synagogue', which stood in Duke's Place, London, the *Jewish Chronicle* reported that

> On Sabbath morning last [19 November 1853], the eldest son of Baron de Rothschild M.P., having attained the age of thirteen years, was called to the reading-desk, during the Reading of the Holy Law, and read a portion, according to the custom on such occasions. The amount of offerings on the occasion was about 130L. The Baroness being in the twelve months' mourning for her mother, the event was celebrated in the mere family circle, but ever watchful to do good when and where good can be done, the Baroness has determined to apprentice as many poor boys (13) as was the age of her son.[16]

At the same time, Natty's growing maturity and new sense of responsibility is demonstrated by the admonitions contained in the greetings to his younger brother Leopold on the occasion of his eighth birthday, although the letter is also suffused with fraternal warmth.

> Many happy returns on your birthday dearest Leopold. I wish you may always be happy, good and wise. You are now entering your eighth year and I hope you will turn over a new leaf and be very attentive to your lessons and good towards all your teachers. Your brother who loves you very much & hopes you will improve. Natty de Rothschild.[17]

Natty was fast absorbing some of his mother's conscientiousness and perfectionist streak. Nor was this altogether surprising, as Natty and his slightly

15   Lucy Cohen, *Lady de Rothschild and her Daughters 1821–1931* (London, 1935), p. 81.
16   *Jewish Chronicle* 25 November 1853.
17   RAL 000/12 Natty to Leopold Rothschild 22 November 1852.

younger brother Alfred were subjected to a strict tutorial regime. Alfred seems to have been bright but lazy. For the period 1852–3 a journal survives in which the two boys' daily lessons were recorded by a tutor with the marks allotted and comments added if they fell below the standard expected. Thus, on Monday 21 June 1852 Natty was studying French, German, Arithmetic, Latin Grammar, Latin translation, and doing exercises in the same language. The comment was that 'There are good marks for Lat [in] Translat [ion] and French, but only half marks for Arith[metic]'. On the same day for Alfred it was recorded that 'For French there is a very bad account; for Music very good. For Latin a good one'. What is certain is that Natty continued to benefit from private tuition at home and Niall Ferguson's suggestion that he attended a gymnasium in Frankfurt for three years must be discounted. It appears to arise from a confusion between Natty and his Frankfurt namesake Nathaniel Mayer Rothschild, who was born in 1836. The other surprising feature of the journal was that both Natty and Alfred continued their secular educational studies on a Saturday including an arithmetic lesson which must have involved writing and thus not even a minimal attempt at observance of the Sabbath.[18]

As he advanced through the years of adolescence, Natty made progress in his studies and Charlotte reported in 1855 that he was interested

in a variety of things & pursuits; in business & in politics, in curiosities of every kind & sort, in farming, in the cultivation of fruit, flowers & vegetables. He reads diligently and likes both history & poetry. He is studying botany, and wishes to resume his drawing lessons, which I am delighted to hear ... He improves I am told in his Latin & mathematical studies & knows arithmetic well, also history but is less quick than Alfred ... He rides better than he did and has a beautiful handwriting.[19]

A year later, Charlotte asserted that

Natty continued to take great interest in botany, agriculture, the natural history of domestic animals ... He talks to the cook of the price of

18   RAL 000/32/23 Journal of lessons of Natty and Alfred 1852–3; Niall Ferguson, *The World's Banker: The History of the House of Rothschild* (London, 1998), pp. 550 and 1162 note 254. RAL CPHDCM Report of Dr Classen of Frankfurt Gymnasium 5 October 1854.
19   RAL 000/1067 Natty pp. 27–30.

provisions ... the arrangement and management of the stables & of the farm – the kitchen garden – the orchard, the greenhouses claim his attention and he understands all these matters perfectly well.

Accordingly, Natty was not only being trained for a career in the bank with the emphasis on arithmetic and fluency in French and German to carry out financial transactions with his Rothschild relatives without unnecessary glitches, but he was being prepared to oversee the management of a great estate, to live the life of a country gentleman. Even so, 'He was a less good linguist than his brothers.' Natty was

> careful of money, economical even as regards himself but kind & charitable without any ostentation ... he has endeavoured to overcome his shyness, and has yielded to his father's wishes in trying to make speeches on given subjects. I must say that his speeches though not so well delivered as Alfy's have been remarkably good.

He was thus being groomed by his father, on whom he still doted, for a career in public life as a leader of the Jewish community and hopefully – when emancipation came – as an M.P. Charlotte concluded that 'what maternal zeal can do shall be done', rightly understanding that 'Scolding is of no use – perseverance will I trust overcome difficulties.' All this was a very rigorous and effective educational programme, despite Charlotte's doubts and interruptions to her plans for her children's tuition, which would gain Natty admission to Cambridge and prepare him for the wider world.[20]

Charlotte remained solicitous and more than a trifle anxious about Natty's studies before he went to university, writing to Leo that 'dear Natty is laboriously, but I hope, successfully solving problems, which to my dull brain prove terrible stumbling blocks ... Juliana has most kindly invited me to dine in Piccadilly tomorrow, but I do not like to leave Natty alone, and, he, you know, cannot quit his books.' Even if she could not be as loving towards him as the genial Leo, the youngest in the family, she was nevertheless a dutiful and caring mother. A few years later she reminded Leo not to 'forget to congratulate Natty, who attains his majority on the

20 Ibid., pp. 33–7; Constance Battersea, *Reminiscences of Lady Battersea* (London, 1922), p. 38.

8th ... and, if you can, send him a letter worthy of the occasion, of him, and of yourself'.[21]

In October 1859 Natty went up to Trinity College Cambridge, probably to study Mathematics rather than Moral Science, a subject which then embraced moral philosophy, political economy, modern history, general jurisprudence and the laws of England.[22] Not being entitled to the exemption then granted to aristocrats, Natty had to sit for an examination known as the 'Little Go', which was taken at the end of the fifth term. This preliminary examination had a strong mathematical content, so that entrants had to master various books of Euclid, elementary algebra and mechanics as well as Latin and Greek set texts, including one of the Gospels in Greek, and an anti-Deist tract, William Paley's *Evidences of Christianity*.[23] Having emerged from a very structured form of education at home, Natty took his studies seriously and soon settled into a disciplined and somewhat strenuous routine. Writing to his family during his stay in Cambridge, Natty described how he spent his day as follows:

> I breakfast every morning at 8 and work in my rooms till 11 from which time till 2 I am engaged with the College lectures & Wright [his coach], 2–4 is devoted to exercise 4–5 to dinner 5–6 to the *Times* and letter writing 6–7 to Wright, 7–8 to sleep 8–1 to Paley and Sophocles, and in order to accomplish the last named fact I have taken to drinking strong Green tea, except on Saturday nights when I take more sleep and read the weekly newspaper. Baillie comes to breakfast in the morning and Wood, Fitzwilliam, Bourke, Fletcher & Henniker to dinner at 4, except when out with the Drag [hounds] or in the Hall.[24]

A drag is a scent laid by an attendant prior to the hunt, not the 'scent of a live fox or hare'.[25] On another occasion, he told his parents that he did

not care much about the Greek but like the Greek history connected

21   RAL Fam C/21 Charlotte to Leo 6 September 1859 and 6 November 1861.
22   Ferguson, *The World's Banker*, p. 741.
23   RAL 000/12 Natty to his parents undated 1860 item 90.
24   Ibid., Natty to his parents undated 1860 item 57.
25   Jane Ridley, *Bertie A Life of Edward VII* (London, 2012), p. 51.

with the time very much. Till now the [George] Grote has not made its appearance. I shall only want the XI & XII volumes [of the History of Greece] which I suppose I must read ... I am at present engaged in reading Todhunter's Trigonometry, and so far as it goes is amusing and easy that is for a book on mathematics.[26]

Such a hectic and sustained work pattern without a period in the afternoon set aside for relaxation could not be endured for long and soon Natty was explaining to his parents why he had varied it, by giving more time to exercise and outdoor activities, as well as the Amateur Dramatic Club. He complained about

the *complete* misconception you have of what is conducive to my work and health here; last year I followed your advice and took no tiring exercises of any kind. My work did not improve; on the contrary grew gradually worse and my condition and health suffered materially as my feeble efforts in the hunting field during the vacation showed. I have found by experience that in order to get on here at all it is *absolutely* necessary to take 2 hours at least of violent exercise *per diem*, so that if I do not go with the drag [hounds] I must do something else in the same way, but as riding after hounds for a short time suits my taste better than being knocked down at football by Bob Lang or Sir G[eorge] Young than rowing in a bad boat or following the foot drag unless I have your positive commands *to the contrary* [I shall follow this pursuit], and all the more particularly as I see in those who read hard take far more exercise than I do.[27]

After enduring some more criticism from his parents when he became stage manager of the Amateur Dramatic Club, Natty protested that

The ADC takes up some time, but I have found I do not one bit more if I do nothing but work and only destroy my health, and make the life here a curse and plague, in addition to which, I have very little to do with the theatricals whilst some of the actors will be in for the Little Go at the time and three or four are men likely to take high honours.[28]

26 RAL 000/12 Natty to his parents undated c. 1860 item 111.
27 Ibid., Natty to his parents undated, probably 6 November 1860 item 7.
28 Ibid., Natty to his parents probably 26 February 1860 item 78.

Natty struggled hard to pass this preliminary examination, telling his parents in the spring of 1861 that 'Half of the University are busy with approaching examinations ... I was rather sorry to see that you had mentioned the Little Go in the Metropolis as it is more than doubtful if I shall get through.' Once plunged into the examination, Natty told his parents that 'I am by no means sanguine about the result of Little Go, as the worst part is to come and I fully expect to get plucked, at all events to run a very close race.' But gradually, as he became immersed in the examination, his confidence grew and he reported to his parents that

> yesterday morning I went in for the first time and as we were examined in the highest branch of mathematics I stayed in the necessary time ... hitherto I have done pretty well in the Gospel viva voce and in solid Geometry and as I shall be able to do something tomorrow and on Friday, I suppose I shall get through.

His forecast proved to be accurate and he did pass the Little Go examination.[29]

Natty, as a Jew, did not find life in Cambridge entirely congenial. First there was the compulsory attendance at chapel, even if at times he was allowed to restrict it to a bare minimum. His tutor Joseph Lightfoot 'promised to do all he can about Chapel but at present [William] Whewell [Master of the College] is the stumbling block in the way of reform'. Sydney Smith quipped about Whewell that science was his forte and omniscience his failing, so the Master was prepared to grant Natty little leeway. Nevertheless, Natty advised his parents in 1862 that

> The Trinity Dons have just made themselves very unpopular by threatening to gate everyone who refuses to take the sacrament in Chapel; the consequence of this new rule is that a very large number absented themselves from chapel today; and will get into trouble for breaking an important college rule.[30]

Then he had to regurgitate the turgid arguments of William Paley's *Evidences of Christianity*. At the beginning of 1861, Natty informed his parents that

29   Ibid., Natty to his parents undated spring of 1861 items 10, 11 and 94.
30   Ibid., Natty to Lionel undated 1860 item 62; Natty to his parents 16 February 1862 item 17.

I have been trying my hand at Sophocles and Paley, I never was very successful in the former line and the Evidences of Christianity are the most absurd conglomeration of words I ever broke my head over, so that there is *no* danger of my being converted as many up here have prophesied.[31]

Reflecting on the situation, Natty asserted that:

In order to effect anything in the way of reform here [in Cambridge], it will be necessary to wait some time for as long as the universities are looked upon as seminaries for the Church of England, or as part of the established church itself, it will be impossible to do anything more for dissenters ... Each college is allowed to regulate for herself and to refuse admittance to anyone they may object to ... but what certainly ought to be done away with is the necessity to take orders after seven years or the total abandonment of the fellowship ... it is very hard for a conscientious individual ... to be deprived of his fellowship, because he will not declare himself a member of the Church of England. I never could see why a national institution like this which is the stepping stone to legal and political preferments as well as ecclesiastical ones should be ruled by priests as if it were a Jesuit's seminary or a Talmudical school.[32]

Natty in his early days at the university was also upset by an anti-Semitic speech in the Cambridge Union, telling his parents that

My blood boiled with rage when he [the speaker] quoted as a solitary instance of the too great power of the House of Commons the passing of the Jew Bill. I had hoped that the day was gone by for all distinctions of this kind and if I had spoken at once I might have aroused religious passions, not so easy to quell as arouse.[33]

So too, Natty's brother Leo, on a visit to a friend at Worcester College Oxford, recalled a dinner party, mostly consisting of clergymen and college fellows, where the conversation was 'very "shoppy" and turned to 'the mysteries of theology of various doxies, until at last I was so puzzled that I did not dare to open my lips'.[34] His friend feared 'That they might

31   Ibid., undated 1861 item 12.
32   Ibid., 1 February 1860 item 83.
33   Ibid., c. 1860 item 82.
34   RAL 000/22/32 Leo to his parents undated c. 1865.

forget my presence & make some attack upon the Jews!' Fortunately such incidents were uncommon, even if the close relationship between the Church of England and the ancient universities made Jewish students sometimes feel unwelcome. As has been mentioned, Natty's religious mentor was Dr M. M. Kalisch, a truly remarkable figure in Victorian Anglo-Jewry. Before taking up his appointment as religious instructor to the wider Rothschild family, he had been the Chief Rabbi's secretary. On Passover in Lionel's home, where the multifarious members of the Rothschild family assembled, Dr Kalisch presided over the Seder service.[35] From his pen flowed commentaries on the Bible which at first were in the traditional mode but later included a two-part treatise on the Book of Leviticus, in which he argued that the priesthood and sacrificial cult should be dated to the post-Exilic period, thus anticipating the Higher Critical theories of Wellhausen.[36] From time to time, Dr Kalisch visited Natty to give him some form of religious instruction. 'I expect to see Alfred and the Doctor down here on that occasion', Natty told his parents, when referring to some new productions envisaged by the Amateur Dramatic Club. 'I will be killing two birds at one throw, as I am sure Trinity expects my religious instructor to make his appearance periodically'.[37] When on a vacation study session with William Aldis Wright, his mathematics coach at Scarborough, Natty declared that 'Mr Wright is anxiously looking forward to a Hebrew conversation with the little Dr', who was coming on a visit. On another occasion in 1862 he told his parents that Wright went 'the round of the Professors here [in Cambridge] and has mentioned ... Doctor ... [Kalisch's Hebrew] grammar. Wright thinks it would be advisable to present the 6 professors with a copy of the grammar.'[38] It is clear that Dr Kalisch's tuition strengthened Natty's commitment to his Jewish faith, so that he was not unduly worried by confronting an interlocutor with missionary intentions. 'I have just been interrupted by the master of the British & Foreign schools', he reported to his parents,

---

35   Battersea, *Reminiscences of Lady Battersea*, p. 22.
36   *Dictionary of National Biography*, Vol. 30 (Oxford, 2004), p. 867.
37   RAL 000/12 Natty to his parents undated c. 1861 item 129.
38   Ibid., items 85 and 87 and c. 1862 item 54.

who called about a little Jew boy and not content with obtaining an audience for his protégé inflicted me with his own presence for an hour expatiating on the Hebrew language & other subjects in which I flatter myself, I floored him completely.[39]

Natty was in any case brought up in a traditional Jewish manner, even if this was interpreted in a very loose way. According to Stanley Weintraub, Charlotte was reluctant to dine at venues at which non-kosher food was served, but did so, a fact which indicates that there must have been a minimal observance of the dietary code in her own home.[40] On the other hand, Charlotte, when referring to Wilhelm Carl's daughters' kosher diet remarked that 'To eat as they do, means not to eat at all; it is worse than doing penance; while away from home, the ladies seem to me never to get a comfortable meal.'[41]

Nevertheless, Yom Kippur, the fast on the Day of Atonement, was kept strictly. On 14 September 1869 Charlotte wrote to Leo that 'This is a very shabby letter; pray forgive me; I have nothing further to say. Uncle Mayer and Natty fast at New Court, dear Papa, Alfred and I under this roof ...' During Tabernacles, the festival of the ingathering of the harvest and Rejoicing in the Law, Natty was accustomed to keep an *etrog* (citron) and *lulav* (palm branch and appurtenances) in his room at New Court, while for many years Dr Kalisch was at hand to ensure that the Seder service at Passover was conducted properly.[42]

As Natty continued with his studies at Cambridge, he was soon complaining that his new coach, Walton, was very angry with him, as he had only obtained 56 marks out of 350 in a test but that he was

certain he is right when he says to get on here one must be wedded to mathematics and think of nothing else and go nowhere and see no one ... One has very little time for real work here as quantities of time are taken up by lectures talk etc and private coaches. In fact to get into the First Class in May I must not only go to Walton's classes but must be there every day for 2 hours writing out additional papers.[43]

39 Ibid., undated c. 1860 item 111.
40 Weintraub, *Charlotte and Lionel*, p. 130.
41 RAL RFAMC/21 Charlotte to Leo 26–8 September 1864.
42 Ibid., Charlotte to Leo 14 September 1869; *Jewish Chronicle* 4 November 1910, pp. 23–4.
43 RAL 000/12 Natty to his parents undated 1862 item 110.

In a letter to his parents on 24 March 1862, Natty apologized for having

> to lock myself up every night but the interruptions were so numerous last
> week that I really must devote every night to Mathematics till Passover
> ... The academical year finishes on 7 June and the only arrangement
> Lightfoot and Whewell will agree to for the Long Vacation is the
> residence of a Master of Arts in King's Parade with me.[44]

After all this, he advised his parents later in the year that 'Walton is always
telling me I shall be plucked', and then a slightly more hopeful forecast from
his tutor, saying that if Natty 'remained up here and read *very* hard I might
just *scrape* (scrape was the word) through'.[45] But as his tutor's optimism
faded for his success in the final examinations Natty decided to leave
Cambridge at the end of 1862 while his honour was still intact, returning
briefly in January 1863 to settle some outstanding bills.[46]

While at Cambridge, Natty made some new friends and cultivated the
friendship of young men from families who were already part of his father's
circle, such as the Duke of St Albans and Augustus and Arthur Guest of
the iron-making dynasty. The ninth Duke of St Albans, who was descended
from Jacob Israel Bernal, a treasurer of the Bevis Marks Synagogue, was
already a friend of his father and grandfather; and it was natural for Natty
to gravitate into the company of his son, the tenth Duke, and through him
to be introduced into the circle of Edward, the Prince of Wales, who came
up to Cambridge in January 1861. Edward was installed by the Prince
Consort at Madingley Hall, a country house four miles from Cambridge,
under the supervision of General and Mrs Bruce and his Oxford tutor, the
historian Herbert Fisher. At the University of Cambridge during 1861 and
1862 he was tutored in a wide range of subjects, including science, law and
history.[47] As Natty informed his parents,

> The Prince is ... obliged to do everything General Bruce tells him and
> cannot even ask anyone to Madingley, the General only allowing his
> royal pupil to call on St. A[lbans] alone. He has rooms at the Lodge

44 Ibid., 24 March 1862 item 20.
45 Ibid., Natty to his parents undated c. 1862 items 55 and 134.
46 Ibid., 18 January 1863 item 30.
47 Ireland, *Plutocrats*, pp. 75–7, 177–8 and 353; Chaim Bermant, *The Cousinhood* (London, 1971), p. 14; Sidney Lee, *King Edward VII: A Biography* (London, 1925), pp. 113–16.

where the different Regius Professors come and lecture to him, they
say he is not allowed to take any notes but has to write out the lectures
when he gets back to Madingley. I fancy the little spirit he ever had
is quite broken, as his remarks are commonplace and very slow ... St.
A[bans] from a congeniality of disposition and mind is a great favourite
at Windsor and plays tennis every day with the Prince (if indeed either
can play tennis). They say he rode very well yesterday so far as his seat
is concerned, he is excessively fond of the chase but Windsor does not
approve of the national sport and allows him but one hour, and does
not even find horseflesh for his equerries. He is very fond of riddles and
strong cigars and will I suppose eventually settle down into a well disciplined German Prince with all the narrow views of his father's family.
He is excessively polite and that is certainly his redeeming quality. If he
followed the bent of his own inclination, it strikes me he would take to
gambling and certainly keeping away from the law lectures he is obliged
to go to now.[48]

This was a very astute summing up of the Prince's indolent character
and disposition. Natty pointed out several other less pleasant characteristics of Edward, who did not impress him overmuch, particularly
his bullying of 'the weak'. 'Yesterday', Natty reported to his parents, 'the
Prince went out in a boat with some friends and gratified the majority
of his companions by throwing St. Albans into the muddiest and dirtiest
part of the river'.[49] In the summer term, the Prince varied his programme,
by arranging 'a weekly luncheon & cricket party at Madingley every
Wednesday, on which occasion ... the Prince delights in bowling at the
legs of his competitors'. On one occasion the Prince was Natty's partner
in a game of whist which they won by a slim margin. 'We ought to have
won three times as much but his Royal Highness threw away the game,'
an exasperated Natty wrote to his parents. On another occasion Natty
reported that 'Those who played with him on Friday [at a card game] say
he is the worst loser ever seen.'[50] At a drag in the proximity of Newmarket
some thirty Cambridge undergraduates, including Natty, turned out to
accompany the Prince, who

48   RAL 000/12 Natty to his parents undated 1861 item 12.
49   Ibid., items 117 and 128.
50   Ibid., items 93 and 120.

piloted by St. Albans kept to the road, we went over nine miles of ground in 35 minutes and five of the nine miles were over a fine line of country. I never saw anything to be compared to [the Prince of]Wales's riding but I cannot say much for either of his companions as they both seemed to think they were riding on the heath and went off at a pace which soon brought them to eternal grief.[51]

Nevertheless, the Prince did have some redeeming qualities, securing an invitation for Natty when he was not invited to a ball sponsored by the Earl of Hardwicke, a leader of county society, and acting 'as a scarecrow on the Proctors [at university races], who left us alone and did not interrupt the proceedings'. He teased Lady Diana, St Albans' spirited sister, who 'shocked her mother and brother by smoking one of the Prince's cigarettes'.[52] At the end of 1861, Natty advised his parents that 'The Prince told me of the Prince Consort's illness, it seems they are afraid that Gastric fever is epidemic at Windsor, and therefore they will not allow the Prince of Wales to return' there. A few days later he wrote that

you will have heard the very sad news of the Prince Consort's death. On Friday last in the hunting field the Prince was rejoicing over the good news from Windsor and he little expected when we parted at ... Toll Bar that four hours afterwards he wd have to leave a gay party to attend his father's death bed [Prince Albert dying on 14 December 1861].

What is clear is that Natty's sympathetic concern over Albert's illness drew him closer to the Prince of Wales, though he was never on such intimate terms with the Prince as his more affable brothers, Alfred and Leo, or his cousin Ferdinand. For the Rothschild brothers, this sustained friendship with the Prince 'was a social breakthrough' which gave them access to the royal court.[53] Many of Natty's new friendships were formed at the Athenaeum, an exclusive club to which he was elected a member, and the Amateur Dramatic Club, where he was stage manager and in charge of the finances, filling both roles with aplomb. He informed his parents that the end-of-term production of the ADC took place on a Friday and

51 Ibid., Natty to his parents undated item 6.
52 Ibid., items 60, 79 and 102.
53 Ibid., Natty to his parents undated December 1861 items 8 and 9; Ridley, *Bertie*, p. 51.

was I believe a great success; we sold altogether 360 tickets, which brings in £70, the donations for the improvement fund amounts to £123 which with the surplus in hand and the subscriptions make a sum total of £300; our expenses are very heavy this term and will I fancy swallow up all the assets.

The ADC staged 'farces and extravaganzas' and enjoyed the Prince of Wales' patronage which strengthened its position with the university authorities. In one such burlesque, William Everett, son of the former American Minister to the Court of St James, by a virtuoso acting performance 'brought down roars of laughter and peals of applause'. Natty agreed with his brother Alfred, 'that the effect of our theatricals was somewhat marred by the men who acted women's parts, as that is a defect which cannot easily be remedied, we always think ourselves lucky if any one of the women pleases the audience'.[54]

Natty sometimes also participated in the debates in the Cambridge Union, which was a testing ground for later parliamentary and political success. During his student days, Natty was an ardent supporter of Free Trade and Gladstone; though Disraeli was a frequent visitor to Lionel and Charlotte's home, Natty was not enamoured of him. Writing to his parents about one parliamentary debate, he noted that 'Gladstone was quite wonderful, and is another of the frequent instances of the pupil exceeding the master, Dizzy must have been reminded not altogether pleasantly of [18]44 & Sir R[obert] Peel.' As regards Gladstone's 1861 Budget speech, Natty

> was very pleased to see that the City people were pleased with the extension of Free Trade. I was immensely struck by the wonderful eloquence of the Chancellor of the Exchequer and comparing it with the recollections of Dizzy's last budget oration thought it infinitely superior, at the same time even if the eloquence had not been so great, it is a greater speech regarded as a financial statement. I did not expect to see so much done for the lower classes by the present budget and on the whole it is very satisfactory, at the same time one cannot feel quite at ease when the expenditure of the country increases at the rate of 50 per cent.[55]

54 RAL OOO/12 – undated items 6, 130, and 134; Lee, *King Edward VII*, p. 116.
55 RAL OOO/12 Natty to his parents 12 February 1861 item 13 and undated item 78.

On another such parliamentary interlude Natty surmised that 'I do not see how Dizzy can be pleased with himself or with Cobden and if the latter says Ld Palmerston has cost us £100,000 he is cheap at the price, if we have regained our influence in the world.'[56] Elsewhere he remarked that he had 'always thought that one of the chief reasons of Dizzy's unstatesmanlike reputation was his want of patriotism'. 'On Saturday [at Gunnersbury]', he confessed to brother, 'we were honoured by the visit of the great Mr Disraeli who was in very good spirits and is going to Aylesbury on Wednesday next on which occasion I am sorry to say I shall have to meet him there.'[57]

Natty concluded that 'the principle of protection is dead and gone and now it is no longer a question of free trade but of peace on earth and a further diminution of taxes ... Manchester has produced nothing besides cotton, the great Peel, Cobden and last though not least Gladstone'.[58] At a Madingley dinner attended by Natty in 1861,

> the principal topic of conversation was the [prospect] of war with America, it seems that a large number of troops are to be sent to America ... The Prince is very anxious to join his own regiment in Canada and emulate his younger brother's fame ... They talked of our annexing Maine and Portland, but I cd not make out what generals and admirals were to do all these wonders.

On the other hand, Natty observed 'from the positions Lee and Jackson had taken up the Federals will soon be surrounded. I only hope the Confederates will not have it all their own way or else when they have finished with the North, they might make an attempt on Cuba & Mexico.'[59] Natty's attitude was balanced, neither wishing for an expansionist British policy, nor applauding the potential imperialist thrust by the Confederate armies, an attitude similar to that of Karl Marx. Natty's brothers followed him to Trinity College Cambridge, Alfred in 1861 and Leopold – better known as Leo – in 1863. Owing to a confusion with King's College School, which Leo attended, Richard Davis was misled into thinking that Natty's

56   Ibid., item 116.
57   Ibid., Natty to Leo undated item 142.
58   Ibid., Natty to his parents undated items 80 and 90.
59   Ibid., 67 and 97.

brothers attended King's College Cambridge.[60] Alfred was a star of the Amateur Dramatic Club but was indifferent to his studies and after a bout of a prolonged illness left after one year. Leo, a keen student of equine form, stayed the course at Cambridge, though he equally neglected his classical studies, for which he was reprimanded by Natty. 'I was rather disappointed that you had acted so in opposition to my wishes', Natty explained, 'you know I am always glad when you amuse yourself but as I told you on Saturday last the best thing for you to do is to work with your coach'.[61] Like his brother Alfred, Leo was an indifferent student, and wrote to his parents explaining how he spent his day at Cambridge, as they were anxious to know.

> We generally have breakfast at about 9 o'c[lock] & by quarter to ten I begin to read & continue my work until 2 o'c[lock]. As yet my occupations have been of a varied kind, I generally do a paper every day once in Greek the next day in Latin besides this I do some composition & prepare some translation for Mr Foster [his coach], we have been reading the hard passages in the Iliad and the Odyssey & also the difficult Epigrams in Martial one of which is generally set in the Tripos. My worthy coach seems to think that I have been reading very well & is pleased with my work which is a great satisfaction. At 2 o'c[lock] we have dinner & at ten & between those hours I read the papers under the trees & am afraid spend a very idle afternoon – And in the evening I read for an hour & a half or so & then return to bed at 10 o'c[lock]'.

Feeling that he had not sufficiently appeased his parents, he again wrote to them justifying his working habits and telling them that his 'coach seems to be satisfied with what I am doing; I am sure you do not understand that it is not the quantity of classical books which I read through but rather the number of good papers wh. I do that will be of use to me in my Tripos'.[62] As the time approached for his examination results to be declared, Leo told his parents to lower their expectations.

> I really begin to feel sure of getting through the examination, but do not anticipate much more – as Myers reassured me to getting plucked but

60   Davis, *The English Rothschilds*, pp. 110 and 115–16.
61   RAL OOO/12 Natty to Leo undated items 141 and 149.
62   RAL 000/22 Leo to his parents undated items 49 and 77.

told me that my papers were very moderate at best! I am beginning to have a much higher opinion of the difficulties of getting even into the third class of the Classical Tripos ...

When the results of Leo's Tripos examination were announced and he was found to have graduated with third-class honours, Natty did his best to mollify his parents. 'I can assure you my hopes were not very great,' he declared, 'as the Dons told me that the most arduous reading would only have enabled Leo to be in the middle of the second class ... I hope that you will congratulate Leo on having got through as in addition to his disappointment he is afraid you may be displeased.'[63] Leo, unfortunately, was clever but lazy. Natty emerged from this childhood upbringing and university education as a somewhat shy but self-confident young man. Looking back in old age, his cousin Constance, three years his junior, painted a portrait of him as 'rather stiff and stand-offish when we were children ... [with a wonderful] knowledge on many subjects', but his cousin Annie's childhood journals, as we have seen, convey a different picture.[64] His sense of fun never left Natty, even if in adult company it could metamorphose into a barbed witticism, though it was more in evidence in the company of children, to whom he could relate in an easy manner, showering them with sweets, fairy stories, and unexpected gold coins. He was also very attached to his dogs, particularly a pet called Snip.[65] His letters to his parents from Cambridge University show a great sense of political maturity, a set of clearly conceived liberal political principles on free trade, low levels of taxation, and a strong yet not aggressive foreign policy. As he remarked to his parents, 'Dizzy cannot have liked the quotations from *Coningsby* altogether, Bright seems to have been very good and although I am not a peace at any price man, yet I think the estimates might with proper administration be greatly diminished.' On another occasion, he condemned 'a very warlike speech of Lord Palmerston which cannot have a pleasant

---

63 Ibid., Leo to his parents item 87 8 February 1867 and RAL 000/12 Natty to his parents undated item 72.

64 Battersea, *Reminiscences of Lady Battersea*, p. 22; Cohen, *Lady de Rothschild and her Daughters*, p. 81.

65 Miriam Rothschild, *Dear Lord Rothschild: Birds, Butterflies & History* (London, 1983), pp. 47–50 and 207–8.

effect in the City'.[66] What confidence he had was derived from his father's unstinting affection, but he remained somewhat secretive, anxious to avoid the too-close scrutiny of his mother, whom he loved and longed to impress. Natty had been trained for a career in managing a country estate, for a life as a member of the landed gentry with an interest in agriculture and the hunt, and earmarked for a political career, after his father Lionel took his seat in the House of Commons on 28 July 1858. Above all, Natty through his education, had developed habits of industriousness and concentration which stood him in good stead when he entered the family bank, work habits his brothers shared to a lesser degree.

66   RAL OOO/12 Natty to his parents undated items 80 and 126.

2

Natty Joins the Bank and becomes a Country Gentleman

After leaving Cambridge and settling all his outstanding accounts by the beginning of 1863, Natty joined the family bank, N. M. Rothschild & Sons, in St Swithin's Lane close to the Bank of England and other major financial institutions in the City of London. As Natty ordered that his private correspondence was to be destroyed on his death, it is difficult to reconstruct what happened in his early days as a raw recruit to the bank, how his father taught him to judge the downturns and upswings of the markets and passed on to him an understanding of the finer points of international relations, something that is essential for a banker who, like Lionel his father, was to specialize in state loans.

Soon afterwards, Natty was joined in the family enterprise by his brother Alfred and then, a few years later, by Leopold. What is clear from the few items of his brothers' correspondence that survive is that Lionel was a strict disciplinarian, though not without a sense of humour, who drove his sons hard. They were soon plunged into a wide range of the bank's financial activities. Writing to his father on 13 August 1863, Alfred regaled him with the news that

> We sent for Cazenove this morning & have sold 25,000 Mexicans at 39 & 28,000 at 39 1/8 for the end of the month;

they leave off 30¾. The fact is that all the markets have been rather dull ... [August]Belmont [the Rothschilds' American agent] proposes to ship the gold from *New York* to Mexico ... Will you please telegraph what you wish to be done as tomorrow is the day for writing to America. The State Bank remits £26,000 & draws £11,000. We sent £60,000 of gold into the Bank and sold £10,000 of silver at 61 today ... Wagg thinks he can place a large quantity of Turkish loan at 102. Shall we do anything ... [?].[1]

We can see that Alfred was still learning and was very reliant on his father, but learning fast. Writing to Leopold in 1867, using a variant of his nickname of Poodle, Lionel remarked that

We have had a busy day as regards talk, and hope tomorrow to have a profitable one; we just sold a few Italians at a good price considering what they were yesterday, but still much too low — Your brothers are very industrious and have a good deal to do, while others are amusing themselves at Balls.[2]

By the end of 1863, Natty was not only immersing himself in all the Bank's financial activities, but mixing with the City elite, as Lionel reported to Leo. 'In the City today there was the Lord Mayor's show and no business ... Natty is going to the dinner'.[3]

Part of the reason for Natty's limited success as a banker was that, as a third generation Rothschild in the London bank, he was content to follow the business practices of his father, Baron Lionel de Rothschild (1808–79). In a tribute to his friend, John Delane, editor of *The Times*, noted that Lionel's

judgment as to the moment for buying and selling, his delicacy in feeling the pulse of the market, were almost universally deferred to. It may be mentioned that the Irish Famine Loan in 1847 ... was negotiated by Baron Lionel de Rothschild; he raised £16,000,000 for the English Government in 1854, and was for 20 years the agent of the Russian Government. He took a large share in the successful funding of the United States' debt. He provided the funds for the instant purchase of the Suez Canal shares, and managed the business of the group of

1   RAL 000/40/8 Alfred de Rothschild to Lionel 13 August 1863.
2   RAL 000/40/50 Lionel to Leo 11 July 1867.
3   RAL 000/209/34 Lionel to Leo 9 November 1863.

bankers who guaranteed to the German Empire the permanence of the exchanges, and facilitated the payment of the French indemnity.[4]

Nevertheless, Lionel's management style was flawed in certain respects. He relied on state loans as a principal source of business and was reluctant to seek out new opportunities, failing to invest in railways in Britain or to adequately put money into the fast-growing and changing market in the United States. Since the 1850s, the Rothschilds had been reducing their stake in the cotton trade and shifting into other, more profitable American banking operations. Yet, as the eminent economic historian David Landes pointed out, 'The failure to make the United States an integral part of the family network was surely the Rothschilds' biggest strategic mistake ...'[5] In the spring of 1870, August Belmont begged Natty to interest his father in an expansion of their American business, but to say nothing if this would irritate him. 'I have, for the last few years,' Belmont assured Natty, 'offered to your House a variety of trans-actions and negotiations, all of which safe and without risk, some of them paying handsome commission and others would have paid brilliant profits.' Natty chose to ignore this request. Three years later, Belmont told Despard that 'The London House has such immense operations and Government negotiations of a profitable nature always on hand, that I can well understand the small importance which the Baron attaches to the American business ...'. Shortly after Lionel's death, Belmont returned to the same refrain, exclaiming that

> If you had, in 1873, accepted the loan to Mr Vanderbilt, which we offered to you, you would not only have made the handsome commission of 5% on that transaction without *any outlay or risk whatever*, but you would have secured the business of the extensive system of R.[ail] Roads under the Vanderbilt control, both in placing their Bonds ... and in supplying them with Railway iron and other material'.[6]

4   *The Times* 4 June 1879.

5   Kathryn Boodry, 'August Belmont and the Atlantic Trade in Cotton 1837–1865' in *The Rothschild Archive Review 2009–2010*, pp. 13–19. David Landes, *Dynasties* (London, 2008), p. 57.

6   RAL T59/29 August Belmont New York to Natty 27 April 1870; Belmont to Despard 20 May 1873; and Belmont to N. M. Rothschild & Sons 28 October 1879.

Because of the firm's focus on financing international loans, Lionel tutored his sons in diplomacy, so that they would be able to evaluate the stability of regimes and the risks of conflict with all its unpredictable consequences. Thus on 6 July 1870, Natty deciphered a telegram from the Paris House, relaying a message from Napoleon III which stated strong French objections to Prince Leopold of Hohenzollern, the Prussian choice, being offered the vacant Spanish throne. Natty hurried to Carlton House Terrace where he found Mr Gladstone, the Prime Minster, who was 'leaving for Windsor, and [I] drove with him to the railway station. For a time Mr Gladstone was silent. Then he said he did not approve of the candidature, but he was not disposed to interfere with the liberty of the Spanish people to choose their own sovereign.' Lord Granville, the new Foreign Secretary, persuaded the Spanish government to withdraw their candidate, allowing the Rothschilds to send a telegram to Gladstone, which reads as follows: 'The Prince has given up his candidature. The French are satisfied.' Against the wishes of the British government, France insisted on a guarantee of Leopold's candidature never being renewed, leading to an outbreak of hostilities between France and Prussia. At the age of thirty, Natty had a ringside seat at the secret diplomatic negotiations that ultimately failed to avert a major European war.[7]

As an even younger man of 22, Natty had been introduced to Napoleon III when he visited Ferrières, the chateau outside Paris belonging to his Uncle, Baron James de Rothschild. With his cousin Alphonse, Natty rode to the railway station on 16 December 1862 to greet the Emperor on his arrival. As he explained to his parents:

> I must say it was one of the most disagreeable rides I ever had as the road was like a pane of glass ... If it had been in England the populace would have been much more enthusiastic, as it was the cries of *Vive l'Empereur* were for the greater part uttered by paid agents. On his arrival at the castle his majesty inspected everything and had all the members of the family introduced to him. I thought him the most perfect gentleman I had ever seen and certainly his suite make a great show ... after breakfast which lasted some time and would have been excellent if it had only been warm, the sportsmen adjourned to the Park. There was an enormous

7   John Morley, *Life of Gladstone* Vol. 2 (London, 1903), pp. 325–35.

show of game, but as most of the shots had drunk 10 or 12 different kinds of wine they shot very badly. Altogether some 800 pheasants were murdered, they ought to have killed 1,500. The Emperor who shot with English-made loaders shot wonderfully well, and killed only cocks and I believe he killed 250.

It has been suggested that the presence of Natty, with his sisters Leonora and Evelina and his Uncle Anthony plus the British ambassador to meet the Emperor, indicated a serious attempt at improving Anglo-French relations.[8]

On 6 July 1905, Lucien Wolf went to see Lord Rothschild to question him about the British government's purchase of a huge block of shares in the Suez Canal, taking copious notes at the interview as Natty, at his father's behest, had been involved in the negotiations. 'Very shortly after Mr Disraeli came into office in March 1874' Natty recalled:

> he ... went to see Baron Lionel de Rothschild, and told him that he regarded the question of the Suez Canal as one of his chief problems in his Foreign Policy. He thought it absolutely essential to British interests that a large interest in the Canal should be secured, and he said that he would not shrink even from the purchase of the whole concern. On this, Sir Nathaniel de Rothschild ... was sent to Paris to see M. de Lesseps, and he made definite proposals for buying up the Suez Canal Company. These proposals were declined ... [Furthermore,] proposals were actually made to the Khedive by Messrs Rothschild for the purchase of his shares long before Mr Greenwood's visit to the Foreign Office on November 15th, 1875 ... In regard to Henry Oppenheim, Lord Rothschild told me that he believed his action was due to information he received from his Egyptian house [Oppenheim, Nephew & Co], warning him that the Rothschilds were making overtures for the shares. He thereupon came to New Court to see Baron Lionel ... to persuade him to let him participate in the purchase.[9]

In the end, the Rothschilds secretly advanced the sum of almost £4 million to allow the British government to buy the Khedive's block of 44 per cent

8   RAL 000/12/26 Natty to his parents 17 December 1862; Ferguson, *The World's Banker* pp. 620–1.
9   Yivo Archives, David Mowshowitch Collection, reel 2, note by Lucien Wolf 6 July and 8 July 1905, 11 January and 29 January 1906.

of the shares in the company that controlled the Canal, a contract being signed on 25 November 1875. Everything was done covertly so as not to alert financial competitors and the French government. Through Britain insisting that the five per cent interest on the purchase money was to be a first charge on the Egyptian finances, further scope was given for outside interference in that country's affairs. Natty was a full participant in these negotiations so the current interpretation of this transaction is coloured by Natty's reminiscences.[10]

As Leonore Davidoff has recently pointed out, the nineteenth century witnessed the revival of the extended family in Europe among the middle classes, particularly in its upper ranks, as families grew healthier and larger because more children survived.[11] The characteristics of these families has been well summarized by Adam Kuper in a review of her book.

> There were more and more brothers and sisters, and consequently more brothers- and sisters-in-law, uncles and aunts, and cousins. Because brothers and sisters remained close, uncles and aunts became quasi-parents. Cousins were quasi-siblings and so too were brothers- and sisters-in-law, and these relatives could and did marry one another ... Close relatives had rarely married in pre-industrial Europe. Now in bourgeois circles in England, one marriage in five was with a relative. Cousin marriages, even between first cousins, were respectable and popular.

The inter-related families

> developed lifelong bonds, lived as close to one another as they could after their marriages, and made sure their sons and daughters treated their cousins as brothers and sisters. Their children and grandchildren often intermarried, and repeated marriages linked families over gener-ations. Cohesive clans developed, the men often clustering in particular professions as bankers, merchants, lawyers, clergymen, and civil servants and collaborating in religious and political movements.[12]

So far from being unusual, the Rothschilds were, in many respects, a typical

---

10 Ferguson, *The World's Banker*, pp. 820–7; Lucien Wolf, *Essays in Jewish History*, ed. Cecil Roth (London, 1934), pp. 287–308.

11 Leonore Davidoff, *Thicker Than Water: Siblings and Their Relations 1780–1920* (Oxford, 2012).

12 Adam Kuper in *Times Literary Supplement* 18 May 2012, pp. 12–13.

example of the Victorian bourgeois family – cousin marriages were common, the friendship between cousins was often like that of siblings, their country houses were located within easy distance of each other in Buckinghamshire and so were their town houses in the West End. They cooperated closely in running their bank as a joint enterprise, and Natty, Alfred and Leo acted together in their sponsorship of Anglo-Jewish charities.

Cousin marriages were frequent among the Rothschilds. Natty's older sister Leonora had married Alphonse, son of Baron James, in 1857 at Gunnersbury. Charlotte and Lionel were hoping that Natty would marry Constance or Annie, his English cousins, the daughters of Sir Anthony and Lady Louise de Rothschild. The high-spirited Evelina had teased her cousin Constance some years earlier, asking her whether or not she was in love with Natty, but the only response she drew was that Constance liked him. Charlotte had half-expected that Natty 'would fall in love or glide into that delightful feeling and make the excellent Baronet [Anthony] supremely happy by proposing to one of his daughters'. In turn it had been intended that Emma, the daughter of Mayer Carl (otherwise known as Charles) von Rothschild and Louise Lionel's sister, who lived in Frankfurt, would marry James Edouard of Paris, Nat's son, but it never happened.

At the outset of the Austro-Prussian War in 1866, Mayer Carl moved with his wife and five daughters to Paris and then visited Gunnersbury, the home of Lionel, his wife's brother, and of Charlotte his own sister.[13] There Natty and Emma fell dizzily in love. On 25 September 1866 Constance recorded in her diary: 'No secret about Natty & Emmy. I am very glad, hope they may be happy.' Evelina wrote to her sister Laury, who was married to another cousin Alphonse in Paris, that there was an informal engagement between the pair, that Natty was 'fidgeting for letters from Emma' and becoming 'spoony', i.e. foolishly amorous. So Emma was doubly Natty's first cousin, being the daughter of Charlotte's younger brother and of Lionel's sister Louise. It was the attraction of two like-minded persons: the sensible hard-working Natty and the strait-laced Emma. She was much in the mould of his own mother, someone he was desperately anxious to please, but found difficult to do so – it seems that unconsciously he chose a wife very much

13 Weintraub, *Charlotte and Lionel*, p. 209; BL. Add. MS 47913 Diary of Constance de Rothschild, 10 August 1858; Ferguson, *The World's Banker*, p. 762.

like his mother. As the most gifted of her sisters, Emma 'spoke five languages fluently, drew and painted, played the piano with considerable skill, and in her youth was an expert swimmer and horsewoman'. As a young girl, Emma was privately coached by a university lecturer in optics and physics, subjects of her own choosing.[14] She was concerned as to how Charlotte, who was also her aunt, would react to her sudden engagement, and on her return to Frankfurt penned a long letter of sincere gratitude:

> Pray let me thank you for all your kindness and love – my heart was too full when at Gunnersbury to permit me to express all the deep thankfulness I felt for your affectionate welcome. I only hope to show you my gratitude one day by true filial devotion and trust I may not prove unworthy of the numerous proofs of tenderness you have shown me ... and hope you will see in these lines the tender and affectionate heart which dictates them.[15]

Then, without warning, Charlotte and Lionel and their family were suddenly plunged into mourning and the deepest gloom. Evelina ('Evy'), a gracious and vivacious young woman, who brought so much joy to family and friends, died. Married to her cousin Ferdinand ('Ferdy') from the Austrian branch of the family, Evelina, while heavily pregnant, was seized with convulsions and gave birth to a still-born child on 4 December 1866, dying herself a few minutes later. The death may have been the delayed result of a train accident in which Evelina had been involved a short time before; alternatively, the cause of death may have been toxemic pre-eclampsia.[16] Upset at losing a close friend, Constance de Rothschild noted that Evy's death 'now seems to me improbable. We were very busy & therefore very happy down in the school when the telegram came.'[17] Ferdy was heartbroken at losing a wife whom he had loved since she was a little girl, pouring out his grief to a very receptive Leo.

> Mine is a loss which years cannot repair, nor any accidental circumstances relieve. Ever since childhood I was attached to her. The older I

---

14   Ibid., p. 209; BL. Add. MS 47913 Diary of Constance de Rothschild 25 September 1866; Rothschild, *Dear Lord Rothschild*, pp. 58–9; *The Times* 11 January 1935.

15   Rothschild, *Dear Lord Rothschild*, p. 10.

16   Weintraub, *Charlotte and Lionel*, pp. 207–8; Rothschild, *Dear Lord Rothschild*, p. 10.

17   BL. Add. MS. 47913 Diary of Constance de Rothschild 4 December 1866.

became, the more we met, the deeper I loved her and in later years she had so grown into my heart that my only wishes, cares, joys, affections, whatever sentiments in fact a man can possess were directly or indirectly wound up with her existence. I can find no consolation in the future. It may partly come from the past, in the recollection of those happy bygone days, when she lived, when we were so intensely happy.

Ferdy never remarried and Charlotte and Lionel, Evelina's parents, remained inconsolable, the visits and messages of sympathy from family and friends being of little avail.[18] It was not the first taste of bitterness that the family had endured, as there had been recriminations between two sides of the family when Alphonse and Laury's infant son René had died in 1861, shortly after he was circumcised. Alphonse blamed some defect in the child from birth, while Charlotte attributed the death to an outbreak in Paris of erysipelas, an infectious disease, and wished that 'the ceremony could be abolished'.[19] On the surface, the relationship between Natty and Ferdy was cordial enough, but below it there were tensions and a degree of animosity. Perhaps Natty unconsciously blamed Ferdy for his sister's death.[20]

In February 1867, Natty travelled to Frankfurt, where he rekindled his love for Emma and arranged the wedding date with her family, proceeding to Paris before returning home. To his parents, Natty wrote that 'I need not tell you that all here will be very pleased that the day they have selected should meet with your approval. I have not written to anyone but yourselves about this as I was waiting until I heard positively from you.' At the same time, the letter was interspersed with business news, showing how quickly Natty was learning his craft as a banker.

As I wrote to you yesterday the market for all sorts of Austrian securities improves daily [now that the Hungarian difficulties are nearly settled]; yesterday at one of the cafés at which the faithful congregate there was a great demand for the last Austrian loan and the House sold 500,000 florins without at all affecting the market. They reported here that the

---

18   Ferguson, *The World's Banker*, p. 762.
19   RAL RFam C/21 Charlotte to Leo 4 and 6 November 1861.
20   Davis, *The English Rothschilds*, pp. 124–5.

Portuguese loan was to make its appearance today, they said Hope was to bring it out in Amsterdam and that it would meet with great success.

He concluded by asking 'Please let me know at Paris if there are any commissions for me to execute'.[21]

After a stormy passage across the Channel, accompanied by Leo, and a drive in a carriage along the Rhine, Natty arrived in Frankfurt in mid-April 1867 for his wedding, where he was later joined by his other brother and his sister Laury, though not by his parents, who were still in mourning for Evelina. To Charlotte and Lionel, he reported with genuine enthusiasm that

> I have this instant given your beautiful jewels to Emmy. I need hardly tell you that wonder and amazement was depicted on the faces of all who saw them and each ornament came in for its share of praise. I think that the pearl necklace and ruby tiara excited the more astonishment, they all agreed that the pearls were like pigeons' eggs and that the tiara was super.

So too, Leo reported that Emma's family 'seem to be delighted with the jewels which they say reflect so very much your good taste'. But 'Everywhere they talk about the war & all the railway officials talk of nothing else to one another & one man amused Natty by telling him, that if the "worst came to the worst" they [the Prussians] would most certainly "lick the French".'[22]

The next day, Leo informed his parents that he was

> very glad to hear that the prices in the City are so much better, let us hope that the darkened horizon of the political world may clear & that we may not have any European war – Uncle Charles [Emma's father] returned from Berlin ... [where] he had a long interview with Bismarck ... [He] was as you know tremendously feted but of all his parties & functions he was most amused at Uncle Salbert's where he found a circle of rabbis & priests who proved an excellent audience ... [for] his stories and in their turn cracked many jokes – Laury & Alfred arrived by the midday train from Paris looking none the worse for their long train

---

21 RAL 000/12/43 Natty to Charlotte and Lionel 3 and 4 February 1867.
22 RAL 000/12/ 42 Natty to Charlotte and Lionel undated, probably 15 April 1867 and RAL 000/22/93 Leo to the same 15 April 1867.

journey ... Laury brought a cargo of presents from Paris which (with the exception of her own locket which is quite lovely) are not as successful as the London ones ... The Frankfurt ladies have each sent Emma a cushion so that she has 24 pieces of embroidery and besides many chairs![23]

Natty praised Uncle Anselm of Vienna for selecting a beautiful locket for Emma made by Biederman; otherwise the gifts, apart from his sister's pretty locket, 'were all chosen with more or less bad taste ... Uncle Nat was kind enough to send me £300 and I believe that Uncle James intends presenting me with £1,000'. Natty, having spoken with his future father-in-law, confirmed that the diplomatic omens were 'not so good'. Bismarck appears to have told him [Uncle Charles] that 'the German Confederation being united, he never could give up Luxembourg and having a well organized army he is not afraid of France ... I must say it strikes me more than ever that we should go with France in the Luxembourg question and thus prevent any difficulties about Belgium'. Because Uncle Charles had been elected to the Parliament of the new North German Confederation and was compliant by always voting with the government, his 'subserviency' endeared him to Bismarck, enabling him to obtain a remission in the payment of 4,000,000 thalers by Frankfurt and 'a great many other boons they were anxious to obtain'.[24]

When writing to his parents on 16 April 1867, Natty added that

This will be almost the last letter I shall have the pleasure of writing to you as a bachelor and I wish I could express to you in good terms all my gratitude for your past kindness and for the care and attention which you have always lavished on me ... I only hope and trust that it may be in my power by fulfilling all your wishes to repay you in a slight way for all you have done for me.[25]

At five in the afternoon, the couple were married in a civil ceremony in a small office, only large enough to accommodate them and the witnesses. Alfred remarked that 'Emma looked extremely handsome, and was dressed in a lilac dress, a white bonnet and an Indian shawl which suited her

23   RAL 000/22/89 Leo to Charlotte and Lionel 16 April 1867.
24   RAL 000/12/44 and 45 Natty to Charlotte and Lionel 16 April 1867; Ferguson, *The World's Banker*, p. 668.
25   RAL 000/12/44 Natty to Charlotte and Lionel 16 April 1867.

uncommonly well; Natty is radiantly happy and God grant that they may be as happy as they deserve to be.' In the evening, the family guests were entertained to dinner by Baron Charles.[26]

The next day, on 17 April 1867, Natty and Emma were married under a *chupah* (wedding canopy) in the house of her parents in Frankfurt in a religious ceremony conducted by a rabbi, 'who came very late'. According to Leo, the rabbi 'made an excellent speech in German, as he said everything to the point & was not at all pompous. The house is filled with beautiful flowers & the dining table decorated with beautiful cakes.' As for the young couple,

> the bride looked very handsome in her white dress covered with the usual thick lace & the bridegroom appeared to great advantage – Natty was not very nervous but showed much feeling whilst of course Emma was rather upset. I shall not weary you with a description of the ladies' dresses but darling Laury looked as usual lovely in violet & white lace.

Before the marriage ceremony the ever-sensitive Leo told his parents that he could:

> easily imagine what your feelings must be on such a day. May God give you strength to bear up against your afflictions & may he mitigate grief by sending you every blessing. Today you will gain a new daughter who can never hope to replace the darling we mourn but who will by her affection & devotion prove a great joy to you my beloved parents. May God give our dear Natty & his bride every blessing to enjoy a long life of sunshine & happiness. As you may suppose, they are radiant with joy & you can have no idea what a handsome pair they make. Emma looked beautiful last night & Natty no unworthy match.

At the conclusion of the festivities, which were somewhat subdued because of Evelina's death, Uncle Salbert proposed Natty's health and the newlyweds left for Heidelberg and their month-long honeymoon at 5 o'clock.[27]

Her cousin Constance envied Emma's romantic union, noting in her diary that 'another young happy creature full of life & vigour gives herself to the man of her own choice, to the man of her heart ... [Natty and

26 RAL 000/22/89 Leo to Charlotte and Lionel 16 April 1867 and RAL 000/40/17 Alfred to the same 16 April 1867.
27 RAL 000/22/94 Leo to Charlotte and Lionel 17 April 1867.

Emma] did not require a party. I see more that a quiet wedding is therefore happiest & the best.'[28]

Part of Natty and Emma's honeymoon was spent in Italy, visiting the architectural and artistic sites of Florence and Genoa. Clasping Murray's handbook, the happy young couple continued their inspection of churches, monuments and pictures [in Florence] and in the afternoon they 'drove to a Villa ... which is situated on a hill and overlooks the town. The house is a bower of roses and there are several acres full of beautiful flowers all around'. Despite being on his honeymoon, Natty took time off to confer with Horaz Landau, the Rothschilds' extremely experienced agent in Turin, warning his father that Landau advised him that

> there is nothing to be done in American tobacco. The Government want now only Hungarian tobacco and will only purchase on condition that the tobacco is delivered here. I cannot find out anything about the Italian budget but everybody here seems to agree that a powerful admin-istration is wanted to save the country from ruin.[29]

On 3 May 1867, Natty and Emma, accompanied by Landau and Baron Kubeck, left for Genoa by train, the latter in particular wished to be remembered to Lionel and was 'anxious to find out who was to represent Austria at the Conferences'. In Genoa, they stayed in a hotel overlooking the marketplace with the harbour in the distance. Their next stop was Nice and then homewards to Paris, where they were to celebrate the seventy-fifth or seventy-sixth birthday of Baron James at the Rue Laffitte. Meanwhile, Natty reported that 'Italian stock is flat and I suppose will fall again'.[30]

The family correspondence is a curious amalgam of news about the wedding and honeymoon, business, share prices and political and diplo-matic gossip. Leo, for instance, advised his father that a Rubens he wanted to purchase was being sold at auction in Paris, while a collection of etchings and engravings by Albrecht Dürer had also come on to the market.[31]

What is apparent is that all three brothers had received a thorough

28 BL. Add. MS. 47913 Diary of Constance de Rothschild 17 April 1867.
29 RAL 000/12/46 Natty to Charlotte and Lionel 2 May 1867.
30 RAL 000/12/41 and 47 Natty to Charlotte and Lionel 4 and 16 May 1867.
31 RAL 000//22/94 Leo to Charlotte and Lionel 17 April 1867.

grounding in the business of banking from Lionel, with particular reference to state loans which included an intimate grasp of the minutiae of politics and diplomacy. Even so, until his death in 1879, Lionel micro-managed the bank, attending to every small detail and not allowing Natty to use his own initiative and acquire sufficient confidence in his own judgement. Just before his death, Lionel sent Natty to Paris on a business trip. Natty confessed to Disraeli that 'I was with him late on Friday night and during the whole of Saturday taking his instructions previous to my departure ... I admired and appreciated ... the greatness of his judgement and the lucidity of his mind.'[32] Though a man of almost 40, Natty was in awe of his father.

The other overriding influence on Natty was Benjamin Disraeli. Disraeli struck up an intimate friendship with Natty's parents, Lionel and Charlotte de Rothschild, listening to the former's advice when he was Chancellor of the Exchequer and flirting with Charlotte, as well as portraying the family in romantic terms in his novels. Hannah Arendt and Isaiah Berlin have both suggested that 'Disraeli's racial chauvinism [which emerged in the mid-1840s] was a compensatory counter-myth, forged to combat his feelings of social inferiority through assertions of an ancient racial lineage nobler than that of the English aristocracy.'[33] Paradoxically, the Anglican Disraeli not only stiffened Natty's pride in being Jewish, but led him to reorient his views on foreign policy so that, like his mentor, he became convinced that the Turkish Empire had to stay intact as a bulwark against Russian expansion – a view that put him at odds with Gladstone and his fellow Liberal M.P.s.

Natty, having been elected as the Liberal M.P. for Aylesbury in Buckinghamshire in 1865, was very partisan and still critical of Disraeli, writing to his parents, 'From what I hear ... by fair means or foul, Dizzy will tide over this session.'[34] After the Suez Canal episode in 1875, when Lionel advanced the money for the British government to purchase a significant block of shares in the Canal Company, the Rothschild family grew somewhat estranged from Gladstone and closer to Disraeli. In 1877,

32 Bodleian Libraries, dep. Hughenden 141/3 ff.162–3, Natty to the Earl of Beaconsfield 7 June 1879.

33 Todd M. Endelman, 'The Emergence of Disraeli's Jewishness' in *Broadening Jewish History: Towards a Social History of Ordinary Jews* (Oxford, 2011), pp. 201–24.

34 Ferguson, *The World's Banker*, p. 844 and Weintraub, *Charlotte and Lionel*, p. 221.

Natty assured Monty Corry, Disraeli's secretary, 'pro-Turkish as I have always been, I am astonished at the Turkish feeling everywhere'. A year later, he apologized for accidentally voting with his fellow Liberal M.P.s in a censure vote against the Conservative government, telling Corry, 'I write this to you although you know I wd. sooner have cut off my hands than do such a thing.'[35]

When Lionel died in 1879, Natty told Disraeli that his father 'always laid the greatest store in your love and friendship and hoped and trusted that it would be extended to his sons'.[36] By December 1879, Natty was referring 'to that arch fiend Gladstone', the very expression which Disraeli used in private when sometimes mentioning his rival. A little while later, Natty sent Disraeli good wishes for the New Year, ending his letter with the comment that 'I hear that a great many Liberals are disgusted with Gladstone, that he will do you good and himself harm is ... [my] wish.'[37]

By the 1850s, Lionel and his brothers, Mayer and Anthony, had established themselves in the Vale of Aylesbury in Buckinghamshire which was sometimes dubbed 'Rothschildshire'. Their rolling acres in the countryside gave the Rothschilds tremendous political clout, so it was not altogether surprising when Natty, who was staying with his uncle Sir Anthony at Aston Clinton, stood as the Liberal candidate for Aylesbury at the 1865 election, something for which he had been in training since his youth. Writing to his parents, Natty remarked that he was

> very glad to receive such good accounts from you ... both with regard to the health of all the invalids and with regard to the City election. Here everything is going on as well as possible. James came to me in a great fright because Watson has been sent for by Lord Carrington, it was however only for the county election.

Describing the election campaign, Natty informed his parents that

> We drove over to Missenden and were met by a large party, who promenaded me through the town and over the Hills and far away like a tame bear, friend and foe we called upon alike. I made up my mind

35 Bodleian Libraries, dep. Hughenden 141/3 f.110 Natty to Monty Corry 31 August 1877 and f.160 – c. 1878.
36 Ibid., ff.162–3 Natty to the Earl of Beaconsfield 7 June 1879.
37 Ibid., 141/3 f.136 Natty to the Earl of Beaconsfield 9 December 1879 and f.140 – c. 1879.

before starting that at 4 o'clock I would leave off and when the time came I told them in distinct terms that I intended to go home to keep well for the nomination day, luckily they were all of the same opinion and had had walking enough themselves.[38]

As the core of the Liberal party in the constituency was composed of Dissenters, they demanded the abolition of church rates, and when Frederick Calvert, another prominent Liberal, refused to give such a pledge, the Dissenters switched their support to Natty, who was returned unopposed, as was the Conservative candidate, S. G. Smith.[39] At succeeding contests Natty sought to continue his electoral pact with Smith. Howell, an advanced Liberal, challenged Natty to join forces with him in Aylesbury in the 1868 and 1874 elections but he refused to do so for fear of losing the famers' support, and countering that Howell had incited labourers against employers, a step too far.[40] Natty was to hold a seat in Buckinghamshire as an increasingly disillusioned Liberal until 1885, when he was raised to the peerage.

Disraeli had a much more positive view than his young protégé of the Jews' place in the modern world and was more sceptical of claims that anti-Semitism was provoked, in large part, by self-indulgent and provocative behaviour on their part. When Lionel was asked what he and Disraeli chatted about, he replied 'The race as usual,' and after the birth of Lionel's son Leopold, Disraeli congratulated him, adding: 'I hope he will prove worthy of his pure and sacred race.' Paul Smith has asserted that 'So far as there is a coherent principle in [Disraeli's novel] *Tancred*, it arises ... from the spiritual ascendancy of the eastern race. 'All is race there is no other "truth", says Sidonia.' In Smith's illuminating phrase, Disraeli regarded race rather than class as the prime motor in Western history.[41] A large component of Disraeli's construction of race was the importance he attached to Judaism. Cecil Roth, in his examination of Disraeli's Jewishness, concluded that 'it seems as though the Christianity which he professed, quite sincerely, in his own mind was not that of the established

38   RAL 000/12/106 and 107 Natty to Charlotte and Lionel c. 1865.

39   Davis, *The English Rothschilds*, pp. 119–20.

40   Richard Davis, *Political Change and Continuity 1760–1885: A Buckinghamshire Study* (Newton Abbot, 1972), pp. 208–11.

41   Paul Smith, *Disraeli* (Cambridge, 1999), pp. 101–4.

Church, but a Judaic ethical monotheism, of which the Jew Jesus was the last and greatest exponent'.[42]

In the mid-1840s, Disraeli was already proclaiming that 'the children of Israel ... baffled the Pharaohs, the Assyrian kings & the Roman Caesars; to say nothing of the Crusades & the Inquisition'. More than three decades later, his outlook remained unchanged – if anything, his racial identification with the Jews was even firmer when referring to the Jews and himself. On 21 November 1880, Disraeli, having stepped down as Prime Minister, wrote to Natty,

> What does Bleichroder [Bismarck's banker] say about the Jewish persecution [whipped up by Stoecker]? Or is he & his prosperity one of the causes of it? We have beaten the Pharoahs, the Assyrians & the Romans – & even the Middle Ages– & I have no fear they will ever extinguish us – but I foresee the chance of much misery and perhaps devastation. Plunder is at the bottom of it.[43]

To this, Natty responded by arguing,

> There is no doubt that Bleichroder himself is one of the causes of the Jewish persecution ... There are also a great many other reasons which we can discuss at full length when we meet again; among them the constant influx of Polish, Russian and Rumanian Jews who arrive in a state of starvation and are socialists until they become rich. The Jews are also proprietors of half the newspapers particularly of those papers which are anti-Russian. A good deal of money has no doubt been sent from St. Petersburgh to stimulate this persecution.

In a magisterial aside, Fritz Stern claimed that the Rothschilds had 'a certain penchant for blaming the Jews for anti-Semitism'.[44]

Disraeli did not agree with this analysis, seeing an uglier, greedier, irrational side to anti-Semitism. He wrote back to Natty that

---

42   Daniel R. Schwarz, '*Mene, Mene, Tekel Upharsin*: Jewish Perspectives in Disraeli's Fiction' in Todd M. Endelman and Tony Kushner (eds), *Disraeli's Jewishness* (London, 2002), pp. 49–50.

43   Smith, *Disraeli*, p. 102; RAL 000/848/37 Earl of Beaconsfield to Natty 21 November 1880.

44   Bodleian Libraries, dep. Hughenden 141/3 f.146 Natty to Earl of Beaconsfield 22 November 1880; Fritz Stern, *Gold and Iron: Bismarck, Bleichroder, and the Building of the German Empire* (London, 1980), p. 521.

> I am anxious & disquieted about the German affair ... When *Hep* was
> shouted in the Middle Ages, I doubt whether the Governments, dark as
> they were, favoured it at first. The value of the House of Israel was felt
> by all of them. It was the university students that set it [going] & may
> again – the Govt. remaining frigid and indifferent.[45]

Natty had somewhat ambivalent views on the causes of anti-Semitism
and a strong sense of public duty, believing that Jewish bankers sometimes
shirked their duty to the wider community, thus stirring anti-Semitic sentiments at large. '"Public life!" I almost remember the rasping vehemence
with which Lord Rothschild conveyed to me his remedy for anti-Semitism'
recalled Israel Zangwill. 'He had been telling me about the rich Hungarian
Jews, whose one thought was to hunt and shoot over their estates with the
local nobility.' Public service, in Natty's understanding, meant displaying
innovative farming techniques to the wider agricultural community,
treating his tenant farmers well, and building model dwellings for his farm
labourers, but it also entailed the eradication of slums in the cities by the
construction of affordable housing and supporting hospital funding.

When Natty and Emma were first married, they shared accommodation with his parents at 148 Piccadilly and in the country. Other members
of the Rothschild family were already well established in Buckinghamshire,
Mayer Amschel having acquired Mentmore in 1842, while Anthony came
into possession of Aston Clinton in the early 1850s; at the same time,
Lionel started buying farms at Hulcott and the Manor of Bierton with
its large estate. Ferdinand, from the Austrian branch of the family, having
settled in England in 1859, built Waddesdon in the vicinity of the family's
other country houses. The political influence wielded by the owners of
these estates allowed Natty to become the M.P. for Aylesbury in 1865. So it
made political and commercial sense for Lionel to purchase Tring Park for
£230,000 in 1872, when the property came on to the market. Tring was an
estate situated in Hertfordshire bordering on to Buckinghamshire. Miriam
Rothschild has suggested that it was Constance, a great friend of Emma,
who probably persuaded her father, Sir Anthony de Rothschild, to broach
the question of the purchase to his brother Lionel.[46] The country house at

45 RAL 000/848/37 Earl of Beaconsfield to Natty, 1 December 1880.
46 Rothschild, *Dear Lord Rothschild*, p. 5; Ireland, *Plutocrats*, pp. 295–8.

Tring was a magnificent example of Wren architecture, which was altered so as to become a more commonplace, but exceedingly comfortable, Victorian mansion. Although the size of the estate is often stated to have been 15,000 acres, it has been suggested that its extent at its height was double this in acreage, though this hypothesis is not altogether convincing.[47] Just as Lionel exercised total control in the running of the bank, so he and Charlotte supervised the first stages in the remodelling of the house and its furnishings and decor. In a letter written by Emma to her mother-in-law on first moving into Tring around 1874, she extolled its virtues, saying that she could not:

> find words to express to you how much I admire this beautiful house and its perfect arrangements. Everything is so charming and combines elegance with comfort. I am writing in my bedroom which is so magnificent I can hardly believe myself to be its occupant. I have often longed to possess the carpet which is described in the Arabian Nights and to be transported to fairyland but I have obtained that and without the carpet, for Tring is quite fairyland and I cannot thank you enough for all the trouble and care you have bestowed on this house and for you and Uncle Lionel and your kindness in allowing us to live here. The dining room is a perfect success and the pictures look as if they had always been placed there. The blue room is too lovely and I could not imagine the beauty when you showed me the paper and the chintz at M ...[entmore]! It would take too long to enumerate all I admire but I see a predominance of my favourite Chinese and Indian ornaments – one prettier than the other. Thousand thousand thanks! I hope that my inadequately expressed words will not lessen the assurance of my deeply felt gratitude. The children's rooms are too beautiful and Baby [Evelina] looks at the pictures with delight ...Walter thanks you very much for furnishing all so nicely. This is his own message.[48]

In later years Natty remodelled the house still further, but at this stage he and Emma were hardly consulted, not even on the decoration of the baby's room.

From a photographic album compiled by H. Bedford Lemere in 1890, we can view part of the interior of the house – the over-ornate

47 Ferguson, *The World's Banker*, pp. 748 and 1203, note 64.
48 RAL 000/33 Emma to Lionel and Charlotte circa 1874.

morning-room lined with bookcases and filled with chairs draped in antimacassars and the rather more austere dining room, its walls displaying beautiful paintings.[49] Natty had a 'group of pseudo-Greek marble figures' placed over the fireplace in the smoking room. Around the walls there 'were matching, bas-relief white marble plaques' of semi-nude classical figures which Natty had come across in Italy and arranged to have copied at immense expense. Emma was a super-efficient organizer and managed her huge staff with aplomb and concern for their welfare – a servant prepared twenty-four coal scuttles during the night to assist the five housemaids in lighting the fireplaces in the property because Natty and his wife were always entertaining. As Natty was out riding by 6.00 am, the indoor staff at Tring were up an hour earlier, but as a concession they were allowed to have alternate afternoons and evenings off.[50] Whereas Lionel and Charlotte were friendly with a small circle consisting of Disraeli and his wife, the editor of *The Times*, Delane, the banker J. Abel Smith, Bernal Osborne and C. P. Villiers, Natty and Emma were hosts to a wider circle of Liberal and Conservative party politicians and members of the aristocratic elite, plus an assortment of relatives and leading figures from the Jewish world. On 15 April 1885, Edward Hamilton noted

> Had an interesting dinner at the N. Rothschilds tonight. The Russian Ambassador was there in very good humour and was tackled in the evening by Sir William Harcourt There were also present the Bretts, Lady C. Beresford, Du Canes, Wolff, A. Balfour, Leighton, J. Morley, G. Russell &c. Sat between Leighton and J. Morley, who both made themselves very agreeable.

Emma had a knack of inviting interesting people to her dinner table and hired the elder Grosstephen, one of the most talented chefs in Europe, to preside over her kitchen.[51] Constance de Rothschild, Emma's great friend, lived nearby at Aston Clinton with her parents, and there was constant

---

49 RAL 000/880 Photographs of Tring Park by H. Bedford Lemere, architectural photographer to the Queen, October 1890.
50 Rothschild, *Dear Lord Rothschild*, pp. 3, 8 and 21.
51 Ireland, *Plutocrats*, p. 336; Dudley W. R. Bahlman (ed.), *The Diary of Sir Edward Hamilton* Vol. 2 (Oxford, 1993), p. 839; Rothschild, *Dear Lord Rothschild*, p. 30.

bustle and social or political activity in each of the numerous Rothschild country houses in Buckinghamshire that would entertain the young couple. On 5 March 1868, the Prince of Wales paid a visit to Mentmore, home of Natty's Uncle Mayer, Natty and both his uncles being on hand to greet Prince Edward at Cheddington Station. 'After a very short interlude breakfast was served', Natty observed:

> there was ample time for partaking of all the delicacies of and out of season and H. R. H. ate as if he did not mean to go out hunting. At Wingrove there were a good many people assembled to do honour to their future sovereign but as the deer van had been sent on ... and the deer had been turned out long before our arrival, the deer went away over the heart of the Vale and gave an excellent run of an hour and three-quarters. The Prince went very well and considering that the pace was terrific and the best riders fell on every side, he was very lucky to escape without any accident at all. He was delighted with his run ... and with his reception, he enquired particularly after Laury, said he was very glad she had a son and heir ... The Prince is certainly marvellously strong. During the last week he has been sitting up night after night smoking etc and has never had more than 4 hours sleep and there he was yesterday riding about all day and when he returned to London he went to pay some visits where I know not ... the party at the Gladstones was dull and very hot. I am happy to say Emmy is very well and so is the little boy.

Natty's friendship with the heir to the throne continued to flourish. A few days later, Natty went to the House of Commons to hear the Irish debates and afterwards he and Alfred were invited by the Prince to Marlborough House, where a concert was being held to mark Edward's wedding anniversary.[52]

Natty, and Baron Ferdinand at Waddesdon in particular, were model landowners. 'The farms at Tring Park have long had a high reputation for the excellence of the general management, but it was in the breeding of pure-bred stock that Tring Park achieved the greatest distinction' declared *The Times* in its obituary of Natty.

RAL 000/848/33 Lady Rothschild's Alphabetical Visitors Book 1896 and 1899 and Visitors Tring 1912–1915.

52   RAL 000/12/50 and 51 Natty to Charlotte 6 March and 10 March 1868.

To describe fully the late peer's enterprise in stock-breeding would be to write a history of the breeds of Shire horses, Dairy shorthorn and Jersey cattle, and Hampshire Down sheep, as well as poultry-keeping and dairying ... It is no exaggeration to say that Tring Park was looked upon ... as a centre in agricultural activity which afforded an example to the whole industry ... and in every section of the work Lord Rothschild himself took a keen personal interest.

A sale of sixty head of Jersey cattle in March 1892 from Lord Rothschild's herd that were reputed to be excellent dairy animals and better adapted to the British climate than their island dams fetched £1,195, 8s 6d.[53] With his brother Leopold, a notable racehorse owner, Lord Rothschild was the joint master of a pack of staghounds, keeping kennels at Ascot, Leighton Buzzard, Leopold's estate, and hunting over the Vale of Aylesbury in Buckinghamshire. From his father, Natty had inherited a love of horses and 'was a good rider, and in his younger days was an enthusiastic rider to hounds. He ... [helped to maintain] a famous pack which was kept up in princely style, the huntsmen and whippers-in being splendidly mounted ... and the deer are preserved under conditions that ensure a good run at each meet.'[54] Natty was an exemplary landlord, building fifty model cottages at Tring. These new homes were generously let to the tenants of condemned properties at their old rents. In addition, he not only offered to buy the condemned properties from poorer owners at a fair valuation, but to compensate them on terms laid down by an independent assessor. Furthermore, Natty built as many as four hundred cottages on the Tring Park estate itself, while Lady Rothschild built and maintained eight small houses for retired employees of the estate.[55]

Many of the welfare activities on the Tring Park estate were organized by Emma. From Lady Rothschild's personal accounts, it is apparent that she gave money generously for the supply of winter fuel and clothing, the apprenticeship of young men and women, assisting emigration, compensation for personal injuries of employees and for multifarious

53 The Times 1 April 1915 and Bucks Herald 26 March 1892.
54 Jewish Chronicle Special Memoir 2 April 1915 p. iv and David Kessler, 'The Rothschilds and Disraeli in Buckinghamshire', Jewish Historical Studies Vol. XXIX (1982–6), pp. 231–52.
55 Daily Telegraph 1 April 1915; Rothschild, Dear Lord Rothschild, pp. 20 and 44.

medical expenses. Employees of the Tring Park estate received free medical attendance and nursing, free medicine and access to a nursing home which Emma opened and equipped. On payment of a subscription of £1 a year, the residents of Tring could obtain the same benefits. Any man in Tring could find employment in the woods of the estate; there were also allotments for hire at a token payment with a gift of a joint of beef and a pair of rabbits at Christmas. All the children of Tring received a free hamper at Christmas, toys and a shilling; on royal birthdays and the New Year, children were handed a mug stuffed with sweets and a shilling. Emma subscribed to 177 local charities connected with Tring, including convalescent homes, lying-in societies, needlework guilds, the Church Girls Union, the Young Women's Christian Association, the Tring United Band of Hope (a temperance society) and many others, besides subsidizing the repair of local churches.[56]

From the few records from Tring Park that survive, it is reasonable to infer that Bateman was correct in suggesting that the estate was approximately 15,000 acres in size during the 1880s, as it yielded gross profits of £13,642 6s. 3d. in 1882 and £15,152 11s. 2d. in 1886. The estate comprised farms, allotments, shops, cottages and the Buckinghamshire County Cricket grounds. However, particularly in the early years of ownership, Natty authorised lavish expenditure to ensure that the estate was kept in a good state of repair. There was the thatching of Goodchild's cottage at Longwick, digging and draining, tiling, plumbing, repairs to fences, the installation of new gates, stone-picking and the cost of labour. All this expenditure resulted in Natty being left with a net profit of £5,301 2s. 6d in 1882 and £9,046 13s. 9d. in 1886.[57]

At Tring Park, Natty and Emma brought up their three children, Walter, Evelina and Charles, instilling in them a love of animals and the countryside. On a visit to the house in August 1874, their grandmother Charlotte noted that it

> felt cool and the gardens looked bright with flowers and birds. Walter, who was lively, talkative and very active, insisted upon showing me his favourites. It was delightful to see the little boy so pleased and happy,

56   Rothschild, *Dear Lord Rothschild*, pp. 19–20.
57   RAL X/1/4/1 Tring Park Estate Ledgers for 1882 and 1886.

feeding the tame partridges and pheasants that are being brought up on the lawn, stroking the white parrots that are swinging in round iron rings and half hoops under the large elm tree, and helping ... the attendant to prepare the daily puddings of rice, currants, potatoes and eggs for the more delicate birds in the temple, and in the aviaries of the conservatory.[58]

Unfortunately Walter, who was minimally brain-damaged at birth, was so delicate that his mother decided to isolate him from other children, apart from his sister, to prevent him from picking up an infection, and he spoke slowly and with difficulty. Yet he was a precocious child with an uncanny ability to recognize differences 'between the insect fauna of Germany and England' at the age of ten and with a passionate interest in the different species of plants and animals which won him the friendship of Dr Gunther, the Keeper of Zoology at the Natural History Museum. In contrast to his brother Charles, who went to Harrow and made friends for life, Walter was tutored at home and had no close companions of his own age. He was brilliant at zoological classification and had an obsessive interest in natural history that greatly irritated his father. He had all the symptoms of what today would be thought of as someone suffering from Asperger's syndrome.[59] All his life, Walter was protected by his mother and was the despair of his father, who nominated his second son Charles to succeed him at the bank.

Natty had sat as the Liberal M.P. for Aylesbury since 1865 without attracting much public attention. In 1869 and again in 1871 and 1872 a series of South American loans was issued, characterized by inflated premiums generated by the contractor for the loan buying up large quantities and then unloading them without warning; all these loans defaulted. Behind the Honduras loan stood the dubious figure of Charles Lefevre, who was associated with the issuing house of Bischoffsheim & Goldschmidt. A Parliamentary Select Committee on Loans to Foreign States was appointed in March 1875 before whom Natty was called to testify. When questioned by the committee about the rigging of the market, Natty refused to suggest any remedies, but claimed that the panaceas put forward were unworkable.

58 Ireland, *Plutocrats*, p. 351.
59 Rothschild, *Dear Lord Rothschild*, pp. 52–5, 57–8, 60 and 64.

If financiers were compelled to state the price at which they had taken on the loan from a government, then such business would be diverted from London to Continental bourses. As for the suggestion that the Stock Exchange should be told the terms of a contract, he bluntly countered that 'You have no more right to ask me at what price I have got a loan than you have to ask a man what price he gives for a horse' and that any such provision would be 'Very easily evaded'. Further, Natty was of the opinion that the majority of people who took up loans were not country clergymen and widows but did so 'because ... [having] made a good deal of money by former foreign loans', they expected 'the new loan ... was as equally as good as its predecessors'. Like Natty, the Select Committee had less confidence in legislative redress and more 'in the enlightenment of the public as to their real nature and origin'.[60] Natty's mother Charlotte was pleasantly surprised by the impression he had made by his performance in front of the Select Committee, writing to Leo that 'Natty, who is very modest, must nevertheless be pleased with his evidence before the loan committee; it has given general satisfaction in the Bank of England, the Stock exchange, etc and Mr Delane [editor of *The Times*] wrote to congratulate Papa.'[61] Nor did it end there, as two years later Natty was selected to sit on a Royal Commission to inquire into the objects and constitution of the Stock Exchange. Natty was becoming recognized as an authoritative City voice.[62]

In vain did Gladstone try to keep Natty loyal to the Liberal party, by raising him to the peerage in 1885, making him the first Jew to be admitted to the House of Lords. Queen Victoria had earlier baulked at the suggestion, when Gladstone requested her to confer a peerage on Lionel. The radical journalist Henry Labouchere bemoaned the fact that Gladstone had seen fit to make hereditary peers out of a number of brewers, such as Guinness, Allsopp and Bass, who had accumulated large fortunes, as well as some of the great financiers, such as Rothschild and Revelstoke. 'Some people are turning up their noses at the Rothschild Peerage,' remarked Edward Hamilton, 'but I am very pleased it has been

60 *Select Committee on Foreign Loans*, pp. xlix and l; evidence of Sir Nathaniel de Rothschild qq. 5767–858; David Kynaston, *The City of London: A World of its Own 1815–1890* Vol. 1 (London, 1994), pp. 270–5.

61 RAL RFamC/21 Charlotte to Leo 14 and 15 May 1875.

62 Ferguson, *The World's Banker*, pp. 742 and 1202, note 28.

conferred. The stake which the remarkable family hold in this country amply justifies royal recognition; and it removes the last remnant of religious disqualifications.' As a friend of the Prince of Wales, Natty was invited by Edward to join the Privy Council on the occasion of his coronation as King in 1902, thus confirming Natty's paramount influence and status.[63]

On 6 May 1889 Lord Salisbury, the Conservative Prime Minister, wrote to Natty that he wished to appoint him Lord Lieutenant of Buckinghamshire in succession to the Duke of Buckingham. 'The proposal is naturally suggested by the position you occupy in the county: but I may add that it is made with the approval of Lord Hartington [the Liberal Unionist leader]: so that you will not be guilty of any dereliction of political allegiance in accepting it.' The Prince of Wales apologized to Lord Carrington, Natty's friend and neighbour, for overlooking his own claim to fill this vacancy, exclaiming: 'it would have been strange ten years ago, but times change. He is a good fellow and a man of business, and he and his family own half the County!'[64] But the Rothschilds were also the biggest donors to the coffers of the Liberal Unionists, whom Salisbury was eager to propitiate. Because of the political friendship existing between Natty and Hartington, the latter wrote to Lord Salisbury, then Prime Minister, on 3 April 1889 pressing the claims of Natty to be made Lord Lieutenant of Buckinghamshire, a suggestion that appears to have been acted upon. In the early 1890s, a Liberal Unionist fund for the 1892 election was initiated, to which Natty contributed £5,000, Alfred and Leo jointly added another £5,000 and their cousin Ferdinand another £700.[65]

Natty was the first Jew to occupy the position of Lord Lieutenant, the premier rung in county society. Prior to this, his uncle, Mayer Rothschild had been appointed High Sheriff of Buckinghamshire, a minor position in the county hierarchy.[66] One of Natty's major new duties was to appoint

63   *The Times* 1 April 1915; Algar Labouchere Thorold, *The Life of Henry Labouchere* (London, 1913), p. 218; Bahlman (ed.), *The Diary of Sir Edward Hamilton 1883–1885* Vol. 2, p. 899.

64   RAL 000/848/37 Lord Salisbury to Natty 6 May 1889, and Anthony Allfrey, *Edward VII and his Jewish Court* (London, 1991), pp. 31–2.

65   T. A. Jenkins, 'The Funding of the Liberal Unionist Party and the Honours System', *English Historical Review* 105 (1990), pp. 920–38.

66   Ireland, *Plutocrats*, pp. 247 and 305.

magistrates to sit on the bench, which he did with the assistance of an advisory council. Among Lord Rothschild's correspondence is a letter from the Bishop of Oxford, declaring that he was writing to his Lord Lieutenants to become 'Vice-Presidents of our Diocesan Sustentation [sustenance] Fund'. So too, as an estate owner, his brother Leopold responded to a request for financial help from a congregant of a church near his home, by promising to contribute £100 per annum towards the curate's salary. Natty was also heavily involved in the implementation of Haldane's Territorial Army reforms. Like his Uncles Mayer and Anthony, Natty was much more embedded in the role of a rural magnate unlike his father, Lionel, who had inherited the property at Gunnersbury, a place within easy reach of the City by carriage; Lionel sat as an M.P. representing the City of London.[67]

The Prince of Wales, anxious to avoid parliamentary censure for requesting an increased allowance from the Civil List, became increasingly reliant on Rothschild largesse. 'My dear Natty', Edward stated in 1883, 'I cannot find words too extreme [in] gratitude for your kindness and liberality, which you may be convinced will never be forgotten by me.' A cash advance of £100,000 was obtained by Edward from the Rothschild Bank in 1889 by taking out a mortgage on the Sandringham Estate, followed by a further advance of £60,000 in 1893. It is interesting that Natty's promotion to Lord Lieutenant occurred simultaneously with the first mortgage advance on this property. It is not certain that these loans were ever fully repaid.[68]

At first an ardent supporter of Free Trade and the Liberal party, in 1886 Natty switched his allegiance to the Liberal Unionists, a break-away faction of Whig aristocrats and businessmen, led by the Marquess of Hartington, heir to the Duke of Devonshire, his style of life and sympathies being more akin to their own. Within the Liberal Unionist party which won 78 seats in the 1886 general election, the Rothschild family exercised great financial clout and growing influence. Edward Hamilton recorded in his diary on 31 August 1887 that he

Went down to dinner at Gunnersbury which is now the joint possession

---

67   RAL 000/848/37 Bishop of Oxford to Natty 27 June 1897, Cecil Roth, *The Magnificent Rothschilds* (London, 1939), pp. 223–4 and George Ireland, *Plutocrats*, pp. 344 and 346.
68   Ridley, *Bertie*, p. 269.

of the three brothers Rothschild ... I had a good deal of talk with N. Rothschild whose judgment on political affairs may not always be good but who has a wonderful knowledge of what is going on. According to him, Hartington will be Prime Minister very soon, and the Prime Minister of the real 'Liberal' party, of which the so called Conservatives are now the proper representatives. Hartington would never again be made to do the dirty work of the Radicals.[69]

Another misplaced judgement of Natty's was the confidence he placed in the political durability and effectiveness of his friend, the erratic Conservative Cabinet Minister Randolph Churchill. According to Roy Foster, Randolph Churchill became friendly with Sir Anthony de Rothschild, staying at Aston Clinton in 1873 and praising the cuisine: 'Like all Jews' places it is a wonderful house for eating, every kind of food.' By 1888 there was a 'growing intimacy' between Churchill and Natty, 'to whom he entrusted Cabinet secrets, the interests of whose firm he pressed in Persia, India, and Burma, who was – to general discomfiture – his closest adviser as Chancellor of the Exchequer, and to whose bank he owed £66,000 when he died'.[70] When he hastily and thoughtlessly resigned his position at the Exchequer in December 1886 after only five months in office, Lord Salisbury accepted his resignation and his political career was finished.

What fuelled the secession of the great landowners from the Liberal party were fears over enhanced rights for the tenants of Irish estates and the potential danger this posed for landowners in England. Natty voted with Whig aristocrats against Gladstone's Irish Land Bill (1880), as he regarded the compensation paid to tenants as equivalent to confiscation. Other votes followed against the Compensation for Disturbance Bill.[71] Although the actual split in the Liberal party developed over the Home Rule Bill for Ireland, Natty's disenchantment with Gladstone had been growing for some time, not only over his Bulgarian atrocities campaign in 1876 which was anti-Turkish and in part anti-Semitic in orientation, but also over the issue of social reform. It was pointed out that 'Liberals, like Goldwin Smith,

69 Donald Southgate, *The Passing of the Whigs* (London, 1965), p. 420; Bahlman (ed.), *The Diary of Sir Edward Hamilton 1885–1906* (Hull, 1993), p. 64.
70 R. F. Foster, *Lord Randolph Churchill: A Political Life* (Oxford, 1981), pp. 30 and 395.
71 Ferguson, *The World's Banker*, pp. 851–5.

E. A. Freeman and T. P. O'Connor, insisted that Disraeli *was* pursuing racially inspired Judaic policies that conflicted with Britain's Christian mission, so for them there could be no question of irrational anti-Semitism', but other historians would dispute this, claiming that the anti-Semitic venom of the campaign was in no way 'superficial'.[72] The Liberal party had once stood firmly for Jewish emancipation, but that cause had been won and now that the party hosted a nest of vociferous anti-Jewish agitators, there was little to keep Natty within the party fold; this was particularly the case when questions of state intervention, rather than private philanthropy, were starting to emerge, questions such as the compulsory purchase of land to provide allotments and old age pensions.[73]

72 Endelman and Kushner, *Disraeli's Jewishness*, pp. 11–14.
73 Davis, *The English Rothschilds*, p. 199.

3

THE IMPERIALIST PHASE

Discussing the standing of the Rothschild Bank at the end of the nineteenth century, the financial journalist J. Hall Richardson concluded that Natty, Alfred and Leopold 'kept their own hands on the pulse of the money market from day-to-day, and their firm was by no means a back number, although it was not so prominent as an issuing house in the "nineties" as it had been in the "seventies". Naturally, the rise of the South African magnates drew public interest towards such firms as Wernher, Beit and Company and Barnato Brothers'. Assessing Lord Rothschild's career in 1915, *The Times* similarly noted that:

> According to the general belief of the best-informed people in the City, the fact that, since 1890, New Court has taken a less active part in the loan business of London than previously was due as much to the dislike he felt to undertake new business unless all three partners were in thorough agreement as to his own prudent temperament. 'Councils of war do not fight' it was said by the energetic people who wanted the great firm in St. Swithin's Lane to take the lead in the financing of China in the 90s and to go into new fields. It is probably true that London as a money centre, though enormously powerful, was not so powerful as it would have been if the Rothschilds had thought fit to initiate and control some of the big new business of the last 25 years. But it may be that London has

been safer for this conservative attitude adopted by Lord Rothschild and his brothers.[1]

While it was true that the bank was undergoing a gentle decline, it was not the case that it was so effete as to be unable to proceed in some fresh directions, particularly in southern Africa. Having worked in close association with his father for almost twenty years Natty, as the senior partner in the bank, was insufficiently self-reliant to take hard business decisions without the input of his fellow partners, his brothers. Their training had equally accustomed them to exercise caution and to avoid taking bold decisions, even as the market for the bank's services was changing. Natty revealed that it was his bank's business practice when allotting shares in a new loan to 'separate the applications as far as we can, dividing those we consider *bona fide* from those we consider to be of a speculative nature, and we begin by allotting to the *bona fide* subscribers as much as we can.'[2] New business opportunities were mishandled. In 1879, Natty responded to an offer to participate in funding operations in the United States by responding that 'we were ready to go into the matter, and would willingly take hold of it, but on one condition only, that we were not willing to join any American syndicate and be at their mercy or command, and would only take it up if we were given the lead to work it our own way with a group of friends around us, as in my father's time'.[3] On 14 January 1880, Edward Guinness had an interview with Natty, requesting him to assist in the disposal of the family brewery 'by the issue of the capital [to the public] under the auspices' of N. M. Rothschild & Sons, but the terms offered by Natty for undertaking this transaction were not acceptable and the Guinness family looked elsewhere. When Natty was asked whether he had any regrets about turning down the chance of floating Guinness as a limited liability company, he replied that

> I go to the bank every morning, and when I say 'No' to every scheme and enterprise submitted to me, I return home at night care-free and contented. But when I agree to any proposal, I am immediately filled

1   J. Hall Richardson, *From the City to Fleet Street* (London, 1927), p. 173. *The Times* 1 April 1915.
2   Select Committee on Foreign Loans 1875, evidence of Sir Nathaniel de Rothschild q. 5856.
3   Stanley Chapman, *The Rise of Merchant Banking* (London, 1984), p. 87.

with anxiety. To say 'yes' is like putting your finger in a machine – the whirring wheels may drag your whole body in after the finger.[4]

So, too, the Paris house followed Natty's lead in rejecting a proposition to participate in the construction of a section of the London Underground railway.[5]

In addition, Natty was increasingly deaf in middle age and had an unappealingly gruff manner which deterred prospective clients, with whom interviews tended to be terse, limited to a few minutes. Revelstoke, a banking rival, dismissed the Rothschild brothers as 'so unreasonable and lazy it is difficult to ensure a business being properly carried through under their direction. They refuse to look into new things and their intelligence and capacity is not of a high order'. So too, the brilliantly innovative banker Ernest Cassel assessed the brothers in 1901 as being 'absolutely useless & not remarkable for intelligence'. These wholly negative assessments of the brothers were somewhat too dismissive, however.[6]

Natty and his brothers had a partners' dining room at New Court, where they sometimes lunched with guests. Otherwise they were to be found 'in the great oak-lined [partners'] room, with windows fronting the Court', reported J. Hall Richardson,

> in which were placed, at some distance apart, a little table, assigned to Mr Alfred, and, nearer the window, the table occupied by Mr Leopold, and at the other end of the room, the big table at which Lord Rothschild, portly, rather gruff, very deaf, sat. To this table I was taken on special occasions only, when a conference was deemed desirable. There was a continual incoming and outgoing of heads of departments. It was in the days of Carl Meyer ... and he, too, was sometimes present. Members of the Stock Exchange, money-brokers, merchants and City men came and went, quoting prices in a jargon, which fortunately was intelligible to me from my early Stock Exchange training.

4   RAL 000/96B Edward Guinness to Natty 17 January 1880 and to S. N. Braithwaite 21 January 1880; Cecil Roth, *The Magnificent Rothschilds* (London, 1939), pp. 98–9.
5   RAL T16/57 Alphonse in Paris to London cousins, 9 April 1894.
6   David Kynaston, *The City of London: Golden Years 1890–1914* Vol. 2 (London, 1995), pp. 271–2.

Most observers reckoned that Natty was the decisive figure in the triumvirate, though Lord Suffield claimed in 1901 that Alfred 'carries more weight in the firm than even Lord Rothschild, his advice being the one followed in financial matters'; a year later, Cassel made much the same comment, remarking that it was Alfred to whom the other two brothers deferred. Leopold was considered to be more of a sportsman than a financier, yet shrewd enough to deal with business issues when Alfred was away.[7] Nonetheless, correspondence from the 1880s indicates that both Alfred and Leo were reluctant to take a final decision in any matter of importance without Natty's approval. When Baring Gould visited the Rothschild offices in 1888 in Natty's absence, he explained that Central 'wanted to raise £500,000 in Debentures, he talked of 5½% interest at par, redeemable in 5 years at par and 1½% commission ... we told him we did not think there was a chance of your agreeing to this', Alfred advised Natty,

> but possibly one of the 2 following propositions might lead to business, viz a 5½% debenture at par less 2% commission, redeemable at *103*, spread over 7 years, or a 6% debenture at 98 less 2%, redeemable at par, and likewise spread over 7 years ... but naturally we did not make him any firm offer – we simply mentioned these 2 alternatives as a *point de depart* for future discussion.[8]

'Throughout his career, with all its great and multifarious duties and interests, Lord Rothschild was a City man of the best type. He was to be found in New Court during a considerable portion of nearly every day, except when engaged on important business elsewhere or when taking a well-earned holiday from City business', averred *The Times*. Even Leopold, in his early days as a partner, sometimes put in lengthy hours in the office, writing to his wife on 15 September 1881 that 'I have been very busy & have been hard at work from half past ten o'C[lock] till half six – but as I had two long holidays, I must not complain.'[9] Junior office staff and

---

7   Hall Richardson, *From the City to Fleet Street*, pp. 168–9 and Kynaston, *The City of London* Vol. 2, p. 271. CZA H1/2111-25-2. Israel Zangwill to Theodor Herzl, 21 November 1901.
8   RAL X1/109/127 Alfred to Natty 2 February 1888.
9   *The Times* 1 April 1915, and RAL 000/2019/34 Leo to Marie de Rothschild, 15 September 1881.

family members who were being trained as potential partners always had to function at a hectic pace. One of the clerks, Carl Meyer, grumbled to his wife in the mid-1880s that

> It is nearly half-past 6 and ... I have been working ever since this morning ... His lordship [Natty] asked me to lunch with him in the private dining-room – so you may imagine how I have worked ... I have been extremely busy again all day long and shall continue to be so if I want to get away on Friday evening. But it MUST be done ... I have very little to tell you, except the old story that I can hardly hold my pen, so busy have I been all day long ... I am really too beastly overworked.[10]

Natty's son Charles

> often complained of the strain which his financial and social duties were for him, and it was not without interest to hear that his bringing up under the supervision of his father ... had been very strict, and that he had to work like an ordinary employee of the firm, morning and afternoon, only a few hours remaining free for relaxation. His occupation in the firm allowed him only a short holiday, which he usually spent at Peszer or on the estate of his wife.[11]

With Natty at the helm, N. M. Rothschild & Sons was a smoothly functioning, efficient machine in the 1880s, 1890s and the early years of the twentieth century. Consequently, Ronald Palin's evidence of a lethargic state of affairs at the Bank before the First World War, with Leo arriving at 11.00 a.m., lunching at 1.30 p.m. and returning home at 5.00 p.m., and with Alfred arriving at 2.00 p.m., lunching at 3.30 p.m. and spending much of the afternoon dozing should be largely discounted. Palin only joined the bank after the War, so that what he heard was gossip about the final years of Alfred and Leo, when their energy levels and health went into decline.[12]

10 David Kynaston, *The City of London* Vol. 1 (London, 1994), p. 355; Carl Meyer Papers, Carl to Adele Meyer 3 August 1885.

11 RAL 000/848/25 *Peszer Lloyd* November 1923 'In Memory of Nathaniel Charles Rothschild'.

12 Ferguson, *The World's Banker*, pp. 752–3.

To understand the world in which Natty and his brothers operated, it is necessary to see them as key players in the late Victorian phase of empire-building. P. J. Cain and A. G. Hopkins have formulated the concept of gentlemanly capitalism, a theory that held that British imperialism was driven by business interests in the City of London rather than by provincial manufacturers and strategic geopolitical considerations. This overturned Ronald Robinson's and John Gallagher's interpretation, which emphasized the interplay between strategic factors as perceived by ministers and officials in London and the collaboration or resistance of the local population to empire-building. Further, Cain and Hopkins believed that industrialization had developed in a much more fragmented and uneven fashion than had previously been supposed. From the eighteenth century onwards, they argued, 'an alliance was forged between the City, southern investors and the landed interest which was to play a leading role in British overseas expansion until well into the twentieth century'. Hence

> The period 1880–1914 was one of precarious equipoise, when the power of finance, growing increasingly cosmopolitan, reached a transitory equality with that of land, whose agricultural base was being slowly undermined by the free trade internationalism on which the City flourished; after 1914, financial power was clearly more potent than that of the land.

Networks centred on the City of London ensured that the gentlemanly capitalists exerted a powerful influence on government policy and the decision-makers. It was 'The growth of the service sector, including the financial institutions centred upon London [rather than industry, which] was the chief influence upon Britain's presence overseas after 1850.'[13]

The Rothschild family, and Natty in particular, were prime examples of this concept of 'gentlemanly capitalism'. As Cain and Hopkins have suggested:

---

13   Andrew Porter, '"Gentlemanly Capitalism" and Empire: The British Empire since 1750?', *Journal of Imperial and Commonwealth History* 18:3 (1990), p. 266; P. J. Cain and A. G. Hopkins, *British Imperialism: Innovation and Expansion 1688–1914* (London, 1993), p. 131; Roland Robinson and John Gallagher, *Africa and the Victorians: the Official Mind of Imperialism* (London, 1981).

The most eminent figures in the Square Mile were those who had access to information which was either denied to others, including fellow members of the City fraternity, or which reached them at a later date. Privileged information, from which large fortunes and high standing flowed, came principally from contact with those who controlled the machinery of state. Once in the charmed circles of power, bankers gained both immediate profit and entry to a network of contacts and information that opened up additional prospects; as their connections multiplied, so too did their prestige and authority. As confidence in selected bankers grew, they were entrusted with the savings of the elite ... The greatest bankers were able to amass huge fortunes without having to mobilise vast stocks of their own resources because they were able to channel the capital of others ... For these reasons the relations formed between the upper reaches of the financial world on the one hand and high society and high politics on the other were rooted more in face-to-face contact and personal understandings than in perfect market competition or in the cold rationality which Weber associated with modern bureaucracy and with modernisation itself.[14]

This explains the wining and dining by Natty and his brothers of influential ministers and higher grade civil servants outside successive Liberal and Conservative administrations. It also explains why one little girl thought Natty 'lived at the Foreign Office, because from my schoolroom window I used to watch his carriage standing outside every afternoon – while in reality he was closeted with Lord Balfour'.[15] Between 1865 and 1914, of the £1.48 billion issued in foreign public sector issues in London, Niall Ferguson calculated that three-quarters of this business was handled by the Rothschild Bank, alone or in partnership. Thus, the Rothschilds dominated the market for the issue of foreign government bonds. Yet, during the same period, N. M. Rothschild & Sons accounted for only a quarter – £1,085 million – of the public issue of foreign securities in the London market. Despite the involvement of Natty and his brother Alfred in the politics of imperialism, Ferguson wondered why imperial issues only comprised six per cent of the Rothschilds' business. Part of the answer

14 P. J. Cain and A. G. Hopkins, *British Imperialism 1688–2000* (Cambridge, 2002), pp. 41–2.
15 Rothschild, *Dear Lord Rothschild*, p. 38.

may lie in Natty's very profitable personal investment in South African diamond and gold mines.[16]

Shrewd observers grasped that the purchase of shares in the Suez Canal would inevitably lead to the British government assuming financial control over Egypt and eventually political authority. As the crisis in the Egyptian government's finances worsened, it was agreed that the Khedive's domain lands which encompassed one fifth of the Egyptian agricultural land should be mortgaged to raise another loan. Charles Rivers Wilson, a civil servant at the Treasury, was made Egyptian Minister of Finance with Monsieur de Blignières as the Minister of Public Works to ensure that a new, stricter regime was enforced. Under the terms of the Khedive's decree of 26 October 1878, N. M. Rothschild & Sons and the French house of Rothschild Frères were empowered to issue a loan of £8.5 million at five per cent.[17] Natty had prepared the prospectus for this share issue beforehand, sending it to his French cousins for their approval and with Rivers Wilson's help sorted out the terms of the Khedive's decree.[18] Claiming that the new regulatory regime was unpopular with his subjects, the Khedive dismissed it. Meanwhile, Rivers Wilson proposed that the Rothschilds should withdraw their loan and, at the same time, exert pressure on the British government to compel the Sultan to dismiss the Khedive. Hence, on 10 April 1879 the British Prime Minister was informed that 'The Rothschilds object strongly to Wilson's proposal to withdraw the loan, which they would consider a very dishonourable proceeding. They wish to work in close cooperation with Her Majesty's Government.' In other words, the Rothschilds fell into line with the Rivers Wilson's second suggestion.[19]

Lord Salisbury complained to the British ambassador to France that

> It may be quite tolerable and even agreeable to the French Government
> to go into partnership with the bondholders, or rather to act as sheriff's
> officers for them ... We have no wish to part company with France,
> still less do we mean that France should acquire in Egypt any special

16 Ferguson, *The World's Banker*, pp. 813–15.
17 D. C. M. Platt, *Finance, Trade and Politics in British Foreign Policy 1815–1914* (Oxford, 1968), p. 166; Caroline Shaw, *The Necessary Security: An Illustrated History of Rothschild Bonds* (London, 2006), pp. 20–1.
18 RAL 000/96B Natty to his cousins Paris 26 October and 6 November 1878.
19 Davis, *The English Rothschilds*, pp. 181–2.

ascendancy; but subject to these two considerations, I should be glad to be free of the companionship of the bondholder.

What happened was that Britain, working in close co-operation with France and the other European powers, compelled the Sultan to dismiss the Khedive and replace him with his eldest son. D. C. M. Platt concluded that the Tory administration 'was concerned primarily with stable government in Egypt – preferably native government – in the interests of Imperial commerce and strategy [safeguarding the Suez Canal and the route to India]. Its policy had no relation, except incidentally, with the interests of the British bondholders'.[20]

To reassure bond-holders, three commissioners nominated by Britain, France and Egypt were placed in control of the Commission of Management of the Domain lands, which were held as security for the Rothschild loan. The British commissioner was Francis Rowsell, the former superintendent of naval contracts at the Admiralty, who worked not only closely with his French colleague Monsieur Boutcron but with the ailing Baron Lionel and Natty who was assisting him. Prior to his departure overseas, Rowsell was fully briefed by Baron Lionel and Natty.[21] 'We are setting the central house in order ... he reported to the bank after arriving in Egypt,

> by the suppression of useless [cotton] ginning mills with their staff ... each one doing some 30 days work a year – whilst two mills kept going can do ... all the work of the estates, cheaper & better in 100 days. In the purchase of stores – coal etc – large savings will be made by simply acting according to common sense, and passing by the den of thieves at Alexandria & elsewhere.

The European Commissioners soon protested vigorously against the imposition of a *corvée* on the labour of the estates under their management, securing the exemption of two-thirds of these properties, though elsewhere they had to seek exemption from the tax by paying a redemption fee of 15 francs per head. This new burden, Rowsell estimated, could amount to £35,000 per annum. Then there was a revolt of army officers demanding

20 Platt, *Finance, Trade and Politics*, pp. 169–71.
21 RAL 000/96B Natty to his cousins in Paris 31 December 1878 and Francis Rowsell to Baron Lionel 1 January 1879.

immediate payment of arrears of pay, forcing the Commissioners to advance a huge sum in francs.[22] Rowsell was worried that

> while fights for place are going on in Cairo, public works are neglected & the canals are left uncared [for]. There is promise of an excellent harvest of grain, if only the people be left alone to garner it, and not taken for the new levy of 15,000 men for the army – or for *Corvées* or other drafts on labour. You may rely upon the united best efforts of my colleagues & myself to keep the interests of the loan safe ... It will be for the Governments & yourselves to decide our future action.

Problems were also encountered with the claims of prior mortgagees on the state lands.[23]

Following on these difficulties, there was a fresh, unwarranted demand for £55,000 in taxes claimed by certain provinces, to which Rowsell responded by saying that 'Of course we shall not pay, for we have not the means'. The Khedive's Minister was given to 'understand that he would get nothing till after the wheat harvest, & further until we could see that the December coupon was secured'.[24] A week later, Rowsell wrote to Baron Lionel that

> The true cause of the [budgetary] deficit, however, is I am sure, to be found in the items of wages & cattle purchases, & cattle maintenance ... But the practical conclusion at which I arrive is that the sooner the lands are put in hirings sufficient to pay the coupons & to give a surplus towards amortisement, the better ... The cost of a corporation must almost necessarily be greater than those of private persons doing the same thing – I hope to have an opportunity of discussing these points fully with you next month.

In the meantime, he was warned to keep these observations on the budget private.[25]

The correspondence shows how determined the British financial representatives in Egypt were to protect the interests of the bondholders and how closely Rowsell coordinated his policy with that of the Rothschild bank.

22   Ibid., 6 and 22 March 1879.
23   Ibid., 12 April 1879.
24   Ibid. Francis Rowsell to Baron Lionel 19 and 26 April 1879.
25   Ibid., 3 May 1879.

Towards the end of 1881, Arabi Pasha's nationalist party gained the ascendancy in Egypt, exciting fears of instability among British politicians. A joint note from France and Britain sounded very much like an ultimatum and Alexandria was bombarded in July 1882 following a riot in which fifty Europeans were killed. Due to British military intervention and the crushing of the nationalists, Britain was forced to occupy Egypt after September to ensure good government and to prevent any other European power gaining control of vital strategic assets. A. G. Hopkins challenged this interpretation by arguing that British officials based in Egypt and particularly Auckland Colvin, the new Controller-General, were pressing in 1882 for a more robust form of intervention, influencing the politicians and press in London. Furthermore, Hartington, the Secretary of State for India, and Dilke, the Under-Secretary at the Foreign Office, demanded that the Liberal government adopt a more robust policy as regards Egypt, even if this resulted in its occupation. Britain now had a considerable economic stake in Egypt. In 1880, Britain absorbed eighty per cent of Egyptian exports and supplied forty-four per cent of her imports, much of this being the exchange of Manchester cotton goods for Egyptian raw cotton; by 1873, British investors, who were sinking their money into infrastructure projects, were owed more than half the public debt.[26] Even Gladstone himself had a dark secret, namely his large holding of Ottoman Egyptian Tribute Loan bonds which amounted to thirty-seven per cent of his entire portfolio and which climbed steeply in value after the British occupation. One important point overlooked by Hopkins was that the British and French governments were using the Rothschilds – Natty and his brother-in-law Alphonse in Paris – as a channel for back-door communication, by way of coordinating their policy towards Egypt with the result that the two governments took an increasingly tough line against the regime. Alphonse was extremely pleased with the bombardment of Alexandria, pointing out that 'England can now no longer withdraw until law and order are re-established all over the country; this is the best guarantee ... to all those with legal interests in Egypt'.[27] On 7 September 1882, Granville informed Gladstone that

---

26 A. G. Hopkins, 'The Victorians and Africa: A Reconsideration of the Occupation of Egypt, 1882', *Journal of African History* 27:2 (1986), pp. 363–91.

27 Ferguson, *The World's Banker*, pp. 834–6 and 840.

> Brett has written to Dilke to tell him that Tissot had asked Nat
> Rothschild, what were the plans of the Gov as to Egypt, and whether we
> should like to renew the Treaty of Commerce – & that Rothschild had
> answered that he could not say anything as to the 2d question but as to
> the first, it was clear that England must secure the future predominance.
> To which Tissot answered 'naturally'.

Niall Ferguson further claimed that it was 'difficult to avoid the conclusion
that the Rothschilds encouraged the British government to override
Gladstone's conscientious scruples and ... forcibly to "put down Arabi",'
but this was to ignore the plethora of patriotic political forces within the
government and the civil service and diffuse economic interests in the
country pushing for the occupation of Egypt and Gladstone's own dark
secret.[28]

It was a widely held view in radical circles in Britain that the government
had intervened to protect the interests of the bankers and bondholders. As
Wilfrid Scawen Blunt observed, Rivers Wilson believed that he had

> the full support of the London Foreign Office ... and the interest and
> power of the house of Rothschild. On this last he knew he could rely, for
> he had just persuaded them on his passage through Paris to advance the
> fatal loan of nine millions on the Khedival Domains which was to bind
> them to the cause of European intervention whenever necessary on the
> part of the bondholders.

But it might be suggested that Baron Lionel was too canny a financier not
to know when an ill-considered financial proposition was being placed in
front of him. Blunt further embroidered this fanciful story, by alleging that
the Rothschilds tried pulling strings in London and Paris, but on account
of the situation in South Africa – the Zulu War – the British government
was reluctant to take any action. Because of this impasse, Blunt continued,
the Rothschilds turned to Bismarck,

> who ever since his Frankfort days had extended a certain contemptuous
> protection to the great Hebrew house, and not in vain. The French and
> English Governments were given to understand by the then all powerful

---

28 Agatha Ramm (ed.), *Gladstone – Granville Correspondence, 1876–1886* Vol. 1 (Oxford,
    1962), p. 417; Ferguson, *The World's Banker*, p. 836.

Chancellor that if they were unable to intervene effectively in Egypt in the bondholders interests, the German Government would make the cause their own.

Hence the British intervention in 1879, and again in 1882, when Bismarck stirred up the situation in Egypt – as if Bismarck would be acting in great power relations at the behest of the Rothschilds.[29] Where Blunt's account was misleading was his supposition that the aims of the Rothschilds and the British government were incompatible, while he ignored Britain's growing economic ties to Egypt.

Francis Rowsell, the British Commissioner, was in regular communication with Natty about the running of these estates, which at first required additional borrowings to keep them functioning, sending him accounts and information from the other Commissioners. By 1884, he had become convinced that the mortgage over the domain lands should be redeemed.

> But it would be so popular a thing to abolish the Domain administration. I know everybody, from the highest pasha down to the last cowherd would be delighted to get these estates into native hands ...
> I look forward to more trouble and confusion for that unfortunate Egyptian country, cursed in its protection.

Alfred assisted his brother in the handling of the Egyptian loan by the bank and Charles Rivers Wilson, the Khedive's Finance Minister, was a frequent visitor to Alfred's country house.[30] The Egyptian economy rapidly benefited from the efficient administration supplied by Britain. When, in 1885, Britain wanted to float a new loan of £9.4 million at three per cent to be guaranteed by the six Powers represented in the *Caisse de la dette publique*, Bismarck insisted on the participation of the German banks in the issue, thereby precluding the involvement of the Bank of England. Salisbury decided that N. M. Rothschild was the obvious choice for the loan, as it had branches in London, Paris and Frankfurt and enjoyed amicable relations with Bleichroder. When Rowsell died prematurely, Natty's prior approval

29 Wilfrid Scawen Blunt, *Secret History of the English Occupation of Egypt* (London, 1907), pp. 42, 65–6, 255 and 276.
30 Caroline Shaw, 'Egyptian Finances in the Nineteenth Century: A Rothschild Perspective' in *The Rothschild Archive* report 2005–6, pp. 34–8; RAL 000/96B Lord Tenterden to Natty 16 November 1879.

was sought on the appointment of a new British Commissioner, Mr Gibson, who took office in 1886 at a reduced salary. In all, the Rothschilds issued four Egyptian loans between 1885 and 1893, totalling £50 million.[31] Under British administration, Egypt flourished. 'Thanks for your congratulations about my budget of 1891, the results of last year are extraordinarily good, Egypt has never had such a large revenue as that of 1890', wrote an official to Lord Rothschild. By 1894 'The various Reserve Funds reached a total of £E3,554,000' boasted Alfred Milner in the preface to 'England in Egypt' (1894), a bestseller among investors that rapidly went through five editions.[32]

Baron Lionel had initiated the Egyptian loan business which proved to be a valuable learning experience for Natty given the numerous difficulties he had to surmount; ultimately it became a profitable one. As Milner stated in reference to one matter of contention in 1891, 'It is not worth anybody's while, considering the magnitude of the relations between the Egyptian Government and your House, to have a serious dispute about a comparative trifle.'[33] It was not so much falling profits in Egypt but a failure of nerve and vision on Natty's part as a third-generation member of the Rothschild Bank that prevented investment in lucrative infrastructure projects once the economic situation had stabilized, thus allowing Cassel to replace it.

Stanley Chapman noted that the Rothschilds, in the tradition of Court Jews, were interested in bullion dealing, quicksilver and precious stones. Hence, after Britain added Burma to its empire, the Rothschilds successfully floated the Burma Ruby Mines in the 1880s, and this became a profitable enterprise.[34] Although Natty fumbled when it came to seizing offers to float leading enterprises, he was quick to exploit the new opportunities arising from the discovery of diamonds and gold in South Africa. Fortuitously after the Californian gold rush of 1849, the Rothschilds despatched a relative of theirs, one Davidson, to the United States, enabling them to become large-scale importers of gold and establish important

---

31 Ferguson, *The World's Banker*, pp. 838–9 and Stern, *Gold and Iron*, pp. 422–3; RAL 000/96B Julian Pauncefote to Natty 15 February 1886.
32 RAL T15/78 E. Palmer to Lord Rothschild 9 February 1891. Alfred Milner, *England in Egypt* (London, 1894), p. vi.
33 RAL T15/79 Alfred Milner to Lord Rothschild 27 July 1891.
34 Chapman, *The Rise of Merchant Banking*, p. 25.

connections with the mining engineers. In 1881, Natty commissioned Hamilton Smith, who was trained in the new, more scientific, mining techniques, to prepare a report about the El Callao gold mine in Venezuela. Natty was so favourably impressed with the report that he persuaded Hamilton Smith to settle in London, where, with Edmund de Crano, he opened a thriving mining consultancy which in 1886 became the Exploration Company. While this company was originally set up for the express purpose of assessing the potential of mineral finds, it was reconstituted as a joint-stock company three years later with the objective of company promotion. Natty, Alfred and Leo were the major shareholders in the Exploration Company between 1886 and 1914, though the size of their holding shrank from a third in 1890 to 7.6 per cent in 1914 because there were other, more profitable, forms of investment. The original twenty members were entitled to half the profits after ten per cent had been distributed, but there was an outcry from other shareholders against this blatantly unfair method of distribution. So, in 1895, founder shares were scrapped and, by way of compensation, the original members were allotted half the capital in the company at par. The close relationship between the Rothschilds and the Exploration Company was indicated by the fact that an early office was sited in St Swithin's Lane, close to New Court, and the fact that the Company's extraordinary meetings were held at the bank's premises.[35]

As early as 1882, Natty had despatched Albert Gansl, his former San Francisco agent, to Kimberley to report on the Anglo-African Diamond Mining Co., which owned part of the Dutoitspan diamond mine. On 16 November 1882, Gansl informed him from Kimberley that 'The largest proportion of the [diamond mining] Companies being represented in London and finding it urgent that immediate steps should be taken for united action and possibly for prompt amalgamation, I intend to return to Europe ...' asking for his message to be relayed to the Paris house. He recommended a vast reconstruction scheme to merge a hundred small companies, but this proved to be unworkable.[36] In 1885,

35 Robert Vicat Turrell with Jean-Jacques Van Helten, 'The Rothschilds, the Exploration Company and Mining Finance', *Business History* 28:2 (April 1986), pp. 183–6.
36 RAL T43/1 Albert Gansl to N. M. Rothschild & Sons 16 November 1882; Ferguson, *The World's Banker*, p. 881.

Charles Roulina, the owner of a large diamond-cutting plant in Paris, put forward an alternative amalgamation scheme, but this foundered on the opposition of the major diamond mine-owners in Kimberley, including Cecil Rhodes. Unable to compete with some of his major competitors, who were mining at deeper levels, Rhodes ignored safety rules and ordered his men to continue working regardless of the consequences. This led to a disaster in 1888, when 178 African labourers and 24 white miners perished. Meanwhile, in 1887, Rhodes had appointed Gardner Williams, an American mining expert associated with Smith and de Crano, as general manager of his De Beers mining company as a means of securing financial backing from Lord Rothschild due to Williams' links to the Exploration Company. Despite the fact that Rhodes' competitor, Kimberley Central, was in a stronger position financially, Gardner Williams' recommendation was crucial in tipping the scales in Rhodes' favour and winning over Natty's support for the takeover of the *Compagnie Française*, the leading independent company that owned a multitude of rich claims. Rhodes, by restructuring the Kimberley board, also secured the adhesion of Alfred Beit, an influential diamond-broker and financier, and Harry Mosenthal to his side.[37] To set up a meeting, Williams sent a detailed report to Hamilton Smith and de Crano, begging them to secure an audience for Rhodes with Lord Rothschild. Carl Meyer, an astute and increasingly influential senior clerk, working for the London Rothschilds, read Gardner's detailed memorandum and was convinced by his arguments, in turn persuading Natty. Thus the ground was prepared when Natty met de Crano and Rhodes at New Court. On leaving the meeting, as Rhodes and Williams had gone on ahead, Natty said to de Crano: 'You may tell Mr Rhodes that if he can buy the French Company I think I can raise the million pounds.' With this part of his mission completed, Rhodes went on to Paris to confer with Jules Porges, a founder of the *Compagnie Française* and a business associate of Beit; there was also a helpful business connection between Harry Mosenthal of the Exploration Company and Porges.[38] N. M. Rothschild & Sons guaranteed the sum of £750,000

37   Rob Turrell, 'Rhodes, De Beers, and Monopoly', *Journal of Imperial and Commonwealth History* X:3 (May 1982), pp. 327–33; Turrell, 'The Rothschilds, the Exploration Company and Mining Finance', p. 187.
38   Paul H. Emden, *Randlords* (London, 1935), pp. 50–1.

required by De Beers to purchase the company in August 1887, for which they were handed a commission of £100,000, but in addition to this, the Rothschild syndicate profited from a share option scheme, so that 'in effect … [they were] paid £250,000 for advancing £750,000 for the purchase'. In the autumn of 1887, Carl Meyer was despatched to Paris to oversee the negotiations for the liquidation of the French business. The opposition of Kimberley Central, a rival company under the control of Barney Barnato, was bought off by De Beers offering them the prize of the *Compagnie Française* for 35,600 £10 shares in the Central together with £300,000 in cash. Thus the titanic struggle between Rhodes and Barnato was an elaborate charade, as the latter had already secured sufficient inducements from Rhodes to collaborate with him. Rhodes assured Stow that

> The great comfort I feel now is that the goal is reached. Barnato, who has 8,000 De Beers and 1,500 one hundred Centrals or roughly £600,000 of parent stock is working in everything with me and has given his pledge to go to the end with me and Baring-Gould though a weak man has made up his mind to go with the tide. Whatever Porges may be I feel for self interest alone Beit has burnt his boats and would sooner quarrel with his home firm than sell me and he is working heartily for the same object.

During October, Rhodes and Beit held secret discussions with Barnato and Baring-Gould to arrange the amalgamation of Kimberley with De Beers. To ensure this merger succeeded and the formation of De Beers Consolidated Mines Limited Rhodes, with the help of Barnato, bought shares in Central and later joined the Rothschilds and others in netting shares at bargain prices when the stock market boom collapsed. Unification of the two companies, did not take place, however, until February 1889 because of continuing shareholder disputes.[39]

In Paris, Baron Gustave, after a briefing from Carl Meyer in October 1887, complained of being left out of the complete picture of the negotiations, taking umbrage – according to Meyer – because the Paris House was not as busy as its London rival. 'We are delighted', he advised his English cousins,

39 Turrell, 'Rhodes, De Beers, and Monopoly', pp. 330–3.

to see all now being settled by some sort of amalgamation of De Beers with Kimberley. However, we expect to have, as you have, a voice in that matter and that you will oppose the formidable association so as to prevent using its strength in order to overpower the Anglo-African for the sake of buying more profitably their shares.[40]

Natty issued £2.25 million debenture stock in De Beers to wipe out the debts that had been incurred in the past and to purchase leases in mines in Dutoitspan and Bultfontein; and the injection of cash continued unabated through the Exploration Company in 1889, with some later assistance from the London Rothschilds who, in 1894, issued De Beers debentures worth £3.5 million. At the same time, Carl Meyer, who was developing an expertise in South African mining affairs, was appointed in 1888 to the London board of De Beers to exercise a watching brief on behalf of N. M. Rothschild & Sons, who held 31,666 shares, the second-largest holding in the company.[41]

From the first, there were clashes between the London board of De Beers, dominated by Natty through his nominee Carl Meyer, and their Kimberley counterparts led by Rhodes over the business and financial practices of the company. Rhodes wanted to use the company's resources to fulfil his imperial ambitions, whereas Natty and Meyer were determined to adhere to more orthodox canons of conduct. Apart from this worthy objective, Natty believed – somewhat naïvely – that it was the function of the Hatton Garden diamond merchants to set up a syndicate to control wild fluctuations in the price of diamonds, rather than leaving this to the directors of the Kimberley board. Rhodes had taken a great gamble to bring about the amalgamation of the Kimberley diamond mines, so the fruits of such a merger were not going to be surrendered lightly by him. Natty reprimanded Rhodes on 7 August 1891, exclaiming that:

> I had a long visit or visitation the other day from Mr Roulina who came to complain of the fall in the price of diamonds which was ruining him and he wanted the [De Beers] Company to store all their diamonds for a long time and not pay any dividends. I told him I had nothing to say

40 RAL T43/11 Baron Gustave Paris to his cousins 5 October 1887; T43/16 Carl Meyer to N. M. Rothschild & Sons even date.
41 Ferguson, *The World's Banker*, p. 833.

in the management of the concern but if I were asked I would strongly advise you not to do anything of the kind as you had duties as great, if not greater, towards your shareholders as towards the trade and that I considered you had no right to speculate in diamonds but were bound to sell as best you could. But I added he had the remedy in his own hands, if he wished to ensure a high and stable price for diamonds he need only form a syndicate, deposit caution money, and guarantee you a certain price for a certain quantity for a long time to come ... I have heard nothing from him since but all this talk does the De Beers Co'y a great deal of harm and the shares are lower than ever. I hope you will soon hold your meeting, make a brilliant speech and restore confidence among your shareholders. And above all, I hope you will husband the resources of the Company and make them as financially strong and as powerful an association as they deserve to be.[42]

Otherwise, Natty wanted to distance himself from the day-to-day running of De Beers, allowing Rhodes and his fellow directors to guide the direction of the company. He informed Rhodes that

As regards Debeers you know I do not like to interfere in their internal administration, and only hope that the Company will be able to pay a good dividend and gradually diminish their indebtedness. The Reserve Fund is no doubt an element of great strength to them'.[43]

When Natty and Carl Meyer discovered, in 1891 that Rhodes had assembled a secret reserve of diamonds to keep up the price level they were furious as was the Liberal press in London and eight Kimberley firms left the syndicate. Natty cautioned Rhodes against the syndicate trying 'to force up the price of the article too much'.[44]

Another source of friction with Rhodes was the system of Life Governors that had been instituted by him to appease Barnato, entitling these appointees to a certain share of the profits exceeding thirty-six per cent. The issue continued to simmer as a matter of contention. In the next year Rhodes wrote to Natty that

42 S. D. Chapman, 'Rhodes and the City of London, Another View of Imperialism', *The Historical Journal* 28:3 (1985), pp. 647–66 and particularly p. 654.
43 Rhodes House, Rhodes MSS, Af.S 228 C.9 f.36 Natty to Rhodes 12 July 1892.
44 Chapman, 'Rhodes and the City of London', p. 655.

> Your statement practically amounts to this ... that the Life Governors have drawn from the Company more than their due ... If, as I gather, the resolution of the Board adopted on the 4th May 1898 did not express the views of yourself and the majority of the French shareholders who you state represent the larger portion of the Company's capital, then I think the question should be reopened and settled on its purely legal merits ...[45]

On 4 May 1899, following another board meeting, Carl Meyer, who was a tough negotiator, noted that Rhodes 'appeared flushed with his triumph on Tuesday, and began his violent abuse of me again. After we called each other liars and duly put it in the minutes he proceeded to formulate his demands and as they were moderate we agreed on all points so that now I hope we shall have peace for some time.'

Gradually the areas of disagreement were whittled down. By 1901 Meyer noted that

> Rhodes was very amiable for once and as pleasant as one could wish, his heart trouble seems to have softened the harshness and bitterness to some extent and he never once said a disagreeable thing. I may say that we nearly came to an agreement on all questions. And have since been to New Court where the agreement arrived at meets with their approval so I think we shall carry it through on Wednesday after which Rhodes wants to be off ... to Egypt ... The outcome is that the Life Governors will be bought out by means of an issue of new shares worth at present prices about 3 millions sterling! Not a bad haul for them.[46]

The final point of contention between Natty and Rhodes was the pace and direction of British imperial expansion which Natty held was on no account to be subsidized from the ample coffers of De Beers, though he was a foundation shareholder of the British South Africa Company (1889) and the Matebele Concession Syndicate (1890). The former company was set up by Rhodes to colonize an area which later became known as Rhodesia.[47] While not discussing the subject with any of the other De Beers directors, Natty poured out his thoughts in candid fashion to Rhodes in 1892:

45 Ibid., p. 656.
46 Carl Meyer Papers, Carl to Adele Meyer 4 May 1899 and 7 October 1901.
47 Davis, *The English Rothschilds*, pp. 212–13.

Let us say at once that our first and foremost wish in connexion with South African matters is that you should remain as the head of affairs in that colony that you should be able to carry out that great imperial policy which has been the dream of your life – I think you will do us the justice to admit that we have always loyally supported you in the carrying out of that policy, and you may rest assured that we shall continue to do so ... you are the only judge as to whether the Cape Government ought to take over the Northern Territories; that is not our business, and we do not wish to offer any opinion on the subject. You must know how far your Charter would be violated or not by such a policy, and whether it would meet with the approval of Her Majesty's Government. But what we do say, is, that if it is your policy, and you require money for the purpose, you will have to obtain it from other sources than the cash reserve of the Debeers Company. We have always held that the Debeers Company is simply and purely a diamond mining company ... It is quite possible that the Articles of Association may give you a loophole, but nowadays, people are disposed to construe the articles of association more severely than they used to do ... If you must raise money for the maintenance of the Chartered Company, and require increased revenue for that purpose, we can only say that sooner than let Debeers Co subsidize the Charted Company, we would prefer putting a small export tax on diamonds ... And this raises the point if the time has come for you to consider whether the Cape Government should take over the Diamond Mines and buy out the shareholders ... at a fair and equitable price.[48]

Rhodes had a gargantuan vision of Britain dominating the globe. He believed in the possibility of 'the occupation by British allies of the entire Continent of Africa, the Holy Land, the valley of the Euphrates, the islands of Cyprus and Crete ... the whole of South America, the islands of the Pacific, the whole of the Malay Archipelago, the seabord of China and Japan'. So too, the United States would rejoin the British Empire. There was a danger that if Britain did not seize Bechuanaland and the Matabele territories fast enough, the Transvaal Republic and the Germans in South-West Africa would link up and block British expansion northwards. At first, Rhodes was confident that Natty fully shared his vision of an active British

48   Rhodes House, Rhodes MSS C3b f.201a Natty to Rhodes 15 January 1892.

policy for southern Africa. He entrusted him as the executor of his fourth and fifth wills with the formation of a secretive and educated elite to foster the expansion of the British Empire, suggesting on 2 June 1888 that Natty take for his model the Jesuit Constitution, substituting the words 'British Empire' for 'Roman Catholic Religion'. Natty was required 'to establish a society of the elect for the good of the Empire'.[49] In 1891, J. Astley Cooper, editor of the periodical *Greater Britain,* put forward a scheme for students from the colonies to study at British universities. T. Hudson Beare, an Australian based in Britain, suggested that 100 scholarships should be awarded for youth from the Empire who were eager to complete their higher education in Britain. Alerted to these possibilities, Rhodes, in his sixth will, allotted part of his fortune for scholarships for students from South Africa to study in Britain, recasting the scheme in his final will for the endowment of Oxford scholarships for young men from all parts of the English-speaking world.[50] Although Natty remarked that 'Oxford will be able to offer inducements to Colonials, even Americans, to study on the banks of the Isis and to learn, as Rhodes did there, to love his country and to make it big and prosperous', it is doubtful whether he had anything to do with reshaping the scheme along more practical lines, as he had been removed as a trustee from Rhodes' final testament. Even before that had happened they had drifted apart, as Rhodes began to doubt Natty's steadfast commitment to his vision, castigating him in 1891 to Reginald Brett as 'Honest but without sufficient brains'. Rhodes was tormented by the thought that 'if I die, all my money will pass into the hands of a man who, however well-disposed, is absolutely incapable of understanding my ideas. I have endeavoured to explain them to him, but I could see from the look on his face that it made no impression ... and that I was simply wasting my time'.[51]

On the Witwatersrand, the Exploration Company was a key inter-mediary between the Rothschilds and Wernher, Beit & Co, which established control over gold production in the Central Rand. In 1887, Rhodes and Charles Rudd formed Gold Fields of South Africa, in which

49   Philip Ziegler, *Legacy: Cecil Rhodes, the Rhodes Trust, and Rhodes Scholarships* (New Haven, 2008), p. 10; Davis, *The English Rothschilds*, p. 213.

50   Ziegler, *Legacy*, pp. 16–17.

51   Davis, *The English Rothschilds*, pp. 213–14. Ferguson, *The World's Banker*, pp. 887–8.

the Rothschilds purchased 13,000 ordinary shares by 1898, though by 1914 they had almost halved their investment in the company. Rhodes was, in any case, not a talented gold mine developer, failing to grasp the potential of reefs on the Rand and falling out with men who possessed such knowledge. Writing to Natty on 29 October 1888, Rhodes lamely pleaded that the negotiations over the De Beers amalgamation had taken up so much of his time that he had 'missed the best part' of the Rand and that 'at present prices there is not much margin for profit'.[52] In addition, Rhodes had vastly exaggerated hopes of the potential of mines in Matabeleland, declaring in 1888 'As to the gold all my reports only verify previous statements the gold bearing reefs are simply endless'.[53] In 1890, the much more commercially astute Alfred Beit became convinced of the potential of deep-level gold mining and started buying up concessions in the Central Rand which became the sites of deep mines.

Rhodes, as we have seen, was determined to encircle the Transvaal with British possessions, becoming disappointed when Natty failed to cajole Portugal into ceding Delagoa Bay, its port on the coast of Mozambique, as this was a vital export link for the Transvaal. Under the terms of the Sivewright agreement, the Cape railways were almost given the monopoly of trade with the goldfields of the Rand. While on his trip to Southern Africa, the invaluable Carl Meyer advised Natty to confer with Rhodes and advance a loan to the government of Transvaal for the construction of an extension to their railways. In May 1892, after a positive survey by Hamilton Smith and no doubt the enthusiastic endorsement of Meyer, the London Rothschilds purchased 9,000 shares in the increasingly valuable Wernher, Beit deep-level gold mines on the Rand.[54] Carl Meyer, on a trip to South Africa at this time, had already reported in glowing terms to New Court, declaring that

52   Robert V. Kubicek, *Economic Imperialism in Theory and Practice. The Case of South African Gold Mining Finance 1886–1914* (Durham, NC, 1979), pp. 86–7 and 112; Rhodes House, Rhodes MSS,t.14 f.319 Rhodes to Natty 29 October 1888.
53   Rhodes House, Rhodes MSS Aiv.t.14 f.315 Rhodes to Natty 20 January 1888.
54   Kenneth Wilburn 'The Nature of the Rothschild Loan, International Capital and South African Railway Diplomacy, Politics and Construction 1891–1892', *South African Journal of Economic History* 3:1 (March 1988), pp. 4–19.

looking at the different Gold mines and other properties ... I am becoming quite an expert in mining ... I have no hesitation in saying that, in my opinion, these fields have an enormous future before them and that the country altogether will, for the next 10 or 20 years, offer a greater scope for European capital than South America and similar countries. Here is a fine country, lovely climate, inhabited by Dutch and Anglo-Saxons, only beginning to be developed and replete with every mineral as well as adapted for every branch of agriculture. I feel that it would pay for the House of Rothschild to have a clever representative here who would be able to do plenty of good business.[55]

Meyer was obviously angling for an enhanced role in the operations of N. M. Rothschild & Sons, an approach that was spurned. In July 1892, on the strength of his advice, Natty agreed to advance Kruger a loan of £2.5 million so long as he undertook not to borrow

more money for the Natal extension, and as you [Rhodes] will see from the prospectus, we insisted upon the money being spent exclusively within the limits of the Republic [thereby thwarting the extension under Kruger's own auspices into Portuguese territory]. Naturally we shall never let them think that we are acting at your suggestion.[56]

Both Rhodes and the British government continued to believe that because of the financial exigencies of the Boer Republic, the port of Delagoa Bay would in the course of time slip into their own hands, thus giving them a stranglehold on Transvaal.

On 17 January 1893, the Rothschilds' mining expert Hamilton Smith wrote a widely quoted article in *The Times,* which claimed that the Rand held gold reserves worth over £300 million. Shortly afterwards, in February 1893, Rand Mines was launched with a nominal capital of £400,000, in which Wernher, Beit and their Johannesburg representatives took half the shares; it was a giant holding company which bought a number of deep-level claims and a majority holding in five smaller mining companies.[57]

55   RAL T43/5 Carl Meyer to N. M. Rothschild & Sons 26 March 1892.
56   Rhodes MSS Afr.S.228 C9 f.36 Natty to Rhodes 12 July 1892.
57   *The Times* 17 January 1893 and Turrell, 'The Rothschilds, the Exploration Company and Mining Finance', pp. 187–8.

Deep-level mines started to proliferate, as Goldfields of Mashonaland came into production, followed in 1894 by Jumpers Deep Levels and the Transvaal and General Association. The Rothschilds were allotted 27,000 out of 100,000 shares in Rand Mines, later in 1897 taking £35,000 in bonds.[58] With the growing prosperity of the Boers, British hopes of the easy incorporation of these territories evaporated and Rhodes' policy grew increasingly confrontational. In the meantime, relations between Natty and Rhodes cooled, so much so that Natty was not taken into Rhodes' confidence when he made preparations for the Jameson raid, an abortive coup in December 1895 against Kruger's Afrikaner regime in the Transvaal that ended in disaster.[59] Rhodes was one of a number of charismatic personalities; others were Disraeli, Lord Randolph Churchill and Theodor Herzl. These men captivated the more prosaically minded Natty, kindling hidden passions which he was often too frightened to express; but the more grandiose Rhodes' vision grew, the greater the lack of comprehension on Natty's part.

Still the Rothschilds persisted and Alfred tried a new tactic, making fresh overtures to Portugal, approaching their envoy, Luiz de Soveral, again in 1896 for a concession for an extended Transvaal railway. Earlier, when he had enquired whether the Portuguese government would sell 'Delagoa Bay & Railway, he [the envoy] replied that this was not possible but indicated that there might be some other way of securing your object', though he would not say 'what this alternative might be'. Joseph Chamberlain adumbrated other possible courses of action which would be open to the Portuguese government, including the sale to the British government of a 99-year lease on the disputed territory in exchange for payment of a lump sum, or a sale to a private company domiciled in Portugal but controlled by British shareholders. Nothing, came of this diplomatic initiative, however.[60]

Natty liked to establish a listening-post in each British administration with easy access to the Prime Minister and ministers, by way of passing on foreign news and diplomatic gossip and for sounding out whether a new

58 Ferguson, *The World's Banker*, pp. 877–8; David Kynaston, *The City of London* Vol. 2, pp. 82–4; Kubicek, *Economic Imperialism*, p. 64.

59 Wilburn, 'The nature of the Rothschild loan', p. 10; Richard, *The English Rothschilds*, pp. 216–17.

60 RAL 000/182 Joseph Chamberlain to Alfred 28 July 1896.

foreign loan to the Transvaal or Russia would meet with official approval. During Lord Salisbury's first two administrations, he tried the direct approach and offered his profuse thanks and personal favours, such as procuring 'a carriage for you at Boulogne or Calais'. When Natty asked for a financial concession on behalf of his friends the Sassoons, Salisbury replied that 'the Government will be prepared to grant a Charter to the Arabian Bank, if the terms ... which are admittedly faulty, are altered in a manner to make it satisfactory to the Treasury'.[61] But during Salisbury's third administration, Natty relied increasingly on conferring with Schomberg McDonnell, his Lordship's principal private secretary, whether it was to pass on a warning about the Brazilian government's designs on Trinidad, a message in 1897 that Turkey would quit an occupied part of Greece 'on payment of a million and a half, or two millions' or that the Bank of England should, in various ways, support the Chinese Loan brought out by the Hong Kong and Shanghai Bank.[62] In 1897, Natty advised McDonnell that 'It will be impossible to place the Loan [for the Sudanese Railway] on the English market at less than 4%. To bring it out at 3½% would mean failure, and would make my House look ridiculous. He called up Alfred Rothschild ... and said the same only more strongly'.[63] By the end of 1898, he was alerting Salisbury to

the internal condition of France as very dangerous ... Prince Louis [Napoleon] is said to have raised funds sufficient for a *coup d'etat*, mainly owing to the Duchess of Rivoli and Madame Murat (both Jewesses by blood) ... who want to shew themselves more Catholic than the Pope, in establishing an Empire based on the Army and the Church.[64]

Although the hardline policy of Joseph Chamberlain, the Colonial Secretary, and Sir Alfred Milner, the High Commissioner, inevitably led to the Boer

61 Hatfield House, 3 Marquess, Rothschild file, Natty to Lord Salisbury 18 September 1885 and 25 February late 1880s; Lord Salisbury to Natty 29 June 1889 and Natty to Lord Salisbury 2 July 1889.
62 Hatfield House, 3 Marquess, Rothschild file, notes of Schomberg McDonnell 21 October 1895, 20 August 1897 and 23 February 1898; Natty to Schomberg McDonnell 23 February 1898.
63 Hatfield House, 3 Marquess, Rothschild file, note of Schomberg McDonnell 4 December 1897.
64 Hatfield House, 3 Marquess, Rothschild file, note of Schomberg McDonnell 31 December 1898.

War in 1899, Alfred de Rothschild and Natty in Britain and their business associate, Sammy Marks, in the Republic acted as peacemakers. At first Chamberlain, was open to suggestions, writing to Alfred in June 1899 that 'I admit that I was not very sanguine that representations will have much effect on Mr Kruger. But I do not see that your letter from an independent source can possibly do any harm, & I sincerely hope that it may do good.'[65] Marks was a diamond dealer and entrepreneur based in Pretoria, the creator of the South African steel industry and a huge coal-mining enterprise and the founder of a distillery; he enjoyed good relations with President Paul Kruger.[66] On 13 June 1899, Marks was cabled by Isaac Lewis, his London-based partner, asking him to approach Kruger secretly, informing him that the London house of Rothschild wanted to act as intermediary between him and the British government to facilitate the efforts for peace. Lewis felt that this 'opened a door for the President to enable him to secure without any loss of dignity, peace and prosperity for the country'. Natty was also sanguine about the prospects for peace, telling Lord Salisbury's private secretary: 'I enclose a cable from Pretoria ... I think it shows they will ultimately settle all outstanding questions but you are better able to judge than I am.' Kruger was convinced, however, that Natty, who in 1898 had attached onerous conditions to a new loan, was working closely with Chamberlain and Rhodes to rob the Republic of its independence. Nothing Marks said could shake Kruger's obduracy, as he was certain that 'England will never be satisfied until she has the Transvaal and this idea has such a hold on the Old Man that no argument I may address seems to shake it.' A few weeks later, the Rothschilds renewed their offer, only to be rebuffed by Kruger once again. Lewis informed Marks that

> There is not the slightest doubt as to the enormous influence they [the Rothschilds] hold, and that they should have volunteered their services to assist in bringing about a peaceful solution seemed to me a wonderful step to have gained. I am the more surprised therefore and disappointed that their intervention should in the end have been so badly received.[67]

65 RAL 000/182 Joseph Chamberlain to Alfred 13 June 1899.
66 Richard Mendelsohn and Milton Shain, *The Jews in South Africa* (Johannesburg, 2008), pp. 54–5.
67 Richard Mendelsohn, *Sammy Marks: 'The Uncrowned King of Transvaal'* (Athens, OH,

On 6 July 1899 Chamberlain was informed by Natty that Kruger was willing to make major concessions on the franchise under which the Uitlanders (the non-Boer residents) would be given a 'seven years' retrospective and retroactive franchise' which 'would be accepted with acclamation by the non-British Uitlanders who it feared expect Lord Salisbury to go to war'. The crisis seemed to be over, yet Marks remained suspicious of the Colonial Secretary, suggesting that 'Chamberlain and party do not care so much whether the franchise is granted as they would make believe'. His prediction proved correct, as Chamberlain made a speech in the House of Commons on 28 July 1899, stating that Britain had the right to intervene in the internal affairs of Transvaal, fanning Kruger's distrust. At Hartington's suggestion, Natty sent a telegram on 25 September to Marks, outlining fresh proposals:

> Government of Great Britain are anxious Peace. If agree to 5 Year Franchise without conditions Government of Transvaal have no reason to fear friendly discussion subsequently arranging details. Positively no further demands shall … be sprung. War occur now it is his [Kruger's] fault not Government of Great Britain … We are assured by N. M. Rothschild & Sons Government of Great Britain and England or the British do not wish interfere integrity Transvaal … Most strongly urge you to do utmost secure franchise *without conditions*. In our opinion only way war can be prevented.

The proposal was scotched both by Kruger and the British Prime Minster Salisbury, who feared the outcome of such unauthorized negotiations.[68] Natty clung to a desperate hope for peace until the last, misreading the impasse in the negotiations with the Boers. Writing to McDonell on 29 September 1899, he observed that 'As a matter of course you will go on with your preparations but it strikes me that if Steyn has asked you what you want, it must be with the knowledge of Kruger & would show a desire for peace.'[69]

1991), pp. 111–12; Hatfield House, 3 Marquess, Rothschild file, Natty to Schomberg McDonnell 24 July 1899.

68 Ferguson, *The World's Banker*, p. 891; Mendelsohn, *Sammy Marks*, pp. 113–14; Hatfield House, 3 Marquess, Rothschild file, cables Lewis to Marks 26 September 1899 and Marks to Lewis 27 September 1899.

69 Hatfield House, 3 Marquess, Rothschild file, Natty to Schomberg McDonnell 29 September 1899.

Despite Natty's efforts for peace, J. A. Hobson, the liberal journalist, blamed Jewish financiers and mine-owners for the war, claiming that

> recent developments of Transvaal gold-mining have thrown the economic resources of the country more and more into the hands of a small group of financiers, chiefly German in origin and Jewish by race. By superior ability, enterprise and organization these men, out-competing the slower-witted Briton, have attained a practical supremacy which no one who has visited Johannesburg is likely to question.

He went on to observe that

> When it is borne in mind that this great confederation of press interests is financially cemented by the fact that Rand mining magnates are chief owners of at least two important London daily newspapers, and of several considerable weekly papers, while the wider and ever-growing Jewish control of other organs of the press warrants a suspicion that the direct economic nexus between the English press and Rand finance is far stronger than is actually known, we shall have a clear comprehension of the press conspiracy which has success-fully exploited the stupid jingoism of the British public for its clearly conceived economic ends ...

Two years later, in *Imperialism: A Study* (1902), he questioned whether anyone could 'seriously suppose that a great war could be undertaken by a European state ... if the House of Rothschild and its connections set their face against it?'[70] Natty warned Rhodes to

> be careful in what you say regarding the conduct of the war and your relations with the military authorities. Feeling in this country [is] running high at present over everything connected with the war and there is a considerable inclination, on both sides of the House, to lay the blame for what has taken place on the shoulders of capitalists and those interested in South African Mining.

---

70 Albert S. Lindemann, *Esau's Tears: Modern Anti-Semitism and the Rise of the Jews* (Cambridge, 1997), pp. 362–3; John Allett, 'New Liberalism, Old Prejudices: J. A. Hobson and the "Jewish Question"', *Jewish Social Studies* 49:2 (Spring 1987), pp. 99–114; Claire Hirshfield, 'The Anglo-Boer War and the Issue of Jewish Culpability', *Journal of Contemporary History* 15:4 (October 1980), pp. 619–31.

Once the war had started, Natty was for its vigorous prosecution, including the interdiction of provisions going to the Boers at Delagoa Bay.[71]

Robert Kubizek distanced himself from the view of Cain and Hopkins, who asserted that 'British-led diamond- and gold-mining imperialism, and ultimately the [Boer] war itself, served the City of London financial and service sector interests ...' Kubizek, by contrast, suggests that Chamberlain then (Secretary of State for Colonies) and Alfred Milner (British High Commissioner to the Cape), in working up to a conflict with Paul Kruger (President of the Transvaal) over the Uitlander question, acted *against* the dominant will of City financiers (as represented by the Rothschilds) who favoured a peaceful solution. This simplified summary of Kubizek's comments, noted Raymond Dumett, 'merely demonstrates how difficult it is effectively to separate out the "gentlemanly capitalist' financial/services element in imperialism from political and strategic considerations and (to cite another alternative theory of causation) the purely idiosyncratic acts of wilful politicians and vainglorious 'men on the spot'.[72]

Cain and Hopkins' rejoinder to this rebuttal of their thesis was to claim first that the gentlemen capitalists benefited from their South African mining shares and that at the request of the Colonial Office the international banks in London tried to create difficulties for the Transvaal government in 1898, when it attempted to borrow money. Natty informed the Colonial Office that 'any loan could be stopped and would be in London and possibly in Paris, but we cannot influence the market in Holland or Germany'.[73] Secondly, Cain and Hopkins suggested that

> more important agents [of conflict] were the imperial government and, indirectly, the mine-owners. Neither wanted war; both exerted the pressures that brought it about. The imperial government knowingly adopted a high-risk policy ... Britain's determined stance owed little to strategic considerations: by the 1890s her interests and ambitions in South Africa had far outgrown the requirements of a naval base ...

71 Ferguson, *The World's Banker*, p. 892 and Hatfield House, 3 Marquess, Rothschild file, Natty to Schomberg McDonnell 18 October 1899.

72 Raymond E. Dumett, Introduction in Raymond E. Dumett, ed., *Capitalism and British Imperialism: The New Debate on Empire* (London, 1999), p. 23.

73 Cain and Hopkins, Afterword, p. 210 in Dumett, ed., *Gentlemanly Capitalism and British Imperialism*; Cain and Hopkins, *British Imperialism 1688–2000*, p. 325.

[at Simonstown] ... Nevertheless, the mine-owners played their part in a dangerous game. They pressed their grievances against Kruger's government in 1899, generalised them to include political questions, and associated themselves with Milner to an extent that compromised the search for a peaceful settlement.

Further, they argued that 'the principal motive [of the British government for the war] was the more general one of preventing a union of South Africa under the leadership of the Transvaal, creating what Lord Selborne called a

> "United States of South Africa", which might have damaged Britain's economic interests in the region and harmed her broader geopolitical commitments ... If the outcome is judged by the subsequent trade and investment figures, and by South Africa's support for the war effort in 1914 and 1939 ... the strategy was equally successful.[74]

Ultimately, after the Boer War broke out, Natty and the other gentlemen capitalists decided that their interests coincided with that of the government and called for the war's vigorous prosecution. What this revealed was that, whereas the British advance into Egypt was a more clear-cut example of gentlemanly capitalism, the reasons for the involvement of Britain in South Africa were more complicated, though in the last analysis this still upholds the Cain/Hopkins thesis.[75] In addition, as we shall see in the next chapter, Natty, the gentleman capitalist, was very much in favour of the foundation of new small Jewish colonies so long as they became an integral part of the British Empire.

Apart from this, Natty fully supported Lord Randolph Churchill's trip to South Africa in 1891 in search of gold, providing his mining engineer, H. Perkins, for the expedition and facilities at the bank for the Syndicate. To finance this expedition, Churchill had formed a syndicate which raised nearly £16,000. He held a stake of £5,000, which he borrowed from Lord and Lady Wimborne, who invested another £2,000 on their own account; his other sister, Lady Sarah Wilson, contributed £1,000 to the Syndicate and the Duchess of Marlborough a similar amount. The mining magnate Beit travelled with the expedition, while Rhodes offered Churchill hospitality in Cape Town.

74   Cain and Hopkins, *British Imperialism 1688–2000*, pp. 325–6.
75   Dumett, Introduction in Dumett, ed., *Capitalism and British Imperialism*, pp. 22 and 23.

The whole affair was an excellent example of gentlemanly capitalism.[76] But the search was so fruitless that, on his return to London, Churchill denounced the prospects of Mashonaland and the mining exploration syndicates. On one occasion at Tring, he told Natty to his face that Rhodes was 'a sham', so incensing him that he left the room until his fury abated.[77]

According to Cain and Hopkins 'the adherence of successive governments to the gold standard and free trade strengthened sterling's role as an international currency, reinforced the City's position as a global financial centre, and entrenched Britain as the world's leading shipping, insurance and brokerage market'. As far as the majority of voices in the City of London were concerned, free trade and the gold standard underpinned the flow of goods in international commerce; but in the 1880s and 1890s and into the Edwardian era, bimetallists disputed the efficacy of the gold standard, blaming it for the fall in prices and deflation. Instead, they advocated a freely convertible bimetallic standard which would stem the import of cheap foodstuffs from South America and ease competition in the Indian market for manufactured cotton articles, thereby generating a fierce political controversy.[78] Although E. H. H. Green questioned the strength of the argument that gentlemanly capitalists in the City and elsewhere successfully blocked the bimetallists' campaign, he conceded one of the strongest contentions of Cain and Hopkins. This was that 'given the City's geographical position and centrality to government finance, most senior politicians, administrators and bankers "inhabited the same mental world"'.[79] Since 1868, Alfred de Rothschild had served on the Court of Directors of the Bank of England, the first Jew to do so, resigning on grounds of ill-health in 1890. His retirement was regretted by his colleagues, showing that his contribution to their financial deliberations

76   Foster, *Lord Randolph Churchill*, p. 372; RAL, T15/84 and 86 Randolph Churchill to Natty 22 March and 17 May 1891.

77   Ferguson, *The World's Banker*, p. 886.

78   E. H. H. Green, 'Gentlemanly Capitalism and British Economic Policy, 1880–1914' in Dumett, ed., *Gentlemanly Capitalism and British Imperialism*, pp. 44–67 and particularly 45; E. H. H. Green, 'Rentiers versus Producers? The Political Economy of the Bimetallic Controversy c. 1880–1898', *English Historical Review* 103 (1988), pp. 588–612; and A. C. Howe, ''Bimetallism, c. 1880–1898: A Controversy Re-opened?' 105 (1990), pp. 377–91.

79   Cain and Hopkins, Afterword in Dumett, ed., *Gentlemanly Capitalism and British Imperialism*, p. 199.

was valued and that he was not sitting on the board as a mere figurehead. So when the Chancellor of the Exchequer, Sir William Harcourt, wanted a safe pair of hands to serve on the British delegation to the International Monetary Conference in 1892 in order to counter the bimetallists in the Commons, he chose Alfred.[80] Writing to Natty, Sir William Harcourt, Chancellor of the Exchequer, who was a family friend, asked him to

> express to Alfred my sense of his kindness in desiring to help me out of what is certainly a most awkward situation – The name of Rothschild will carry a weight which no other could command in the monetary world ... I take for granted that he is a good sound staunch monomet-allist ... who will uphold to the death the single gold standard which has been maintained in England now for nearly a century & which has, I believe given her the command of the money markets of the world and has been the sheet anchor of her commercial and financial prosperity.

Natty assured Harcourt of Alfred's reliability, also forwarding him a letter addressed to the station master at Cologne to ease Harcourt's journey to take the waters at a spa, while Alfred sent him a much longer letter, confirming that there could not be found a 'stauncher supporter of Monometallism than myself'; and enclosing a memorandum he had written in 1886, when requested to outline his views on the subject by the Governor of the Bank of England. His sound views had been formulated before 'the great fall in the price of silver and the corresponding depreciation in the value of the rupee'. Thanking Alfred, Harcourt remarked that 'this currency question has never been in a more ticklish situation or one that requires more firm & intel-ligent handling'.[81] After busily studying the question, Alfred concocted a compromise formula, whereby the price of silver would have been stabilized without giving it a status similar to gold. Niall Ferguson concedes that this was the most 'practicable' of the three schemes to be submitted to the confer-ence.[82] However, until his doctor, Dr Broadbent, came to the conference

80 Davis, *The English Rothschilds*, p. 228; Ferguson, *The World's Banker*, pp. 743 and 874–5.
81 Bodleian Libraries, Harcourt MSS dep. 166, f.59 Natty to Harcourt 31 August 1892, f.61 Harcourt to Natty 1 September 1892, f.66 Natty to Harcourt 2 September 1892, f.68 Alfred to Harcourt with 1886 memorandum ff.70 and 71, 2 September 1892, f.76 Harcourt to Alfred 5 September 1892; f.87 Alfred to Harcourt 5 October 1892.
82 Ferguson, *The World's Banker*, p. 1226n. 74.

in Brussels on receipt of an urgent summons, Alfred was too nervous and agitated to be effective, though afterwards he became more operational. His aide from the bank, Carl Meyer, who loyally supported him, reported that

> we have endless small meetings, discussions, visits ... The worst of it is that Alfred won't go to see anyone & always sends others which with some of the swells produces a certain friction and coolness. As usual the French are the most disagreeable. But our worst enemy is Bertram Currie, one of the English delegates who is jealous of Alfred and tries to thwart his plans ... besides it changes every day like a kaleidoscope. One thing is certain and that is that nothing DEFINITE will come out of all this – at the best only a basis for future diplomatic negotiations between the Powers.

Alfred's plan with two other older schemes were submitted to a sub-committee. Carl Meyer remained of the view that Alfred's scheme would not be 'adopted as it is open to any number of objections but Alfred was the hero of the hour having brought forward the ONLY practical suggestion & he is naturally as proud as a peacock – he is quite a different man since Broadbent came as he has more confidence in himself'. To Alfred's annoyance, his old friend Sir Charles Rivers Wilson, the Comptroller General of the Public Debt Office, and another member of the British delegation, made a speech against his plan, while the devastating onslaught of the French delegate 'shattered the remnants of' Alfred's 'hopes'. Although there was a proposal to adjourn the conference until the summer of 1893, Harcourt instructed the British delegates not to agree to this to ensure that the discussions came to a halt.[83] Even before this point had been reached when it became apparent that the American plan 'to discontinue their yearly purchase of 54 Million ounces of silver' or 'to go on with them' in return for European concessions was going nowhere, Alfred was pleading to be allowed to return home. He had to be dissuaded from a premature departure by a flattering missive from Harcourt, who wanted the conference to end in a 'euthanasia' and praised Alfred's contribution to this end for 'the able and intelligent manner in which you have represented a great nation'.[84]

83 Carl Meyer Papers, Carl to Adele Meyer 4 October, 27 and 28 November, 9, 11 and 16 December 1892.
84 Bodleian Libraries Harcourt MSS dep.167 f.5; Alfred to Harcourt 5 December 1892;

Another area in which the Rothschilds heavily invested was copper. During the late 1880s, the Paris and London banks bought a controlling interest in the Rio Tinto mines in Spain which produced more than ten per cent of the world's copper, introducing open-cast mining and quadrupling production within ten years.[85] Adding to their investment in this area, the English Rothschilds, through their investment vehicle the Exploration Company, bought a controlling interest in the Anaconda copper mine near Bute, Montana in 1895, which produced twenty-five per cent of North American copper, so that by the close of the century it is reckoned that the Rothschilds controlled almost forty per cent of world copper production. After receiving a report from their mining engineer E. Cumenge in February 1898, however, who forecast that profitability of the Montana mine would fall steeply, the Rothschilds sold their interest. Having helped to stabilize world copper production and to keep up the price level, the Rothschilds installed their employee, Charles Fielding, as a board member and later as chairman of Rio Tinto in 1904. Under his leadership, the company introduced many technological advances in copper production and the manufacture of superphosphate used in chemical fertilizers.[86] With a dividend level of 69.05 per cent between 1897 and 1913, the performance of Rio Tinto was astonishing and by 1912 it was the world's 'thirteenth largest company in terms of its capitalization'.[87] The American banker Jacob Schiff introduced the Guggenheims to the mining engineer Hamilton Smith of the Exploration Company, leading the way to the Rothschilds. By 1900 M. Guggenheim & Sons of New York, with their silver and copper mines, was a favoured client of the London bank, their account showing a turnover of £7.1 million.[88]

At the turn of the twentieth century, the energy level of the three Rothschild brothers was declining and Natty suffered from a prolonged

ff.7–14 Harcourt to Alfred 6 December 1892.
85 Ferguson, *The World's Banker*, pp. 878–9; Raymond Carr, *Spain 1808–1939* (Oxford, 1966), pp. 265 and 391.
86 Miguel A. López-Morrell, *The House of Rothschild in Spain 1812–1941* (Farnham Surrey, 2013), pp. 245–51.
87 Ibid., p. 252.
88 Cyrus Adler, *Jacob H. Schiff: His Life and Letters* Vol. 1 (New York, 1928), pp. 155–6; Chapman, *The Rise of Merchant Banking*, p. 24.

bout of ill-health in 1901, necessitating a lengthy diet of 'milk and biscuits'. At the same time, there was no injection of fresh talent into the leadership of the bank. Natty's heir Walter, who was autistic, was found to be unsuited to banking and Charles, his second son, was young and untested while in any case remaining a reluctant banker. Nor were Leo's sons particularly talented as bankers.[89] Apart from this, Natty's financial touch was not so sure-footed as it had been in the past. Despite organizing the rescue of Barings, he pooh-poohed the rumours that the rival merchant bank was in trouble, assuring Randolph Churchill until the last minute that all was well. Churchill wrote to Alfred 'What a time you must have had in the City last week. Fancy the Barings brought so low. Natty told me when I was at Tring that they were allright.'[90]

Sixteen years later, Mount Stephen blamed Lord Rothschild for the loss of income incurred in selling Argentinian bonds, when the latter was treasurer of the hospital charity, the King's Fund.[91] On the other hand, our account reveals that Alfred, despite his hypochondria, had been a useful second-in-command at the bank, both for financial negotiations and diplomatic overtures. Nevertheless, by 1905 his rudeness to staff was becoming insufferable, treating 'men of 30 years service like office boys'.[92]

Spurned by Natty and his brothers when he had asked to be made a partner in the bank, Carl Meyer, who possessed the requisite ability, transferred his business allegiance to Ernest Cassel in 1897, though he still remained on friendly terms with his former employers. According to Edward Hamilton, the Rothschild brothers believed that Meyer had grown 'too big for his boots'. Cassel financed the construction of the Aswan Dam, helped set up the National Bank of Egypt and arranged for the purchase of the Daira Sanieh Sugar Co, all ventures which the Rothschilds deemed too risky to handle. Cassel worked closely with Meyer, who had an office in the London headquarters of the National Bank of Egypt and grew immensely wealthy. Meyer also had business interests in China. Without

---

89   Carl Meyer Papers, Carl to Adele Meyer 3 September 1901.
90   RAL T15/58 Randolph Churchill to Alfred 17 November 1890. Philip Zeigler, *The Sixth Great Power: Barings, 1762–1929* (London, 1988), pp. 244–53.
91   F. K. Prochaska, *Philanthropy and the Hospitals of London: The King's Fund 1897–1990* (Oxford, 1992), pp. 42–3.
92   Chapman, *The Rise of Merchant Banking*, p. 25.

the momentum supplied by Meyer, it is difficult to explain why the Rothschilds became so active and so successful in southern Africa after 1887, when the brothers usually had a much more passive approach to new business opportunities.[93] Behind the riches reaped by the London house in the 1890s and beyond in the diamond mines and goldfields was the guiding hand of Meyer. As Natty explained to Rhodes in 1901,

> the history of the Debeers Company is simply a fairy tale. You have succeeded in establishing a practical monopoly of the production of diamonds, you have succeeded in establishing a marvellously steady market for the sale of your production, and you have succeeded in finding a machinery capable of carrying this through.

Meyer served on the board of De Beers shortly after its inception and was vice-chairman from 1888 to 1921. The French Rothschilds, however, were less successful than their London cousins, when it came to investing in gold mines.[94]

In the recent past, the Rothschild brothers had been both feared and respected in government circles, though these comments by a scion of a rival banking dynasty should be treated with a degree of caution. Sir Evelyn Baring informed Goschen that

> The disadvantages of dealing [with the Rothschilds] are that, so far as my experience goes, they are very difficult and not over pleasant people to deal with, and that they expect large profits. The advantage is that their influence is so great that they can go far to prevent anyone else competing with them. I am rather sceptical of being able to float a loan without the Rothschilds ...[95]

In 1897, Meyer transferred his allegiance and investment acumen elsewhere, good business ventures were missed, and the London house of Rothschild fell into relative decline, as rival banking houses seized a larger share of the market for loans and company flotations. The 'Rothschilds' reduced role in the financing of the Boer War was an ominous development', Niall

---

93 Pat Thane, 'Financiers and the British State: The Case of Sir Ernest Cassel', *Business History* (1986): 35–61.

94 Rhodes House, Rhodes Papers Af.S.228 C7b f.313 Natty to Rhodes 20 August 1901. Ferguson, *The World's Banker*, p. 877.

95 National Archives, FO 633/9 Baring to George Goschen 11 February 1888.

Ferguson noted. In the United States, the investment outlook was less gloomy, as the Rothschilds briefly poured money into the Anaconda copper mine and linked up with the Guggenheims, though their venture into the Interurban Street Railway Co. of New York was more problematic.[96] Moreover, Natty formed a syndicate in 1901 which controlled the mining of nickel in Canada; nickel was essential if the corrosion of armour plate and guns was to be prevented.[97] With hefty profits from diamond mines and copper, the Rothschilds were still a significant player in the City at the turn of the century; and with the establishment in 1897 of the Pekin Syndicate, originally an exploration company, but which gained huge concessions in China in the first decade of the twentieth century the Rothschilds' appetite for imperial adventures seemed unabated.[98]

Natty and his brothers, in their participation in the British scramble for Africa, namely in Egypt and South Africa, best exemplify the contentions of Cain and Hopkins about the role of gentlemen capitalists as the driving force behind Great Britain's quest for empire.[99] The Rothschilds financed the mergers of Maxim-Nordenfelt and Vickers, leading armaments manufacturers, companies which underpinned the expansion of the British Empire.[100] They were not only bankers but members of the landed interest with an ear close to leading politicians and senior civil servants, embodying all the characteristics of this form of capitalism. Their role as leaders of City opinion was equally significant in halting the campaign of the bimetallists in 1892 and maintaining the gold standard. Nor was the Rothschilds' role limited to the expansion of the formal empire, they were prominent players in areas of informal empire in South America. Despite the area succumbing to the general economic crisis of 1873, the Rothschilds successfully placed an issue of Brazilian bonds on the London market and, between 1858 and 1914, the Bank issued Brazilian bonds totalling £140 million for the government, railways and port facilities. Likewise between 1886 and 1914,

96 Ferguson, *The World's Banker*, pp. 892–4 and Adler, Jacob H. Schiff Vol. 1, pp. 167–8.
97 Anthony Allfrey, *Man of Arms: Sir Basil Zaharoff* (London, 1989), pp. 107–8.
98 Ferguson, *The World's Banker*, pp. 914–15 and 918; Frank H. H. King, 'One Letter and a New Understanding: The Rothschild Archive and the Story of the Pekin Syndicate', *The Rothschild Archive Review* (2006–7), pp. 41–7.
99 David Cannadine, 'The Empire Strikes Back', *Past and Present* (May 1995), pp. 190 and 192.
100 Allfrey, *Basil Zaharoff*, pp. 46 and 51.

the Rothschilds issued bonds for Chile worth £33 million on the strength of its export of nitrates.[101]

---

101 Caroline Shaw, *The Necessary Security: An Illustrated History of Rothschild Bonds* (London, 2006), pp. 28–30, 36; Cain and Hopkins, *British Imperialism Innovation and Expansion 1688–1914*, pp. 300, 303, 305 and 310; Anders L. Mikkelsen, 'With a Little Help from their Friends: The Maintenance of Brazilian Credit, 1889–1898' in The Rothschild Archive report 2010–11, pp. 20–5.

4

NATTY AND JEWISH INTERVENTION IN RUSSIA: THE FIRST PHASE

On 27 April 1881 the first pogrom in the wave of mass attacks on Russian Jews in 1881 and 1882 occurred in the city of Elisavetgrad (Kirovgrad) in the Ukraine during the week after Easter. The assassination of Tsar Alexander II, a month earlier, added to existing religious tensions and created a febrile atmosphere. John Klier has characterized the pogroms of 1881–2 as mainly an urban phenomenon spread by modern means of communication, the 'railroads, telegraph, and ... the printing-press' and noted that they could be best understood 'within the general model of an ethnic riot'.

The pogroms spread throughout the south-western provinces of the Russian Empire, jumping from the cities into the surrounding villages. The number of fatalities may not have exceeded fifty, however, of whom half were rioters fired upon by troops trying to suppress the disturbances. The violence was chiefly directed against Jewish-owned property. The

> city [of Elisavetgrad] presented an extraordinary sight: streets covered with feathers and obstructed with broken furniture which had been thrown out of the residences; houses with broken doors and windows; a raging mob, running about yelling and whistling in all directions and continuing its work

of destruction without let or hindrance, and ... complete indifference displayed by the local non-Jewish inhabitants to the havoc wrought before their eyes.

In addition, there were isolated but extensive pogroms against Jews in July 1883 and June 1884, followed by occasional outbreaks of violence. Recent research by Hans Rogger, Michael Aronson and John Klier has indicated that the pogroms were neither instigated nor tolerated by the Tsarist authorities, contrary to the belief of contemporaries.[1] If the local authorities failed to suppress violence rapidly, this may be attributed to the short-comings of the police and the reluctance of the army to become involved in civil disorders, rather than due to the malevolence of the authorities.

When reports of these disturbances first reached England, the Board of Deputies and the Anglo-Jewish Association sent a joint deputation on 24 May 1881 to Lord Granville, the Foreign Secretary in Gladstone's administration. Baron Henry Worms M.P. asked Lord Granville to 'make such representations to the Russian Government as to show that the voice of the country not only of the Jews, but the public generally, is undoubtedly against measures which are only worthy of the barbarism of the middle ages and which are a disgrace to the civilization of the present day'. This was a familiar theme in nineteenth-century Anglo-Jewish discourse, when urging the British government to take action after some anti-Semitic riot overseas. Arthur Cohen, the president of the Board of Deputies and a Rothschild relative, added that

> I know you will use all the influence you can bring to bear on the Government of Russia to induce that Government to do all in its power to put a stop to these outrages. I do not know whether your Lord has seen that a Jewish deputation [led by Baron Horace Gintsburg] has been received by the Russian Emperor, and that they have been delighted with their reception. That being the case, it would be a bad policy ... to express at this moment, the slightest mistrust as to the conduct of the Russian Government ... it may strengthen the hands of the Russian Government

1   S. M. Dubnov, *History of the Jews in Russia and Poland* Vol. 11 (Philadelphia, 1946), p. 250; Hans Rogger, *Jewish Policies and Right-Wing Politics in Imperial Russia* (University of California Press, 1986); John Doyle Klier, *Russians, Jews and the Pogroms of 1881–1882* (Cambridge, 2011), pp. 59, 79 and 412.

if they are informed of what is really the feeling not only of British Jews, but of the British public.

Natty's brother Leopold repeated this last point, while also stressing that 'by extending his mercy to the poor Jews, he [the Tsar] might feel that he can regain the confidence of his subjects and forget the terrors of Nihilism'. Given that the true extent of the outrages was unknown in Western Europe, the Foreign Secretary gave a non-committal reply, suggesting that it would be injudicious to make representations to the Russians. He thought that 'in many instances it might weaken the hands of the Government, who, I believe, are infinitely more enlightened than the mass of the people on the subject. I feel very strongly that if any representations are made they should not be official representations, and moreover they should not be made public.' Doubtless, few representations were made in private to the Russian ambassador and the pogroms continued unabated until a new initiative was taken by the Kovno circle.[2]

In the meantime, Sir Moses Montefiore wrote to his nephew, Arthur Cohen, on 24 May 1881 offering at the age of 96 to go to Russia and plead with the Tsar on behalf of his Jewish brethren.

> When I had the honour of an audience with the Emperor Nicholas in ... 1846, His Majesty observed the laws of Russia did not permit Jews to sleep in St. Petersburg. I said, 'I trust your Majesty will see fit to alter them' and the reply was, 'I hope so'. Twenty-six years later, on my again visiting St. Petersburg to seek an audience of the late Emperor Alexander, I found 12,000 of my coreligionists there ... On my arrival there, I was asked by a person of high authority what my object was in seeking an audience of the Emperor. I replied that it was to convey my gratitude to His Majesty for having realised the hope expressed to me by his father ... I am fully convinced that it is only by mild and judicious representation ... that you have a chance of your application reaching the throne of the Emperor.

According to Montefiore's biographer, 'This magnificent pig-headedness, this faith in the goodwill of the Romanovs and the ability of providence

---

2   *Jewish Chronicle* 27 May 1881 pp. 12 and 13; Raphael Langham, *250 Years of Convention and Contention: A History of the Board of Deputies of British Jews, 1760–2010* (London, 2010), p. 114.

and the British government to promote his efforts, [nevertheless] disguised a devout resignation. It was also a complete misreading of the situation, of Montefiore's ability to make any deep impression on the Russian autocrats. Unable to visit Russia, he sent a gift to the Jewish schools there 'to celebrate the coronation of the new tsar'.[3] But within the newly formed Russo-Jewish Committee, the proposal continued to be mooted to send a delegation to Russia 'to intercede with the Tsar on behalf of his Jewish subjects, to endeavour to procure an abrogation of the laws which at present oppress the Jews in Russia, and generally to take such steps as may be found expedient to improve the condition of the Jews'. At a later stage, the Committee also planned to ask about emigration.[4]

On 11 and 13 January 1882, *The Times* published two sensational articles describing the pogroms in Russia, which had been compiled from eyewitness accounts gathered by a special correspondent of the *Jewish World*.[5] The Tsarist authorities had managed hitherto to conceal from the outside world the extent and gravity of these disturbances. Under the guidance of Yakov Lifschitz, Rabbi Elhanan Spector of Kovno and his son started collecting accounts of the pogroms, which they were persuaded to transmit to Dr Asher Asher (1837–89), secretary of the United Synagogue who, in turn, would pass them on to Sir Nathaniel de Rothschild M.P. Dr Asher was a confidant of the Rothschild family, as well as their medical attendant and unofficial almoner, and it was the material forwarded from the Kovno circle that formed the basis of the articles in *The Times*. In coded language, Dr Asher acknowledged receipt of the letters and said he had 'placed them on the tables of kings and before my pure red dearly-beloved [red shield = Rothschild], a shield that defends all who shelter in his shade, and with his consent I shall pour forth fountains and not a single word shall fall to the ground'. Natty was expected to hand over the letters to the editor of *The Times*, with whom he enjoyed good relations, for publication with the aim of stirring public opinion in England and Western Europe; and it

---

3 *Diaries of Sir Moses and Lady Montefiore* Vol. 2, Louis Loewe ed. (London, 1983), p. 300 and Abigail Green, *Moses Montefiore: Jewish Liberator, Imperial Hero* (Cambridge, MA, 2010), p. 411.

4 Klier, *Russians, Jews and the Pogroms of 1881–1882*, p. 244.

5 *The Times* 11 and 13 January 1882; Klier, *Russians, Jews and the Pogroms of 1881–1882*, p. 404.

was also intended that he should bring the distress of the Jews in Russia to the attention of the British government and representative non-Jewish public figures. Through Dr Asher, Lifschitz hoped to appeal more widely to Rabbi Samson Raphael Hirsch in Germany and the Chief Rabbi of France Zadoc Kahn and in turn to their respective communities.[6]

Natty, as chairman of the executive of the newly constituted Russo-Jewish Committee, a body set up jointly by the Board of Deputies and the Anglo-Jewish Association (AJA), was well-placed to insert an account of the recent atrocities in Russia in the British press; it should also be noted that Dr Asher was honorary secretary of the AJA. Natty's father Lionel had enjoyed a close relationship with, John Delane, editor of *The Times*, a relationship that his son continued to cultivate with his successors.[7] What the Russo-Jewish Committee wanted was to draw the attention of the British public to the series of outrages that had occurred in 160 towns and villages in southern Russia, involving spoliation of property, murder and widespread rape. A sub-committee, under the direction of Dr Hermann Adler, then assistant Chief Rabbi, compiled a report from material supplied by the Alliance and the Russian rabbis for insertion in *The Times*, promising to republish it later in pamphlet form.[8] From 45 places in Russia, the Kovno circle had collected detailed information which its members sent to London, reporting 23 murders of men women and children, 17 deaths caused by violence, and 225 cases of rape. A constant complaint in many places was that the Tsar was alleged to have issued a *ukase*, granting the peasantry the right to take possession of the property held by Jews, a falsehood that was sometimes printed on placards. The Russian Jews also complained about the tardy response of the authorities to impending attacks or in dealing with disturbances once they had happened.

> The culpable neglect of the military authorities of Warsaw in refusing to
> make use of the 20,000 men forming its garrison, finds its counterpart

6   Israel Oppenheim, 'The Kovno Circle of Rabbi Yitzhak Elhanan Spektor: Organizing Western Public Opinion Over Pogroms in the 1880s' in Selwyn Ilan Troen and Benjamin Pinkus, eds, *Organizing Rescue* (London, 1992), pp. 91–125.

7   *Jewish Chronicle* 18 November p. 7 and 2 December 1881 p. 9; Ferguson, *The World's Banker*, pp. 533, 540 and 626.

8   LMA, ACC/2712/RJC/1 Russo-Jewish Committee 19 December 1881 and 9 January 1882.

in the similar behaviour of the Governors of Kieff, Elizabethgrad, and Odessa earlier in the year. The behaviour of the police, who are described as only interfering to prevent the Jews from protecting themselves, exactly tallies with their behaviour elsewhere.

Worst of all were the widespread attacks on Jewish property, the wrecking of Jewish homes in street after street and the deliberate razing of whole areas in towns, by setting them on fire – the latter act was expressed in vivid terms by the peasants, when claiming that the 'red cock is crowing'.

> By the end of June [1881] the 'red cock' had crowed over 15 towns in Western Russia, including Mohilew (Mogilev), containing 25,000 inhabitants, Witebak, with 23,000 and Slonim, with 20,000, as well as smaller towns ... on July 3 6,000 Jews lost their homes by fire at Minsk, 4,800 being deprived of every means of subsistence at the same time. The town of Pinsk, in the same province, suffered a like fate ... the Jews of Russia are only allowed to reside in 28 of its provinces, often only in certain towns, and the number of permits to reside is, at least theoretically limited. For the last 20 years, however, these barbarous laws have been somewhat allowed to fall into desuetude ...

though now they were being more rigorously enforced. After the publication of these accounts in *The Times* and in pamphlet form, they received widespread coverage in the European press.[9] John Klier claimed that later investigations by British consuls published in Blue Books 'presented an account of events at great variance from that offered by *The Times*. In particular they denied the high incidence of rape'.[10]

Within the Russo-Jewish Committee, Natty exercised his leadership in a somewhat timorous fashion, for which he was sharply criticized at a Council meeting of the AJA. An editorial in the *Jewish Chronicle* wondered what was the best course of action, a memorial to the Tsar or a deputation, before directing its attention to a third course of action – 'Public Meetings that have been found so efficacious in the case of the Roumanian Jews, and, outside our ranks, in the more nearly parallel case of the Bulgarian Horrors.' Natty, secretive by nature, thought that behind-the-scenes diplomacy

9   *The Times* 11 and 13 January 1882 and Oppenheim 'The Kovno Circle of Rabbi Yitzhak Elhanan Spektor', p. 92.
10 Klier, *Russians, Jews and the Pogroms of 1881–1882*, p. 405.

would be most effective and kept in contact with the Russian ambassador in London. A delegation was to go to St Petersburg to intercede on behalf of Russian Jewry and to plead for emigration restrictions to be relaxed. Shortly afterwards, Natty, as chairman of the Russo-Jewish Committee, called on the Russian ambassador, Prince Lobanov, on 17 January 1882, with an amended memorial to Tsar Alexander III demanding equal rights for his co-religionists in Russia and the abolition of the Pale of Settlement, while saying nothing about emigration; but after taking instructions from his government the ambassador refused to accept it – a calculated snub.[11] At the same time, the *Jewish Chronicle* bemoaned the lack of leadership in Anglo-Jewry. 'Why have we not a Sir Francis Goldsmid now to act with energy and decision in the midst of aimlessness and lethargy? It is in his true spirit of devotion to the Jewish cause, that his widow issues from her seclusion and directs the Jewish community which he so often led [to hold a public meeting].' Natty was as yet unready to assume leadership of the Anglo-Jewish community from the ageing titan Sir Moses Montefiore, so that the latter remained its titular head until his death in 1885. With a groundswell of opinion building up in England after the reports in *The Times* and the recent riot in Warsaw, Natty was compelled to give in to the demands of the AJA and agree to a large public meeting being held before the start of the parliamentary session. His other option, a joint delegation of European Jewish leaders to call on the Tsar, had been foreclosed by the reluctance of his continental colleagues to participate, but more of this later. As Oswald John Simon remarked:

> The undivided judgment of the most eminent prelates, members of the press and other leading public men is that the only means of touching Russia is by the free outspoken public opinion of English Christians expressed at public meetings to be held in the metropolis and all the chief towns in England. The fifteen gentlemen of that Committee meeting in closed doors think otherwise.[12]

11 *Jewish Chronicle* 6 January p. 5 and 13 January 1882 p. 11; *The Times* 25 January 1882; Klier, *Russians, Jews and the Pogroms of 1881–1882*, pp. 244–5; Steven Gilbert Bayme, *Jewish Leadership and Antisemitism in Britain, 1898–1918*, Columbia University PhD 1977, p. 261; LMA, ACC/2712/RJC/1 Russo-Jewish Committee 30 January 1882.

12 *Jewish Chronicle* 13 January p. 5 and 20 January 1882 pp. 5, 11 and 12. Langham, *250 Years of Convention and Contention*, p. 115.

The Damascus Affair of 1840 was the first occasion on which Christians – Evangelicals, Quakers, City men and anti-slavery activists – had rallied on behalf of a Jewish cause 'in the name of "humanity" and "civilized" values'. In turn, Montefiore had been chosen in 1861 as chairman of the Syrian Relief Fund, an almost wholly Christian concern with few Jews among its leading members. In 1872, when Sir Francis Goldsmid formed the Romania Committee, he gathered together a grand Christian coalition headed by the social reformer Lord Shaftesbury and the bishop of Gloucester to stage a protest meeting at the Mansion House on behalf of the Jewish inhabitants, deploring the lack of liberty and the trampling of civilized Christian values in that country.[13] With much the same message, the Council of the Evangelical Alliance on 19 January 1882 issued a statement which was forwarded to the Foreign Secretary, viewing

> with horror and indignation the atrocities recently committed upon the Hebrew race in certain parts of Russia. Remembering that the displeasure of God has been repeatedly manifested against those who have oppressed and persecuted the Jews ... and on grounds of our common humanity, the Council would express their deep compassion and heartfelt sympathy with the sufferers and those who have been so cruelly bereaved.[14]

On 28 November 1881, the executive of the Russo-Jewish Committee, meeting under Natty's chairmanship, resolved to send a deputation to the Tsar consisting of the leaders of the Jewish communities in Paris, Berlin and Vienna, to intercede on behalf of his Jewish subjects, to endeavour to obtain the abrogation of the laws which were oppressing them and to improve their condition generally, but first they had to seek the agreement of the Continental leaders to this plan.[15] In his reply, Gerson Bleichroder, Bismarck's banker and a former Rothschild agent, stated that he had advised the Alliance Israélite Universelle in Paris that 'their emigration plan seemed ... utterly impracticable, for of the 4 million Jews in Russia they want to despatch to America precisely the strong and healthy ones leaving the old and infirm to a lot likely to be all the more wretched in consequence'. He

13 Green, *Moses Montefiore*, pp. 140, 229, 291 and 372.
14 *Jewish Chronicle* 27 January 1882 p. 6.
15 LMA, ACC/2712/RJC/1 Russo-Jewish Committee 28 November 1881.

had 'likewise told the Anglo-Jewish Association ... not to take any steps with your Government with a view to inducing them to make representations to the Russian Government, because the German Government would take no similar steps, and because the relations between England and Russia are not very brilliant, so that the former might receive a very unpleasant answer to their representations'. When a delegation of Russian-Jewish leaders met the Tsar, he 'referred them to Ignatieff [the reactionary Minister of the Interior] and appointed a Commission composed in his sense to investigate the complaints, and everything remained as before'. No government would 'run the risk of interfering in the affairs of a Great Power' except in a 'mild' way. 'Were Germany to do so, the answer would be: how are matters with you, and England would be reminded of Ireland'. In addition, Bleichroder subsequently wrote that the German authorities were doing nothing to check their own 'anti-semitic movement'. When he had raised the matter in the past with Russian officials, their rejoinder was, 'What is the Government in Germany doing *for* the Jews; not more, not only not more, nay even less than we'.[16] Baron Alphonse, Natty's cousin in Paris, was nonplussed and could not suggest an answer. The Viennese Jewish community was also reluctant to participate in a delegation because it was unlikely 'to find a favourable reception' in St Petersburg, nor would the 'arguments of humanity' appeal, as Russian officials were familiar with them and 'extremely sensitive ... to any pressure [criticism] from abroad'.[17] So this option was dropped and subsequently the presentation of a memorial to the Russian ambassador was rebuffed, leaving the Russo-Jewish Committee with no alternative but to agree to a large public demonstration.

On 21 January 1882 a galaxy of stellar Victorian names, including Lord Shaftesbury, the Archbishop of Canterbury, Cardinal Manning, Charles Darwin, Benjamin Jowett and Matthew Arnold signed a manifesto calling on the Lord Mayor of London to hold a meeting at the Mansion House in connection with the persecution of the Jews in Russia. The signatures had been collected at the Carlton Club by Baron Henry de Worms, M.P. A week later, the Lord Mayor presided over a large and enthusiastic meeting on a

16 Ibid., 19 December 1881 annexed correspondence, Gerson Bleichroder to Natty 2 and 14 December 1881; and Berlin Jewish Community to Natty 7 December 1881.
17 Ibid., 19 December 1881 and as a appendix, Dr Kuranda Vienna to Natty 12 December 1881.

platform graced by the philanthropist Baroness Burdett-Coutts and Louisa Lady Goldsmid 'to express public opinion upon the outrages inflicted upon the Jews in various parts of Russia and Russia[n] Poland'. Alfred Lord Tennyson, the Poet Laureate, who was unable to attend the gathering, sent a letter, expressing dismay at 'the reports of this madness of hatred against the Jews (whatever the possible provocation), and of the unspeakable barbarities consequent'. Lord Shaftesbury moved the first resolution, deploring 'the persecutions and outrages which the Jews in' Russia have suffered and which are an affront to 'Christian civilization'. He hoped that 'the humane and civilized prince' who now sat on the Russian throne would feel the force of this expression of English public opinion. 'Are we not asking him to restrain violence, murder, outrage, spoliation? ... and to let the oppressed go free!' Cardinal Manning asserted that 'there are laws larger than any Russian legislation, there are laws which are not one in London and another in St. Petersburg ... they are the same in every place – I speak of the laws of human nature the laws of God are the foundation of every law of man'. Professor James Bryce M.P. moved a resolution, calling upon Gladstone, the Prime Minister, upon receipt of these resolutions 'to exercise a friendly influence with the Russian Government'. Because he had played an active role in the agitation against the Bulgarian atrocities, he had been asked to speak today. He thought that they were bound to express their opinion 'of those who had been guilty of horrors in Russia, more openly than any other country is bound, because it is England which was the first to admit the Jew to the privileges of full political and civil equality ... A meeting of this kind is a far better representative of feeling in England than diplomatic action'. This phenomenon of race hatred was not confined to the uncivilized peoples of South-Eastern Europe, but had erupted in 'a nation like Germany, which had rendered such great services to learning and science'. While recognizing 'the difficulty of diplomatic action ... [he hoped] that it will not be far distant when English influence will be used not only with Russia, in the cause of humanity'.[18] This meeting rekindled the key phrases of liberal, mid-Victorian Britain, the more general imposition of Christian, civilized values and the championing of humanity across the globe.

18 *Jewish Chronicle* 27 January p. 6 and Supplement 3 February 1882 pp. 1–4; Eugene C. Black, *The Social Politics of Anglo-Jewry 1880–1920* (Oxford, 1988), p. 254.

At the meeting, Natty proposed a vote of thanks to the Lord Mayor which was seconded by Serjeant Simon M.P., a spokesman for Jewry in the House of Commons. At the same time, the Lord Mayor, Sir John Whittaker Ellis, launched the Mansion House Relief Fund and, by the autumn, the sum of £108,759 had been collected for the relief of Russian Jewish refugees in England and on the Continent. A large slice of the fund was contributed by the Rothschild family. Natty handed over £10,000 – £5,000 from the London bank and £5,000 from the Paris house – while there was a further donation of £1,200 from the Dowager Baroness James de Rothschild.[19] As chairman of the Russo-Jewish Committee, Natty was one of those eminent persons who conferred with the Lord Mayor to ensure that the future fund was utilized for emigration and to ensure that not too many of the refugees settled permanently in Britain.[20] In addition to the assembly at the Mansion House, mayors called meetings in all chief cities throughout the length and breadth of the land, including Liverpool, Glasgow, Manchester and Birmingham, at which letters were read from John Bright and Joseph Chamberlain, and at Oxford and Cambridge. As in the past, Christians fully participated in the fund-raising, Joseph Chamberlain contributing £50. Alfred de Rothschild, Natty's brother, sat on the committee of the Mansion House Fund as representative of the Rothschild family, but he did not serve on the executive nor did he initiate policy. Of the funds collected, much of the first £85,000 was expended on assisting 15,000 victims of the Russian persecution to emigrate between 1882 and 1885, 'at first by special organisation, at Brody, Lemberg [Lvov] and Liverpool, and later by the continued activity of the Conjoint Committee of the Fund and the Jewish Board of Guardians of London'. In 1891, £5,000 was forwarded to the Central German Committee, who dispensed it to their organization in Hamburg, so that in July and August 1891, 22,000 refugees were diverted away from the British Isles; but, in all, between 1886 and 1891, £12,500 was expended on emigration and settlement. The aim was 'to prevent any increased congestion in the overcrowded districts of London in conse-quence of the expulsion of so many victims of Russian oppression', a polite

19   *Jewish Chronicle* Supplement 3 February 1882 p. 4 and 17 February 1882 p. 14; Geoffrey
     Alderman, *Modern British Jewry* (Oxford, 1998), p. 113.
20   *Jewish Chronicle* 27 January 1882, p. 9.

way of saying that Russian Jews were to be deflected away from emigrating to Britain. Apart from this, the Jewish Board of Guardians repatriated 50,000 individuals back to Russia between 1880 and 1914.[21]

Money was also earmarked by the Fund towards the founding of six agricultural colonies in the United States and Canada, where the refugees could find employment. Natty was most deeply involved in the establishment of the agricultural colony in Canada. Sir Alexander Galt, the Canadian High Commissioner in London, approached him in January 1882 to encourage the settlement of Jewish agriculturalists in north-west Canada. What he and Sir John Macdonald, the Canadian Prime Minister, really wanted was to use this Jewish colony as 'a link, missing link ... between Canada and Sidonia [the house of Rothschild]'. Macdonald complained to Galt that 'After years of ill-concealed hostility of the Rothschilds against Canada, you have made a great strike by taking up the clo' cry [a disparaging remark about Jewish old clothes sellers], and going in for Jewish immigration into the Northwest'. Macdonald's underlying motivation was to gain access to Rothschild finances for the Canadian Pacific Railway, then under construction, and for developing the interior.[22] In preparation for agricultural pursuits, Natty placed a number of young Russian Jews in 1886 on farms around Aylesbury for training before they were sent to the new agricultural settlements in the United States and Canada; it is claimed that he paid the travelling costs of 200 families who migrated to Canada, though no source for this assertion is cited.[23] It seems unlikely, however, because the Rothschild family had already made the largest contribution to the Fund. The Jewish Board of Guardians' archives contains a questionnaire dating from 1886 which mentions that the Mansion House Committee proposed 'to draft 12 persons to Lord Rothschild's farm at Aylesbury and

21 *Jewish Chronicle* 10 February 1882 pp. 4 and 9; Mowshowitch Collection, Yivo reel 10 'Mansion House Fund for the Relief of Russian Jews' Report 1886–91, pp. 1–4; Vivian Lipman, *A Century of Social Service: The History of the Jewish Board of Guardians* (London, 1959), p. 94.

22 Benjamin Gutelius Sack, *History of the Jews in Canada* Vol. 1 (Montreal, 1945), pp. 180–2; Gerald Tulchinsky, *Taking Root: The Origins of the Canadian Jewish Community* (Hanover, NH, 1993), pp. 113–14.

23 'Mansion House Fund for the Relief of Russian Jews' Report 1886–91 p. 3 and Rothschild, *Dear Lord Rothschild*, p. 19.

12 to Mr H. Landau's farm at Tunbridge Wells'. The selection of candidates appears to have been undertaken by the delegate Chief Rabbi Dr Hermann Adler.[24] The younger men who left for Canada worked on the construction of railways and the laying of sewers, while twenty-six families founded a colony near Moosomin on land placed at the disposal of the Mansion House Fund by Galt. This colony, called New Jerusalem, failed because the soil and climate proved to be uncongenial and too remote from the markets, Winnipeg being two hundred miles distant. Galt unfairly blamed the settlers for the failure, denouncing them in 1888 as 'vagabonds', and claiming they ' have sold their cows – the cattle I gave them – and turned to their natural (!) avocation of peddling'.[25] When a fire destroyed their crop of hay, the colony was wound up because of the difficult conditions.

Asher Isaac Myers (1848–1902), then proprietor of the *Jewish Chronicle*, put extra pressure on Gladstone, the Liberal Prime Minister, to do something about the outrages being perpetrated against the Jews in Russia. 'Since the receipt of your last letter', Gladstone told him 'an account of the most shocking nature has come under my eyes entitled "Persecution of the Jews in Russia 1881"'. This was a reprint of *The Times* articles in pamphlet form. Gladstone seemed inclined to take some form of action, but was then dissuaded from this course by his Foreign Secretary and by Madame Olga Novikov, an aristocrat and a family friend of Gladstone's, as well as an unofficial representative of Pan-Slavic and reactionary circles. She held court in Claridge's Hotel for leading politicians and publicists, while defending the Russian government in the press from charges of mistreatment of its Jewish population. She denounced the pamphlet as 'nothing more than a Jewish compilation, concocted to excite bad feelings against my country'. Gladstone then instructed his Foreign Secretary to tell Myers that in the Prime Minister's opinion 'the interference of foreign Governments in such cases is more likely to do harm than good'. A letter in similar terms was sent by Gladstone to the Lord Mayor, who had forwarded him the resolutions passed at the Mansion House gathering. Colin Matthew declared that Gladstone claimed, disingenuously, that when he had criticized government reluctance to intervene over Naples in 1851 and Bulgaria

---

24 Southampton, MS 173, 1/11/1 undated questionnaire circa 1886.
25 Tulchinsky, *Taking Root*, p. 119.

in 1876 he had done so as a private citizen but now that he had ample opportunity to do something positive he failed to act.[26] In the House of Lords, Earl Granville repeated that 'Her Majesty's Government had always resisted any attempt on the part of foreign Governments to interfere with the internal affairs of the Kingdom and was expected to pursue the same policy with regard to other nations. He had, however, made communications in a non-official capacity'. This was only true with regard to a group of major European powers; elsewhere in the Balkans, the Near East and North Africa, Britain showed no reluctance in making its views known.[27]

Through the official *Journal de St. Petersbourg* and through Madame Novikov, the Russian government denied the charges of complicity and the extent of the violation of Jewish women during pogroms, declaring that, by their exploitation of the peasantry, the Jews had brought these troubles on themselves. Support for this campaign of denial came from the British consuls in Russia, who felt that their reputations had been impugned by the articles printed in *The Times* and the Foreign Office reprinted their reports in a Blue Book. Consul-General Stanley declared that 'there had been little loss of life, and violations of women have, I believe, been most rare'.[28] In response to this campaign of disinformation, witness statements were taken from twenty-five refugees who passed through Britain and fresh evidence was collected from sources in Russia which Dr Asher, on behalf of the Russo-Jewish Committee, sent to *The Times*. Dr Asher appealed to the Kovno circle to collect well-documented accounts of the outrages to rebut the charge that these were isolated incidents. The Circle enlisted the help of the German rabbi Ruelf of Memel and the radical *maskil* (Jewish scholar) Yehalel. Having done so, statements were compiled to show that the accounts of the murders and rapes in particular were not exaggerated. These precise and detailed rebuttals, signed either by the violated women or the relatives of those who had been murdered, were again published in *The Times* under the *imprimatur* of Sir Nathaniel de Rothschild M.P. For instance, seven residents of Brezowka signed a letter which was attested to by their rabbi that some of their wives and daughters had been raped and

---

26 *The Gladstone Diaries Volume X*, H. C. G. Matthew, ed. (Oxford, 1990), pp. lxiii, 197 and 200–6; Stanislawski, *Zionism and the Fin de Siècle* (Berkeley, 2001), pp. 36–9.

27 *Jewish Chronicle* 10 February 1882 p. 10.

28 Klier, *Russians, Jews and the Pogroms of 1881–1882*, p. 240.

a Russian notable confirmed 'the large number of outrages on Women ... giving heart-rending details as to the violation of 20 women in Berezowka'. Another respondent from the town who arrived in Britain stated that it was common knowledge among the Jewish community that over 20 girls had their names inscribed at the local *Beth Din* (Jewish court of law) as having been violated, to guard against charges of unchastity at some later date.[29] Undoubtedly there were inflated reports from certain towns, as in the case of Kiev where, in four of the six cases cited, the victims denied that any outrage had been inflicted upon them. Elsewhere, there were substantial accounts of violations of Jewish women and statements were obtained from doctors who had attended victims of rape.[30] Unfortunately, the late Professor Klier failed to examine all the available documents in the Ruelf collection in the Central Zionist Archives which contains material that refutes his claim that 'the rape narrative that appeared in the West was, in fact, more legendary than factual', though he concedes later that 'there were unquestionably rapes' during the pogrom in Balta. In all the ensuing media campaign, Natty's role seems to have been low key, his crucial role being to ensure that *The Times* published these counter-claims early in March 1882.[31]

A second Blue Book was issued on behalf of consular officials to rebut the claims contained in the 'Supplementary Statement' sponsored by the Russo-Jewish Committee. *The Times* stood by its allegations, however, claiming that 'what was believed before is now proved – unless, that is to say, we are to assume that a whole community has banded together to lie in the face of the world in a matter affecting the honour of its women'. Then came the Balta pogrom of 29–30 March 1882, forcing British consular officials in the second Blue Book to admit that the Russian authorities

29 *Supplementary Statement Issued by the Russo-Jewish Committee in Confirmation of 'The Times' Narrative* (London, 1882), pp. 22–5 and 28–9; *Jewish Chronicle* 10 February 1882 p. 10.

30 *Russia No. 2 (1882) Correspondence Respecting the Treatment of Jews in Russia* PP.LXXX1 1882, pp. 7–8.

31 Oppenheim, 'The Kovno Circle of Rabbi Yitzhak Elhanan Spektor', pp. 110–12 and Jonathan Frankel, *Prophecy and Politics. Socialism, Nationalism, & the Russian Jews 1862–1917* (Cambridge, 1981), p. 75; *Jewish Chronicle* 3 March p. 7 and 10 March 1882, p. 15; Klier, *Russians, Jews and the Pogroms of 1881–1882*, pp. 11–13 and 405–9.

had lied about the extent of injury to persons and damage to property, undermining the credibility of their previous reporting, while the coverage of the Balta pogrom seemed to substantiate all the past accusations. Even the sensational stories of the joint rape of mothers and daughters appeared to have gained additional credence. Although this was a triumph for the Russo-Jewish Committee in the propaganda war, it was otherwise a defeat, for the Russian government would not yield to outside pressure and alleviate the condition of its Jewish subjects.[32] On 27 April 1882, the Russo-Jewish Committee deliberated 'with a view to the mitigation of the fresh outrages in Russia' and 'discussed the propriety of taking further action, but no proposal being forthcoming the meeting adjourned'. It was the last time this particular organization convened. Natty and the other communal leaders were bankrupt of ideas, no fresh diplomatic initiatives were forthcoming.[33]

In 1869, and on four other occasions in the early 1870s, the London and Paris Rothschild houses floated loans for the Russian government, but after 1875 the previously good relations between the Rothschilds and the Tsarist regime were interrupted for a number of years because of great power rivalry in the international sphere with Britain. In such fraught circumstances, the London house could not raise loans for the Russian treasury. From 1881, there was the added complication of the brutal persecution of their co-religionists by the Russian state. On 27 March 1882, Baron Alphonse informed London that 'this issue is all the more sad because there is no visible remedy'. What were the Rothschilds to do, when intervention with St Petersburg would prove fruitless? The answer was, Alphonse concluded, to refuse to participate in floating loans for the Russian treasury, this being the source of the new policy. In April 1882, Nikolai Bunge, the Russian Minister of Finance and a determined opponent of Ignatiev in the Council of Ministers, observed that 'Rothschild recently announced to anyone who would listen that he would not buy Russian state bonds; these words of Rothschild carry very heavy weight on all European stock exchanges, and the consequence was an unusual decline in the value of our

32 Klier, *Russians, Jews and Pogroms 1881–1882*, pp. 407 and 409. *Russia No. 2 (1882) Correspondence Respecting the Treatment of Jews in Russia*, p. 37.
33 LMA, ACC/2712/RJC/1 Russo-Jewish Committee 27 April 1882.

issues, and the stock market as a whole'. In vain, did the Russians employ unofficial emissaries, such as Elie de Cyon in June 1882, to persuade Baron Alphonse to change course, hinting that there would be concessions for his co-religionists, if money was forthcoming. So too, Baron Horace Gintsburg, the leader of Russian Jewry, appealed in October 1882 to Baron Alphonse to respond more favourably to the offers of the Tsarist regime, but without any transformation of the situation on the ground all these overtures were politely brushed aside by the Rothschilds, the London and Paris houses were of one accord. As Baron Alphonse explained to Gintsburg, 'unhappily it can't be done because of the persecution of our coreligionists in Russia'. When a new Minister of Finance, Ivan Vishnegradsky, came into office in 1887, the Paris house of Rothschild, with the approval of London, participated in the raising of new loans for Russia in that year and again in 1889. Moreover, the London house was willing to take a share in the £12 million loan issue in 1890.[34]

On 3 May 1882, the Tsar ratified laws forbidding Jews from settling anew outside towns and small towns, from buying or leasing land elsewhere, and from participating in business activities on Sundays and Christian holidays. A 'crackdown' was initiated against Jewish tavern owners. Yet the laws were so clumsily framed that they provided ample loopholes for evasion. Throughout the rest of the decade, emigration from Russia continued apace, though at a reduced rate. In 1890, Jews were expelled from large Russian cities such as Moscow and Kiev, and earlier laws were enforced more harshly, setting off increased waves of migrants. A great public protest meeting was held at the Guildhall in London on 10 December 1890.[35] Once again, the great and the good assembled in the Guildhall under the leadership of the Lord Mayor, Alderman Savory, who

34 Eliyahu Feldman, 'The Rothschilds and the Russian Loans: High Finance and Jewish Solidarity' in Jonathan Frankel, ed., *Reshaping the Past: Jewish History and Historians: Studies in Contemporary Jewry* Vol. 10 (New York, 1994), pp. 231–7; Fritz Stern, *Gold and Iron: Bismarck, Bleichroder and the Building of the German Empire* (London, 1981), pp. 443–5; Klier, *Russians, Jews and the Pogroms of 1881–1882*, pp. 250–51; Ferguson, *The World's Banker*, p. 906.

35 Salo W. Baron, *The Russian Jew under Tsars and Soviets* (New York, 1987), p. 47 and Lloyd P. Gartner, *The Jewish Immigrant in England 1870–1914*, p. 44; Klier, *Russians, Jews and the Pogroms of 1881–1882*, pp. 224–7.

was of Huguenot descent, to affirm that 'religious liberty is a principle which should be recognised by every Christian community as among the natural human rights'; once again, the same Victorian tropes about humanity and the basic principles of Christian civilization were given a fresh airing. Strong support came from all sections of the Christian community, with the Bishop of Ripon giving the keynote address. Cardinal Manning, who was ill, sent a long, eloquent letter, the Revd Hugh Price Hughes spoke for the Nonconformists, and Sir Joseph Pease and Sir Robert Fowler added their voices on behalf of the Quakers. The Bishop of Ripon remarked that 'the amelioration of the misery and oppression of humanity belongs to the politics of the world', while Cardinal Manning held that 'we refuse to accept the modern theory of non-intervention, which had its first expression in the question, "Am I my brother's keeper?"'[36]

Once again, the Russian government and Madame Novikov ran a campaign of disinformation and damage limitation to counter Jewish claims. Before the Guildhall meeting, Novikov questioned the concern of the English for the fate of Russian Jewry, suggesting that they should rather be focusing on the misery of the submerged poorest tenth of the population described in General Booth's 'Darkest England' or on the horrors inflicted in Africa. 'And thousands and tens of thousands [of poor Russian Jews] will sell all they have and come over to experience the first fruits of the generosity which promises them a new land of Canaan in the City of London.'[37] A few weeks later, Madame Novikov warned in *The Times* that Russia was 'a great military Power, having at her disposal an army of two millions of well disciplined and drilled soldiers'. She implied that 'the Jewish religion teaches people to hate their enemies', to which the Revd Dr Adler responded 'What a shameful libel on Judaism, the religion that taught the world the command "Thou shalt love thy neighbour as thyself"'. Novikov claimed that the Guildhall meeting would result in a fresh wave of migrants from Russia and that on 24 November 1890, 300 destitute Jews had already arrived. Replying to her, the Duke of Westminster answered that 'the numbers did not exceed 60, and that most came with luggage and were not dependent, nor did they all remain in the country'. As for

36 *Jewish Chronicle* 12 December 1890 pp. 21–7.
37 *The Times* 22 November 1890.

protest meetings, she had not objected to the gathering held at St James's Hall on 8 December 1876 over which he, the Duke, had presided, when the Bulgarian Christians were persecuted by the Turks.[38] In the summer of 1891 Sir Robert Morier, the liberal British ambassador to St Petersburg, discounted 'the report that a society has been formed in Russia for ... transporting 60,000 Jews to England in the ... summer ...; the scare produced' had its 'origin in an ironical article inserted in one of the Russian papers and copied in others to the effect that seeing how tenderly the British Public loved the Hebrew race it would be an act of Christian charity to send the destitute Jews of whom Russia wished to rid herself to Britain. There was no need for inflated accounts, the truth concerning the current situation was "so bad as to be almost incredible".[39]

Having considered all their options as to the best approach to Alexander III, the Lord Mayor and his advisers decided to send the memorial from the Guildhall by registered post, only to have it returned by the Tsar through his ambassador. Britain's representative in St Petersburg had been forbidden by Prime Minister Salisbury from touching the protest 'with a pair of tongs' so as not to upset Anglo-Russian relations. Neither Natty nor his brothers attended the Guildhall meeting, though the platform was graced by their cousin, Baron Ferdinand de Rothschild M.P. Natty had been ennobled as Lord Rothschild and his absence from the Guildhall meeting 'was a significant fact' on which the *Jewish Chronicle* deliberately 'made no comment at the time'. Later it reported that he was motivated by a desire to give 'the public demonstration ... every possibility of achieving the object in view'. The *Jewish Chronicle,* perhaps relying on inside information commented however that 'the Rothschilds thought that on this occasion there was more to be done by personal diplomacy than by the democratic machinery of public meeting'. The principal source of pressure on the Russian government emanated from Natty's cousin in Paris, Baron Alphonse de Rothschild, with whom he worked closely. 'Baron Alphonse ... is credited with having specially exerted himself to expose the ruinous economical consequences which must follow to Russia from further persecution of the Russian Jews', that is, that the

38   *Jewish Chronicle* 12 December 1890 p. 27.
39   National Archives, FO 65/1398 Sir Robert Morier to Lord Salisbury 11 June 1891 No. 153.

Tsarist government was made aware that it would encounter insuperable difficulties in raising a state loan on the Paris market. 'Whether by public or private representations, some sort of respite seems to have been gained. M. Vishnegradsky, the Minister of Finance, himself interposed to stay this reproduction of a peculiarly baseless calumny, and the telegrams have stated that a period of delay is interposed between the conception and the execution of some of the projected' measures against the Jews.[40] What the Paris Rothschild archives reveal is that, after Baron Alphonse wrote to the Minister in August 1890, warning him against anti-Jewish measures which would reduce several million people 'to misery, despair, and perhaps even to death', he received assurances that no further restrictions were contemplated.[41] In fact, as late as April 1891, Baron Alphonse pleaded privately with his cousins to tell Sir Julian Goldsmid, chairman of the reconstituted Russo-Jewish Committee, and his allies to curb their public protest meetings, as this would worsen the situation of the Russian Jews.[42]

Unhappily, the understanding between Baron Alphonse and the Russian Minister of Finance broke down in May 1891. The *Jewish Chronicle* castigated the Rothschilds and Bleichroder on 1 May for participating in a consortium to raise money for the Tsar. Sir Robert Morier reported that Vishnegradsky had been notably successful 'in having exchanged the French market for the German for the series of loans he is bringing out in order to convert the Public Debt of Russia at reduced interest. The *entente cordiale*, which it seems to be the interest of many influential people in Russia as well as France to [promote] ... seemed to exclude all prospect of an interruption in the flow of French capital towards the Russian Treasury. Without any premonitory symptom whatever ... the Paris House of Rothschild suddenly withdrew the loan, every detail of which had been agreed on and which was on the eve of signature'. Among other motives, the withdrawal of the loan was precipitated 'by a wish to enter a protest against the revolting form of persecution announced in the Decree for the Expulsion of the Moscow

40   Andrew Roberts, *Salisbury: Victorian Titan* (London, 2000), p. 71 and *Jewish Chronicle* 13 February 1891, pp. 12 and 13.
41   Herbert R. Lottman, *Return of the Rothschilds* (London, 1995), pp. 97–8.
42   RAL XI/101/22 Baron Alphonse to London cousins 23 April 1891; *Jewish Chronicle* 10 January 1896, pp. 14–16.

Jews is quite certain. A very strong feeling, I am told, was beginning to spring up in the great body of the Jewish community at the compliance of the great financing Jews and their greediness in making large profits by assisting the Russian Government financially. Pressure has been used to force their hand and cause them to make a demonstration'. Furthermore, the French market became unfavourable to raising this loan due to the failure of a loan to Portugal.

> Now the Jews being absolutely necessary for his operations, it had become from an early date indispensable for him [Vishnegradsky] to conciliate them and for this purpose he had telegraphed to the Paris Rothschilds as far back as January last to say that he could give the assurance that for three years at least all further measures against them would be abandoned.

This flagrant breach of faith was used by his enemies in Russia to oust him.[43]

The Paris correspondent of *The Times* had another explanation for the impasse, observing that 'As this conversion [loan] was to have occurred on the initiative of the houses of Rothschild, Bleichroeder and other great Jewish financiers, and as in England – owing to the reception in Russia of the representation of the Mansion-house meeting – the barbarity of these expulsions ... has been felt more keenly than elsewhere, Lord Rothschild took the first step in protesting to the members of his house against the support given by Jewish financiers to a Government which has devoted itself to such persecution. Accordingly, on 2 May, the house of Rothschild telegraphed to the Russian Minister of Finance, not that it did not wish to take part in the conversion – a thing which it could not do – but that for the moment the situation of the market rendered the operation difficult, if not impossible'.[44] Lucien Wolf repeated the claim in his *Notes on the Diplomatic History of the Jewish Question* that 'as soon as the news of the persecutions reached New Court, Lord Rothschild resolved to break off negotiations. At his insistence ... the Russian Finance Minister was informed by the Paris House that unless the oppression of the Jews was stopped they would be

---

43 *Jewish Chronicle* 1 May 1891. National Archives, FO65/1398 Sir Robert Morier to Lord
    Salisbury 13 May 1891 No. 124.
44 *The Times* 9 May 1891.

compelled to withdraw from the loan operation.'[45] Thus a false interpretation of the rupture in relations between the French Rothschilds and the
Russian government gained credence, thereby boosting the reputation of
Lord Rothschild as the foremost champion of world Jewry. This explanation
of the motivation is untenable, though until the missing correspondence of
the London house with its Parisian counterpart is found, there will be no
conclusive answer. The fact that the London house was of the opinion that
'Alphonse could not have done otherwise' than reject the loan, however,
because of the 'medieval barbarities' which had been inflicted suggests
that the London Rothschilds followed the lead of their French cousins.
Equally, the story in *The Times* could have been an attempt by the Paris
house to distance itself from the main share of the blame for its withdrawal
from participation in the loan. It is likely that Baron Alphonse was furious
when Vishnegradsky claimed that he could no longer intervene with the
Emperor to alleviate the restrictions on the Russian Jews, and that cousin
Natty's strong feelings in the matter reinforced his view that he should not
proceed with the contract. As he had told Natty earlier, on 8 April 1891, he
agreed to the Russian request for a loan 'to take care of the situation of our
poor coreligionists, who have no other champion except for the minister of
finance'.[46]

Alphonse reiterated to his agent, Adolph Rothstein, a banker who was
the intermediary with the Minister of Finance on 22 April that if the press
continued to publish reports of persecution, he could no longer continue
to do business with Russia. A week later, Baron Alphonse warned that he
was not participating in the loan because of broken assurances on behalf of
the Russian Jews, but he cited the poor condition of the money market as
his ostensible reason for doing so. In this way, he hoped to avoid the Tsar's
wrath falling on the Jews. On the envelope containing the documents
relating to the abortive loan, the Parisian Rothschilds summarized the
episode in a note: 'The 3 per cent loan, 1891 – renounced. Issued by the
Crédit Foncier de France and the Etablissements de Crédit. We refused
because of antisemitism in Russia'.[47] Alphonse's despair regarding the plight

45   Lucien Wolf, *Notes on the Diplomatic History of the Jewish Question* (London, 1919), p. 55.
46   RAL XI/101/22 Baron Alphonse to London cousins 8 April 1891.
47   Feldman, 'The Rothschilds and the Russian Loans', pp. 238–41; Eliyahu Feldman, 'The
     French Rothschilds and the Russian Loan of April 1891', *Zion* 56:2 (1991), pp. 162–72.

of the Russian Jews emerged later, when he railed that the Tsar's 'intolerance must bring about in Russia the same corruptness as did the intolerance of Louis XIV and of Philip II of Spain'.[48]

Following reports of the renewed harassment of Jews, including the news that on 28 March 1891 20,000 Jews were ordered to leave Moscow and in April similar expulsion orders were expected in St Petersburg, there was an upsurge of interest in emigration schemes and agricultural colonies to absorb the refugees fleeing from Russia. Natty was involved in a number of these projects as an alternative to emigration to America. Throughout the spring and summer, there was talk in political circles of Baron Hirsch's plan to move vast numbers of Jews from Russia to agricultural colonies in undeveloped regions elsewhere which excited Natty's rivalry and competitive spirit. Writing to Cecil Rhodes on 31 July 1891, Allick Grey advised him that:

> Ld Rothschild is prepared to spend £40,000 in transporting to S. Africa & establishing on good Agricultural Land within easy access of the sea a carefully selected No. of Russian Jews – He proposed that these Jews shall be taken exclusively from a class who have proved themselves to be successful & persevering Agriculturalists – I had been under the impression wh. I fancy is very prevalent, that the Jew who is content to make an honest living out of tilling the soil was a Fiction, but I am assured that this is not correct, & that in certain agricultural Colonies founded I believe in the South of Russia by the Emperor Nicholas the Jews have shown themselves to be made of the stuff which makes good & desirable Colonists ... the great thing is that they seem to possess those attitudes wh. wd. make them a desirable addition to any young Country such as Cape Colony wh. has more Land than Population ... Rothschild therefore says that while he is prepared to spend £40,000 in transporting 400–500 Families to S. Africa & establishing them there, he will not spend One Penny unless you [Rhodes] give your approval to the scheme – Now here comes a possible Rub. Just as Arnold White has been selected by Hirsch to organise the colossal Emigration of Russian Jews to the Argentines, in which work he, Hirsch, is prepared to put

Appendix with copies of correspondence between Baron Alphonse and the Russian Treasury and other parties. Ferguson, *The World's Banker*, p. 907.
48 RAL T16/18 Baron Alphonse to London cousins 22 April 1892.

£3,000,000 sterling & more if necessary! so Rothschild also proposes to put the managt. of his suggested S. African experiment ... in the hands of ... Arnold White ... [who] is I am aware not a Persona Grata in C[ape] Colony. White wants your approval of the proposed project before he sends you more details.'[49]

Nothing appears to have come of this scheme, nor of a petition to Lord Rothschild from the London members of Hovevei Zion (Lovers of Zion, the first Zionist organization) for the colonization of Palestine which he agreed to present to the Prime Minister, Lord Salisbury.[50]

Baron Maurice de Hirsch (1831–96), a leading railway entrepreneur, first assisted the Russian Jews fleeing to Brody in Austrian Galicia in 1882 by building shelters for them and instructing his local agents to come to their aid but, unable to do anything for Jews within the country after negotiations with the Russian government collapsed, he determined to make the waves of migrants leaving Russia more productive by settling them in agricultural colonies in Argentina.[51] For this purpose, he established the Jewish Colonization Association (ICA). The ICA was incorporated as an English company on 10 September 1891 rather than being set up as a trust, as company law granted it greater flexibility. Arnold White had reported favourably for Baron Hirsch on the Jewish agricultural settlements in southern Russia and was sent to St Petersburg on a second mission, where he obtained satisfactory concessions for would-be emigrants. Hirsch endowed the company with £2 million in paid-up capital and on his death bequeathed them a further large sum, though this was reduced to £5,872,104 after payment of death duties. Among the earliest shareholders chosen by the Baron were Lord Rothschild, Sir Ernest Cassel, Sir Julian Goldsmid and Frederic Mocatta, who were each allotted a single £100 share. In addition, N. M. Rothschild & Sons were appointed as the company's bankers, although the Rothschilds and Baron Hirsch had sometimes been at loggerheads.[52] Hence Natty had good insider information on the company's affairs and

49   Rhodes House, Rhodes MSS Afr.S.228 C3a f.184 Allick Grey to Rhodes 31 July 1891.
50   *Jewish Chronicle* 29 May 1891 p. 8; Cecil Bloom, 'Samuel Montagu and Zionism', *Transactions of the Jewish Historical Society of England* XXXIV (1994–6), pp. 17–41.
51   *Jewish Chronicle* 24 April 1896, pp. 9–11.
52   Theodore Norman, *An Outstretched Arm: A History of the Jewish Colonization Association* (London, 1985), pp. 19–22.

the prospects for Jewish emigration to Argentina. In the same year, 1891, American-Jewish leaders began to intervene forcefully for government action with regard to the situation facing Russian Jewry. They felt that there was no need for a large public demonstration against Tsarist policy because their government was responsive to their demand for a protest to Russia through official channels. Indeed, James G. Blaine, the Secretary of State, warned Oscar Straus and Jacob Schiff that to hold such a meeting would be counter-productive, as Russian officials would interpret American initiatives as being swayed by outside pressure, rather than representing their real concerns. On 19 January 1891, Schiff told his cousin Ernest Cassel that the American–Jewish leadership was 'working very effectively here through the press and the Department of State to exert wholesome influence in St. Petersburg' and that the Secretary of State had reiterated that he would 'make representations to the Russian Government on behalf of our oppressed Russian coreligionists'. On 18 February 1891, Blaine despatched a note which was to be read to the Russian Foreign Minister, drawing attention to the enforced migration to America 'upon whose shores are cast daily evidences of the suffering and destitution wrought by the enforcement of the edicts against this unhappy people'. President Harrison touched on the plight of the Russian Jews on 9 December 1891 in his annual message to Congress, when he protested that

> the banishment, whether by direct decrees or by not less certain indirect methods, of so large a number of men and women is not a local question. A decree to leave one country is in the nature of things an order to enter another – some other. This consideration, as well as the suggestion of humanity, furnishes ample ground for the remonstrances which we have presented to Russia ...[53]

By the early twentieth century, American Jewish leaders were becoming more closely attuned to the ideas of their European colleagues about a banking boycott of Russia and were an increasingly important factor in Jewish international diplomacy. The Anglo-Jewish establishment headed by Lord Rothschild was determined to impede the arrival of huge number

---

53 Gary Dean Best, *To Free a People: American Jewish Leaders and the Jewish Problem in Eastern Europe 1890–1914* (Wesport CT, 1982), pp. 20–41.

of Russian Jews into Britain, and believed, somewhat naively, that they had succeeded. As the *Jewish Chronicle* reported on 8 May 1891,

> Mr Arnold White and others associated with him in the 'Anti-Alien movement' should know that Lord Rothschild, Sir Julian Goldsmid and Mr Samuel Montagu are giving anxious thought to the problems how Jews expelled from Moscow and other cities without the 'Pale of Settlement' can be assisted without coming to any congested districts in London or elsewhere.

A month later, speaking at the Council of the United Synagogue, Natty explained his position. The 'Jewish community could not conceal from itself the fact that it was just now entering upon a period of difficulty – for there was reason to apprehend the influx of a large number of destitute coreligionists.' He for one did not believe, however, that there would be any very large immigration into this country. In his opinion, the great number of fairly well-to-do Russian Jews who were driven from their homes would seek places of refuge other than England, in view of the condition of the labour market here. As for their poorer brethren, every effort had been made to inform them of the hardships that would probably await them in this country. For this reason he did not anticipate any large arrival in England, 'unless the English Jews were to adopt some scheme of relief, and that was not very probable. There was, however, one paramount duty devolving upon the Jewish community – the task of Anglicizing the number of their foreign brethren at present living in the East End of London'.[54] Hence Natty's support of two vital Anglo-Jewish charities, the Jews' Free School and the Four Per Cent Industrial Dwellings Association, to ease the integration of immigrants into the host society.

No new loans were extended by the Rothschilds to Russia until November 1894, when Tsar Nicholas II succeeded his father and there was a new minister of finance, Sergei Witte. In addition, there had been a Franco-Russian entente since 1891 and a military alliance since 1894. Baron Alphonse brushed aside Natty's suggestion that direct negotiations should be started with Witte for a loan, as this would give them no leverage

---

54 *Jewish Chronicle* 8 May 1891 p. 5; *The Times* 3 June 1891.

as regards the situation of the Russian Jews. Through Rothstein, his agent in St Petersburg, Baron Alphonse stipulated that he would float a Russian loan, provided no new hostile measures were adopted against the Russian Jews and, on receiving adequate assurances from Witte, he signed a contract on 29 November. All three Rothschild houses – Paris, Frankfurt and London – participated in the consortium for the 1894 loan and London did not oppose the 1896 loan.[55]

In August 1898, Natty advised Lord Salisbury's secretary Schomberg McDonnell that

> Witte intends to visit Paris in October and that he has arranged to see Baron Alphonse de Rothschild there ... the object of M. de Witte's visit is to ascertain what prospect exists of Russia raising money in France, and more especially whether there is any likelihood of the House of Rothschild bringing out any Loan for Russia ... It would neither be in accordance with the interest nor the inclination of Lord Rothschild to encourage M. De Witte, unless Y[our] L[ordship] thought it desirable that he should do so.

Salisbury agreed that at the time 'it is not our interest to encourage the borrowing operations of Monsieur de Witte. But it may, by some unforeseen turn of events, become so: & therefore it would not be prudent to show reluctance to help him too manifestly'.[56] When Salisbury enquired of the English Rothschilds, through his secretary, in January 1899 whether they would assist in the raising of a large loan for Russia on the London market, he was told that 'Mr Alfred Rothschild, who is extremely Russophobe says, No, on no account. Lord Rothschild is less decided: he thinks his House could make or mar such a loan; if they brought it out it would not be particularly lucrative, and his inclination is adverse to the operation.'[57] In 1901, the French Rothschilds headed a consortium which floated a large Russian loan. Then came the Kishinev pogrom, in April 1903, with the loss

---

55 Feldman, 'The Rothschilds and the Russian Loans', pp. 241–4; Ferguson, *The World's Banker*, p. 909.

56 Hatfield House, 3 Marquess, Rothschild file, Schomberg McDonnell to Lord Salisbury 25 August 1898, and Lord Salisbury's reply.

57 Davis, *The English Rothschilds*, p. 231; Hatfield House, 3 Marquess, Rothschild file, Schomberg McDonnell to Lord Salisbury 3 January 1899.

of 51 Jewish lives, causing the attitude of the Rothschilds to sponsoring Russian loans to harden.

Natty's status as a leader of world Jewry had a shaky start in the 1880s and 1890s. He could not decide whether or not to organize a massive protest meeting at the Mansion House in January 1882, leaving the initiative to Baron Henry de Worms, and when earlier he tried to present a memorial to the Russian ambassador in London requesting equal rights for his co-religionists, he was rebuffed. In December 1890, he failed to attend a second, well-organized protest meeting in the City, fearing that the Tsar would ignore public appeals and trusting to private entreaties. Natty's older French cousin and brother-in-law, Baron Alphonse de Rothschild (1827–1905), took the lead in inaugurating a new policy of refusing to raise loans for Russia in 1882 and again in 1891, when the situation of their co-religionists deteriorated, a policy which Natty fully supported. He regarded his older cousin as his mentor on this issue. But Natty, like his cousin, thought that it was useless to antagonize the Tsar unnecessarily, as it would only provoke harsher measures against the Jews and unleash a flood of migrants overseas, something that he was determined to avoid. If a new Tsar came to the throne or a new minister of finance were appointed, who might assist in the lifting of restrictions on Russian Jews, Natty was prepared to reconsider his policy of curtailing loans. In addition, Natty was of a younger generation than the two Prime Ministers, Gladstone and Lord Salisbury, and the influence he could exert on their foreign policy as regards the Jews in Russia was minimal, as they were not particularly sympathetic to his concerns on this issue. Although he helped to inaugurate a new policy of deflecting East European immigrants from entering Britain, once they had arrived he believed that they should be given a fair chance of settling permanently in their new homeland and that they should be Anglicized without delay.

5

NATTY AND THEODOR HERZL

Natty's predictions about Jewish emigration from Russia proved to be somewhat erroneous, as the Jewish population of Britain soared from 60,000 in 1880 to 250,000 or just under 300,000 by 1914.[1] Meanwhile, anti-alien agitation had been gathering momentum in the 1890s. It was supported by Lord Salisbury who, as Prime Minister in July 1891, had placed a confidential report prepared by Arnold White for Baron Hirsch before his Cabinet on a scheme for setting up agricultural colonies in Argentina as a means of relieving Russian Jewish emigration pressure. Salisbury wrote to the British ambassador in Russia in 1892, asking him to do what he could by representations outside the official despatches to halt the migration of Jews into Britain and, in a private capacity, he introduced his own Aliens Bill in 1894.[2] In 1896 the Prime Minister promised legislation in the Queen's Speech, but nothing was done, though it became part of the Unionist party's programme. Faced with a 'rise in immigration, a worsening of the East End situation, and the onset of an economic recession' together with continued sniping from

1   Alderman, *Modern British Jewry*, pp. 103 and 120.
2   Roberts, *Salisbury*, p. 71 and Alderman, *Modern British Jewry*, p. 133. National Archives, FO/65/1398 Sir Robert Morier to Salisbury 10 July 1891 No. 184 with enclosures reprinted as a Cabinet Paper 31 July 1891.

his own backbenchers, Gerald Balfour, as President of the Board of Trade, appointed a Royal Commission on Alien Immigration in 1902.

Although the commission was chaired by the ailing and fair-minded Liberal Unionist Lord James of Hereford, Balfour, in an attempt to placate opponents, deliberately packed it with a built-in anti-immigration majority. Foremost among these was Major William Eden Evans-Gordon M.P., the leader of the restrictionist pressure group, the British Brothers League, who was aided by his colleagues on the Commission. Among the Commission's members were two Jews, Henry Norman, Liberal M.P. for Wolverhampton, and William Vallance, clerk to the Whitechapel Board of Guardians.[3] Opposed to their colleagues on the Commission were Lord Rothschild, the leader of British Jewry, and Sir Kenelm Digby, the permanent Under-Secretary at the Home Office, a liberally minded gentleman appointed by Asquith. As Natty informed Arnold White, 'I did not seek a seat on the Commission, and accepted one very reluctantly; and I am perfectly certain that I have very little or no personal influence with the Members thereof'.[4] But that is not how White, one of the leading journalistic exponents of restriction, saw the situation in the spring of 1902.

> When I consider that the Royal Commission does not contain one single representative of the views I share is equipped with a knowledge of the history and bearings of the case, I cannot conceal from myself that the report of this Commission is more likely to justify the Government in their abandonment of the proposed measure of 1896 than to arrive at a solution of the difficulty. Major Evans-Gordon has been a member of Parliament for a little over a year and although his industry and tact are admirable his interest in the subject is recent and of political origin. Mr Henry Norman who, I believe, also shares my views has no special knowledge of the subject and comes to it practically as a new man ... Under these circumstances the influence of your Lordship on the Commission is simply overwhelming.[5]

3   Bernard Gainer, *The Alien Invasion: The Origins of the Aliens Act of 1905* (London, 1972), pp. 67 and 183–4.
4   NMM, WHI/166 Natty to Arnold White 21 May 1902.
5   NMM, WHI/166 Arnold White to Natty 17 May 1902.

One of the first witnesses to be called to give evidence to the commission was Arnold White, who appeared at the urging of Lord James of Hereford, its chairman. White was opposed to the admission of large numbers of Jews from Russia on grounds that they competed unfairly with English workmen and because they would 'not mingle their blood with ours'.[6] Replying to a question from Lord James, he stated that his

> objection about the race is absolutely strong. So long as the community in England is comparatively small, I think it is a very great advantage to the country and a distinct strength, but, in consequence of this aloofness, if they become very strong and very powerful, I should expect to find the consequences in England which I observe in other countries, that is to say, they would become masters – dominant.

White wanted a certificate of fitness signed by a consul before settlers could gain entry to Britain and on arrival they were to be subject to the same entry regulations as existed in New York.[7] In a sharp exchange with White, Natty accused him of making 'insinuations' or giving 'the impression 'that the government 'has been obliged to build new synagogues on account of the large number of criminals who came with the aliens', when this was not the case. The phrase 'a lie' was bandied about, to which White took strong exception and which Natty later withdrew. Natty pointed out privately that 'the Synagogues [at Wormwood Scrubbs and Pentonville], if you like to call them by that name, were instituted more than thirty years ago' before the period of mass Jewish migration.[8] Nor was Natty deterred by White's threat to start an 'agitation on the subject of restricting alien immigration' should the commission not report in a favourable sense, even if this resulted in 'violence'.[9]

Since their earlier meeting in 1891, White had been trying to cajole Natty into agreeing to curb the mass migration of Russian Jews into England. 'I share with you the opinion', Natty observed,

> that an influx of persons of foreign birth, likely to become a public charge by reason of physical incapacity or mental disease, is most undesirable

6   *R.C. on Alien Immigration* P.P. 1903 IX q.q. 1148, 1152 and 1153.
7   *Jewish Chronicle* Supplement 9 May 1902 cross-examination of Arnold White.
8   *R.C. on Alien Immigration* q.q. 1106–8. NMM, WHI/166 Natty to Arnold White 21 May 1902.
9   NMM, WHI/166 Arnold White to Natty 17 May 1902.

and should be discharged. I have no reason to believe that such persons come here in number sufficient to justify legislation. If reliable evidence were forthcoming to the contrary, I should be willing to consider the situation in the light of the fresh evidence produced.

During a cross-examination in 1902, White claimed that Rothschild had originally used words to the effect that 'When I consider that alien immigration has attained serious proportions I shall be prepared to take action', but Natty strongly denied this and was also unwilling to bar entry to a vague category of immigrants whom White designated as 'undesirables'.[10] Almost alone within the Royal Commission, Natty battled on behalf of the Jewish immigrants, despite having few allies on it other than Sir Kenelm Digby. Natty was well briefed on the current situation of the Jewish immigrants in England and tried to steer some of the Anglo-Jewish communal experts, such as Henry Herman Gordon and Joseph Prag, along the lines of evidence which he hoped would convince members of the Royal Commission not to restrict the entry of Jewish immigrants into Britain. Leonard Cohen referred, in his evidence, to the six months' residence rule before a foreigner could be assisted by the Jewish Board of Guardians, to prevent the dispensation of charity becoming too great an attraction for the new arrivals. Nathan Joseph, chairman of the executive of the Russo-Jewish Committee, added that the rule 'did not apply to the cases of Russian Jews dealt with by the Conjoint Committee, in consideration of them being sufferers from religious persecution. He also gave interesting figures proving that overcrowding was not an evil brought about by the aliens, and mentioned a number of streets in East London which were hot-beds of criminality before the aliens came into them'. Hermann Landau, President of the Jews' Temporary Shelter, and the superintendent 'both proved in their evidence the futility of the Board of Trade immigration figures; at one point during Landau's evidence, 'Lord Rothschild was overheard to say in undertone "Poor Landau is so full of *Rachamanoth* (compassion)"'. Guided by Natty, Henry Gordon rebutted the suggestion that immigrants were

10 Kerstin Warnke-Dakers, 'Lord Rothschild and his Poor Brethren: East European Jews in London 1880–1906', in Georg Heuberger, ed., *The Rothschilds: Essays on the History of a European Family* (Sigmaringen, 1994), p. 123; NMM, WHI/166 Arnold White to Natty 17 May 1902.

attracted to Britain by the profligate way in which the proceeds of charity
were handed out, while Joseph Prag refuted in his 'evidence the statements made by other witnesses that the overcrowding in certain districts
was entirely due to the incursion of the alien', showing that in St Pancras,
where there were no Jews, conditions were worse than Stepney. Prag also
noted that the Jewish worker embarked on 'the mantle, boot and shoe,
clothing, fur, cap-making, cabinet-making, cigar and cigarette, trimming
and waterproof clothing trades, and other trades which, before his advent,
were new in the country, e.g., the blouse-making trade'.[11] When questioned
by Lord Rothschild, Canon Barnett, the founder of Toynbee Hall and a
denizen of the East End for thirty years, agreed that 'It is better, measured
by moral standards. People are more comfortable, they are better clad and
better shod, and their pleasures are more sober'.[12] An *Express* reporter, who
had watched Lord Rothschild's reactions during the sessions of the Royal
Commission, remarked 'How great was the pain he felt when evil words
were spoken about the Eastern European Jews! How delighted he was to
hear praise for the Jewish population! How his face would light up when
anti-Jewish evidence was contradicted.'[13]

If the entry of Russian Jews into Britain was growing less secure,
additional outlets were being sought, particularly in Palestine. For this
reason, it is necessary to interweave the accounts of counter-measures
adopted to thwart the anti-aliens campaign and the story of the advance of
the Zionist movement in Britain, in each of which Theodore Herzl played
a significant role. Originally, the Austrian branch of the Rothschilds had
failed to respond to a lengthy letter addressed by Theodor Herzl to the
whole family, so, in February 1896, he republished it in pamphlet form
entitled 'The Jewish State'. In the autumn of 1882, Baron Edmond de
Rothschild of the French banking house began supporting the fledgling
Jewish colonies in Palestine with money and with an expert agronomist to
offer advice. As early as 1884, the Baron had assured one of the founders

11 LMA, 4184/02/05/001/001 A. Munday, *Some Reminiscences of the Shelter's Activities for
    the Last Quarter of a Century* undated pp. 46–7. *R.C. on Alien Immigration* evidence of
    Gordon q.q.17601 and 17604 and Prag q.q.17828 and 17829 Vol. IV summary of Prag's
    evidence p. 123.
12 *R.C. on Alien Immigration* evidence of Canon Barnett q. 17554.
13 Warnke-Dakers, 'Lord Rothschild and his Poor Brethren', p. 121.

of Rishon-Le-Zion that his aim was not merely philanthropic, 'I have set out on this enterprise to see whether it is possible to establish Jews on Palestinian soil'.[14] On 20 July 1896, Baron Edmond, in the presence of the President of the Alliance and Emile Meyerson of the Jewish Colonization Association [ICA] rejected Herzl's request for help, claiming that the movement was more nationalistic in focus than religious and doubting whether sufficient capital could be raised for the project and whether the Sultan's cooperation could be obtained.[15] When members of the New York branch of the Hovevei Zion Society wrote to the Anglo-Jewish Association in 1890, recommending that it should make the establishment of agricultural colonies in Palestine its priority, rather than settlement in the United States or Canada, they did not receive a very enthusiastic response.[16] In the past Natty had contributed financially to the upkeep of the Lionel de Rothschild School for boys and the Evelina School for girls in Jerusalem as well as to the funds of the Hovevei Zion. Through the British government he had petitioned the Sultan for a colony, but that was as far as he would go.[17] Two years later, in 1892, Samuel Montagu noted that

> Mr Landau had some plan of farming in Essex with Russian-Jewish labour [and] we were successful in teaching a dozen Jews farming in Aylesbury, but this course might be adopted systematically ... I may be able to help your [English] society financially but doubt if Lord Rothschild would be inclined to give for Palestine colonization unless Lord Salisbury gives satisfactory encouragement to the schemes.

Montagu informed Herzl that he had petitioned the Ottoman ruler to grant 250,000 acres east of the River Jordan for Jewish colonization and had won Gladstone's support, but that Lord Rothschild had 'pencilled [such a scheme]out of existence'.[18]

---

14 Howard M. Sachar, *A History of Israel* (Oxford, 1976), pp. 26–32 and Simon Schama, *Two Rothschilds and the Land of Israel* (London, 1978), pp. 17 and 54–87.

15 David Vital, *The Origins of Zionism* (Oxford, 1975), p. 307 and RAL T45/1 Baron Edmond to cousins London 11 October 1898; Schama, *Two Rothschilds and the Land of Israel*, pp. 145–7.

16 Southampton, AJ95/ADD/6 AJA executive minutes 25 February and 29 April 1890.

17 Josef Frankel, 'Herzl and the Rothschild Family', *Herzl Year Book* Vol. III (1960): 217–36.

18 Cecil Bloom, 'Samuel Montagu and Zionism', *Transactions of the JHSE* Vol. xxxiv (1994–6): 17–41 and in particular 26 and 27. Amos Elon, *Herzl* (New York, 1986), p. 172.

After refusing earlier requests to meet Herzl, despite pleas from Sir Francis Montefiore, J. L. Greenberg and Israel Zangwill, Natty felt the time was ripe in the summer of 1902 for such an interview. It was at this juncture that Major Evans-Gordon and Arnold White, the leaders of the anti-alien campaign, whom Natty regarded as 'jackasses' had summoned Herzl before the Royal Commission in the hope that he would declare that 'a Jew could never become an Englishman', thereby embarrassing Natty in front of his fellow commissioners. Natty, on the other hand, was determined to ensure that Herzl would only deliver anodyne remarks, so that the proceedings before the Commission would run smoothly. At the same time, Herzl was entranced by the depth of Natty's hidden power and connections, admitting that 'I took you only for a rich man. But in the course of years I have come to know your power. I believe that outside of yourself only few people have such knowledge of your power as I have.'[19]

The two of them had their first encounter on 4 July 1902 at New Court in the bank's office. At the outset, Natty declared that 'he did not believe in Zionism ... We would never get Palestine, etc. He was an Englishman and wanted to remain one. He "desired" that I should say this and that to the Alien Commission, and not say this and the other.' To Natty's amazement, Herzl shouted him down so loudly that 'he held his tongue, astounded and dazed'. Herzl persisted in his onslaught, saying that 'I will tell the Commission what I think proper and what I am convinced of. That has always been my custom, and I shall stick to it this time, too.' He would tell them about the misery that existed in Eastern Europe, that matters were dire, too, in Austrian Galicia, where 700,000 destitute persons would soon be on the move. Natty riposted: 'I do not wish you to tell the Commission that. Otherwise there will be restrictive legislation.' Herzl interjected undeterred that 'Certainly I shall say it! Most certainly! You can depend on that.' Surprised and hurt, Natty rang the bell to summon his brother Leopold to join them. Denouncing charity as a stratagem for 'stifling the cries of distress', Herzl continued that he had a scheme to place before the Commission which would prevent the flood of immigrants into Britain. At lunch in the dining room, they were joined by Alfred,

19 Raphael Patai, ed., *The Complete Diaries of Theodor Herzl* Vol. IV (New York, 1960), pp. 1273–4 and 1291.

who said: 'Colonization, fine! But why in Palestine? "Palestine sounds too Jewish."' Herzl then moved his chair closer to Natty's good ear, as he was becoming increasingly deaf, and told him that what he wanted was 'to found a Jewish colony in a British possession'. As there were other people in the room, Herzl wrote on a piece of paper 'Sinai Peninsula, Egyptian Palestine, Cyprus', all territories adjacent to Palestine, obtaining an enthusiastic response from Natty.[20] Natty's friendships with Randolph Churchill and Cecil Rhodes ended on their deaths in 1895 and March 1902, lacking in imagination he was seeking anew a charismatic personality with as great a visionary streak and was instantly drawn to Theodor Herzl, who seemed to embody in himself the very qualities he lacked.[21] Natty at once respected Herzl, who treated him as an equal, something which most other Jews were too in awe of the noble lord to do.

A day later, Natty wrote to Herzl, acknowledging his:

> letter with the lengthy details of your various Colonization schemes, which will require a good deal of study; but, on the face of it, I may as well tell you at once that the large scheme appears to be quite impracticable; being as it is, not only of a vast & complicated nature, but also involving the outlay of several millions and, quite apart from all the difficulties it presents, I do not see where the necessary financial support could be obtained on the large scale required. A smaller scheme for colonization in Sinai or anything similar on a small scale in other countries might perhaps be carried out ...[22]

On 7 July 1902, Herzl appeared as a witness before the Royal Commission on Alien Immigration. His testimony was not a success. As he noted, he 'was out of sorts, spoke and understood English badly, and made a number of mistakes due to caution'. He was also, no doubt, upset by Natty's tepid response to his grand plan. He repeated much of what he had told Natty at their interview, namely, that charity was no panacea, nor would intermarriage and assimilation solve the problem of the Russian Jewish immigrant. Since Herzl had written the pamphlet, in which he referred to 'the black cloud gathering in the East', he assured the commission that the overall

20 Ibid., pp. 1291–4.
21 Frederic Whyte, *The Life of W. T. Stead* Vol. 2 (London, 1925), pp. 208–9.
22 Central Zionist Archives, H1\100-4-1 Natty to Herzl 5 July 1902.

situation of the Jews had worsened, particularly in Romania and Galicia. The programme formulated by the Zionists at the Basle Congress in 1897 was 'to create a legally assured home for the Jewish people in Palestine'. Lord Rothschild pressed on Herzl the point that philanthropic gentlemen had established colonies in Palestine, to which he replied 'They did not succeed'. Natty continued that the Turks would not allow them to succeed, to which Herzl answered lamely that he would 'prefer not to speak about the Turkish Government here' and that he would put his views privately to the chairman.[23] Earlier in the evidence, Natty had tried to retrieve the situation and clarify Herzl's position, by asking, 'Do you think it is possible that a Jew should be a disciple of Dr Herzl and a Zionist ... and at the same time a good citizen, and a good Englishman or a good American or a good Austrian?' To this, Herzl responded robustly, stating that he was 'deeply convinced of it, and you have proof of it in the last war. I know of Zionist societies who ... as a body, were in your Army'.[24] He conceded to another commissioner that, as far as America was concerned, he had 'heard of difficulties of emigration and that they are overcrowded with Jews'.[25] Baron Hirsch's endowment which had been spent on schools and 'several small agricultural stations', mostly in Argentina, was money wasted. The experiment was 'a failure because when you want a great settlement, you must have a flag and an idea. You cannot make those things only with money'.[26]

After giving evidence to the commission, Herzl hurried to a Rothschild garden party at Gunnersbury, to which he had been invited by Leo. Here he 'was seen and perhaps did Zionism more good among the *upper Jews* by that than by all my previous speeches and actions'. The next day, he recorded in his diary that

> I repaired the bad impression which I felt I had made at the Commission hearing on Lord James, its chairman, by calling on him and telling him frankly everything that I had cloaked with reserve at the session. He thought that I could carry out the Sinai–El Arish–Cyprus plan

23 *R.C. On Alien Immigration* q.q. 6337 and 6422–6.
24 Ibid., q. 6418.
25 Ibid., q. 6476.
26 Ibid., q.q. 6365, 6368–70 and 6373.

only with the aid of Lord Rothschild. The Rothschilds ... were highly respected here, where there was no anti-Semitism.[27]

With Sir Kenelm Digby, the liberal appointee at the Home Office, Natty dissented from many of the recommendations of the majority on the commission and signed a Minority Report, stating that he was 'opposed to the adoption of restrictive measures, because even if they are directly aimed at so-called "undesirables" they would certainly affect deserving and hard-working men, whose impecunious position on their arrival would be no criterion of their incapacity to attain independence'. Within the Commission, Natty also had to rebut suggestions from witnesses that Rothschild largesse was attracting unwanted Jewish immigrants from Eastern Europe.[28] In fact, whenever there was an upsurge in the influx of foreign Jews to British shores, as in the case of the Romanians in 1900 and of Russian Jews in 1904–5 during the Russo-Japanese War, the Rothschilds played a leading role in ensuring that a place of refuge was found for them overseas.

Calling on Lord Rothschild at the bank on 9 July 1902, Herzl was ushered into a private room, where he explained his colonization scheme, taking care to avoid including any plans for Palestine, as the banker objected to colonization there. Natty firmly believed that mass settlement in Palestine would lead to the disintegration of the Ottoman Empire, something which he had been anxious to avoid since, like Disraeli, he regarded the integrity of the Sultan's possessions as the great bulwark against Russian expansion. Natty demanded that Herzl put this scheme down in writing and that any colony be limited in size to 25,000 inhabitants. He would then broach the matter with Joseph Chamberlain, the Colonial Secretary. On 12 July 1902, Herzl confirmed to Rothschild that his plans for 'a great Jewish settlement east of the Mediterranean will strengthen our prospects for Palestine. The Jews in the English colony of the Jewish Eastern Company will be as loyal Zionists as Hirsch's remote colonists in Argentina.' If his plans for a Jewish colony in a British possession were to fail to come to fruition, he suggested founding a colony in Mesopotamia then under Turkish suzerainty, but here

27   Patai, ed., *The Complete Diaries of Theodor Herzl*, p. 1295.
28   *R.C. on Alien Immigration*, Dissenting Report of Digby and Rothschild, p. 52. Warnke-Dakers, 'Lord Rothschild and his Poor Brethren', pp. 121–2.

there were 'fewer political assurances for the future'. He wanted Natty to call together a meeting of five or six financiers in order to set up the Jewish Eastern Company with a working capital of £10 million, but he was quickly rebuffed.[29]

Natty agreed with Herzl that 'the Hirsch millions have not been spent as judiciously as they might have been ... I am at work now, and I am in great hopes that the money will be spent in a better and more judicious way. If I am successful and the results are satisfactory, it will be possible to enlist more sympathy [for your schemes] and to work perhaps on a larger scale ... Of one thing I am convinced – that the dream of Palestine is a myth and a will-of-the-wisp'.[30]

Natty was forthright in his opposition to Zionism, replying to Herzl on 18 August 1902 that:

> I tell you very frankly that I should view with horror the establishment of a Jewish Colony pure and simple ... It would be a Ghetto with the prejudices of the Ghetto; it would be a small petty Jewish State, orthodox and illiberal, excluding the Gentile and the Christian. And what would be the result; ten, fifteen or fifty thousand Jews would live in comparative happiness and ease, their habits and their example would be quoted and their co-religionists and brethren at home would be more oppressed and more ground down on the principle of 'Do unto others as you would be done by' ... I wish the Jew wherever he lives to be a prosperous and good citizen and you cannot attain that object by establishing a few orthodox communities in scattered parts of the world. By all means encourage emigration. Find new homes for Jews, but let them live among their Christian brethren, by the streams of Babylon or elsewhere, but let one and all of us beware of the impossible.

In the meantime, differences of opinion among the directors of the Hirsch Fund had been referred to arbitration; and he was hopeful that as a result, 'a very considerable sum will be devoted annually to emigration'.[31] Once again, Natty did not fully comprehend the dimensions of the potential disaster in Russia and the necessity for Jewish large-scale migration running into

29   Patai, ed., *The Complete Diaries of Theodor Herzl*, pp. 1300–303.
30   Central Zionist Archives, H1\ 1815-3-1 Natty to Herzl 29 July 1902.
31   Central Zionist Archives, H1\1815-4-1 Natty to Herzl 18 August 1902.

millions, thinking instead of a small migration rather than the establishment of a place of refuge. Herzl responded that he did not accept that a 'Jewish commonwealth' would have

> to be small, orthodox, and illiberal ... Were the founders of the states which are now great mightier, cleverer, better educated, wealthier than we Jews of today? Poor shepherds and huntsmen have founded communities which later became states. In our time, Greeks, Romanians, Serbs, Bulgarians have established themselves – and should we be incapable of doing so. Our race is more efficient in everything than most other peoples.

To keep Natty abreast with his thinking, Herzl sent him a copy of *Altneuland*, his utopian novel envisaging a Jewish future in Palestine.[32]

Herzl met Joseph Chamberlain on 22 October 1902 to outline his plans. Later that day Herzl discussed the situation with Natty, who would have preferred a colony in Cyprus, but fell in with Herzl's scheme for its location to be El Arish. In any case, Chamberlain had notified Herzl that he would not crowd out the Greek and Muslim inhabitants of Cyprus for the sake of new immigrants. He was nevertheless sympathetic and set up an appointment for Herzl to meet Lord Lansdowne, the Foreign Secretary, who dealt with matters concerning El Arish and Sinai.

Natty was charmed by Herzl, having assured an acquaintance that despite being 'an enthusiast ... [he] is a great man'.[33] Because Natty thought in terms of how best to strengthen the British Empire, he attached little importance to Palestine as a Jewish colony which was, in any case at the time, part of the Ottoman domains; so the alternative choice was El Arish and Sinai but not Cyprus, where previous attempts at Jewish colonization had faltered.[34] When Herzl requested a further meeting in 1903, Natty visited him in his hotel. Herzl informed him that he wanted to obtain £3 million for the Jewish Eastern Company from the ICA for the Sinai scheme; the other £2 million would have to be raised by public subscription. 'Rothschild

32 Patai, ed., *The Complete Diaries of Theodor Herzl*, pp. 1347 and 1357.
33 Ibid., pp. 1360–3 and 1369. Alex Bein, *Theodore Herzl: A Biography* (Philadelphia, 1945), p. 419.
34 John M. Shaftesley, 'Nineteenth-Century Jewish Colonies in Cyprus', *Transactions of the JHSE* Vol. XXII (1970): 88–107; Patai, ed., *The Complete Diaries of Theodor Herzl*, p. 1369.

promised ... [Herzl] to ask Claude Montefiore, [who had some control over the charity's funds] to come and see him, although he ... [did not] like him.' Herzl noted that Natty 'is a fine old man and I am really fond of him'. On 17 January 1903, Herzl had another meeting with Natty who promised to use his influence with Montefiore and Herbert Lousada, another member of the board of the ICA to persuade the charity to participate in the venture. If the ICA directorate did not cooperate, Natty said they could proceed by way of public subscription. Rothschild refused his offer to head the Jewish Eastern Company, saying to Herzl that 'I only want to be your co-worker. I am glad if I can be of help to you'. Herzl hand-picked seven experts to serve on the committee to investigate conditions in the Sinai Peninsula.[35] Two days later, he met Herbert Lousada and, with Rothschild's support, Lousada promised to look into the scheme, when the experts' report had been completed. Natty admonished Lousada, telling him 'to bear in mind that Dr Herzl's plan couldn't be treated so lightly. The Secretaries of State for Foreign affairs and the Colonies had been persuaded.'[36] It is noteworthy that Natty's sons, Walter and Charles, were exposed to Herzl's magnetism and charm at this meeting and that during World War I they became prominent Zionist supporters.

On 10 February 1903 Herzl wrote to Natty saying that your 'wish to help me has pleased me greatly, and I am grateful to you with all my heart for the aid you have already given me. We shall see what effect your inter-vention with ... Claude Montefiore and ... Lousada has had'. As soon as he had more definite news from Egypt, these gentlemen should be encouraged to call a board meeting of the ICA. It would helpful if Lord Rothschild could be in Paris at that time, as he wished to meet Baron Alphonse and Baron Edmond in his presence, to overcome French opposition to his El Arish plans. A few days later, Herzl noted that he had 'received a pleasant letter from Lord Rothschild who enclosed an obsequious communication from the ICA, signed by Leven [its president], which will gladly do his Lordship's bidding if at all possible'.[37] Excited by the quickening pace of events, Herzl informed Kessler that at Easter he was 'to meet in Paris

35   Patai, ed., *The Complete Diaries of Theodor Herzl*, pp. 1385–7 and 1393.
36   Ibid., pp. 1395–6.
37   Ibid., pp. 1409–11 and 1419.

with Lord Rothschild and other gentlemen in order to found the Land Company'. On an equally optimistic note, Herzl reassured Rothschild on 18 March 1903 that the results in the reports and memoranda which had been completed 'show that the territory we have in mind is suitable for a great settlement. In addition, we have received a written preliminary assurance from the Egyptian government, granting the desired settlement to the Zionist movement in principle'.[38] However, the experts' report of 26 March 1903 concluded that existing conditions were unsuitable for European settlement, but if sufficient irrigation were introduced, the area around El Arish could be developed.[39]

To expedite these negotiations, Herzl paid a hurried visit to Cairo, while awaiting the outcome of further deliberations on the supply of water. He returned from Egypt by way of Paris, where he once again conferred with Lord Rothschild in the magnificent mansion of Baron Alphonse. Herzl confided in his diary that Natty's 'intellectual mediocrity is distressing, but he is a man who is truly good and devoted to me'. Rothschild mentioned that he had told the influential ICA members Zadoc Kahn, the Chief Rabbi and Narcisse Leven its president that, through Herzl, they had the chance of 'doing something great'; and Herzl, with Natty's aid, tried to attract the support of Jacob Schiff, the American banker and philanthropist, for a great plan to help their Russian co-religionists. Whereas Baron Edmond was well-disposed to Herzl's plan, his brother Alphonse would not collaborate because he deemed it to be a political initiative.[40] Joseph Chamberlain stated that it was essential that Herzl enlist Rothschild's support, as 'the English government counted on him'. Having spoken to five persons connected with the ICA, Herzl informed Rothschild, on 27 April 1903, that they indicated they would grant one million pounds for the Pelusium project which was dependent on water from the Nile, while he would have to raise the other £4 million by public subscription. He was more interested in El Arish, however, where colonization could be started at once. Some of the misery in Eastern Europe could be alleviated and he could inspire the masses with the good

38 Ibid., pp. 1433–4 and 1437–8.
39 David Vital, *Zionism: The Formative Years* (Oxford, 1988), pp. 152–3.
40 Patai, ed., *The Complete Diaries of Theodor Herzl*, pp. 1467–9 and 1471.

tidings. 'Then, too, it is the beginning of a diversion by means of which we may forestall the Alien Bill'.[41] Nevertheless, the Egyptian government's irrigation expert pronounced against the scheme in May 1903 because of the excessive amount of water that would have to be extracted from the river. This killed the El Arish project.[42]

Meanwhile between 6 and 8 April 1903, there was a pogrom in Kishinev in which fifty-one Jews were killed and much of their property destroyed; the reverberations of this heinous act shook the Jewish world. Places of refuge had to be found quickly for the Jewish masses, who were once more on the move. On 23 April 1903, Herzl set up a fresh appointment with Joseph Chamberlain to assist in the negotiations with British government officials in Egypt. Chamberlain advised him in the course of their discussions that 'I have seen a land for you on my travels [in Africa] and that's Uganda. Its hot on the coast, but farther inland the climate becomes excellent, even for Europeans. You can raise sugar and cotton there. And I thought to myself, that would be a land for Dr Herzl. But, of course, he wants to go only to Palestine or its vicinity', to which Herzl replied that 'Our base must be in or near Palestine. Later we can also settle Uganda. For we have enormous masses to migrate.'[43] In fact, at a subsequent interview with Herzl's lieutenant, Leopold Greenberg, Chamberlain offered the Zionist movement 'an area for colonization large enough for a million souls, with local self- government. Not in Uganda but in its vicinity.' Although the project became known as the 'Uganda Scheme', the land originally earmarked for Herzl by Chamberlain was situated between Nairobi and the Mau Escarpment. Owing to opposition from the white settlers it was suggested that a better location for settlement would be in the Kenya or Nandi districts.[44] By 30 May 1903, Herzl was admitting to Lord Rothschild that his Sinai plan had come to nothing, but that he was not discouraged because he had an alternative scheme 'and a very powerful man is ready to help me'.[45]

41   Ibid., pp. 1474 and 1477–9.
42   Vital, *Zionism*, pp. 153–4.
43   Patai, ed., *The Complete Diaries of Theodor Herzl*, pp. 1473–5.
44   Jehuda Reinharz, *Chaim Weizmann: The Making of a Zionist Leader* (New York, 1985), p. 177.
45   Patai, ed., *The Complete Diaries of Theodor Herzl*, p. 1501.

Despite the backing of Herzl for the East African project, support for it split the Zionist movement. Nevertheless, in the emergency following the Kishinev pogrom, the Uganda offer gained increasing plausibility. At the Zionist Congress in Basle which opened on 23 August 1903, Herzl announced the project and was thrilled to receive a congratulatory telegram from Natty, Lord Rothschild.[46] When Chaim Weizmann met some of the leaders of ICA in France in the autumn, he became convinced that their goal remained Palestine and that only pressure from Lord Rothschild persuaded them to support an expedition to East Africa mounted by Herzl.[47] In fact, since 1900 the ICA had taken over the administration of Baron Edmond's colonies in Palestine and prior to that, urged on by Zadok Kahn and Leven, had allocated one million francs for loans and the purchase of land there.[48] A Hamburg journal reported that the East Africa project was to be taken up by a conference in London or Paris on the initiative of Lord Rothschild. Representatives of the ICA and the Alliance would be attending the meeting together with Lord Rothschild and Herzl.[49] From another perspective, Lucien Wolf criticized the plan as 'an unwise experiment in Jewish self-government' which would indicate their inability to assimilate.[50]

Herzl died on 3 July 1904. Just over ten days later, Weizmann informed Menachem Ussishkin (1863–1941), a Zionist ideologist that the 'African story is not finished, Lord Rothschild and some others stand behind it, and therein lies the strength of Greenberg & Co ... [They] want to take Herzl's place.' Joseph Cowen and Leopold Greenberg were said to be planning 'the setting up of an African syndicate with the participation of the ICA, Lord Rothschild and seven-twelfths of the Jewish Colonial Bank'. In August 1904, rumours still abounded that Lord Rothschild would finance an expedition to East Africa, though this was later denied.[51]

Without Herzl's vitality and drive, the Uganda project foundered,

46 Ibid., p. 1559.
47 Reinharz, *Chaim Weizmann*, p. 187.
48 Derek J. Penslar, *Zionism and Technocracy* (Bloomington, IN, 1996), p. 28.
49 *Jewish World* 6 May 1904, and Meyer W. Weisgal, ed., *The Letters and Papers of Chaim Weizmann* Vol. 3 Series A (date and place needed), pp. 259–60.
50 Robert G. Weisbord, *African Zion* (Philadelphia, 1968), pp. 158–61.
51 Weisgal, ed., *Letters and Papers of Chaim Weizmann* Vol. 3, pp. 282, 297 and 333.

Israel Zangwill and others seceded from the Zionist movement to establish the Jewish Territorial Organization (ITO) to revive this plan and the British government proceeded with their Alien Immigration Bill. In May 1906, Zangwill was still touting an enhanced Uganda scheme. He informed Lucien Wolf that

> I had a long interview with Mr Chamberlain on Friday and he quite accepted the idea (which was new to him) of a Jewish development of the entire East Africa Protectorate. He says, of course, there would be a row at the idea but he is willing to back it up with all his influence and empowered me to let Lord Elgin [the Colonial Secretary in the Liberal administration] know his views. I am also writing to Rothschild about it.[52]

On 11 July 1906, Chamberlain, the former Colonial Secretary, suffered a stroke and became incapacitated and, lacking the support of enough persons of influence, Zangwill's initiative was at an end.[53] A further damper to Zangwill's enthusiasm was a rebuff from Natty. Writing to his French cousins after a visit by Zangwill, Natty said that he 'told ... [him] very frankly that neither you nor we could take any part in a scheme aimed at the establishment of a Jewish Kingdom with a Hebrew Monarch or Stadtholder'.[54] After the demise of the Uganda scheme, Zangwill and Lucien Wolf looked elsewhere to alternative locations, including Mesopotamia and Angola, for their Jewish colony.[55]

Simon Schama gives a somewhat distorted account of Natty's relationship with Herzl, claiming that he 'had shown no enthusiasm for ... [the El Arish approach] or any other similar hare-brained adventures'.[56] What emerges from a close reading of Herzl's diary and other sources is that Natty was a doughty supporter not only of the El Arish project, being kept informed of its precise details, but of the Uganda scheme, for which he did some arm-twisting of French Jewish leaders on Herzl's behalf, as the

---

52 Central Zionist Archives A77/25 Israel Zangwill to Lucien Wolf 6 May 1906.
53 Weisbord, *African Zion*, pp. 229–31.
54 RAL XI/130A/0 Natty to French cousins 13 November 1906.
55 School of Slavonic Studies, Wolf Collection, Wolf to Sir Ernest Cassel 18 November 1913. Adam Rovner, 'A Portuguese Palestine', *History Today* (December 2012): 29–35.
56 Schama, *Two Rothschilds and the Land of Israel*, p. 191.

Zionist leader's most prominent ally. What Herzl had wanted initially was a Jewish colony in the vicinity of Palestine under British protection to be part of the British Empire, so that the Jews would have a forward-base to lay claim to Palestine; even the Jewish East African colony was to be under the British flag, but both schemes were contingent, in the eyes of the British government, on Lord Rothschild's unflagging backing.

Weizmann continued this Zionist pro-British policy when he strove to have the mandate for Palestine granted to Britain. So too, Herzl's British imperial aspirations were in close harmony with Lord Rothschild's ambitions for an expanding empire. Where Natty parted company with the Zionist movement and to some extent with Herzl, was in his reluctance at this point to envisage a Jewish state in Palestine. Josef Fraenkel's presentation of Natty as a crypto-Zionist, as someone who in principle was 'in favour of a Jewish national home in Palestine' under Herzl's influence, was thus misleading. In 1906, Arthur Balfour was 'unable to understand why Rothschild, etc., are so hostile to Zionism', Weizmann remarked to David Wolffsohn.[57] Yet Natty's admiration for Herzl continued long after his death, so much so that he contributed 4,800 kronen towards a Zionist fund for his children.[58]

On 19 May 1904, Lord Rothschild led a delegation from the Board of Deputies, which was received by the Under-Secretary of State for the Home Office, to demand amendment of the Alien Immigration Bill, as the Home Secretary was attending a Cabinet meeting but was anxious to know the views of the Jewish community. Natty observed that the Commission was of the opinion that a system of entry for immigrants

> somewhat analogous to the one in vogue in the United States should be introduced into this country ... Now ... the Bill ... provides no machinery like that which exists in America. It introduces into this country a loathsome system of police officers, of espionage and of passports, of arbitrary power by police officers.

Further, Natty pointed out that, as Sir Kenelm Digby had stated in a letter to *The Times*

57 Meyer W. Weisgal, ed., *The Letters and Papers of Chaim Weizmann* Vol. IV Series A (London, 1975), p. 336.
58 Josef Frankel, 'Herzl and the Rothschild Family', pp. 235 and 238.

the majority of the Commissioners proposed that an enquiry should be held before a Court of Summary Jurisdiction, and ... the order of prohibition should be made by a magistrate ... Your Bill provides that Custom House officers and Coast Guard officers should have the power to prohibit the landing of any passenger pending the decision of the Secretary of State ... my view is – I will not say the view of the Board of Deputies – that all regulations for immigrants ... for deciding upon the fate of the immigrant, can only be carried into effect if, at the port of landing, the State previously provides a place where the immigrants can live, where they will be fed, where they can be medically examined, and where their friends can claim them ... in the case of the Jewish immigrant who arrives in this country, the Jewish community will willingly enter into a bond that he should not become a public charge during the first two years of his new life.[59]

Lord Rothschild's views were, to some extent, ambiguous although, with Sir Kenelm Digby, he had defended Jewish immigration within the commission. He had championed Conservative candidates at the 1900 general election, Evans-Gordon at Stepney and David Hope Kyd, both of whom had pronounced anti-immigrant views, until rebuked by the *Jewish Chronicle*.[60] He had also supported measures directing the main flow of immigrants away from the British Isles and those who nevertheless gained entry were to be made subject to a vigorous new system of state inspection and control, even if it was different from the system devised by the government.

When the Bill was sent to a Grand Committee for examination, a group of Radical Liberal M.P.s 'chocked it with words until the time limit was reached'. Winston Churchill M.P., who had crossed the floor of the House to join the Liberal ranks, also claimed credit for destroying the Bill, telling a correspondent 'Yes, I wrecked the Bill'. He added that the Conservatives were well aware that

the opposition of wealthy and influential Jews in their own party has always prevented, and probably always will prevent, their passing such a measure into law. That men like Lord Rothschild and others of his faith should earnestly strive to preserve a free asylum in England for their

59 *Jewish Chronicle* 27 May 1904 pp. 10–12; *The Times* 2 and 31 May 1904, letters from Sir Kenelm Digby.
60 Alderman, *Modern British Jewry*, p. 136.

coreligionists who are driven out from foreign countries by religious persecution, although the expense must fall mainly upon themselves, is an honourable fact in thorough accordance with the traditions of the Jewish people.[61]

Still hoping to use the measure to attract working class support and under renewed pressure from some Jewish party members, in 1905 the government introduced the Bill in a drastically revised form and it was enacted into law. A former Conservative Chief Whip pointed out in a constituency speech that 'Some [rich Jews] who supported the party financially and otherwise had marked their displeasure by withdrawing their patronage.' Gone was the clause prohibiting certain areas to alien immigrants on the grounds that they were overcrowded. While the Bill still excluded undesirables and destitute aliens, the ill-defined category of immigrants of a 'notoriously bad character' was dropped. The government conceded the rights of religious refugees by a clause which stated that in the case of

> an immigrant who proves that he is seeking admission to this country solely to avoid prosecution or punishment on religious or political grounds, or for an offence of a political character, or persecution involving danger to life and limb, leave to land shall not be refused ... merely [because] of want of means.[62]

In December 1907, the Board of Deputies wrote to Campbell-Bannerman, the Liberal Prime Minister,

> to request repeal of the Aliens Act, not merely its reform, [but] quickly withdrew from this position once it became clear that it did not have the support of Lord Rothschild ... any memorial signed by English Jews which did not include his signature would certainly be considered as a sign of want of unanimity on the part of the Jews themselves.[63]

Lord Rothschild was of the opinion that if the Board asked for the repeal of the Act, there were plenty of M.P.s who would be glad of the opportunity

---

61 John A. Garrard, *The English and Immigration* (London, 1971), pp. 42–3; *Jewish Chronicle* 2 December 1904 p. 12.
62 Garrard, *The English and Immigration*, pp. 44–6; Alderman, *Modern British Jewry*, p. 137.
63 David Feldman, *Englishmen and Jews: Social Relations and Political Culture 1840–1914* (New Haven, 1994), p. 358.

to ask for its penalties to be made stiffer. Further, he pointed out that the funds of the Board of Guardians were insufficient 'to relieve the Jews already in the country', while 'the labour market was overstocked'. When a deputation from the Board of Deputies went to see him, Natty confirmed his refusal to sign the memorial, stipulating that Britain must have the right to exclude criminals and the diseased. The Board might deplore 'the Act as antisemitic in operation & most harshly administered & then proceed to ask for an amendment establishing receiving homes and a right of appeal to the King's Bench'.[64] Hence the Board obtained a series of concessions in the administration of the act from the new Liberal government, such as the opening of 'receiving houses' for immigrants at ports, the selection of more sympathetic personnel to sit on the immigration boards, and allowing the immigrants to receive legal assistance. It was much closer to the American system for receiving immigrants which had been envisaged by Natty. So much so that Lord Rothschild, in a widely publicized letter to Bonar Law, the new Conservative party leader, claimed in December 1910 to 'have no doubt that if you and the party you represent are returned to power, the provisions of the Act will be carried out in such a way to give satisfaction to the Jewish community'.[65] Following the Aliens Act, it was estimated that between 1906 and 1914 an average of 4,000 or 5,000 Jewish immigrants settled in Britain each year, half the previous number but still a significant figure.[66]

It was not until the beginning of the First World War that the question of Palestine was seriously discussed again, when the disintegration of the Ottoman Empire became an issue of practical politics. Before this time, Natty had retained his long-held belief in the territorial integrity of Ottoman domains. As late as 1913 he posed the question to his cousins of 'where would we be today if we had yielded to the persuasions of the different Foreign Offices and had issued a large Turkish Loan in order to give stability to the young Turks when they came into office? We are very sorry for your Credit Establishments that they should be full of short-dated Balkan Notes, but we cannot grieve over the quarrels of Greeks, Bulgars,

64 LMA, ACC/3121/C/13/001/05 Minutes of the Law and Parliamentary Committee of the Board of Deputies 12 and 23 December 1907.
65 Garrard, *The English and Immigration*, pp. 130–3.
66 V. D. Lipman, *Social History of the Jews in England 1850–1950* (London, 1954), p. 143.

Servians as we were always of the opinion that Turkish rule, bad as it might be, was best suited to keep these turbulent races in order'.[67]

Herbert Samuel, a rising star in the Cabinet, had his imagination awakened by Herzl and, despite a loss of faith, still felt a deep connection with the Jewish immigrant population of Britain. He saw the dissolution of the Ottoman Empire as providing an opportunity for the establishment of the Jewish state at the end of the war and a centre that would welcome massive Russian Jewish migration. In January 1915 he circulated a memorandum on 'The Future of Palestine' among his Cabinet colleagues, which opened in ecstatic terms:

> Already there is a stirring spreading with great rapidity that now, at last, some advance may be made, in some way, towards the fulfilment of the hope and desire, held with unshakeable tenacity for eighteen hundred years, for the restoration of the Jews to the land to which they are attached by ties almost as ancient as history itself.

As the 90,000 or 100,000 Jews in the country were incapable of setting up an autonomous state, the solution was to incorporate Palestine into the British Empire, thereby encouraging Jewish immigration. Thus

> in the course of time, the Jewish people, grown into a majority and settled in the land, may be conceded such a degree of self-government as the conditions of the day may justify ... The gradual growth of a considerable Jewish community in Palestine will not solve the Jewish question in Europe ... But it could probably hold in time 3,000,000 or 4,000,000, and some relief would be given to the pressure in Russia or elsewhere ... Let a Jewish centre be established in Palestine; let it achieve, as I believe it would achieve, a spiritual and intellectual greatness; and inevitably, the character of the individual Jew, wherever he might be, would be ennobled.[68]

It is remarkable but almost axiomatic that all global Jewish questions should turn on the issue of what to do about the Russian Jewish population. On

67 RAL XI/130A/7 Natty to his cousins Paris 14 May 1913.
68 National Archives, CAB37/123/43 memorandum on 'The Future of Palestine' by Lucien Wolf January 1915; Isaiah Friedman, *The Question of Palestine 1914–1918: British–Jewish–Arab Relations* (London, 1973), pp. 8–10.

5 February 1915, Samuel wrote to Lord Rothschild that 'with the approval of Sir Edward Grey [the Foreign Secretary] I sent you a memorandum, which has been circulated to a few members of the Cabinet. I should be very grateful if you would give me the opportunity of discussing with you on the subject with which it deals.' A few days later Samuel thanked Natty for his kind invitation to dine and sleep at Tring on Friday, 'and am grateful for the opportunity of discussing with you the subject' of the future of Palestine.[69] What happened when Samuel visited Tring? Isaiah Friedman has suggested that Lord Rothschild and his brother Leopold were so convinced by Samuel's arguments that they supported his pleas for a British Protectorate in Palestine, but it is doubtful whether this extended to sharing Samuel's enthusiasm for a major Jewish settlement there. It is more likely that they agreed with Lucien Wolf's standpoint, that the Jews were to have equality with the native population of Palestine, open access for immigrants, 'a liberal scheme of local government for the existing colonies ... the establishment of a Hebrew University, and ... the recognition of Hebrew as one of the vernaculars of the land', nothing more.[70] Under no illusions Weizmann believed that the Rothschilds considered 'it their patriotic duty as Englishmen to desire that Great Britain should occupy Palestine. The Jewish side of the question is of secondary importance'. Furthermore, Weizmann recorded in his memoirs that 'Old Leopold Rothschild was, like his wife, furiously anti-Zionist, and remained so to the end.'[71] It was the younger generation of Rothschilds, the sons of Natty, Walter and Charles, and James de Rothschild, the son of Baron Edmond and the wives of two of them (Walter remained a bachelor) who all became strong supporters of Zionism. Thus when Charles wrote to Weizmann on 9 June 1915 that 'As you know my late father was strongly in favour of Mr. H. Samuel's scheme', this was to put a retrospective pro-Zionist gloss on Natty's thinking.[72]

After the passing of the 1905 Aliens Act, Natty brokered an accommodation with successive Liberal administrations which allowed a sizeable

69 RAL, 000/848/37 Herbert Samuel to Natty 5 and 9 February 1915.

70 National Archives, FO371/2579 memorandum of Lucien Wolf, 'Suggestions for pro-Allied propaganda among the Jews of the United States' 16 December 1915.

71 Meyer W. Weisgal, ed., *The Letters and Papers of Chaim Weizmann* Vol. VII Series A (London, 1975), p. 148; Chaim Weizmann, *Trial and Error* (London, 1949), p. 205.

72 Rothschild, *Dear Lord Rothschild*, pp. 239–40.

number of Jews to enter Britain each year before the First World War, blocking any attempt at its repeal. Until Herzl's death, Natty was a staunch supporter of his colonization schemes in El Arish and East Africa, so long as these entities were on a small scale and did not include plans for Jewish self-government. When, in 1915, it appeared that the Ottoman Empire might disintegrate, Natty saw this as an opportunity for the absorption of Palestine into the British Empire, not as a potential home for Russia's Jews. In 1918 Lucien Wolf shrank from envisaging a Jewish state in Palestine, for as a nineteenth-century liberal, he was on ethical grounds opposed to uprooting the indigenous Arab peasant population. Doubtless had Natty lived, he would have adopted a viewpoint akin to Wolf that the Jews 'passed out of' Palestine 'because in reality it was too small for their great spirit and [they] took the world for their stage'.[73]

73   Central Zionist Archives A/77/25 Israel Zangwill to Lucien Wolf 30 December 1918 and
     Wolf to Zangwill 31 December 1918.

6

NATTY AND JEWISH INTERVENTION IN RUSSIA: THE SECOND PHASE

As far as world Jewry was concerned, most of Lord Rothschild's interventions were on behalf of Russian Jewry, but he also took action to assist Moroccan, Persian and Romanian Jewry, thereby establishing his credentials as an international leader. In 1893, Natty received a letter from the Foreign Office, confirming that 'the Sultan had reprimanded the Moorish Kaid accused of ill treating the Jews of the Morocco city [Mogador] and ordered him to treat them as favourably as the Mohammedans. The Vizier has also informed the Jewish Community ... and conveyed to them the Sultan's good will'.[1] When, in the same year, he intervened with the British authorities on behalf of the Jews of Hamadan in Persia, Sir Frank Lascelles took the matter up with the Shah, expressing

> regret ... that the persecution had not ceased and he added
> that he feared that a very bad impression would be created in
> England if it were allowed to continue. The Shah said that the
> new Governor of Hamadan had not yet reached his post and
> had not therefore been able to execute the strict orders which
> His Majesty had given him on the subject, but his Majesty
> had no doubt that all complaints would cease as soon as the
> Governor arrived. In a subsequent interview with Sadr-Azam

1   Rothschild, *Dear Lord Rothschild*, p. 33.

[the Prime Minister], Sir Frank Lascelles pointed out to his Highness how unwise and short-sighted a policy it was of the Persian Government to outrage the feelings of the Jewish community throughout the world by action of this kind under the present circumstances of that Kingdom.[2]

Natty was good at the grand gestures. Thus, on 4 November 1889, as Lord Rothschild, he headed a delegation of Anglo-Jewish notables including Sir Julian Goldsmid, Sir Albert Sassoon and Reuben Sassoon in full *levée* dress, who had an audience with the Shah of Persia at Buckingham Palace. After a few introductory remarks in French, Natty handed the Shah an illuminated address of welcome on behalf of British Jewry. Sir Julian Goldsmid added a few remarks in French, while Sir Albert Sassoon held a short conversation with His Majesty in Persian. The Shah, in reply, stated that he was

> pleased to learn that his sentiments towards the Jews in his Dominions were appreciated by their Co-religionists in other parts of the World. He assured the Deputation that they might confidently rely on his efforts to promote their welfare and said that he thought much good would ensue from the establishment throughout the provinces of Secular Schools for the Education of the Persian Jews and that such institutions would receive his hearty support. With regard to certain complaints ... that the Jews in some parts of his Empire were subjected to indignity and oppression, H.M. said that every one of his subjects ... irrespective of creed ... could personally lay any complaints before him with the assurance that they would receive attentive and impartial consideration and if such complaints were substantiated the offenders would be promptly punished.[3]

However, if the two episodes of Natty's intercession in 1893 are examined more closely, it becomes apparent that they were both made when the Earl of Rosebery, who was married to Natty's cousin Hannah, was Foreign Secretary and that the subsequent task of following up these representations to the British government was left to the leaders of the Conjoint Foreign Committee. The latter body sent a memorial onwards to the Foreign Office from the Jews of Hamadan, complaining that they were

2   LMA, ACC3121 C11/2/1 T. H. Sanderson to Natty 26 May 1893; David Vital, *A People Apart: The Jews in Europe 1789–1939* (Oxford, 1999), pp. 483–4.
3   LMA, ACC/3121/A/13 BODS minutes 20 November 1889, pp. 33–4.

forced to wear a distinctive costume which tended 'to lower them in the estimation of the rest of the population and to mark them out as fit ... objects for contempt and violence'. There was also dissatisfaction about Mullah Abdullah, who went around stirring up religious hatred in the town. The Foreign Office assured the Conjoint that 'where the Governor is strong the Jews have little to fear', particularly as the middle class did not join in the agitation, and that as regards the wearing of a special costume, 'it does not appear to be strictly enforced'. Later, a bond was taken from the Mullah when he returned to the town to ensure his good behaviour, though this soon suffered a relapse.[4] The British government, under the Marquis of Salisbury in 1895, was not only compelled to make fresh representations in Teheran to protect the Jews of Hamadan from molestation at the hands of the Mullah, but two years later it had to intervene elsewhere to save the Jews of Isfahan from persecution.[5] Turning to the situation in Mogador, the Earl of Rosebery acknowledged that 'while the reports of Kaid Quida's cruelty are confirmed, the Sultan's intervention has now put a stop to it ... the Jews ... are of the opinion that they would not at present be justified at making further complaints as a reconciliation has been effected with the Governor'.[6] Protracted correspondence with the British government ensued about the Jews of the city extending their quarter without the site reverting to the ownership of the Moroccan government within a short period. In 1905, however, Lord Lansdowne admitted that 'the disabilities from which the Jews in Morocco suffer, and which had been pointed out to the late Lord Salisbury in 1888, had not been removed, in spite of formal promises of successive Sultans; and that the subject might be considered at the forthcoming Algeciras Conference'.[7]

4   LMA, ACC/3121/A/13 pp. 184–5 Earl of Rosebery to Natty 28 November 1892 and Natty to Earl of Rosebery 29 November 1892; ACC 3121 C11/2/1 S. G. Asher to Lewis Emanuel 30 May 1893; Arthur Cohen and Sir Julian Goldsmid to Earl of Rosebery 7 June 1893; Foreign Office to Arthur Cohen and Sir Julian Goldsmid 14 June 1893; ibid., 28 July 1893.
5   LMA, ACC/3121/A/13 pp. 319 and 424 T. H. Sanderson to Conjoint 30 August 1895; ibid., 24 September 1897.
6   LMA, ACC/3121 B2/9/6/7 16 February 1894.
7   LMA,ACC/3121/A/13 p. 351 Arthur Nicholson to Marquess of Salisbury 9 April 1896 and T. H. Sanderson to Conjoint 22 June 1896; ACC3121/ B2/9/6/8 Eldon Gorst to Lewis Emanuel 15 November 1905.

Natty's interventions in individual cases of injustice were sparse but effective. Through his high-level contacts in Brazil, Natty saved the Benichimol brothers from execution for high treason in 1894; and it was 'suggestive' to one historian 'that the intervention of perhaps the foremost banker in the world was required to make the Buenos Aires police remove one girl from a brothel'.[8]

In June and July 1900, ruinous economic restrictions imposed on Jews in Romania caused a sudden exodus of Jews from that country to London, initially by a group of 172 people, followed by a second batch of 196 and the expected arrival of another 200 homeless refugees, which threw the Anglo-Jewish establishment into a state of panic. After a hastily called meeting, Alfred Cohen, Claude Montefiore and Herbert Lousada unanimously decided to appeal to the Alliance to take measures to prevent Frankfurt or Romania sending any more would-be emigrants to Britain, as they would 'refuse absolutely to be the means or conduit pipe for sending any more out'. If Romanian Jews wished to emigrate to Canada or the United States, they would have to leave from Continental ports.[9]

Looking back, Alfred Cohen was of the opinion that 'The Jewish Community did not try last year to cast back capable fugitive coreligionists, but did try to prevent Roumania dumping down here the refuse of that country, people afflicted with disease and with vice and who would never have been sent here had there been the least scintilla of capacity in the people who sent them here'.[10] 'Advice was promptly sought of ... Lord Rothschild and Messrs F. D. Mocatta, Ellis A. Franklin, Claude G. Montefiore, Leonard Cohen (President of the Jewish Board of Guardians) and others, [who] were most prompt in rendering the [Poor Jews' Temporary] Shelter both personal and pecuniary assistance', recalled Abraham Munday. On 3 July 1900, the first batch of migrants who were, in the main, fit young men, was sent by steamer to Quebec to work on farms in Canada. 'These were followed by another party of 183, two of whom were destined for New

8   LMA,ACC/3121/A/13 BODS minutes 6 December 1893 p. 241 and 21 January 1894 pp. 245–6; Lloyd Gartner, 'Anglo-Jewry and the Jewish International Traffic in Prostitution 1885–1914', *AJS Review* 7/8 (1982–3), p. 170.
9   Alliance, AIU Angl. 1/D/17/9964 Alfred Cohen, Claude Montefiore and Herbert Lousada to Narcisse Leven 6 July 1900.
10   LMA, C11/2/2 Alfred Cohen to Lucien Wolf 11 June 1901.

York, and the rest for Winnipeg, Canada … whilst a third group of 144, of whom 42 were sent to various places in Canada, and 102 to the United States, sailed on 17 July 1900.' None could be defined as the human material so denigrated by Alfred Cohen. In all 426 out of the 650 Romanians left the United Kingdom within five weeks of their arrival and it was likely that the bulk of the remainder migrated overseas.[11] Despite the suggestion by Eugene Black that Lord Rothschild had participated in the discussions and the subsequent correspondence with the Alliance, there is no evidence from the archive that he signed any of the letters, as the signature purported to be his is, in fact, that of Herbert Lousada, so that it is more likely that Natty's assistance was confined to financial aid.[12]

Having co-ordinated their action with other European Jewish relief organizations to stem the influx of Jews from Romania, the Anglo-Jewish leaders turned to diplomatic action to exert pressure on the Romanian government. In 1902, the Romanian Parliament passed a law forbidding foreigners from practising a handicraft in their country, unless the parent state of these artisans accorded similar privileges to Romanian citizens. If enforced, this act would have deprived Jewish artisans of employment, as Jews were classed as foreigners without a parent state. As early as June 1901, Lord Rothschild brought Romania's attempt to flout the provisions of the Treaty of Berlin (1878) which protected Jews to the attention of Lord Lansdowne, the British Foreign Secretary, who tried to persuade the powers signing the treaty to intervene.

The idea for this intervention was probably conceived by Lucien Wolfe, who drafted an elaborate and brilliantly worded memorandum in its support, which so pleased Lord Rothschild that he offered to pay Wolfe his incidental expenses for compiling it.[13] Natty communicated his action to the leaders of American Jewry, the politician Oscar Straus and the banker Jacob Schiff, who secured the support of President Theodore Roosevelt for Lansdowne's initiative. In July 1902, John Hay, the U.S. Secretary of State, formulated a powerful indictment of the Romanian government's

11 LMA, 4184/02/05/001/001 Abraham Munday, *Reminiscences* pp. 35–6.
12 Eugene C. Black, *The Social Politics of Anglo-Jewry 1880–1920* (Oxford, 1988), p. 260.
13 LMA, ACC/2805/3/1/4 Lord Lansdowne to Natty 13 June 1901. LMA, C11/2/2 Eric Barrington to Wolfe 14 June 1901, S. G. Asher to Wolfe 14 June 1901 and Benjamin L. Cohen to Wolfe 17 June 1901.

policies; three weeks later, American ambassadors in the key capitals were instructed to communicate this note to the governments to which they were accredited, in order to ascertain the action they proposed. No longer feeling unsupported, in September 1902, Lansdowne sent a circular to the Treaty Powers, proposing combined representations at Bucharest to protest against the infringement of the treaty, with the result that the Romanian government promptly rescinded the offending law. Without Jacob Schiff's powerful intervention, Lord Rothschild's efforts to stir the British Foreign Office into action would have been futile, though it was noted that Lansdowne felt more strongly about the Romanian Jews 'than the Cabinet did'. A subtle realignment of the centres of Jewish power was occurring, in line with the growing financial and industrial strength of the United States.[14] Attempts by the Conjoint Committee to participate in the negotiations were brushed aside by the Foreign Office because Natty had taken the matter up.[15]

Such interventions in the Muslim lands on behalf of Jewish relief have been called the 'imperialism of human rights' by Abigail Green and perhaps the term could also be applied to Romania at the time, but Britain was wary of taking forceful action against Russia, one of the great powers, whatever humiliations they inflicted on their Jewish population, apart from pointing out the negative impact this was having on British public opinion.[16]

In addition to the grave concerns about the infringement of the human rights of Jews living overseas, what most concerned Anglo-Jewish leaders in the closing decades of the nineteenth century was the resurrection in Central Europe and the Mediterranean world of the blood libel – the fantastic charge that Jews required the blood of slaughtered Christian infants in order to bake *matzot* for Passover. To the Victorians, the revival of these barbaric medieval notions was an affront to the new world order of civilized values

14 Lucien Wolf, *Notes on the Diplomatic History of the Jewish Question* (London, 1919), pp. 36–43; Naomi W. Cohen, *Jacob Schiff: A Study in Jewish Leadership* (Hanover, NH, 1999), p. 131; Ron Chernow, *The Warburgs: A Family Saga* (London, 1995), p; 100. Baron von Eckardstein, *Ten Years at the Court of St. James 1895–1905* (London, 1921), p. 170.

15 LMA, C11/2/2 T. H. Sanderson to Joseph Sebag Montefiore and Claude Montefiore, 2 June and 8 July 1902.

16 Abigail Green, 'The British Empire and the Jews: An Imperialism of Human Rights?', *Past & Present* 199 (May 2008), pp. 175–205.

they were trying so hard to create. Sometimes the death of a Christian child or youth was sufficient to ignite the charge and attract the attention of Jewish notables; sometimes the publication of a book or pamphlet purporting to offer substantial proof of the veracity of the legend was enough to activate Anglo-Jewish leaders. Among the episodes they had to deal with were those in Alexandria, Egypt (1881), Tisza-Eszlar, Hungary (1882), France (1889), Xanten, Germany (1892), Malta (1892) and Polna, Bohemia (1899).[17] Usually, the Chief Rabbi or the intervention of the lay leadership of Anglo-Jewry, could be mobilized to rectify the situation, but there were occasions when the added diplomatic weight of the Rothschilds was found to be necessary.

Despite the fifty-one deaths, the hundreds of injured, and the massive destruction of Jewish homes and shops in the Kishinev pogrom of 19 and 20 April 1903, it has been interpreted as an isolated incident – apart from another later disturbance at Homel – as it did not lead to a wave of further pogroms in Russia.[18] Nevertheless, the anti-Jewish violence shocked opinion in Western Europe and the United States as did a prior newspaper campaign accusing Jews of ritual murder. A letter protesting against the outrages committed in Kishinev, signed by the presidents of the Board of Deputies of British Jews and the Anglo-Jewish Association (AJA) was published in *The Times* on 18 May 1903 and, at the same time, a Kishinev Relief Fund was inaugurated, but both these bodies and the Russo-Jewish Committee were opposed to the Lord Mayor calling a public meeting at the Guildhall.[19] Contributions to the Relief Fund poured in, not only from Anglo-Jewry, but from South Africa (£1,500) and Australia (£700 2s 0d).[20] A mass meeting of Jews and others attended by 5,000 persons in Mile End passed a resolution against the cruelties and anti-Semitic excesses perpetrated at Kishinev and elsewhere against Jews and the revolutionary Social Democratic movement; a labour demonstration was held in Hyde

---

17 Maurice Samuel, *Blood Accusation: The Strange History of the Beilis Case* (Philadelphia, 1966), p. 4.

18 Klier, *Russians, Jews and the Pogroms of 1881–1882*, p. 60; Edward H. Judge, *Easter in Kishinev: Anatomy of a Pogrom* (New York, 1992), p. 140.

19 *Jewish Chronicle* 22 May, pp. 8 and 9 and 29 May 1903, pp. 14 and 19.

20 LMA, ACC/2805/3/1/16 C. S Joseph to Hermann Adler 6 and 22 May 1903; and H. Liberman, Cape Town to Hermann Adler 1 July 1903.

Park and a Zionist Federation protest meeting in the East End.[21] Leopold de Rothschild had recently been invited to become a Vice-President of the Board, because his attendance was desired 'as the interpreter of Lord Rothschild's views'. Leo confessed that he 'had very many duties and, he was ashamed to add, many pleasures also [his love of the turf], which would prevent his [constant] attendance'. In this instance, he could tell them that 'His Lordship's opinion was that a [public] meeting would be inadvisable, and he thought that it would do more harm than good ... Had it been possible for a meeting to be held, convened by the Great Christian statesmen and dignitaries of the Church, the community would welcome it with feelings of gratitude.'[22] Without Natty's blessing, the call for a protest meeting was a non-starter. Nor was it inconceivable that Lord Rothschild had arranged private discussions with the Foreign Office to ease the situation. A Conference called by the *Hilfsverein* of European Jewish organizations in Berlin, including the AJA, 'unanimously decided not only not to support emigration from Russia, but to oppose it in every possible way ... It was pointed out that there were no funds for the purpose and that emigration at this juncture would result in a terrible catastrophe.'[23]

American Jewry took a more active and positive stance. On 27 May 1903, a great protest meeting called by the Mayor of New York, Seth Low, took place at the Carnegie Hall, the speakers including former President Grover Cleveland. At an audience, the leaders of the B'nai B'rith convinced President Theodore Roosevelt of the necessity of sending a petition to the Tsar condemning the Kishinev massacres and Roosevelt, after further consultations, decided to ask the Russian government, in a note incorporating the petition, if it would accept it, only to have this government pre-empt him by declaring informally that that it would refuse to do so. Having, by its action, broken diplomatic protocols, the Tsarist regime jeopardized its position and the President ordered Secretary of State Hay to publish the full instructions to the U.S. ambassador in Russia, including details of the autocratic regime's manoeuvres. Roosevelt informed Congressman Littauer that 'I think we did that business pretty well. We certainly went to the limit

21   *The Times* 22 June 1903 and *Jewish Chronicle* 5 June 1903, p. 17. Langham, *250 Years of Convention* p. 119.
22   *Jewish Chronicle* 3 July 1903, p. 10.
23   *Jewish Chronicle* 10 July 1902, p. 10.

in taking the lead on behalf of humanity.'[24] This certainly was the view of the *Jewish Chronicle*, which saw 'the hegemony of the Hebrew race passing to the Jews of the United States'. True that 'At the time of Damascus blood accusation, it was English and French Jewry which took the lead. In the case of the Russian horrors of 1882, also, the leadership lay with European Jews. But in the latest and most brutal of Russian outbursts, it has been left to our American brethren to make a stand for justice to the Jew.'[25] All these diplomatic developments in Washington were also closely monitored by the British Foreign Office, an indication of their concern, despite their quiescence.[26]

Towards the end of 1903, there were rumours that fresh excesses were about to occur in Kishinev and Lord Rothschild and the Chief Rabbi attended a meeting to voice their concerns. David Lindo Alexander, the President of the Board of Deputies, advised the Chief Rabbi that he had seen Leopold de Rothschild, who did not think that there was any purpose in calling a meeting of the Conjoint Committee at that time. Leo drew his attention to certain despatches which appear in today's 'Morning Post' which, so far as they go, are satisfactory as they shew the Americans are quite alive to the seriousness of the position & are stirring in the matter. Lord Rothschild is not in the City today as he is not very well, but Mr Leopold will see him this afternoon & shew him the despatches in the 'Morning Post' & tell him of his interview with me, & he will then ask Lord Rothschild if he sees his way to write a letter to Lord Lansdowne.[27]

It was then decided to call a meeting of the Conjoint Committee on Friday afternoon at New Court, which the Chief Rabbi was urgently requested to attend.[28] Late in December, Oscar Straus contacted President Roosevelt about reports in *The Times* of London that there had been renewed violence against Jews in Kishinev, urging him to check with the

24 Best, *To Free a People*, pp. 71–85.
25 *Jewish Chronicle* 7 August 1903 p. 15.
26 FO 181/796/2 T. H. Sanderson to Sir Charles Scott 29 July 1903 with accompanying despatches from Arthur S. Raikes to Lord Lansdowne.
27 LMA, ACC/2805/3/1/16 M. S. Isaacs to Hermann Adler 28 December 1903, and D. L. Alexander to Hermann Adler 30 December 1903 with a press cutting from the *Morning Post*.
28 LMA, ACC/2805/3/1/16 Charles Emanuel to Hermann Adler 31 December 1903.

American diplomatic mission in Russia to discover whether or not this was true. In reply, the American consul in Odessa assured the President that the rumours lacked substance.[29] Additional pressure was put on the President by Jacob Schiff and Natty thanked him for persuading the President to obtain assurances from the Russian government that there would be no further disturbances in Kishinev, but Schiff advised Natty that the credit for this should be given to the sharp comments in the American press, in which the Hearst newspapers took the lead.[30]

In the following spring, Lord Rothschild contacted the Foreign Secretary in order to persuade him to protest to the Russian government about the volatile situation in Odessa which could lead to violence akin to the rioting at Kishinev. Natty asked Jacob Schiff to ensure that the State Department made similar representations. Schiff replied that, in the past, the Russian banker Rothstein had been sent by Count Witte as an intermediary with promises of assistance for

> the repeal of the so-called May Laws, not to speak of the pecuniary advantages to my firm, if we would assure him of our cooperation with the Russian Government in its financial plans. This we flatly refused, telling Mr Rothstein that promises were cheap, and that action would have to precede Russia's application to the American money markets before our cooperation could be had, and that until then we should bring all the influence we could command to bear against Russia getting a foothold in the American money markets.

Natty assured Jacob Schiff on 7 April 1904 that the London bank had not handled a Russian loan since 1875 and that Russia had no prospects of obtaining loans on the London market from other Jewish or non-Jewish firms. He was less hopeful about the Continent, but the Paris house of Rothschild remained anti-Russian.[31] Natty's remarks were not strictly accurate, however, because the London house had participated in loans floated in Paris in 1889 and 1894; and though Alfred had dismissed a visit of Rothstein in 1900 with the remark 'I won't see this *chuzpe ponem*

---

29 Best, *To Free a People*, p. 87.
30 Cyrus Adler, *Jacob H. Schiff: His Life and Letters* vol. 2 (New York, 1928), p. 119; telegram to Hermann Adler from the *New York Journal* 7 January 1903.
31 Cohen, *Jacob Schiff*, p. 135; Adler, *Jacob H. Schiff* vol. 2, pp. 120–3.

[Yiddish for impudent fellow]', Natty had given him a hearing; but in the spring of 1903, a German embassy official claimed that financial circles in London, including the Rothschilds, were more favourably disposed towards Russia. However, despite the efforts of Rothschild and Schiff to close the British and American money markets to Russia, the Bleichroders in Berlin and the Banque de Paris et des Pays-Bas took up Russian loans in October 1904 and in May 1905.[32] Moreover, the attitude of the London house remained somewhat equivocal until the spring of 1905 with talk of Lord Rothschild raising a loan in the City to help Russia pay an indemnity to Japan to end the war.[33]

During 1904, the Russian government sent emissaries to the Paris Rothschilds with avowals of better treatment for Russian Jews in return for a loan, blandishments which Baron Alphonse resisted. 'We have invariably replied', he informed his London cousins on 20 July,

> that Russia is a great power, while we have no such pretensions, not considering ourselves a power; that it is for the Russian government to do what justice, equity and its own interest recommended; that as for us, we make no conditions, and that we can only accept gratefully any serious improvement in the lot of our coreligionists which the government might feel itself duty-bound to make ... All that you [in London] have to do is to hold on to that terrain which you and we share; and in reply to all hints that we accept all signs of goodwill with great satisfaction, and that we should be delighted if the Russian government were to put them into practice.[34]

Later in the summer of 1905, during talks to end the Russo-Japanese War, Schiff met Sergei Witte, later appointed as Prime Minister, who recalled in his memoirs that he had

> never met such a Jew as Schiff. Proud, dignified, conscious of his power, he declared to me solemnly that so long as the Tsar's government would

---

32   A. J. Sherman, 'German Jewish Bankers in World Politics: The Financing of the Russo-Japanese War', *Leo Baeck Year Book XXVIII* (1983), p. 69; von Eckardstein, *Ten Years at the Court of St. James 1895–1905* pp. 170–1; Marina Soroka, *Britain, Russia and the Road to the First World War* (Surrey, 2012), p. 61.

33   Ibid., p. 164.

34   Feldman, 'The Rothschilds and the Russian Loans', p. 245.

continue its anti-Jewish policy, he would exert every effort to make it impossible for Russia to get a kopeck in the United States. He banged the table with his fist and declared that a government, which indulged in massacres and in inhuman persecution on religious grounds was not to be trusted.[35]

Again Natty approached Lord Lansdowne in April 1905, when he learnt

> from a trustworthy source ... that on the Russian Passover there would probably be massacres, not only of Jews, but also of other non-Orthodox persons in many parts of Russia. His idea seemed to be that steps might be taken, perhaps through the Press here [in line with what happened in the United States previously] with the object of warning the Russian government of the disastrous effect which would be produced were they to tolerate any such proceedings.

Lansdowne promptly scotched the idea.[36] Bolstered by the support of his French cousins and the defiant attitude of Schiff, Natty also adopted a more robust approach, telling the Russian ambassador a few months later that he would not be a participant in any loan until there was an improvement in the position of its Jews.[37]

One of the difficulties in the situation was that it was hard for Anglo-Jewish leaders to obtain accurate details of the plight of their co-religionists in Russia because of the censorship prevailing there. Thus, the President of the Board of Deputies shared the Chief Rabbi's view that 'it will be advisable to postpone writing to Baron Gunzburg [Gintsburg] until he arrives in Marienbad. You will then have a free hand as to the questions you can put to him & he will be able to answer them without restraint.'[38]

During the Russo-Japanese War of 1904–5, the Anglo-Jewish establishment faced a new emergency, when 11,000 Russian Jews sought refuge in Britain, to which the answer, as usual, was to send them overseas. According to Abraham Munday, secretary of the Jews' Temporary Shelter,

---

35 Cohen, *Jacob Schiff*, p. 138.
36 National Archives, FO800/141 Lord Lansdowne to Charles Hardinge 14 April 1905.
37 Feldman, 'The Rothschilds and the Russian Loans', p. 245.
38 LMA, ACC/2805/3/1/4 D. L. Alexander to Hermann Adler 30 June 1905.

The first difficult problem to overcome was that of finance, and it was quickly solved by the noble house of Rothschild, who immediately issued appeals for funds, heading the list themselves with a munificent donation, and by the Russo-Jewish Committee and the Jewish Colonization Association, both of which bodies contributed largely towards the expenses entailed in assisting these refugees. The Committee ... were able to devote their entire energies to the feeding and lodging arrangements and to the planning of a scheme for the ultimate disposal of the refugees, which after a number of conferences at New Court, was decided to be emigration to the Argentine, Canada and the United States of suitable cases and repatriation after the war of unsuitable ones.

Of the 10,540 refugees who were interviewed under the scheme, thirty per cent proceeded to Argentina, forty-six per cent to various places in Canada, twenty per cent to the United States, one per cent were assisted to localities in the United Kingdom and the Continent, while two per cent were repatriated to their home towns after the War.[39] Throughout the implementation of these arrangements, Natty played a crucial coordinating role and a notable one as a fund-raiser.

In contrast to the pogrom at Kishinev, the violence of 1905–6 can only be understood in the context of the Russian revolutionary movement when, in a series of major disturbances, 880 Jews were killed in October 1905, but throughout the extended period there were also attacks on other groups depicted as enemies of the regime, such as students and teachers.[40] In November 1905, Carl Stettauer was 'told on good authority that an enormous number of well-to-do Russian Jews are at present staying in the various boarding houses in Berlin'. He was 'convinced that a great many have left in anticipation of coming trouble'.[41] Sporadic violence against Jews continued and there was a pogrom in Bialystok from 1 to 3 June 1906 that claimed seventy victims. Between the autumn of 1906 and the outbreak of the First World War, the pogroms ceased, though the fear of violence lingered among Jewish communities. According to widespread elements within the Tsarist camp and the bureaucracy, Jews formed the backbone of

---

39   LMA, 4184/02/05/001/001 Abraham Munday, *Reminiscences*, pp. 6–8.
40   Klier, *Russians, Jews, and the Pogroms of 1881–1882*, p. 60; Vital, *A People Apart*, p. 571.
41   Southampton, Carl Stettauer Papers Ms128 AJ22 F/2 Carl Stettauer to Samuel Montagu 21 November 1905.

the revolutionary parties, while it was also claimed that they financed the activities of the revolutionaries.

Moreover, hard-line elements within the autocratic regime instigated a charge of ritual murder against Mendel Beilis in 1911–13 to rally the masses behind the Tsar, depicting the Jews as bent on gaining control of the globe and as the carriers of universal evil and the embattled Tsarist regime as being the last bastion of resistance against this world-wide conspiracy.[42]

Furious at the violence of the pogroms, Natty induced the British government on 6 November 1905 to make a protest to Russia through the British *chargé d'affaires* Cecil Spring Rice. It was noted in an internal Foreign Office report that the Rothschilds were 'very unhappy over the antisemitic disorders – hence [the] telegram'. Count Witte was told unofficially that the massacring and plundering of Jewish communities, which were unprotected by the police, was creating an unfavourable impression, and that unless the outrages were checked Russia would lose the support of the 'English press and public' opinion. Arthur Balfour, despite the fact that Natty was a close friend and political ally, toned down the contents of this telegram, amending a passage which read riots 'apparently unopposed if not encouraged by the authorities and police' into something much more bland. A copy of the telegram was sent to Lord Rothschild by Balfour, who added that he hoped this 'would have the effect of stimulating the Central Government to put an end to these atrocious attacks on the Jews.'[43] A few days later, Lord Rothschild, on behalf of the Russo-Jewish Committee, was a signatory to a letter to *The Times* fulminating against 'the unspeakable calamities [which] have befallen the Jews in Russia'. At the same time, Lord Rothschild urged Schiff to ensure that the United States government acted on parallel lines with the British government in exerting diplomatic pressure on Russia, and had arranged for British relief funds to be distributed through diplomatic agents to allay suspicions that 'foreign Jews are fomenting revolution, and

42 Hans Rogger, *Jewish Policies and Right-Wing Politics in Imperial Russia* (Los Angeles and Berkeley, 1986), p. 53.
43 Eliyahu Feldman, 'British Diplomats and British Diplomacy and the 1905 Pogroms in Russia', *Slavonic and East European Review* 65:4 (October 1987), pp. 579–608; National Archives, FO65/1706 Lord Landsdowne to Spring Rice 6 November 1905 and Balfour's amended draft FO65/1705; Rothschild, *Dear Lord Rothschild*, pp. 33 and 325, note 54.

money ... will not be taken away from destitute Jews'.[44] Despite Schiff's plea to the President to take concerted action with other powers to stem the violence in Russia, Theodore Roosevelt refused to move, lamely claiming that any action would do more harm than good.[45]

Reporting back to London and playing down the revolutionary ferment in Russia, Spring Rice remarked that

> the outrages against the Jews are the direct result of the policy pursued by the Government for the last few years. Both clergy and police have been systematically encouraged to hound on the lower classes of people against the liberal elements of society and especially against the Jews who are the head and front of the liberal movement in Russia. This policy is absolutely antagonistic to that which M. Witte represents ... He has caused a severe warning to be addressed to the clergy, has addressed quieting proclamations to the people, and the Government is now, I believe, doing its best to take effective military measures to suppress the riot. But it must be remembered that in many districts ... at least one half of the minor officials and of the population sympathise with the rioters and on the first outbreak of disorders the action of the Government was seriously crippled.[46]

Meanwhile, subscription lists had been opened in Britain by Lord Rothschild and in the United States by Schiff to aid the distressed Jewish communities in Russia that had suffered as a result of the pogroms. The Foreign Secretary was very helpful, allowing an amazing degree of informal cooperation, for which Natty thanked him profusely. After conferring with Lord Lansdowne, Natty decided to remit £10,000 to the Volga Kama Bank to the British *chargé d'affaires* at St Petersburg to distribute through 'the various British Consuls at those places where relief is most urgently required'. This would ensure that 'the fund should be utilised for immediate relief in the immediate scene of the outrage and not for political propaganda or emigration purposes', a very important consideration for Natty; and an equal sum was sent to the British Consul-General at Odessa.[47]

44 *The Times* 9 November 1905 and *Jewish Chronicle* 24 November 1905 pp. 22–3.
45 Adler, *Jacob H. Schiff* Vol. 2, pp. 136–8.
46 National Archives, FO65/1707 Spring Rice to Lord Lansdowne 7 November 1905.
47 National Archives, FO65/1721 Natty to Lord Lansdowne 8 November 1905, enclosing a
    telegram from Natty to Spring Rice; Alfred de Rothschild to Lansdowne 7 November 1905

Even Witte, whose second wife was Jewish and who was liberal-minded, held somewhat paranoid views about the Jewish community, insisting that any charitable funds should be distributed through Baron Horace Gintsburg's committee, and not through the British consular service. 'Any direct communication between H.M. Consuls and the Jewish communities at the present moment would be inadvisable owing to their connection with the extreme socialistic parties'. Spring Rice's advice surely reflected what Witte told him. What also concerned Spring Rice, as he explained to Oswald Simon, was that the regime would claim that foreign governments were distributing funds for the purchase of weapons and bombs. The British proposal appears to have been misunderstood, however, as 'it was not suggested that Consuls should distribute funds, but that they should be authorized to receive remittances to hand them over for distribution to properly accredited Committees'.[48] Spring Rice communicated directly with the Rothschild family, informing it that 'I have seen Gunzburg who having received authority from the Minister of the Interior will distribute funds through [the four] Com[mittee]s formed by him [in Southern Russia] which is most satisfactory', while Alfred assured another official that they would comply with the government's wishes.[49]

In London, in mid-November 1905, within weeks of the October pogroms in Russia, a meeting of leading international philanthropists was held at New Court, called by Paul Nathan of the *Hilfsverein* in Germany, Baron Horace Gintsburg and Jacob Schiff but presided over by Lord Rothschild who quickly assumed the titular leadership of the movement. Because Schiff was too far away in the United States to take on any coordinating role, the other key player in the relief of pogrom victims was the dynamic Dr Paul Nathan, a journalist and aid worker, based in Berlin. The

---

and Lansdowne to Alfred 6 November 1905; Lansdowne to Natty 8 November 1905 and from his secretary to Natty on the same date.

48 National Archives, FO65/1707 Spring Rice to Lansdowne 8 November 1905 and FO65/1706 same to Lansdowne 9 November 1906. Max Beloff, *Lucien Wolf and the Anglo-Russian Entente 1907–1914* (London, 1951), p. 18.

49 RAL 000/182 Lord Lansdowne to Alfred 7 November 1905 and T. H. Sanderson to Lord Rothschild 8 November 1905; Spring Rice to Mr Smith Odessa 8 November 1905. National Archives, FO65/1706 Spring Rice to Lansdowne 9 November 1905 at 2.12 p.m. and 9.00 p.m. and 11 November 1905 and FO65/1721 Alfred to Mr Mallet on two occasions 9 November 1905.

conference resolved to collect funds and to send a travelling commission to Russia, comprising Dr Nathan, David Feinberg of St Petersburg and Carl Stettauer. The Commission should have the power, in case of emergency, to disburse money in the hands of Baron Gintsburg 'for immediate necessaries of life and for the needs of the Hospitals'. A special Bureau was to be set up in Berlin with representatives of the Alliance Israélite Universelle charged with digesting and tabulating all the information coming out of Russia from the towns affected by the outrages; it was to advise the Alliance and the Russo-Jewish Committee of London from time to time of the needs of each locality. To prevent overlapping, all financial aid was to be sent through N. M. Rothschild & Sons of London, who were to keep separate accounts of the money received from the Continental committees.[50] The conference reiterated the commonly expressed opinion that emigration was not the solution for the Russian Jews. As Schiff had put it on a previous occasion, 'Five million people cannot emigrate, and no matter how many Jews may leave Russia, five millions will always remain there. The weal of these people can only be obtained by equal opportunities, equal rights, and equal duties with the rest of the Russian population.' But on the insistence of Paul Nathan, the question of equal rights was removed from the agenda of the conference because in Germany this would be regarded as unwarranted interference in the domestic affairs of another country. The London conference concluded that its goal was 'the prevention of migration so far as may be feasible; no charity, but rather the grant of prompt assistance to those who are in a position to take up their original economic activity, even if only on a modest scale'.[51]

By the end of 1905, Schiff was warning Count Witte that if his government failed to ameliorate the position of its Jews, there would be a mass exodus. He worked closely with Rothschild and Montagu in London and Dr Paul Nathan in Berlin in the collection of funds, amassing almost $1 million in the United States within a month in a nationwide appeal, while the money raised was channelled through the Rothschilds to Russia, where it was distributed through the network established by Baron Horace

50 Southampton, Carl Stettauer Papers Ms 128/AJ22/F/3 Report of the travelling Commission December 1905 pp. 1–2.
51 Vital, *A People Apart*, p. 599; Paul A. Alsberg, 'Documents of the Brussels Conference of 1906', *Michael* 2 (Tel-Aviv 1973), pp. 145–53; Adler, *Jacob H. Schiff* vol. 2, p. 122.

Gintsburg, a wealthy banker and communal leader. He also set up a meeting between Dr Nathan and Count Witte as the representative of the international relief movement.[52]

Having left Berlin on 10 November 1905, the Commission reached St Petersburg on the following day, and met at the home of Baron Horace Gintsburg on 24 November. It was decided to grant assistance to enable victims to resume their occupations, to provide financial relief for those unable to earn a living, and to make provision for orphans. All the affected towns would be allocated to a central committee which would collect the information for its own district and verify its accuracy. The local committees were to prepare lists of persons eligible for relief, the details of which were to be forwarded to the Information Bureau in Berlin and the St Petersburg Central Committee; and after an understanding had been reached between Berlin and St Petersburg, the result as to the amount payable was to be communicated to Lord Rothschild.[53] The travelling Commission reached Moscow on 27 November, then proceeded to Kiev arriving on 29 November. Because the telegraphic and postal services were on strike and railway communication had been partly suspended, the Commission took stock of the situation and decided, with the assistance of the local committee, to grant immediate relief without waiting until it was in a position to consult St Petersburg or London. When the Commission went to the railway station to leave the town, there was a military mutiny and the Vice-Consul, Mr Smith, accompanied them at some risk to his own life to afford them some diplomatic protection. On 1 December, the travelling Commission left for Odessa, where they arrived on the following day and, after four meetings with local representatives, arrived at the amounts to be allocated to Odessa and the places attached to it, with the exception of Kishinev.[54] Here, part of the overseas aid provided after the previous pogrom was spent on local institutions, instead of on relief,

52 Cohen, *Jacob H. Schiff*, pp. 141–3 and Adler, *Jacob H. Schiff*, pp. 134–6; *Jewish Chronicle* 24 November 1905, p. 23 and 1 December 1905, p. 23. Ernst Feder, 'Paul Nathan and his Work for East European and Palestinian Jewry', *Historia Judaica* 14 (April 1952), pp. 3–26.

53 Southampton, Carl Stettauer Papers Ms128/AJ22/F/3 Report of the travelling Commission pp. 1–4.

54 Southampton, Ms128/AJ22/F/3 Report of the travelling Commission pp. 4–7. National Archives, FO65/1721 Carl Stettauer to Lord Lansdowne 10 December 1905.

which reduced the communal financial burdens falling on more affluent members of the community, though this caused resentment and discord. Furthermore, a number of the wealthier members of the community had reneged on their promise to make charitable donations. Nevertheless, the Commission granted Kishinev relief funds of 75,000 roubles, on condition that the local community raised another 25,000 to 30,000 roubles. Unable to reach important towns because of the widespread strikes, the Commission improvised by organizing relief for Ekaterinoslav, Saratov and Rostov through their contacts with representatives of the tea merchants W. Wissotsky & Co., which had branches throughout Russia.[55]

A follow-up meeting of philanthropic organizations after the London conference was held in Frankfurt on 4 January 1906. Here, it was decided that three-quarters of the money collected would be forwarded to the Rothschilds for onward transmission to Russia, while the rest of these funds would be retained locally to assist immigrants crossing the border and to speed them on their journey. Natty advised his French cousins that he had just received a telegram from Frankfurt, stating that 'The Committee on the Continent are quite prepared to work harmoniously with the Committee here.'[56]

At the end of the month, a Zionist-sponsored international conference opened in Brussels, where it was resolved, under pressure from Nathan, that 'the emigration of Jews without any means of existence cannot be recommended at present, or as long as the necessary funds are not forthcoming.'[57]

Misunderstandings about the transfer of funds by the Rothschilds and Samuel Montagu & Co to Russia, however, needed sorting out by Natty. 'I received a telegram from Baron Gunzburg imploring us to send at once money to him on a very large scale', Natty remarked,

> & I should have acquiesced immediately had I not received at the same time a very clear letter from the Foreign Office to the effect that the Russian Ambassador Count Benckendorff had called on Sir Edward Grey [the newly appointed Liberal Foreign Secretary] to inform him, for the benefit of the Russo-Jewish Committee, that the Russian

---

55 Southampton, Ms128/AJ22/F/3 pp. 7–9.
56 Paul A. Alsberg, 'Documents of the Brussels Conference of 1906', p. 151. *Jewish Chronicle* 2 February 1906 pp. 8–9. RAL XI/130A/0 Natty to his cousins Paris 5 January 1906.
57 *Jewish Chronicle* 2 February 1906, pp. 8–9.

Government insisted upon having the control of the distribution of the funds. Under those circumstances I thought it useless to send any more funds today, & have telegraphed to Baron Gunzburg to ascertain the meaning of this peremptory & apparently very barbarous order.[58]

British diplomats ascertained that 'Someone in the entourage of the Emperor seems to have told him that part of the £600,000 subscribed in London for the relief of Russian Jews was being spent in furthering revolutionary aims' and that 'Count Lamsdorff, the Foreign Minister, forgot that he had previously agreed to the arrangements with Baron Gintsburg, when confronted by the Tsar.' The belief also prevailed in official circles in St Petersburg that 'the arms and ammunition found at Moscow in the hands of the insurgents were paid for by foreign money and imported from abroad. The Jewish Bund played a great part in the disorders, and as Count Lamsdorff told ... [Cecil Spring Rice] Jews of both sexes were subsequently found on the barricades.' The role of the Jews in the 1905 Russian Revolution of 1905 was grossly exaggerated in this case. 'The matter was arranged subsequently between Witte and Rothschild by the exchange of private telegrams.' When the dispute was brought to Witte's attention, he was furious at Count Benckendorff's interference and authorized all the funds which the Rothschilds had sent to Russia to be handled by Baron Gintsburg through his bank.[59]

After Dr Paul Nathan in Berlin processed the claims sent by the St Petersburg Central Committee, they were forwarded to London, supported by documentary evidence to be finally adjudicated upon by the Russo-Jewish Committee; the authorized remittances were forwarded by N. M. Rothschild & Sons and Samuel Montagu & Co to St Petersburg. Even so, this still sometimes left open questions as to the correct apportionment of relief and its sufficiency. Consequently, a hurried two-day meeting at Dover was arranged between Dr Nathan and two members of the executive of the Russo-Jewish Committee to sort out these outstanding issues.[60]

58   RAL XI/130A/0 Natty to his cousins Paris 1 January 1906.
59   National Archives Lord Sanderson note for Grey 1 January 1906 and Cecil Spring Rice to Grey 3 and 4 January and Charles Hardinge to Grey 5 January 1906. Henri Sliosberg, *Baron Horace-o de Gunzbourg, sa vie, son œuvre* (Paris, 1933), p. 123.
60   Southampton, Ms128/AJ22/E/1 Report of the Russo-Jewish Committee 1905–6 proof copy.

In all, N. M. Rothschild & Sons received contributions from world Jewry between November 1905 and December 1906 amounting to £474,391 12s 7d, which, with interest, rose to £477,885 5s. 10d for the relief of the victims of the pogroms, though only £408,208 9s 1d was actually remitted to places affected by the pogroms. By far the largest contribution of £240,000 came from the United States, followed by Britain and its colonies with £113,141 2s 0d, Berlin with £39,000, Paris with £31,986 17s 8d and Vienna with £22,101 11s 0d. Significant donations were also received from Brussels, Buenos Aires, Cairo (£1,000) and Tangiers, while Russian Jewry raised 434,028 roubles for the relief of its own stricken communities. Of the individual contributors in Britain, Natty led the way with a donation of £10,000 and there was the promise of £5,000 from Sir Ernest Cassel. Clerical assistance was provided free of charge for the fund by the Rothschild bank and Samuel Montagu & Co, but, whereas the financial contributions were sent to New Court, the bulk of the work of paying the remittances was performed by Samuel Montagu & Co. Despite the instructions to the organizers of relief not to encourage emigration, it was found necessary in practice to be more flexible and to clear the refugees crowding the Austrian frontier towns by forwarding them from Continental ports to Argentina and America. The cost of the operation was borne initially by the Central Fund for 444 persons but, after February 1906, the Jewish Colonization Association shouldered these expenses. It was remarked that

> Terrible as has been the tribulation through which our people have been afflicted by the incidence of the pogrom barbarities, there is one redeeming feature ... that the calamity has evoked a solidarity of sentiment and action among the Jews throughout the globe which has greatly strengthened their brotherhood and made them more than ever anxious to work together for the Jewish cause.[61]

As Natty enjoyed excellent relations with the liberal Russian ambassador, Count Benckendorff, who sometimes visited his country estate and favoured Jewish emancipation, he wished to rely on private exhortations and was strongly opposed to calling a public meeting to protest

---

61   Ibid.; the Russo-Jewish Committee Central Fund accounts 1905–6; National Archives FO 371/121 Natty to Lord Sanderson 3 January 1906; *Jewish Chronicle* 10 November 1905, p. 14.

against the recent disturbances. His viewpoint was echoed by Sir Samuel Montagu, the President of the Russo-Jewish Committee, who claimed that such 'A public meeting might render the situation of the Jews more precarious.' An informal meeting of Anglo-Jewish leaders was held at New Court in the presence of Lord Rothschild and Nathan Joseph, the most influential person on the Russo-Jewish Committee, the consensus being that it was inadvisable to call a public meeting. Again, the matter was discussed at a meeting of the Conjoint Committee; communications of a private nature had been disclosed which later turned out to be untrue but which influenced a negative decision.[62] A day after the annual meeting of the Board of Deputies, its President D. L. Alexander went with Claude Montefiore of the AJA to see Lord Rothschild in order to persuade him to hold a public meeting, only to encounter his continuing opposition to such a proposal.

An increasingly important figure in the campaign on behalf of Russian Jewry was Carl Stettauer (1859–1913), a wealthy leather merchant, who represented Britain on the travelling Commission and, on his return, was co-opted on to the Russo-Jewish Committee. As he was due back in Britain in a few days, Natty agreed to reconsider the matter after consulting with him. Stettauer's view was that 'things were very bad indeed in Russia. It was not a question of one Government but of half-a-dozen Governments ... [His] opinion was that a public meeting would do no good but at the same time it could do no harm.' Thereupon Lord Rothschild withdrew his objection to the holding of such a meeting.[63]

On 8 January 1906, Lord Rothschild presided over a huge public demonstration of support for Russian Jewry in the Queen's Hall – which could hold 2,500 people – reversing his previous policy of persuasion by secret negotiation. The platform was graced by the presence of religious leaders of all denominations, a cluster of peers including Lord Milner, the Lord Mayor and all three Rothschild brothers. Messages of goodwill came from the new Liberal Prime Minister, Sir Henry Campbell-Bannerman, 'expressing sympathy with the Jews in Russia, and horror at the cruelties that have been inflicted upon so many of them', and from Arthur Balfour,

62 *Jewish Chronicle* 8 December 1905, p. 13.
63 *Jewish Chronicle* 22 December 1905, p. 14.

who declared that 'The treatment of their Jewish citizens ... is certainly the darkest blot on the history of Christendom ... I earnestly trust that the outcome of this appalling Russian tragedy may be to make Security, Liberty and Equal Rights, the inalienable birthright of every Russian Jew.'

Natty not only accused a coterie around the Tsar of stirring up the Russian people against the Jews to invalidate the case for reform and a new constitution, but publicly announced himself in favour of equal rights for Russian Jewry. All of the nineteenth century tropes about 'the organised massacres and outrages perpetrated upon the Jews in Russia, which, in the opinion of Englishmen, without distinction of creed or party, are an offence to civilization and a disgrace to humanity' were aired once again, so that the meeting on the surface was a resounding success.[64] The bankers at the helm of the philanthropic organizations, Schiff and Natty, were coordinating their policy, boycotting loans to Russia and begging other bankers not to participate, desperately trying to stem migration into Western Europe and the Americas, and espousing equal rights for the Jews in Russia. Natty decided he had to take care, however, not 'to be too violent or to say anything which might be disagreeable ... to the Czar and Mr Witte'.

Looking back on these events, Nathan Joseph remembered somewhat gloomily that 'There is absolute indifference on the part of the press & the public, even when the worst pogroms are reported. Even a protest meeting has to be artificially "got up" by the Jews and there is a difficulty in obtaining a few speakers – Christians – to speak openly.'[65]

Not everyone among the Russian emigrants to Britain had a flattering appraisal of Natty's response to the pogroms. Writing to Vera, his future wife, Chaim Weizmann vented his rage, exclaiming

> I wish you wouldn't ask how English Jewry is reacting to all this. They are petrified. They are committing a second pogrom. They have given money *on condition* that their unfortunate Russian brethren do not emigrate to England ... Yesterday in Leeds, and 3 days ago in Liverpool, I blasted them before a crowd of three thousand. The meetings were tremendous, such as England had never witnessed before. The squalid Press will attack

---

64 *Jewish Chronicle* 12 January 1909, pp. 20–1. RAL XI/130A/0 Natty to his cousins Paris 9 January 1906. Feldman, 'The Rothschilds and the Russian Loans', p. 245.

65 CAHJP, INV/316 Nathan Joseph to Lucien Wolf 22 November 1907.

me for undermining the authority of 'Lord Rothschild', but I spit on them. I shan't keep my mouth shut[66]

In need of financial support after Russia's disastrous War with Japan and the revolutionary upheavals in Russia, Witte, who was newly installed as Prime Minister in October 1905, tried to secure a massive loan from foreign bankers. For this purpose, he considered the participation of the Rothschilds to be indispensable and sent a succession of intermediaries to Paris and to Natty in London to plead for their assistance. In return for a loan, the French government intimated to Russia that it wanted Russian help in obtaining assurances from the German Emperor of his peaceful intentions and asked for Russia's support at the forthcoming international conference on Morocco; in fact, unless this was forthcoming, France could not sanction a loan. Grey added a note that the British government would be grateful to the Tsar 'for anything he can do in the interest of peace to promote good relations between France & Germany'.[67] When Maurice Rouvier, the French Prime Minister, approached James de Rothschild of the French house 'to join in funding the money for the Russian loan', he was brusquely told that 'the conditions of the proposed loan were an evasion of the Russian law and financially immoral and that for those reasons as well as on account of the treatment of the Jews in Russia the House of Rothschild could not take any part in the transaction'.[68] Like his French relatives, Natty was strongly opposed 'to lending money to a Government', which 'not only cruelly oppresses and massacres the poor Jews, but at the same time pats on the back the chief instigators'.[69]

The first such person to call on the Rothschild brothers at the London bank towards the end of January 1906 was Dr Brandt, an actuary connected with the Russian Treasury,

> an ugly, hump-backed Russian Jew, evidently full of his own importance
> ... The Jew, said Dr Brandt, is an object of horror and detestation to
> everyone in Russia. The Emperor and the Court hate him, hatred which

66 Weisgal, ed., *Letters and Papers of Chaim Weizmann* Vol. 4, pp. 196–7 Weizmann to Vera Khatzman 13 November 1905.
67 National Archives FO371/121 Charles Hardinge to Grey 9 January 1906.
68 FO 371/121 Francis Bertie Paris to Grey 12 January 1906.
69 RAL XI/130A/0 Natty to his cousins Paris 8 January 1908.

is shared by Witte & the Ministers, the Russian people loathe him, and the Duma which is about to be elected will reflect the wishes of the Court and the opinion of the Russian people. You cannot emigrate 5 millions of Russian Jews, and if you do not do something, you may have & probably will have a 'Red Letter' Saturday, a second Saint Bartholomew [massacre], & nearly the whole Jewish Russian population sacrificed to the fury and orthodoxy of the holy Russian people.

Natty declared,

As far as I understand him, the remedy is a very simple one. Make a big loan for Russia, and something may be done for the Jews! I told him ... [with words to the same effect] that he was putting the cart before the horse, namely, that when the Russian Jew has liberty and equal rights, Russian finance would improve and the Treasury difficulties would be considerably less. He said that neither Mendelssohn or Bleichroder [nor] the French bankers had ever mentioned the Jewish question in connection with finding money ...

although this was untrue. On this discordant note, the meeting ended with a 'very cross' Dr Brandt leaving the bank.[70]

Some three weeks later, Arthur Raffalovich, a respected writer on economics, visited Natty. He was being used by the Russians as an agent to offer bribes to influential French journalists in return for which they wrote favourable articles, thus easing the way to the raising of a new Russian loan.[71] Raffalovich

said that 6 months ago his Master, M. de Witte, & the Emperor were anxious, most anxious to ameliorate the fate of the Jewish population in Russia, but that now public opinion in Russia was excited and the Emperor & the Imperial Family, as well as the Ministers were rather hurt & grieved at the fact that the Russian Jews had attempted to defy a just and paternal government, that the Hebrew population were the authors of the Socialistic & revolutionary movement, & that when everything was quieting down in Russia, they alone of his numerous subjects had refrained from sending congratulatory addresses expressing their loyalty & devotion to the throne & their love for the country that treats them

70   Ibid. 23 January 1906.
71   Theodore Zeldin, *France 1848–1945* Vol. 2 (Oxford, 1977), p. 523.

so well! He naturally supposed that we wished to ameliorate the fate of our coreligionists, and that there was only one way of doing so, namely by our consenting to place ourselves at the head of an International Syndicate who would be prepared to accommodate the Crown with untold millions, anything between £60 and £120,000,000! Should we agree to his proposal, he gave us his word of honour that those reforms we have at heart would be immediately effected ...

Natty said he

was bound to remind him of two facts ... the first was that when you made a large financial operation on two occasions for Vishnegradsky, the same or similar proposals had been made to you and that these promises had been broken ... & were never fulfilled. On the contrary, the laws of oppression had been sterner ... when Witte was in Paris [at a much later date] both Edouard & Edmond had interviews with him, and they gathered from their conversation that although Witte might be friendly to the Jews himself, the time was still far distant when equal rights & equal privileges could be granted to them; and that taking all the circumstances into consideration we could not & would not help Russia in her need until she had done for our coreligionists that which would make them happy & reinstated subjects of the Czar & prosperous citizens of the Russian Empire. [Moreover,] I told him [that] it was absurd to suppose that the Jewish population hated the Czar. A large number of alien emigrants wished to go home ... & ... that when the Cesarewitch was born, strange to say, in the ghettos of London & New York, the health of the Czar was drunk, and blessings invoked upon the new born babe.

Raffalovich also carried a message which he wanted Natty to sign, but the latter would not do so without altering it so as to 'lay stress on the Jewish Question'.[72]

The next intermediary despatched by Witte to visit the London bank was a Mr Feld, who came in March. Natty told his cousins that 'He gives a deplorable account both of the state of Russia and of the fate of our coreligionists. His views so far as remedies are concerned are somewhat eccentric, and cannot be entertained, either the political ones or the

72   RAL XI/130A/0 Natty to cousins Paris 14 February 1906.

economical ones, or the financial ones. Like all Russians he harps on the money question, he talks of very large loans for the state.'[73]

Hard-pressed financially, the Russians also sent more envoys to Paris to solicit loans from the Rothschilds. This time, Vishnegradsky, a former Finance Minister, was despatched to the Rothschild residence in the rue Laffitte in connection with a Russian loan. Natty observed that 'the persistence with which the Russian Government keep continually coming to the front, especially at such a critical moment, is a clear proof that they must be excessively hard up'. This persistence was rewarded when, on 3 April 1906, a syndicate of mainly French banks, in which Barings participated, agreed to float a loan of 2.55 billion francs or expressed in pounds as £89 million, of which Barings took £13 million.[74] Keen to reach an Anglo-Russian agreement, Sir Edward Grey, the new Liberal Foreign Secretary, encouraged Barings in March to participate in the negotiations for this loan, stating that 'from a political stand-point he would view with satisfaction Barings' involvement'.[75]

'Numerous reports have been spread about all over Europe that both you [the French house] and ourselves were connected with this Loan. Naturally I have given the most categorical denial', Natty told Edmond and Edouard, 'and I have done all in my power to prevent Jewish writers in the International Press from attacking Russian Finance.'[76] Alfred Mildmay of Barings admitted that 'The demand for underwriting was enormous, and it has been very difficult to avoid offending people ... Some of the Jews, including Sterns, have refused underwriting participation from conscientious scruples, others of the same persuasion have taken the line that the more money they could mulct the Government of the better pleased they would be.'[77] At the end of April, Natty advised his cousins that the issue

73 RAL XI/130A/0 Natty to his cousins Paris 5 March 1906.
74 RAL XI/130A/0 Natty to his cousins Paris 2 March 1906. Feldman, 'The Rothschilds and Russian Loans', p. 245; David Kynaston, *The City of London* Vol. 2 (London, 1995), pp. 419–20.
75 Keith Nelson, *Britain and the Last Tsar. British Policy and Russia 1894–1917* (Oxford, 1995), p. 273.
76 RAL XI/130A/0 Natty to his cousins Paris 5 April 1906 Philip Ziegler, *The Sixth Great Power, Barings 1762–1929* (London, 1988), p. 314.
77 Kynaston, *The City of London* Vol. 2, p. 420.

'hung in the balance for a considerable time, & very large purchases were made here & all over the world in the first two days when the Loan was brought out here'.[78] Lord Revelstoke, however, claimed that 'The Russian government should be pleased to realize that this issue has really appealed to the genuine British investing public.'[79]

After the pogroms of 1905–6, Natty's attitude to raising loans for Russia grew appreciably more robust. He concluded that

> We can have no direct financial interest in the Russian Loan: we should not think of associating ourselves with it until the fate of our coreligionists in that country was assured. We know from very good sources that their present position is as bad as it has been and probably much worse. The present population live in dread of fresh outrages at any moment and particularly when our Passover holiday occurs. The Liberal Party in Russia are also very anxious at the prospect of a large Russian Loan being made in Paris or Berlin fills them with dismay. They think of that money which is often called the 'sinews of war' will in this case be a fresh emblem of aggression.[80]

Having become increasingly disillusioned by Vishnegradsky's broken promises about the amelioration of the condition of Russian Jewry in the 1890s, Natty could no longer trust the repeated assurances of new envoys. At the same time, he did not wish to provoke the Tsar unnecessarily and release a flood of new immigrants to Britain. For some years he wavered, giving the Russian government the benefit of his doubts and even considering the possibility of a fresh loan to Russia in 1899 and towards the end of the Russo-Japanese War, before drawing back from the brink. Outraged at the pogroms in Kishinev in 1903 and the even wider and more violent wave of pogroms in 1905–6, and aware that the flow of immigrants was never ending, Natty adopted a tougher stance and refused to consider the possibility of raising loans for Russia without reforms being instituted beforehand to give Russian Jewry full and equal rights.

From the first, Natty was convinced that the raising of a huge Russian loan was a very risky undertaking from a financial point of view, quite apart from

78 RAL XI/130A/0 Natty to his cousins Paris 30 April 1906.
79 Ziegler, *The Sixth Great Power*, p. 314.
80 RAL XI/130A/0 Natty to his cousins Paris 19 March 1906.

scruples about the welfare of his coreligionists there and the further consideration that it was morally dubious. His analysis of the political situation in Russia was most perceptive, as he realized that it had entered a pre-revolutionary situation, despite the denial of the crisis by other contemporaries.

> A loan of £90,000,000 is a gigantic operation for any State to undertake and although it was often said that when the French Government made their first great loan after the war, the Commune had only just been defeated, yet no living soul could sanely compare the condition of Russia with that of France in 1871. The Duma is about to meet, and the conditions under which it meets, are very similar to, if not identical with those under which the *Tiers Etat* met at Versailles: & it would be very strange if the hungry discontent of the peasants and the demands of the workpeople do not precipitate events in Russia which may be disastrous to all Russian bondholders.[81]

Again, a few days later, Natty reported that

> Messrs Barings closed their list this morning, and they and their friends are very delighted and they say the very success of the operation is by far the greatest financial triumph that has ever taken place, as, without this loan Russia would have been completely bankrupt; but in their jubilation they leave out of all calculations the political events which may occur in Russia when the Duma and the Russian people see how far their political privileges have been curtailed: but all the great geniuses connected with the Loan are in the meantime hugging themselves with delight at the huge profits they have made.[82]

Shortly afterwards he thanked his cousin James for

> the description you gave of the Russian Loan had a very strong flavour of Alexander Dumas' novels with his accounts of ... the famous Mississippi & Louisiana schemes. In the days of the Regent everyone was rich, and huge profits were made until the bubble burst and quite apart from the Jewish Question the bankers and the syndicate who have launched the Large Russian Loan are undertaking a great moral responsibility in guaranteeing the solvency of Russia for many years to come.

81 RAL XI/130A/0 Natty to his cousins Paris 23 April 1906.
82 Ibid., 26 April 1906.

Once Witte had procured the loan and the Russian state was solvent, he was dismissed in April 1906 and Natty predicted that 'the political situation in Russia will soon be awkward'.[83]

Then came reports of a large pogrom in Bialystok. On 18 June 1906, as a result of a telegram from Russian Jewish leaders, a deputation of Alexander, Montagu, Claude Montefiore and Stettauer was received at the Foreign Office by Sir Charles Hardinge, who assured them that 'representations of a non-official character' would be made.[84] Natty had a separate interview with Sir Edward Grey, the Foreign Secretary, to 'ask him if international action cannot be taken [to stop this hideous slaughter of innocent and unoffending people], and on this ground, the continuance of this monstrous policy, will send fugitives in hundreds, if not thousands, to countries where they are not wanted, and where there are many seeking work'.[85] Later in the day of 18 June 1906, Grey telegraphed his ambassador in St Petersburg to say that

> Lord Rothschild and others have received information to the effect that plans are being made for further attacks of a most serious character [in Bialystok]. Much anxiety is felt in this country, and questions have been asked in Parliament. Although we cannot interfere officially in the matter, and although the Russian Government must be well aware of the unfortunate effect which incidents of this kind produce in this and other countries, you should nevertheless take an opportunity of pointing out unofficially to M. Isvolsky [the Foreign Minister] that a painful impression has been created by the outrages reported in the press, and that the sympathy of this country towards Russia, which has so happily increased of late, would certainly be alienated by their renewal.

In response, Sir Charles Hardinge sent Natty the gist of the ambassador's reply, in which he assured London that a new governor had been appointed for Bialystok, that martial law had been declared and that a circular had been sent to governors and police chiefs 'to suppress the least signs of disturbance'.[86]

83   Ibid., 30 April and 3 May 1906.
84   LMA, ACC/3121/A/015 BODS minutes 24 June 1906.
85   RAL XI/130A/0 Natty to his cousins Paris 18 June 1906.
86   National Archives, FO371/125 Samuel Montagu to Charles Hardinge 18 June 1906

On 19 June Grey received a report on the pogrom in Bialystok from Alexander Murray, the British Consul-General in Warsaw, who accepted the official version of events in the city concluding that 'little damage appears to have been done' as troops 'soon put a stop to it'. Murray asserted that two Corpus Christi processions were passing through the streets

> when they were fired upon by Jews from two different houses. The people exasperated against the Jews by a long course of terrorizing to compel them to strike, bomb-throwing, assassinations, and acts of violence, Bialystok being the centre of the Jewish anarchical and red socialistic parties, threw themselves on the Jews, and before the authorities, who, fearing some such occurrence, held troops in readiness, could interfere, Jewish beating was taking place throughout the town.

On the same day, the British ambassador spoke to the assistant Foreign Minister M. Goubastoff, who assured him that steps had been taken to prevent a recurrence of such incidents, but that the blame 'for the late disorders must be attributed to the Jews themselves entirely, and more especially to the younger members of the race'. Sources in St Petersburg were of the opinion that the attacks had been 'engineered by the police authorities', the ambassador noted, though the truth was difficult to establish. Grey minuted 'Shall we communicate to Lord Rothschild the substance of Assistant Minister's reply? It is not very satisfactory' but the permanent secretary remarked that this was not necessary, as Natty had seen the substance of the previous telegram. In fact, Lord Rothschild had only a partial glimpse of the diplomatic despatches passing between Britain and Russia, so that he was unaware that the blame for the current disorders was being placed by the Russian authorities on the Jews.[87]

Nevertheless, Natty wrote to his cousins in Paris that he was not particularly pleased with his interview with Grey. 'Benckendorff, the Russian ambassador, had been down to the House of Commons to see ...

---

enclosing telegram; Edward Grey to Arthur Nicolson 18 June 1906; Nicolson to Grey 19 June; 20 June 1906 minute of Grey and Hardinge; Natty to Hardinge 22 June 1906.

87   National Archives, FO371/125 Consul-General Murray to Edward Grey 17 June 1906; Arthur Nicolson to Edward Grey 19 June 1906; minutes of Grey and Hardinge 20 June 1906.

[Grey] and he told me that they must await definite news from Nicolson and that only unofficial representations could be made.'[88]

A day later, Natty expressed his regret to Edouard that

> you did not think it advisable to speak to your Minister about the outrages in Russia. I never supposed that the French Government would have made an official representation, but they might have spoken unofficially to the Russian Ambassador and it probably would have produced a very good result. The ground they would have taken might have been that these outrages naturally affected the market for Russian securities which were chiefly if not largely held in France. There appears to be no doubt that these outrages were got up by agents of the Government ...'

Since 1894, there had been a Dual Alliance between France and Russia and there was little the French Rothschilds could do to motivate their Foreign Office. Natty 'did not know if anything he had said to Grey had influenced him or whether he had been moved by the general indignation in the Commons, but he had requested a further discussion of the matter'. When they met on 21 June 1906, Grey told Natty that he had authorized 'an unofficial and verbal communication to be made to the effect that a recurrence of these outrages would alienate public opinion and prevent the good feeling which ought to exist between the two countries: this is between ourselves and will not be made public ... He said unless the Emperor took a Ministry from the Duma, everything would go from bad to worse and he was awaiting news as well as authentic details of these horrid massacres.'[89] As instructed, Sir Arthur Nicolson, the British ambassador, advised the Minister of Foreign Affairs, M. Isvolsky, 'that I did not wish for any explanations, and that I had no right to ask for any; nor did I desire to pass any opinion on the occurrences. I simply wished to point out the impression they produced in my country, and how unfortunate it would be if they affected public opinion, which was beginning to be favourably disposed to Russia and her Government.' This reprimand was feeble because Britain was drawing closer to Russia in the European power struggle. Grey rebuked the Russian ambassador in a similar fashion.[90] The *Jewish*

88 RAL XI/130A/0 Natty to his cousins Paris 19 June 1906.
89 Ibid., 20 and 21 June 1906.
90 National Archives, FO371/125 Arthur Nicolson to Edward Grey 20 June 1906; minutes of

Chronicle carried a vague report that 'Mr D. L. Alexander K. C., President of the Board of Deputies, and Mr Claude Montefiore called at the Foreign Office. There they saw Sir Charles Hardinge ... who promised to submit at once to Sir Edward Grey the representations they had made. Shortly afterwards, Lord Rothschild (whom Messrs Alexander and Montefiore had seen earlier in the day) had an interview with Sir Edward Grey. On 22 June, Natty wrote to Hardinge, thanking him for his letter outlining government policy. 'Please convey to Sir Edward Grey my heartfelt thanks for all the trouble he has taken.' To his cousins in Paris, he added that 'the unofficial communications of our Government have produced a certain effect'.[91]

According to the British ambassador, Sir Arthur Nicolson, 'The authorities in St. Petersburg of course attribute the blame [for instigating the outbreak of violence in Bialystok] entirely to the Jews – especially the younger members of the community – who, they assert, goaded the Christians to attack them. The Jews, on the other hand, deny that any blame attaches to their co-religionists, and affirm that the 'pogrom' was got up by the local police at Bialystok. In making this accusation, they admit that the Central Government in St Petersburg was innocent of complicity with the police'. Nicolson also repeated Stolypin's accusation that Bialystok 'had been for years the centre of the Jewish anarchical movement'.[92] Other members of the British diplomatic service, such as Alexander Murray, the Consul-General in Warsaw, were even more inclined to side with the blatantly anti-Semitic explanations of the Tsarist bureaucracy, indulging in stereotypes of Jews as cowards.

> The total number of those who took an active part in the rioting and killing appears to have been about a couple of hundred, and not in any case to have exceeded 300, which brings into relief the spectacle common in anti-Jewish riots of a Jewish population of 60,000 allowing themselves, their wives and children to be robbed and murdered without raising a hand in self-defence.[93]

Edward Grey 25 June 1906.

91 National Archives, FO371/125 Natty to Charles Hardinge 22 June 1906; *Jewish Chronicle* 22 June 1906; David L. Alexander to Grey 25 June 1906. RAL XI/130A/0 Natty to his cousins Paris 22 June 1906.

92 National Archives, FO371/125 Arthur Nicolson to Edward Grey 20 June and 2 July 1906.

93 Ibid., A. P. Murray to Edward Grey 17 June 1906.

Portrait of Nathaniel, 1st Lord Rothschild (1840–1915), by Herbert Horowitz.
Private Collection.

'Pillars of the City – A Scene on Change', sketch by Lockhart Bogle from *The Graphic*, 9 May 1891, showing Nathaniel Rothschild standing in front of a pillar, his son Walter and between them Carl Meyer.

'The Anti-Budget Pageant', cartoon from the *Westminster Gazette*, 16 June 1909, showing Nathaniel Rothschild standing between Arthur Balfour and Austen Chamberlain, the Opposition leaders.

THE CITY PENGUINS.

". . . One of the richest of the Penguins rose and said: ". . . The poor live by the well-being of the rich; that is why the well-being of the rich is sacred. Do not lay a finger on it, it would be gratuitous wickedness. . . ."
—ANATOLE FRANCE's "Isle of the Penguins."

[Lord Avebury, Sir Felix Schuster, and Lord Rothschild were amongst the most prominent figures at the recent Anti-Budget meeting in the City.]

THE WESTMINSTER GAZETTE.

'The City Penguins,' cartoon from the *Westminster Gazette*, 28 June 1909, showing Lord Avebury, Sir Felix Schuster and Nathaniel Rothschild confronting Asquith and Lloyd

Tring Park, country estate of Nathaniel Rothschild. Main entrance, 1889.

Lord Rothschild as Master of Hounds, with Tring Park mansion in the background. John Charlton, 1884.

Lord Rothschild, photographed by Elliott & Fry, c.1910.

From enquiries made by a representative of the American ambassador, 'It would appear ... that a bomb was thrown and some shots fired at a Christian procession. As to the identity of the perpetrators of these acts, versions are contradictory; and I doubt if this point will ever satisfactorily be cleared up.' According to the Governor-General of the town,

> if, during the 'pogrom', there were instances of individual soldiers, or of groups of soldiers without officers, not performing their duties in a sufficiently energetic manner against the rioters, still, on the whole, the troops behaved well, and it is only owing to their self-denying labours and to the fact that they did not permit the inhabitants of the neighbouring villages to enter the town that order was, comparatively speaking, so quickly restored.

Nevertheless, the pillaging and looting continued for three days.[94]

In the autumn of 1905, Sir Charles Hardinge was promoted to the post of permanent Under-Secretary at the Foreign Office in order to foster an entente with Russia, while other officials more sympathetic to Germany had been removed. Hardinge's place as ambassador at St Petersburg had been taken by Sir Arthur Nicolson. To sustain the French alliance, Hardinge realized that the key was friendship with Russia, France's ally. When the Liberal party won the general election in 1906 with a sweeping victory, Sir Edward Grey, the new and inexperienced Foreign Secretary, was dominated by his permanent officials.[95] That was why there was such continuity between the Tory and Liberal administrations and why Lord Rothschild's pleas on behalf of Russian Jewry fell on almost deaf ears at the Foreign Office. The primary motivation of these officials was the move towards an agreement with Russia which came about in 1907; all other considerations were of less than secondary importance, particularly the cries of Jews, some of whom, by their participation in revolutionary activities, were seen as bringing these misfortunes on themselves. Grey instructed his ambassador to Russia, Sir Arthur Nicolson, after the pogrom in Bialystok, on 3 October 1906 that 'I realize you can do nothing by representations about pogroms, and I shall not ask you to make any, though we may send you from time to time the apprehensions that are

94   Ibid., Arthur Nicolson to Grey 25 and 30 June 1906.
95   Ridley, *Bertie*, pp. 400–1.

expressed here. In some parts of Russia there is apparently civil war, carried out by bombs on one side and pogroms on the other'. Nicolson, under the tutelage of Sir Mackenzie Wallace, came to believe that change had to come from above, 'his sympathy for the Jews was also somewhat damped by a closer study of the problem'.[96] King Edward, who took a great interest in foreign policy and was responsible for many of the changes in diplomatic personnel, 'warned Lord Rothschild [after the Bialystok pogrom] ... that the Foreign Office would ignore Jewish complaints'.[97]

Natty's predictions about the political turmoil in Russia and the consequences this would have for that country's financial sector were accurate; this unrest also became

> the chief subject of ... universal conversation. As we have been wise enough to eschew Russian finance for some considerable time and lucky enough not to be inveigled by false promises into taking any part in the last Russian Loan, the fall in Russian securities affects us indirectly and only so far as they may have a considerable effect on the price of other securities. We are naturally much more affected by the fate of our unfortunate coreligionists in Russia and by the barbarities which are again being practised, either at the instigation of General Trepoff or of the two princesses who are supposed to influence the Czar's mind ... and who loudly scream for vengeance on the Members of the Duma who they say misrepresent public feeling, and for the murder of the Jews who they affirm sent these members to St. Petersburg ... the discontent against the Government is so great that no doubt the storm is brewing there which threatens the bureaucracy more than anything else, and that no doubt is the reason why they have got up this modern Saint Barthelemy [massacre] ...

Responding to news about the concern of the French public for the fortunes of Russian stock, he reported a month later that 'So far as the London markets are concerned, I am afraid I can only repeat what I have told you the last day or two, namely that the depression in Russian securities hangs like a heavy cloud over the rest of our market.'[98] In

---

96 Max Beloff, *Lucien Wolf and the Anglo-Russian Entente 1907–1914* (London, 1951), p. 19.
97 Soroka, *Britain, Russia and the Road to the First World War*, p. 124.
98 RAL XI/130A/0 Natty to his cousins Paris 18 June 1906 and 20 July 1906.

September 1906, Leo noted that 'no sooner is order restored in one part of the vast empire than fresh disturbances and riots break out in another ... Reuter says that in Warsaw there is fighting in the streets and much bloodshed and as usual it is the poor Jews who have to suffer ... it is really wonderful that Russian stocks should not be flatter.'[99]

In May and June 1905, Dr Paul Nathan discussed with Lucien Wolf the publication of three journals, *The Russian Correspondence* in London, the *Russische Korrespondenz* in Berlin and *La Correspondence Russe* in Paris, to supply information about the political struggle in that country free of charge to newspapers, politicians and opinion-makers. Wolf wrote to Nathan Joseph of the Russo-Jewish Committee on 11 December 1905 that 'I am most anxious at the present moment to keep up a good feeling between our London millionaires and all classes of the suffering population in Russia, whether socialist or otherwise, and I think that if we can cooperate with them without compromising ourselves, we ought to do so.' Moreover, he pointed out later that

> If I announce the suspension of the 'R.C.' to the Bund [Jewish Social Democratic Party], they will feel that they have been deserted. You must remember that we are doing nothing to help the Jews who wish to help themselves by staying in Russia, and making the land better worth living in. Our relief fund is merely to remedy temporary evils, and when it is exhausted, and the victims of the massacres have been put on their feet again, the future will be as dark as ever. It is only by helping the Russian Jews in their campaign for liberty that we can do anything to assure them a tolerable future, and the best way to do this is with the printing press.

As has been shown, Natty heartily disliked the attacks on Russia's finances in the *Russian Correspondence* as well as the extensive coverage of the socialist parties, particularly the Bund, and made it a condition of continued financial assistance that Wolf support the liberal constitutional parties and stay silent about the financial situation in Russia. On 19 February 1906, Wolf informed Lord Rothschild that

> the Russo-Jewish Committee were then of the opinion that no good purpose was served by continuing the publication but that against this

99 Ibid., Leo to his cousins Paris 10 September 1906.

view the Berlin and Paris Committees – and especially Dr Nathan – strongly protested on the grounds that the publication was actually doing good and that anything that might seem to imply a weakening of the foreign campaign on behalf of the Russian Liberation Movement would encourage the Russian Government to persevere with its reactionary policy. I circulate gratuitously and by post between four and five thousand copies [of the *Russian Correspondence*] weekly. In deference to your wishes, I have lately abstained from criticizing Russian Finances and have given more space to the Constitutional than to the Revolutionary movement. It seems to me that the paper is more than ever necessary now when almost the entire Liberal press in Russia is gagged and the prisons are crowded with reformers, accused of nothing except their Liberalism.

Shortly afterwards, Wolf advised Lord Rothschild that, in deference to his wishes, he had suspended publication of the journal and thanked him for the hundred pounds which he had contributed towards the expenses of publication but, despite this setback, the French and German editions continued to be published under their own editors until the outbreak of the Great War.[100]

At a time when British diplomatic and other ties with Russia were growing stronger, the cessation of publication in English was self-defeating and undermined the efforts of the Rothschilds to put financial pressure on the Tsarist regime. After details of the Anglo-Russian Convention emerged in the press in September 1907, Natty worried that it depended

a great deal upon the action & loyalty of Russian Agents in regions far removed from the Capital ... The agreement is no doubt viewed with considerable disfavour by Ultra-Radicals & should it be attacked by a certain portion of the Continental Press, it will undoubtedly be said that the Press is in the hands of the Jews, & any action of this kind would certainly not be favourable & might be very prejudicial to the fate of our Russian coreligionists.[101]

---

100 Zosa Szajkowski, 'Paul Nathan, Lucien Wolf, Jacob H. Schiff and the Jewish Revolutionary Movements in Eastern Europe 1903–1917', *Jewish Social Studies* XXIX (1967), pp. 18–19. Yivo, David Mowshowitch Collection, reel 4 Lucien Wolf to Natty 19 February 1906 and 23 February 1906.
101 RAL XI/130A/IA Natty to his French cousins Paris 2 September 1907.

In fact, Natty's fear of a backlash to strident criticism of the Tsarist regime in the press made him over-cautious in his actions, too willing to compromise and conciliate. Despite the lack of support from the Rothschilds, Dr Nathan urged Wolf in the summer of 1907 to revive the *Russian Correspondence* as there would be attempts to float a Russian loan in London once the British treaty arrangements with Russia were revealed.[102] Putting to one side his own feelings about Russia because of its anti-Jewish policy, Natty was 'reluctantly obliged to confess [to his cousins] that under some circumstances a very small Russian Loan might probably be successful here [in England], you must bear in mind that Sir Ernest Cassel who is the mentor of Baring Bros is a great adept at obtaining very huge commissions and a still greater adept at obtaining a Loan at a very low price ...'[103]

By the autumn of 1907, the leadership of the Russo-Jewish Committee was in despair as to the growing ties between the British and Russian governments and its inability to have much impact on British public opinion, though it is questionable whether Natty fully shared all the Committee's views. 'Nothing that we may do can I fear, check the F[oreign] O[ffice] efforts for a further Anglo-Russian *rapprochement*', Nathan Joseph advised Wolf.

> On the two occasions when I met Sir C[harles] Hardinge, I could read in him – notwithstanding his sympathetic words – the most complete indifference to the moral question involved in the pogrom grievances. *La haute politique* has quite wiped out *la haute morale*. All diplomatists are essentially opportunists and the F.O. job at present is to neutralise and isolate Germany ... so I can well understand Grey, Hardinge and Nicolson saying – 'Bother the Jews, but let us above all, not say a word that can wound the susceptibilities of the Tsar'. It would not surprise me to see something more than an *entente* – a conditional alliance.

Nathan Joseph doubted whether the *Russian Correspondence* contained enough original material to attract the interest of the West European press. 'What was needed was to prepare, and to hold in readiness, a polygot paper, addressed to the investing public to be launched broadcast by circular and advertisement and placard, at the psychological moment, on the eve of a

102 Szajkowski, 'Paul Nathan, Lucien Wolf, Jacob H. Schiff', p. 19.
103 RAL XI/130A/IA Natty to his cousins Paris 7 October 1907.

projected loan issue showing the rottenness of Russian finance.'[104] Nor did Joseph expect much from the reactionary Third Duma, so that the only hope was for the Russian peasants and people to continue their revolutionary programme until they 'eventually wipe out the present regime by a new reign of Terror in French fashion' – a message to which Natty could hardly subscribe.[105]

During much of the nineteenth century, British and French Jewry were at the forefront in enforcing the human rights of their co-religionists overseas but, at the beginning of the twentieth century, a new era seemed to dawn, when the energetic efforts of the Jewish leaders in the United States eclipsed the action of their European counterparts on behalf of Romanian Jewry and voiced the most incisive protest against the Kishinev massacre. The establishment of a fund by world Jewry for the victims of the pogroms of 1905–6 was the last grand gesture made by Lord Rothschild on the international stage and his enhanced role was somewhat surprising, given that the financial contribution of American Jewry was twice that of Britain and its empire. But Natty had the connection to his fellow banker, Baron Horace Gintsburg, who headed Russian Jewry; and enjoyed a friendship with Lord Lansdowne, who came from a Whig family and was liberal in his inclinations, while he was also a close political ally of Balfour, the Prime Minister, so that British diplomatic officials were anxious to placate him. This enabled Natty to sort out some glitches caused by infighting among the Tsarist bureaucracy which threatened to hold up the distribution of aid. Even so, Dr Paul Nathan of the German charity, the *Hilfsverein*, who was a professional aid worker, was the real organizer of the international Jewish relief effort. In this, he was ably assisted by Nathan Joseph and Carl Stettauer from England and Baron Gintsburg's associate David Feinberg, who travelled to trouble spots in Russia to assess the situation at first hand. Not only were copies of Stettauer's reports while on his mission to Russia sent to Jacob Schiff, but in February 1906 he went to the United States to brief Schiff.[106] Stettauer subsequently visited the Continent many times on behalf of the Russo-Jewish Committee to

104 CAHJP, INV/316 Nathan Joseph to Lucien Wolf 11 October 1907.

105 CAHJP, INV/316 Nathan Joseph to Lucien Wolf 22 November 1907.

106 Southampton, Carl Stettauer Papers, Ms 128 AJ22 F/2 Carl Stettauer to Samuel Montagu 21 November 1905 and AJ22 F/4 Israel Zangwill to Carl Stettauer 6 February 1906.

coordinate the work of the fund. Under pressure from the United States and the Continental committees, it was decided in 1908 to retain the balance of the money collected, amounting to £29,760 10s 8d, because of the precarious situation remaining for the Jews of Russia and future emergencies.[107]

Again, though all the funds from world Jewry flowed into the Rothschild bank in London, most of the distribution was left to the Russo-Jewish Committee and Samuel Montagu & Co. Given their previous success in motivating President Theodore Roosevelt, the failure of Schiff and Oscar Straus to initiate American diplomatic action during the pogroms of 1905–6 was somewhat surprising.[108]

The diplomatic interventions of Lord Rothschild in November 1905 and June 1906, combined with the financial boycott of Russian loans by Jewish banks and the intercessions of the Russian Jewish leadership with their government, staved off a wave of further pogroms by the end of 1906. The visit of Baron Horace Gintsburg and Heinrich Sliozberg to Petr Durnovo, Minister of the Interior, in October 1905 to bring a halt to the pogroms had a successful outcome, and Gintsburg was credited with staving off a pogrom in St Petersburg. Even more fruitful was a visit by the relief committee for pogrom victims two months later to Count Witte, the Prime Minister, which resulted in his issuing orders to try to curtail the pogroms. When fears rose again of widespread pogroms at Easter, a delegation of eight Duma members called on the new Prime Minister Stolypin, strongman of the regime, in April 1907. This resulted in Stolypin issuing orders to governors to suppress future pogroms and threatened dire punishment for those who were remiss in doing so.[109] The Tsarist regime and world Jewry had distorted images of each other, the former maintaining that Jewish leadership and funds fuelled the unrest in Russia and the latter stating that elements of the Tsarist regime directed the pogroms. Both suppositions have been demolished by historical research. Moreover, it was

---

107 *Report of the Russo-Jewish Committee* 1908, pp. 11 and 12.

108 Best, *To Free a People*, pp. 136–7.

109 Vladimir Levin, 'Preventing Pogroms: Patterns in Jewish Politics in Early Twentieth-Century Russia', in Jonathan Dekel-Chen et al., eds, *Anti-Jewish Violence. Rethinking the Pogrom in East European History* (Bloomington, 2011), pp. 97–8. *Report of the Russo-Jewish Committee* 1908 p. 13.

in the interest of the Tsarist regime to crush disorder which, if allowed to continue out of control, would have endangered the rule of autocracy itself.

During 1905–6, the Russian financial situation remained shaky, so that Lucien Wolf's articles in *The Times* in March 1905, questioning whether or not Russia held sufficient gold reserves to be solvent, which was supported by an editorial caused a diplomatic squall.[110] In the following August, Lord Rothschild sent Wolf a letter stating that 'he deprecated another attack on Russian finance as he is afraid of political harm resulting from it'. All that Natty was prepared to let Wolf say in connection with an article on the forthcoming Russian loan was that because of the outrages on the Jews, no Jewish firm would be associated with it but he was not to mention names.[111] In October 1906, *Le Temps* published a leaked confidential report which M. Kokovtsoff, the Minister of Finance, had addressed to the Prime Minister about 'the grave financial condition' of the treasury which upset French investors.[112] This was a wonderful opportunity for Lucien Wolf to renew his questioning of the solvency of the Russian regime which he did on 6 October 1906 in a long letter to *The Times*. 'Terror from above may stave off actual revolution', he noted, 'but it will be at the cost of national bankruptcy.' He then produced figures to show that 'over 700,000,000 roubles of the 1,260,000,000 roubles of the note issue has no metallic guarantee whatever'.[113] The British embassy in St Petersburg, which had been carefully monitoring Russian finances throughout 1906, prepared a fresh report which rebutted Wolf's contentions. Hugh O'Beirne averred that 'this increase in the volume of the currency may be considered a satisfactory symptom, for it points to a development of industrial activity, and it is indeed thought to indicate more particularly the commercial awakening of Siberia as a result of the war'. He dismissed Wolf's wildly inflated figures, estimating that 'the gold reserve' stood 'at 119,400,000 l, as against a total of paper in circulation

110 Lucien Wolf, 'Is Russia Solvent?' *The Times* 11 and 14 March 1905. *The History of the Times: The Twentieth Century Test 1884–1912* Vol. 3 (London, 1947), pp. 408–9.

111 Yivo, David Mowshowitch Collection reel 4 S. H. Archer to Lucien Wolf 1 August 1905 and Natty to Lucien Wolf 10 April 1906.

112 National Archives, FO 371/121 Francis Bertie to Edward Grey 5 October 1906.

113 *The Times* 6 November 1906.

which ... should be estimated at 155,100,000 l'. At the end of the year the British ambassador touched on the financial situation with Prime Minister Stolypin.

> He said that he now felt no uneasiness on that score, and was confident that they would close the year without a deficit. The ordinary Budget for next year would also balance itself, and he would also lay before the Duma an extraordinary Budget, which would be drawn up to meet the very urgent need of greater railway extension, and probably some extra expenditure on military armaments and forts ... If the extraordinary Budget were voted by the Duma, then either an internal or an external loan would be required to meet the extraordinary expenses.

Criticism of the economic competence of the regime was too toxic for the world's financial markets.[114]

Natty's reluctance to turn the screws on the Tsarist regime, by refusing to continue to subsidize the *Russian Correspondence* and by curtailing Wolf's criticism of the financial stability of the regime helped to give it a longer lease of life. This ensured the continuance of autocratic tsarist rule and failure to grant Jews in Russia equal rights as citizens.

114 National Archives FO371/121 Arthur Nicolson to Grey enclosing Hugh O'Beirne's memorandum 12 November 1906 and same to same 30 November 1906.

7

PHILANTHROPY

In the 1870s 'At the very top of the financial pyramid were 250 territorial magnates', David Cannadine noted, 'each with more than 30,000 acres and £30,000 a year to their name ... they were all, by definition, millionaires. The majority held estates in many counties ... owned at least two great mansions in the country, and boasted a grand London house, in Grosvenor or Belgrave Squares, in Park Lane or Piccadilly.' If it were the case that at the height of his career, Natty owned some 15,000 acres, a mansion at Tring Park and a town house at 148 Piccadilly, he approximated to this ideal. Apart from this, Natty and his brothers were active bankers with immense incomes and Alfred and Leo acquired country estates at Halton and Ascott located within easy distance of Tring and London residences at Seamore Place and Hamilton Terrace. William Rubinstein suggested that 'it is difficult to imagine even a single British business figure of the 1870s and 1880s (with the possible exception of the Rothschilds, Lord Overstone and Charles Morrison) whose income from business sources came close to the £200,000–£300,000 per annum of the greatest landowners.'[1] An indicator of their affluence was that the Rothschilds, as a family, were the biggest donors to the Liberal Unionist party at the 1892

1   David Cannadine, *The Decline and Fall of the British Aristocracy* (London, 1992), p. 10 and W. D. Rubinstein, *Men of Property* (London, 1981), p. 196.

and 1895 elections; the amounts contributed by them to the party funds in 1892 have already been noted but, in 1895, they again headed the list, by Natty giving £5,000 and Alfred another £5,000.[2] Natty's wealth was colossal, generating an income of around £200,000 per annum, perhaps a trifle less or perhaps appreciably more, but by how much still remains a moot point. All that it is possible to do is to survey the income and expenditure of his cousin Baron Ferdinand de Rothschild (1839–98) owner of Waddesdon Manor by way of comparison, while noting that Natty's assets were superior because he was very active in business as a top banker. Baron Ferdinand's income fluctuated between £80,000 and £100,000 a year, allowing him to maintain an indoor staff of 24 plus 66 gardeners.[3]

Natty's household staff was of similar size. The Tring Inventory for 1915 showed that there were seven bedrooms in the menservant's quarters on the second floor and eleven bedrooms for the maids, plus three additional bedrooms in the basement for the use of household employees.[4]

From a testimonial presented to Natty on his seventieth birthday in November 1910, we have detailed information about the huge outdoor staff Natty maintained to run his Tring Park estate. In overall charge were a group of twelve employees in the estate office and the lodge-keeper and his family. There was a carriage stables department employing thirteen people, as well as a hunting stables department, employing another eight hands and an ordinary stables department with six employees. His farm labour force comprised 114 men, aided by a carpenters' yard with 62 employees, who also served the needs of the house, and an engineering department of five men to ensure the smooth functioning of carriages and equipment. Natty kept 57 gardeners busy, nearly all of whom were men apart from one female employee. There were two separate game departments, one of eight men under James Street, the other headed by Mr T. Smith with a much larger staff of thirty-five. Because of the welfare conditions of employment insisted on by Natty on his estate, he also funded pensions for 74 former employees and the testimonial lauded him for his 'unvarying kindness and consideration for us and our families, especially in times of sickness.'[5]

2   Adonis, *Making Aristocracy Work*, p. 184.
3   Michael Hall, *Waddesdon Manor* (New York, 2002), pp. 71, 153, 156 and 160.
4   RAL 000/848/19/2 Inventory of Tring Park June 1915.
5   RAL 000/848/6/1 Testimonial from workers on the Tring Park estate, 8 November 1910.

Natty's wife, Emma, with kindly efficiency, presided over a smoothly running establishment at Tring Park and 'was interested in every department of the farm, the stables, the gardens, the carpenters' yard and so on'. During the winter, Emma stayed at Tring Park, leaving Natty to live in some discomfort at 148 Piccadilly as, apart from his study, all the furniture was left draped in sheets. Despite her shyness and a somewhat puritanical streak, Emma was a brilliant hostess, adept at putting her guests at ease.[6] Heading the list of 29 guests on 10 June 1903, with four invitees from the immediate family, were the King and Queen and others who accepted her invitation were the Liberal politicians Earl Carrington, the Earl of Crewe, Viscount Haldane, John Morley and the Liberal Unionist politicians Austen Chamberlain and the Marquis of Lansdowne. This was also an occasion to which Natty could discreetly invite his paramour, Lady Gosford, because her husband held an official position at Court. Other frequent visitors in the Edwardian era were Arthur Balfour, Viscount Milner and the Prime Minister, Herbert Asquith. Viscount Haldane of Cloan was an intimate friend of Natty and Lady Rothschild and was a regular visitor at Tring Park, where he had a room 'which was always reserved' for him.[7] Sometimes the guest list could have a strong aristocratic contingent. On 10 June 1907 among those dining were Georgina Countess of Dudley, Viscount and Viscountess Esher, the Duchess of Montrose, Earl Carrington and the Duke and Duchess of Wellington.[8]

The diaries of Prince George, the Prince of Wales, showed that he dined with the Rothschilds on two occasions in the Edwardian era. For instance, on 18 May 1906 he noted that 'At 8.30 dined with Ld & Lady Rothschild. About 35 people to dinner. Played bridge. Bed at 12.30.'[9] Prince George was also an occasional guest at balls hosted by Natty and Emma. His diary entry for 10 June 1903 stated that 'At 11.O['clock] went with May to Lord & Lady Rothschilds ball. Papa and Mama were also there. Supper at 12.30. Bed at 2.O['clock].'[10]

Tiring somewhat of his wife's straight-laced attitudes, Natty in middle

---

6   Rothschild, *Dear Lord Rothschild*, pp. 16 and 21–2.
7   Richard Burdon Haldane, *An Autobiography* (London, 1929), pp. 162–3.
8   RAL 000/848/32 Visitors Book 10 June 1903, 29 May 1907 and 10 June 1907.
9   RA, GV/PRIV/GVD/1906 and 1909 entries for 18 May 1906 and 10 July 1909.
10   Ibid., 1896 and 1903 entries for 23 June 1896 and 10 June 1903.

age formed an intense relationship with Lady Gosford, whose husband, the Earl of Gosford, was Vice Chamberlain to Queen Alexandra.[11] Lady Gosford was attractive, less prudish than Emma, and more than fifteen years younger than Natty. She was the mother of two sons and three daughters, the last born on 30 June 1883. Like Emma, she was a bluestocking, begging Natty to obtain an English translation of Schopenhauer to take away on holiday in Switzerland.[12] Natty must have met Louisa, who was the step-daughter of Hartington, the leader of the Liberal Unionists and heir to the Duke of Devonshire, in the late 1880s, when the Liberal Unionists were consolidating as a political group and relations at home were strained because of the tensions generated by Walter Rothschild's increasingly wayward behaviour. She was a friend of the whole family, their homes being thrown open to her for discreet encounters, or perhaps liaisons, with Natty; and it is noteworthy that Alfred left her a pair of Sèvres biscuit *garde-à-vous* figurines on plinths, painted with amatory trophies ...' in his will.[13] Even so, despite Natty's attachment to Lady Gosford, he was always loving towards Emma and extremely solicitous of her well-being, an affection that was reciprocated in full measure.[14]

Natty worked as a team with his brothers, attracting more astute financial advice from Alfred and more all-round support from Leo in his own position as the lay leader of Anglo-Jewry. Their mansions at Halton and Ascott in Buckinghamshire and their cousin's estate at Waddesdon Manor, all of which were in close proximity to Natty's abode at Tring Park, helped to recreate the network of Rothschild houses in the county, which had existed in their father's generation, renewing the political power base of the family. Alfred built an extravagant sixteenth-century French *château* at Halton in 1883, evoking this comment from one visitor: 'Oh but the hideousness of the thing, the showiness! The sense of lavish wealth, thrust up one's nose.' Here, he entertained guests with a circus of which he was ringmaster, a private orchestra of which he was the conductor, and the drill

11   Davis, *The English Rothschilds*, pp. 225–6; *The Times* 7 March 1944 obituary.
12   Anita Leslie, *Edwardians in Love* (London, 1972), p. 253 and Rothschild, *Dear Lord Rothschild*, p. 7. *Burke's Peerage* 1871, p. 745 and 1894 p. 613.
13   National Archives, IR 59/522 Inland Revenue file with inventory of Alfred's estate and correspondence with Lady Gosford's solicitors.
14   Rothschild, *Dear Lord Rothschild*, p. 10.

of a fire brigade, of which he was chief. Although he fathered a daughter, Almina, out of wedlock and accompanied her mother to the opera on many occasions, he was happier mixing at weekends with a bunch of bohemian male friends 'from the worlds of art and the theatre'. Autocratic and a hypochondriac, he had a kind nature. Gladstone's secretary Algernon West reported that he was 'told that in the cold bitterness of winter mornings he sent a cart round every morning with hot coffee and bread and butter to every labourer on his estate'.[15] Alfred was a connoisseur of seventeenth-century Dutch art, though he owned no Rembrandts, and also collected paintings by Gainsborough, Romney, Joshua Reynolds and eighteenth-century French masters. As a trustee of the National Gallery and the Wallace Collection, he had strong convictions and behind the scenes encouraged Rosebery to issue a Treasury minute in 1894, stipulating that trustees of the former must be allowed to share with the director in the acquisitions policy for the national art collection.[16]

Alfred's connections may, in part, explain how Natty came to be sitting at the top table at a public banquet in 1901 to celebrate the career of Sir John Tenniel, the illustrious illustrator of *Alice in Wonderland*.[17] Flamboyant and on occasions theatrical, Alfred was nevertheless a successful financier and a competent director of the Bank of England.

Leo stood in for his brothers at N. M. Rothschild & Sons when they were unavailable, but had greater success as a racing enthusiast, producing a Derby winner from his stables in 1904 and deputizing for Natty as a Jewish communal leader. He was an outstanding breeder of race-horses, so much so that his earnings from the turf peaked in 1896 at £46,766 and in 1898 at £40,000. He was a more naturally gifted speaker than Natty and had a more congenial personality.[18]

With his immense wealth from banking and land, Natty not only dominated Anglo-Jewry but was also the most prestigious figure in world Jewry. Speaking in 1953, Redcliffe Salaman recalled that 'Until the close

15 Wilson, *Rothschild*, pp. 256–9; William Cross, *The Life and Secrets of Almina Carnarvon* (Newport, Gwent, 2011), pp. 13–16 and 225.
16 Jonathan Conlin, 'Butlers and Boardrooms: Alfred de Rothschild as Collector and Connoisseur', *The Rothschild Archive Review* 2005–6, pp. 26–33; *The Times* 4 April 1885.
17 RAL 000/182 Table plan of Banquet for Sir John Tenniel 12 June 1901.
18 *Jewish Chronicle* 1 June 1917, Special Memoir of Leopold de Rothschild.

of the First World War, the government of the [Anglo-Jewish] community might be described as a beneficent oligarchy. At its head stood the House of Rothschild, and in several dependent offices one or another member of the twenty odd leading families of the day.' Lord Rothschild was President of the United Synagogue, the premier Anglo-Jewish institution from 1879 until his death in 1915. As a keen foxhunter and a man with a mistress, Lady Gosford, the beautiful daughter of the Duchess of Devonshire, Natty did not hold the usual qualifications to fill this position. In addition, he was principal warden of the Great Synagogue, reading in English the passage from the book of Jonah, usually recited in Hebrew, on the Day of Atonement every year; he was President of the Jews' Free School and Vice-President of the Anglo-Jewish Association, while the Board of Deputies would not make any important move without his prior approval.[19] Once, in 1877, when the Board of Deputies was in disarray, as the United Synagogue had threatened to sever its ties to the Board, Natty's intervention saved that institution from extinction. He not only served as Treasurer of the Jewish Board of Guardians, a key fund-raising function, being succeeded in that role by his brother Leopold, but the Cohens, who were his relatives on his grandmother's side, were successively presidents of the board and shaped its overall policy to the poor. The only person with the financial means and political weight to challenge his leadership was Samuel Montagu, the first Lord Swaythling, who vied with him for control of Anglo-Jewry through his own orthodox Jewish organization, the Federation of Synagogues. In these encounters, Montagu was often worsted, though even when they quarrelled they worked closely together on other issues.[20]

Lord Rothschild was a staunch adherent of the Jewish faith, relishing an address given by his father when he laid the foundation stone of the Central Synagogue.

19 Daniel Gutwein, *The Divided Elite: Economics, Politics and Anglo-Jewry 1882–1917* (Leiden, 1992), p. 5. Davis, *The English Rothschilds*, pp. 225–6. Cecil Roth, *The Magnificent Rothschilds* (London, 1939), p. 266. *Jewish Chronicle* 2 April 1915 Special Memoir. David Feldman, *Englishmen and Jews. Social Relations and Political Culture 1840–1914* (New Haven, 1994), p. 358.

20 Gutwein, *The Divided Elite*, pp. 151, 185, 215, 217 and 273. Langham, *250 Years of Convention and Contention*, p. 77.

198   THE UNEXPECTED STORY OF NATHANIEL ROTHSCHILD

My father told all those kind enough to attend that their civil and religious liberties would be dearly bought if they neglected their religious duties or forgot their Jewish religion. These were the principles which animated him during his lifetime, and these are the very principles he bequeathed to his sons, and which I hope they will carry out on every occasion.

Despite a lack of adherence to the dietary laws and a lax observance of the Sabbath, he remained in the traditionalist, orthodox camp. He opposed the modernizing of services and praised the study of the Talmud. From 1879 until his death, he remained President of the United Synagogue, but in the Edwardian era he gradually relinquished the conduct of Council meetings, leaving such matters in the hands of vice-Presidents due to his increasing deafness; even so, he retained a tight control over the institution's affairs.[21]

It was in an address to a conference in 1912 to select the next Chief Rabbi that Natty came closest to defining his creed.

When I use the word "orthodox" I mean ... [those] who believe in the truths which are inculcated in the Torah and have been handed down to us for many generations. It is, perhaps, invidious to use the word "orthodox", for it is said that orthodoxy is *my* doxy and heterodoxy is *your* doxy (Laughter.) But in defining what I consider to be an orthodox Jew I think there is a very large margin left for individual thought and action, and I hope I shall have the agreement of the Conference when I say that I do not consider it the part of an orthodox Jew to discuss the shape and size of a *mikvah* [ritual bath], or issue an anathema against other people because the *tephillin* they wear are not made in exactly the same way as in Russia and Poland ... It is laid down as a cardinal principle that the Chief Rabbi or any of the gentlemen whom I venture to call suffragan Rabbis, cannot pronounce a *Cherem* [ban] against any members of the congregation because they happen to differ from them.[22]

Natty's faith, like that of the Church of England, was easy-going and tolerant, able to embrace many different strands of opinion and practice. Thus, in 1890, when Hermann Adler was elected as Chief Rabbi, he had made efforts 'to induce the Reform and the Sephardic congregations to

21 *Jewish Chronicle* 4 November 1910 pp. 23–4.
22 *Jewish Chronicle* 19 January 1912 p. 24.

take this opportunity of effecting a closer union with themselves [the other orthodox synagogues]' without success.[23]

Natty chose successive Chief Rabbis, Hermann Adler and Joseph Hertz, working harmoniously with them but dying before there could be any confrontation with Hertz over his support for Zionism. As he grew older, he became increasingly autocratic and less willing to brook any opposition to his viewpoint. A good illustration of this is the preliminary procedure for the election of Rabbi Dr Joseph Hertz as Chief Rabbi in 1913. Many candidates stepped forward, but were rejected for various reasons.

> Then it happened that Lord Milner, in the course of a conversation, mentioned to Lord Rothschild that Dr Hertz, also an aspirant, was a most desirable candidate. Lord Milner reported that, during the Boer War, Dr Hertz, then at Johannesburg, was openly pro-British. He had suffered for his convictions. This was sufficient for Lord Rothschild. He declared the campaign at an end, and proclaimed Dr Hertz as the sole candidate of the United Synagogue. There was, however, a strong opposition. Sir Adolph Tuck was at the head of a committee of men who believed that there were others who would be fit to take up the position of Chief Rabbi, and they tried to postpone the election. The whole committee, on the strength of a public protest, saw Lord Rothschild. Sir Adolph Tuck acted as spokesman, but he was never an eloquent speaker, so he read his statement, which was very lengthy. Lord Rothschild being deaf, did not understand a word. He was nervous and impatient. After a few minutes he lost his temper and shouted. 'Stop! I know all you have to say, but I have made up my mind. The election will take place and unless Dr Hertz is elected I shall resign my chairmanship of the United Synagogue, and shall as head of my house, prevent any of my family from holding office there. I have before me heaps of letters strongly approving the choice which the Executive of the United Synagogue have made, and I will just read you one from a lady who has known Dr Hertz in South Africa during all the years of his appointment out there.' She described him as a scholar of the first rank, and a splendid acquisition for any orthodox community. 'And do you know', he shouted, 'who the lady is? It is Mrs Elsa Cohen, the wife

23 *The Times* 25 July 1890.

of Harry Cohen.' I was nonplussed Elsa Cohen! Our dear sweet little
Elsa, without the faintest conception of anything Jewish an expert on
the qualifications of an orthodox Rabbi![24]

Among the members of the committee who were repulsed by Lord
Rothschild's undemocratic methods were two of Anglo-Jewry's outstanding
intellectual leaders, Lucien Wolf and Dr Redcliffe N. Salaman. Even so,
Dr Hertz was overwhelmingly elected by 298 votes to 39 votes for Dr
Hyamson.[25]

Apart from the United Synagogue, the two institutions to which Natty
devoted most of his time and energy were the Four Per Cent Industrial
Dwellings Company and the Jews' Free School, as he wished to ameliorate
the sanitary conditions of the immigrants and to Anglicize their children
as quickly as possible. The Rothschild family also pumped large sums
of money into the Jewish Board of Guardians and the Jews' Temporary
Shelter, as they were determined to ensure that the Jewish poor did not
become an unseemly burden on the state.

Natty was a long-serving member of the Sanitary Committee, later
known as the Health Committee, of the Jewish Board of Guardians. After
the failure of the Sanitary Committee to improve housing conditions in
the East End by stirring the local authority, Natty became chairman of the
United Synagogue East End Investigation Commission in 1885 and was
determined on action. The Commission reported that the Jewish poor are
'being constantly supplemented by immigrants from abroad, chiefly from
Russia and Poland,[who] are in the main religious and observant'; thus it
would be untrue to speak of them as suffering from 'spiritual destitution'.
What required attention were measures 'to cause the foreign poor upon
arrival to imbibe notions proper to civilised life in this country' and to
improve 'the physical conditions of the poor and their surroundings'. Just
as the Tsarist government had to be persuaded to treat their Jewish subjects
in a less barbaric manner, so the immigrants from Eastern Europe who
arrived in Britain had, by means of evening classes at the Jews' Free School,
to be tutored in the duties of citizenship and by the advice of honorary
visitors to their homes encouraged to adopt 'the civilisation of the country

24 Aubrey Newman, *The United Synagogue 1870–1970* (London, 1976), pp. 100–1.
25 *Jewish Chronicle* 14 February 1913, pp. 13 and 21 February 1913, p. 32.

in which their lot had been cast'.[26] Before the Commission was the example of the pioneering efforts of other philanthropists who had built blocks of model tenements in London, particularly the Metropolitan Association for Improving the Dwellings of the Industrious Classes and the Peabody Trust, and the 'extensive blocks of model dwellings' that had been erected of late by the City Corporation in Middlesex Street, but for which the rents were beyond the reach of the poor. Of more immediate interest to Natty was the scheme in the early 1860s 'initiated by the late Sir Francis Goldsmid, Sir Anthony de Rothschild [his uncle] and others, to improve the housing of ... [Jewish] poor, which resulted in the formation of the Jewish and East London Model Lodging House Association and the erection ... in Commercial Street' of a block consisting of twenty-nine tenements and six shops.[27] Led by Natty, the Rothschild Bank had already lent substantial sums of money to the Peabody Trust, one of the leading philanthropic housing associations in 1881; three years later, Alfred purchased land with Edward Bond on a site in Cartwright Street, on which a block of tenements designed by Nathan Joseph had been erected. To Natty this was also a personal challenge, a means of impressing his highly intelligent and hyper-critical mother, who had been begrudging of praise of his achievements during her lifetime. On her deathbed, in March 1884, she had urged her son to improve the housing of the Jewish working class. Under Natty's guidance, the United Synagogue commission recommended that a company should be formed to provide houses at a reduced rent which would yield a net four per cent return to investors. They were convinced that

> until such healthy houses, with appliances needful for decency and cleanliness, are provided, all means for a permanent amelioration of the conditions of the poor must prove futile and vain ... Each tenement should further have its own separate W.C. No family tenement should consist of less than two rooms, and due provision should be made for a third room in case the exigencies of the families should need the extra accommodation.[28]

26 *Jewish Chronicle* 27 February 1885, p. 8.
27 *Jewish Chronicle* 30 January 1885, p. 5 and 6 March 1885, p. 14. Susannah Morris, 'Market Solutions for Social Problems: Working-class Housing in Nineteenth-Century London', *Economic History Review* LIV:3 (2001), pp. 525–45.
28 Jerry White, *Rothschild Buildings: Life in an East End Tenement Block 1887–1920* (London,

On 9 March 1885, a preliminary meeting was held at the offices of the Rothschild Bank in New Court to set up the Four Per Cent Industrial Dwellings Company. A freehold site had become available in Flower and Dean Street in the heart of the East End which, when developed, could afford accommodation for 186 families at a cost £40,000.[29] The inaugural meeting of the company took place on 1 July 1885, with a board of directors consisting of Sir Nathaniel de Rothschild as chairman, Samuel Montagu and F. D. Mocatta, a well-known philanthropist with experience of model housing schemes. A number of other leading communal figures was also present. Nathan S. Joseph was appointed as architect and Algernon Sydney as solicitor. Of the paid-up £40,000 issued share capital, Natty himself took up a quarter and also arranged for another of his favourite charities, the Jews' Free School, to grant a loan to the company of £8,000 which he himself guaranteed. To make certain the prime site in Flower and Dean Street was acquired promptly, Natty purchased it in his own name from the Metropolitan Board of Works for £7,000 before securing the authorization for the transfer of ownership to the company in August.[30] It was decided to give investors a four per cent return which would enable excellent accommodation consisting of two rooms, a scullery and other conveniences to be provided for a large class of the poor at a weekly affordable rent of no more than five shillings a week, though in many cases this limit was breached to give investors the promised return. The dwellings were opened for occupation on 2 April 1887, the building being appropriately called the Charlotte de Rothschild Model Dwellings or more abbreviatedly the Rothschild Buildings in memory of Natty's mother. The Nathaniel Dwellings incorporating Natty's own name, were later added to the site, so that in a bizarre way he could only grow psychologically closer to his mother after her death.[31]

1980), p. 19. *Jewish Chronicle* 27 February 1885 p. 8. K. D. Rubens, 'The 4% Industrial Dwellings Company Ltd: Its Formation and East End Developments, 1885–1901', in Aubrey Newman, ed., *The Jewish East End* (London, 1981), p. 198.

29 *Jewish Chronicle* 27 February 1885, pp. 10 and 13 March 1885, p. 5.

30 White, *Rothschild Buildings*, pp. 19–21. K. D. Rubens, 'The 4% Industrial Dwellings Company Ltd', pp. 197–8. LMA, 4046/B/02 001 Duparc to Algernon Sydney 3 March 1887 and to Manager London Joint Stock Bank 16 March 1887.

31 *Jewish Chronicle* 3 July 1885, p. 11. White, *Rothschild Buildings*, pp. 22 and 28.

Because of the steady demand for self-contained flats by the Jewish working class, more sites were acquired by Nathan Joseph with the authorization of Lord Rothschild and the other directors and more tenement blocks were erected by the company in the East End. At the end of 1893, the Four Per cent Industrial Dwellings Company reported that the Charlotte de Rothschild Dwellings contained 1,107 inhabitants; Brady Street Dwellings 1,161; and Nathaniel Dwellings 722, making a total of 2,990 persons. When the company started in 1892, it housed 186 families but, by 1901, this number had crept up to 950 families or approximately 4,465 individuals. It was noted then that

> 'There are 948 tenements, divided into one, two, three, four or five rooms. Each tenement (except in the instance of single rooms) has a separate scullery and W.C., and is self-contained. At Brady Street and Stepney Green Dwellings, hot and cold water baths are also provided, free of charge, and an important feature ... at the latter building, is the provision of a hot-water supply at all times for the tenants. There is also a tenants' club and reading-room, which are successfully managed by a Committee of the tenants themselves.[32]

On 28 October 1901, the Mayor of Stepney convened a conference to discuss the congested housing conditions in the East End which, while rejecting the demand for immediate legislation to restrict the entry of destitute aliens, called on the Anglo-Jewish community to try to halt further immigration and promote 'the diffusion and Anglicisation of those already here'.[33]

In line with the long-standing suggestion for the dispersal of the immigrant population, Nathan Joseph had already purchased a site at New Church Road Camberwell in 1899 on which he built the Evelina Mansions in reach of the Borough Jewish Schools and Synagogue; and under his leadership the company went on to acquire a number of other building plots away from the East End. These included a two-acre site in Stoke Newington in 1901 and, in 1903, a slightly bigger plot at Navarino Road, Dalston.[34] Attempts to purchase a larger site in Stratford on which to build

32 *Jewish Chronicle* 2 February 1893, p. 7 and 8 November 1901, p. 23.
33 *Jewish Chronicle* 1 November 1901, p. 20.
34 Hugh Pearman, *Excellent Accommodation: The First Hundred Years of the Industrial*

a village with three-storey cottages containing flats of different sizes were quashed by the reluctance of the West Ham Borough Council to approve the scheme because they objected to a 'colony' of Jews living in their area, and the purchase of another site in Islington was abandoned for reasons that are not altogether clear.[35]

On reaching seventy, Nathan Joseph retired from the architectural practice of Joseph, Son and Smithem, which specialized in designing tenement blocks for a number of philanthropic housing associations, finishing his career with the late Victorian/Art Nouveau building design of Navarino Mansions in Dalston Lane. With the completion of this project and the smaller Mocatta House in the East End in 1905 and the retirement of Joseph, the momentum went out of the company's plans for further expansion before the First World War.[36]

What was Lord Rothschild's role in the company affairs? Twice a year he scrupulously attended the board of directors meeting and the annual shareholders meeting over which he presided, scrutinizing all the company's plans and authorizing the contracts for the purchase of land and acceptances of builders' tenders. Possibly, he oversaw the amendment of the company's articles of association to allow the company to pay interest to shareholders out of capital while the new properties were under construction.[37] Philip Ornstein, in his capacity as secretary of both the United Synagogue and the Industrial Dwellings Company, was able to coordinate the acquisition of sites for development with the building of new synagogues placed within a reasonable walking distance for prospective tenants.[38] Even so, the company was unable to attract Jewish tenants to South London, so much so that Evelina Mansions in Camberwell was occupied almost entirely by gentiles.[39]

Dwellings Society (London, 1985), pp. 74 and 79–83. Jewish Chronicle 8 November 1901 p. 23.
35 Pearman, Excellent Accommodation, pp. 75–8 and Industrial Dwellings Company Minute Book 2: 26 January 1903.
36 Pearman, Excellent Accommodation, pp. 85–7.
37 Industrial Dwellings Company Minute Book 2: 1903–1914 for Lord Rothschild's attendances and 20 May 1903.
38 Jewish Chronicle 8 November 1901, p. 23.
39 Pearman, Excellent Accommodation, pp. 74–5.

Addressing the annual meeting of shareholders in 1911, Lord Rothschild replied to recent newspaper criticism of the honesty of Jewish tenants, by pointing out that the company owned four blocks of flats in the East End comprising 842 families and 3,859 persons. Ninety-five per cent of these families were Jewish. On 31 December the bad debts of these 800 Jewish families amounted to £12 18s. 'The rents actually collected amounted to £13,700, so that the bad debts were less than one farthing in the pound. These 800 families represented 3,800 persons. At Camberwell, the company had a block of buildings where 70 families accounted for bad debts amounting to over £29, or more than 8s per family. The rents collected amounted to £1,400, so that the bad debts were 5d in the £, or twenty times greater than in the East End properties. There were no Jewish families at Camberwell who were responsible to the company for any rent in 1910. At the Stoke Newington and Navarino Mansions the proportion of Jews to Christians was about equal, and there was nothing to choose between either as to respectability and honesty in their dealings. Three hundred families at Navarino Mansions paid £6,200 in rent, and there was not a single bad debt during last year'.[40] At the end of 1913, there were 6,513 persons living in 1,592 of the company's tenements, comprising 3,883 adults and 2,630 children.[41]

Lloyd Gartner has observed 'that the Jews' Free School was able to multiply its capacity many times was largely due to the support of the Rothschilds, who regarded it as a special charity of their own'. Moreover, the Rothschild family supplied four consecutive presidents of the school, extending over a period of 115 years, starting with Sir Anthony Rothschild (1847–75), who devoted their time and energy to the school and its activities. Natty followed his uncle as president of the JFS from 1876 until 1915. Despite a heavy round of business and other communal concerns, Natty, according to the school's historian, Gerry Black

> regularly attended the School's committee meetings – though for his convenience some were held at the Bank's offices at New Court – and was always available at short notice when Angel [the headmaster] and others from the School sought an urgent meeting for advice and help.

40 *Jewish World* 17 February 1911.
41 Industrial Dwellings Company 29 Annual Report February 1914 schedule of properties.

He possessed a profound and detailed knowledge of the work carried on in the School. When, in 1898, F. D. Mocatta led a delegation to seek his permission to call the newly erected addition to the School building 'The Rothschild Wing', he responded by saying that he could not think of anything which would give him so great a feeling of delight.[42]

JFS had 500 pupils in 1823 and by 1856, with its 1,500 pupils, it was the largest school in England, but with the onset of East European immigration in the 1880s there was a quantum leap in enrolment with 3,000 pupils in 1883, rising to 4,250 pupils at the end of the nineteenth century. In 1907, the building in Bell Lane was described as

> the largest of our elementary schools. Where Russian Jews are made into Good British subjects ... the notable edifice raised by the beneficence of the Jewish community for the education of its children of whom no fewer than 2,200 boys and 1,200 girls are pupils. The excellence of its work has gained for it a world-wide reputation while it possesses so great a variety of activities, and so complete an organisation, as to make it almost unrivalled in institutions of a similar nature. A large amount of time is devoted weekly to instruction in the Hebrew language and religion, for the committee has always felt that a thorough grounding in the principles and observances of their faith should form the basis of all educational efforts.[43]

From the days of Nathan Mayer, founder of the English dynasty, the Rothschild family gave generously to the finances of the school, their contributions together with their personal appeals to other donors securing the bulk of its funding. In fact, the *Jewish Chronicle* castigated the community for their over-reliance on the 'princely wealth' of one family for the financial upkeep of the school. When £10,270 was raised at the 1865 anniversary dinner, it was the Rothschild family, led by Natty's uncle Sir Anthony, who headed the list of donors, Sir Anthony, Baron Lionel and Natty himself each giving £1,000, while Baroness Ferdinand, Natty's sister, donated £500. As for the 1869 anniversary festivities, 'Natty

42 Lloyd P. Gartner, *The Jewish Immigrant in England 1870–1914* (London, 1973), p. 221 and Gerry Black, *J. F. S.: The History of the Jews' Free School, London, Since 1732* (London, 1998), p. 58.

43 Ibid., pp. 106 and 149.

said the dinner was bad', remarked Charlotte, 'the room was hot, and the speeches were dull, with the exception of the President's harangue, which was funny and caused the company to laugh.' Natty's mother taught classes of children on a weekly basis, as well as serving on the Ladies' Committee connected with the school and bequeathed the school a sum of £15,000 in her Will.[44] So when Natty immersed himself in the financial management of the school he was following in his parents' footsteps, particularly those of his mother, Charlotte de Rothschild. To cope with the influx of the children of immigrants, some buildings in the old school were demolished and were replaced by 51 classrooms, eight cloakrooms, three stock-rooms and one work-room, all augmenting the existing accommodation, as well as a spacious central hall. On 25 October 1883 the new buildings in Bell Lane, Spitalfields were opened by the Delegate Chief Rabbi Dr Hermann Adler in the presence of Sir Nathaniel de Rothschild, who laid a memorial stone with a silver trowel which was presented to him. Sir Julian Goldsmid in proposing a vote of thanks added that 'Had it not been for the constant and active supervision of Sir Nathaniel, it was doubtful whether the large gathering would have assembled that day to celebrate the opening of the greatest Jewish school in the world.'

The architect of the school was the firm of Nathan Joseph, with whom Natty worked on so many communal projects. A couple of months later, Natty berated the Jewish community for its inadequate financial support of the school, the building fund showing a deficit of £3,800 and the maintenance fund a shortfall of £2,000, warning that it was necessary to increase annual expenditure at the school from £5,200 to £10,000 to be entitled to the full state grant.[45] At the annual prize day in 1885, a portrait of his mother, Baroness Lionel de Rothschild, was presented to Natty, which was hung in a prominent position in the school alongside that of Sir Anthony de Rothschild. When responding, he claimed that it proved that 'you recollect the maternal devotion and care with which she watched over the progress of this school and the love which she felt for this institution'. In 1886, Natty estimated that the annual cost of running the school was £11,000, of which £3,500 was derived from the interest on the school's

44   Ibid., pp. 55–7, 64 and 67.
45   *Jewish Chronicle* 26 October 1883, pp. 6–7 and 21 December 1883, p. 6.

endowment fund, £3,000 came from the government, while the rest had to be raised from donations and subscriptions. Because more ample and up-to-date accommodation was required by the Education department, in 1898, a new wing and a drill hall had to be built for the school at a cost of £20,000, which was named after Lord Rothschild.[46]

'That Lord Rothschild's philanthropy is as wise as it is generous', the *Jewish Chronicle* pointed out,

> is shown by the fact that when it came to his notice a year or two ago that the free distribution of clothing to pupils of the school was leading to undesirable results he promptly acquiesced in an arrangement by which the administration of his annual gift should repose in the hands of a Committee, which now makes grants of clothing only to deserving cases. Lord Rothschild has for years past borne the brunt of the expense of the happy evenings at the school, and it is solely due to his generosity that it was found possible to establish the large evening recreation school, which is proving such a success. The annual outing of the pupils is another of the many ways in which he has shown his desire to promote the happiness of children. Love of children is one of his dominating characteristics, and this love has found the most spontaneous and practical expression in the care and money lavished on the Jews' Free School.[47]

Testifying to a committee of the London School Board in 1871, Moses Angel, headmaster of JFS, spoke in a condescending way about the children in his charge, who 'were ignorant of the elements of sound; until they had been Anglicized or humanized it was difficult to tell what was their moral condition, and many of them scarcely knew their names'. Further, he was upset to have care of children 'who knew neither English nor any intelligible language ... Their parents were the refuse population of the worst parts of Europe, whose first object in sending the children to school was to get them out of the way ... the population among whom his school was placed lived a quasi-dishonourable life [hawking].'[48] In abundantly more measured language, Natty averred that his primary aim was the Anglicization of these children, at the same time boasting of the school's achievements.

46   Ibid., 3 July 1885, p. 8 and 28 January 1898.
47   *Jewish Chronicle* 4 November 1910, p. 23.
48   Gartner, *The Jewish Immigrant*, p. 223.

The large army of children drilled nearly into perfection by their teachers, were reviewed by the Government Inspectors with the following results – 98.8 per cent passed the reading standard, as against 95.1 per cent of the London School Board – (cheers)—97.1 per cent as against 89 per cent passed the writing standard, and 95 per cent as against 87 per cent passed the arithmetic standard. These results are highly satisfactory, especially when you consider that a majority of the children who enter the Free School are foreigners when they come there; they are English boys and girls when they leave, and even that that fact alone would reflect the greatest credit on the teaching staff of the school – (Cheers).[49]

Unfortunately, Natty, like the head teacher at the JFS, had little understanding of the civilization and language of the East European immigrants, urging the appointment in 1912 of a new Chief Rabbi, who 'should be able to speak English, and do all in his power to prevent the teaching and spread of slang and jargon like Yiddish' – a contemptuous and purblind dismissal of a rich culture.[50]

If the Industrial Dwellings Company and the Jews' Free School were Natty's favourite charities, Natty, as head of the English Rothschilds, made his family responsible for ensuring the financial viability of the Jewish Board of Guardians and the Jews' Temporary Shelter, the premier institutions for keeping the Jewish poor from Eastern Europe off the rates and for making certain that sudden floods of Jewish refugees and migrants who had failed to earn a living were sent on their way, without impugning the good name of the Anglo-Jewish elite. Natty served as joint treasurer of the Jewish Board of Guardians from 1874–9, being succeeded by his brother Leopold, who filled the same office for a much longer period of time from 1879–1917.[51] In the ten-year period 1880–9, the Rothschild family contributed over £8,300 to the coffers of the Jewish Board of Guardians, annual contributions usually being kept below £840, apart from the pogrom year of 1881, when a total of £1,740 was raised.

During the following decade, in the early and mid-1890s, the family's contributions rose well above £1,000 pounds annually peaking at £1,692

49 *Jewish Chronicle* 18 June 1886, p. 10.
50 *Jewish Chronicle* 19 January 1912, p. 25.
51 Vivian Lipman, *A Century of Social Service 1859–1959: The History of the Jewish Board of Guardians* (London, 1959), p. 268.

2s 0d in 1892 when this coincided with a renewed outburst of hostility from the Tsarist government but otherwise never amounting to more than £900. In the following decade, 1900–9, Natty and his relatives gave almost £14,600 to the Board, annual contributions peaking in the years after the pogroms of 1905–6 at £2,760 in 1906.[52] Apart from this, the organization received a bequest of £10,000 from Baroness Charlotte de Rothschild in 1884, and there are myriad entries in the Rothschild charity accounts marked Stephany or M. Stephany, indicating special payments to the Board for individuals channelled through its secretary, Morris Stephany.[53]

Another key institution that benefited from Rothschild largesse was the Poor Jews' Temporary Shelter, accommodation mostly for foreign Jewish migrants in transit to other lands, which was opened in 1885. Its principal problem was dealing with sudden surges in demand for food and shelter set off by wars and pogroms. Thus, as a result of the Boer War, 253 refugees came from South Africa, including ten Christians, over half of whom were financially assisted to reach their destinations.[54] In our last chapter, we touched on the assistance rendered by the Shelter to Romanian refugees in 1900 and to Russian Jews, including army reservists, who fled to Britain because of the Russo-Japanese War of 1904–5. Sensing that the Shelter could not cope with the demands for accommodation made on it, Hermann Landau was the driving force behind an ambitious rebuilding scheme, moving the Shelter from 84 Leman Street to next-door premises in the summer of 1906. When the newly refurbished Shelter was opened on 9 July 1906, at a cost of £15,000, Lord Rothschild presided over the proceedings, having helped to raise the funds for the building programme, and for his efforts he was presented with a gold key by Ellis A. Franklin. Meyer Spielmann announced to the assembled guests that 'Lord Rothschild had not told them of the enormous amount of assistance he had given them, especially during the rush when the Russian refugees came to this country, and the Shelter was practically overwhelmed and hardly knew which way to turn.' On observing the inmates of the Shelter after the opening ceremony,

52 Jewish Board of Guardians annual reports 1880–1909.

53 Ibid., 1884 p. 10. Lipman, *A Century of Social Service*, pp. 43 and 268. RAL, VI/16/4 Charity Ledger accounts for 1908.

54 LMA, 4184/2/5/1/3 Poor Jews' Temporary Shelter, executive minutes, 13 March and 24 April 1900.

Leopold de Rothschild was overcome with compassion and instructed the official in attendance to give them 'a substantial dinner on his account'.

It was reckoned by Hermann Landau that £34,000 was expended in 1905 to resettle Russian Jewish refugees in the United States, Canada and Argentina, of which £10,000 was supplied by the Jewish Colonization Association and the Russo-Jewish Committee, the bulk of the remaining money coming from the Rothschilds.[55] Leopold served on the general committee of the Shelter, later becoming its vice-president, and Natty was a regular subscriber to its funds.[56] Although the Board of Guardians at one time carried out more stringent tests on prospective recipients of charity, by 1900 it shared the more flexible outlook of the Shelter.[57]

As we have seen, Natty, from his own experience gained at the Jewish Board of Guardians, was deeply interested in the health and sanitary conditions in which the poor lived and, and in addition, he had strong connections with the voluntary hospitals in the capital, particularly the London Hospital, winning concessions from them for Jewish patients.[58] He was also a friend and supporter of Henry Charles Burdett (1847–1920), secretary of the shares and loan department of the Stock Exchange and a former hospital administrator, who became a remarkable philanthropist. Burdett founded the National Pension Fund for Nurses in 1889 and, a few years later, the Sunday Fund, which channelled donations from churches into the voluntary hospitals. In the nurses' charity, he worked closely with Natty, consulting him on the wording of a press announcement and on whether or not a financial bonus should be conferred on those nurses who were in the initial group to join the pension scheme.[59]

Because of Natty's knowledge and his links to this sector of philanthropy, Prince Edward, the future Edward VII, invited him in 1897 to

55 LMA, 4184/02/05/001/001 Abraham Munday, *Reminiscences*, pp. 65–70. *Jewish Chronicle* 13 July 1906, pp. 25–6. Black, *The Social Politics of Anglo-Jewry 1880–1920*, pp. 252–3.
56 LMA, 4184/02/01/001 Jews' Temporary Shelter annual reports 1909–10, 1910–11 and 1911–12.
57 Gartner, *The Jewish Immigrant in England 1870–1914*, p. 54.
58 Black, *Lord Rothschild and the Barber* (London, 2000), pp. 45–7.
59 Henry Charles Burdett, *Oxford D.N.B.* (Oxford, 2004). Bodleian Libraries, Sir Henry Burdett Papers, Eng.ms c.5926 f.87 and f.112; Burdett to Natty 11 January 1888 and 5 June 1889.

serve as honorary Treasurer from its inception of 'The Prince of Wales's Hospital Fund for London to Commemorate the Sixtieth Year of the Queen's Reign', later known as the King's Fund. This fund to boost the voluntary hospital system was probably Burdett's greatest achievement, but he kept a low public profile in the organization. He cleverly gained both royal patronage for his charities and, with Natty's help, the financial commitment of the City. Between £150,000 to £100,000 was to be raised annually to assist the voluntary hospitals of London. At first Natty was somewhat grudging in his support of the Prince's appeal, seeking the aid of *The Times'* editor 'to make a stand against Burdett's precipitancy, and prevent the Prince from committing himself at once in public in favour of the £100,000 Hospital Endowment'.[60] While Natty was delegated to lobby the financial sector, other targeted groups included the major land-owners, the railway companies, livery companies, leading businessmen and wealthier householders, and the Prince also involved others from his pluto-cratic circle of friends, such as Ernest Cassel and Edgar Speyer. In the course of his involvement with the charity, Natty contributed £15,000 through the Rothschild bank, while the brewing magnate Edward Cecil Guinness donated £60,000. But even in 1902 he remained unenthusiastic about 'the prosperity and potential of the Fund'.[61] As 'Lord Rothschild did not see his way to approaching the rich men, referred to in your letter, with a view to their contributing to the *Endowment Fund*, [the King thought] it would be better to do nothing with them for the present *as regards the latter*'.[62] Despite his friendship with Algernon Sydney, solicitor of the United Synagogue and of the Four Per Cent Industrial Dwellings Company, Natty did little to persuade Ada Lewis, widow of a big moneylender to gift over an annual payment of £10,000 to the Fund from a bequest by her husband, which was initially due to her. Maybe this was because Sydney also happened to be acting for Mrs Lewis. The negotiations were entrusted by King Edward to Lord Farquhar, who was given 'ample time to avail himself of the opportunity to persuade Mrs Lewis to avail herself of the oppor-tunity that now presents itself for doing a great & permanent service to the

60   RAL, 000/848/37 George Buckle to Natty 3 February 1897.
61   RA, PS/PSO/GV/C/C/273/6 Lord Mount Stephen to Prince George 8 March 1902. *The Times* 8 March 1902.
62   RA, PS/PSO/GV/C/C/273/9 Arthur Bigge to Lord Duncannon 31 March 1902.

charity in which her late husband took the deepest interest ... I am afraid we cannot count on Lord Rothschild', Lord Mount Stephen sadly admitted.[63] Edward was convinced that the public favoured voluntary action. 'It is obvious, however, that if these institutions are to be saved from the State or parochial aid, their financial condition must be secured'.[64]

We catch a glimpse of Natty's deferential and circumspect attitude towards the Prince of Wales in the formative year of the Fund. He was very careful to let Edward feel that he was the final decision-maker in regard to the allocation of the money collected between the different hospitals. Writing to Burdett in November 1897, Natty reiterated that as Treasurer, 'It does not rest with me to decide what we ought to do or not. We have to carry out His Royal Highnesses' wishes. At present I take them to be to report how about £30,000 can best be distributed among 10 or 12 leading & needy hospitals.' Burdett at once wrote to Sir Francis Knollys, the Prince's secretary, telling him that Natty had the wrong idea about His Royal Highnesses' wishes and asking for 'an authoritative opinion by Bearer'.[65] After another flurry of correspondence between them, Knollys wrote back to Burdett that 'The Prince of Wales is much pleased at the idea of receiving £38,000 or £40,000 before the end of the year from [the sale of special] stamps and also at the good example of the Fishmonger's Company, and I am sure he will be most reasonable tomorrow [at the Council meeting]'. The Council having met, Knollys informed Burdett that 'I hear the recommendations of the Committees respecting the distribution were unanimously agreed to, and I am very glad to learn that everything passed off most satisfactorily at the meeting.'[66] Burdett and Knollys felt that they had handled their master well, curbing any outbursts of temper and prompting him to make the recommendations in line with their own wishes.

63 RA, PS/PSO/GV/c/c/273/10 Lord Mount Stephen to Arthur Bigge 2 April 1902.
64 F. K. Prochaska, *Philanthropy and the Hospitals of London: The King's Fund 1897–1990* (Oxford, 1992), pp. 19, 20–1, 24, 27, 30 and 38.
65 Bodleian Library, Sir Henry Burdett Papers, Ms Eng. c5939 f.132 Natty to Burdett 21 November 1897 and f.137 Burdett to Sir Francis Knollys 22 November 1897.
66 Bodleian Library, Sir Henry Burdett Papers, Ms Eng. C5939 f.152 Burdett to Sir Francis Knollys 16 December 1897, f.157 Sir Francis Knollys to Burdett 19 December 1896; ff.158–9 20 December 1897.

On 20 December 1897, the Council met at Marlborough House, the meeting being presided over by the Prince of Wales. Natty addressed the Prince in rather florid language, telling him 'I have the honour to communicate a letter from Lord Strafford in which he desires me to present his humble duty to your Royal Highness and to respectfully apologise for him in not being able to attend the meeting'. Here we have the authentic voice of Natty in the royal presence. He continued that:

> The Executive Committee were made aware of the wise resolution of your Royal Highness not to trench on the capital fund for money to be distributed to the hospitals this year ... At the present moment there is at the Bank of England and at other banks a sum of £187,000, a part of which – £99,000 has been invested in securities. That £187,000 consists, first of all of £20,500, which has been received as annual subscriptions and £1,500 interest from moneys we have received, so that of the £187,000 it would be absolutely necessary for your Royal Highness to distribute within a very short period the sum of about £22,000. The remainder, £165,000 would have to be invested. In addition to this sum of £187,000 ... your Royal Highness will receive towards the end of the year £38,000 or £40,000 from the sale of stamps. It gave the Committee a great deal of anxiety and trouble to determine under what head to apportion the sale of stamps ...A great deal has been said in the Press about the mismanagement of hospitals, and the necessity for out-patients paying for the relief they receive there. Although nobody thinks more highly than I do of the Charity Organisation Society ... I must say that on this occasion I differ with them. I myself have a slight acquaintance with the working classes who for the most part are those who go as out-patients to the London Hospitals. I know the difficulties they are placed in, and the thrift they show in belonging to Friendly Societies who give them the money to keep them when they are out of work. And I think that this body here ... would do very wrong if at the outset they tried to impose on the hospitals new regulations for the out-patient department. I think that all the money received for hospital stamps this year might be distributed to the hospitals, if not in accordance with the Hospital Sunday Fund at any rate on those principles.

What is so interesting about Natty's last comment is that it shows that he was not in accord with those Victorian philanthropists who wished to squeeze a contribution out of families struggling to survive above the poverty line.[67]

All was not well by 1906, with the functioning of the finance committee of the King's Fund which operated under Natty's chairmanship; it appears that, as he grew older, Natty was losing his sure touch as a financial investment adviser, so that the income and capital of the fund were needlessly squandered. So incensed was Lord Mount Stephen that he called on Prince George's private secretary, Sir Arthur Bigge (created Lord Stamfordham 1911) to discuss the situation. Bigge advised the Prince that

> Mount Stephen is still annoyed at the way in which the proceeds of the paying off of his gift of Argentine Govt 6% Bonds were reinvested and he blames Lord Rothschild for this, in his opinion [a] great mistake by which the fund has lost £3000 p.a. in income & £100,000 in capital ... He also calls attention to the serious shrinkage in the market value of the invested sums, amounting to £23,462 on £245,583, nearly 10 p[er]. cent – whereas the value of the *Gifts* his and Strathcona's has *increased* by £295,743 on £655,613 nearly 50 p[er]. cent!! ... He attributes this to a lack of real good financial control and he rightly urges that with a capital which before long will amount upwards of £1,500,000 – it is now equal to £1,258,000 ... there is a serious want of a committee of capable financiers ... M[oun]t Stephen said ... that he is prepared to urge that as the bulk of the investments are in American securities it is most important that the members of the Committee should have special knowledge in that branch & Revelstoke, Cassel & especially Fleming are pre-eminently fitted to supply that knowledge.

Because Cassel was 'one of the ablest men in the City of London', Lord Rothschild 'would have to fall in with Cassel's superior knowledge'. Bigge concluded that 'Although I was against the idea of Cassel (merely on account of Lord Rothschild) I really venture to think it would be well if your Royal Highness could agree to him & to Fleming regarding them as in place of Mount Stephen himself' on the finance committee. For reasons

67 Bodleian Library, Sir Henry Burdett Papers, Eng. Ms c.5939 ff.162–72, report of Council meeting of the Prince of Wales Hospital Fund 20 December 1897.

of the King's long-standing friendship with Natty, it was decided not to replace him as chairman of the committee.[68]

Natty 'took a keen personal interest in the efforts made by King Edward's Fund to bring about a uniform system of administration in the London Hospitals, to induce economy and promote efficiency'. He was, therefore, anxious to avoid the duplication of existing charities and the foundation of new institutions, such as the London Jewish Hospital.[69]

Thus, at the Golden Jubilee Dinner of the Jewish Board of Guardians in February 1909, Lord Rothschild launched a mordant attack on the plans for a new Jewish hospital in the East End.

> The people who propose to set up this new charity are discontented with the work of perhaps the greatest and most charitable institution in the world, the London Hospital ... I am not betraying any confidence when I say that their hope that the hospital may be endowed with the money left by the late Mr Henry Barnato is a futile hope. I am sure it will not be given for this purpose. I only wish to tell these kind-hearted but misguided people that the late Dr Asher, who was connected with the Jewish Board of Guardians and the United Synagogue, always had the greatest antipathy ... to any Jewish medical charity. He said, in his terse way, that blue pills and rhubarb had no religion ... I have ventured to address you on this subject in the hope that those who have influence will put their face against a mischievous innovation, and will justify our gratitude to institutions like the London Hospital and the Metropolitan Hospitals who have attended the Jewish sick with so much devotion and success.[70]

Summing up the reasons for Natty's opposition to the Jewish Hospital movement after his death in 1915, Leopold J. Greenberg, editor of the *Jewish Chronicle*, advanced the view that 'If [Lord Rothschild] hated anything more than another it was the doing of a mean trick or an unfair action. As lay head of the Jewish community he had to a large extent pledged the community to support the general hospitals, chief among them being the London Hospital, the bargain being that the general hospitals

68   RA, PS/PSO/GV/C/C/273/60 Bigge to the Prince of Wales 11 September 1906.
69   *Jewish Chronicle* 4 November 1910, p. 22.
70   Black, *Lord Rothschild and the Barber*, p. 67.

would throw their doors open freely to our people. Now when the Jewish Hospital movement was first started it was looked upon ... [by the London Hospital] as something of an impertinence and something of a revolt. 'How dare you ask for this and that, when you are getting the best of everything? We know your Jewish peculiarities, but we cannot bring a great Hospital down to the level of Jewish idiosyncrasies ... one of the means of beating out of the Jews their peculiar idiosyncrasies – idiosyncrasies that are very strong in regard to illness, accident, or death – would be to compel them to conform to the general regulations of a great hospital.' As his heir, Walter Rothschild argued, Natty would not tolerate anything that smacked of Jewish separatism. Thus Natty's views were fully in accord with those of Viscount Knutsford, chairman of the house committee of the London Hospital.

Natty died on 21 March 1915. The foundation stone of the London Jewish Hospital was laid on 14 November 1915, his opposition to a movement with deep roots in the East End population was futile.[71]

Apart from the provision of housing and schools, there was one other area of philanthropy with which the Rothschild family were particularly concerned: the rescue of Jewish girls who had drifted into the sex trade. One evening in May 1885, Constance de Rothschild (Lady Battersea), the daughter of Sir Anthony de Rothschild, was made aware by a Christian friend that there was no home or refuge for Jewish girls who had become prostitutes. Through the summer months of 1885, Constance plunged into a new area of social work, setting up the Jewish Ladies' Association for Prevention and Rescue Work and enlisting the help of her close friend and relative Lady Rothschild, Natty's wife, as President of the Association, and the services of Claude Montefiore, another cousin, and of the Revd Simeon Singer. When the committee of the newly formed Association convened, Constance noted that she 'carried the point by insisting upon the necessity of having some house of refuge for these poor girls'. A home was acquired in Mile End for these girls and for unmarried mothers which, a couple of years later, in 1887, moved to Shepherds Bush.[72] This was followed by

71 Ibid., pp. 45–7 and 77–9.
72 Constance Battersea, *Reminiscences* (London, 1922), pp. 418–23. British Library Add. Ms 47938, Battersea Papers Vol. XXX 18 August 1885 and 6 January 1886.

the opening of a home for respectable working girls, later called Sara Pyke House, and an industrial school for girls who had to be uprooted from an unsavoury locality. When Montefiore House was opened in 1905, the cost of adapting it to become an industrial school for thirty girls was paid for by Lord and Lady Rothschild and the Montefiores. A chief task of the association was the appointment of Yiddish-speaking agents to meet unaccompanied girls at the docks and principal railway stations. In 1889, a committee of gentlemen was established to supervise the work of the society and, in 1896, the organization changed its name into the Association for the Protection of Girls and Women. It widened the scope of its activities when Claude Montefiore secured an annual grant of £1,200 from the Jewish Colonization Association in Paris.[73] Henceforth, the Association moved into the forefront of the organizations combating the international dimensions of the white slave traffic among Jews. Dr Frederick Perugia, a brother-in-law of Leopold de Rothschild, assisted in the establishment of a branch of the association in Buenos Aires, by enlisting the help of the Austrian consul and the police, and persuading Henry Joseph, a businessman and communal leader, to assume the presidency. Meanwhile, in Britain, W. A. Coote, a philosemite and evangelical Christian, formed a national committee against white slavery and summoned an international congress in London in 1899. To promote the organization of the congress and the event itself, which entailed subsidizing Mr Coote's travels and contacts with rabbis, the Rothschilds advanced the necessary funding.[74]

Lady Rothschild fully supported her husband in his multifarious charitable activities both among the inhabitants of Tring and in the Jewish community. Serving on the committee of the Jews' Free School, she was a 'benefactor' and 'true friend' of the school, 'visiting its classrooms and inviting Miss Titleboam, its headmistress, to her home to ascertain what was required. Whenever there was a need for help, whether it was wanted for developments that were of benefit to the whole school or to individuals, she was ready with money, encouragement and with appreciation, which smoothed out many rough places', said her friend in a tribute. She also

73 Lipman, *A Century of Social Service*, pp. 247–55; Edward J. Bristow, *Prostitution and Prejudice: The Jewish Fight against White Slavery 1870–1939* (Oxford, 1982), pp. 236–43.
74 Bristow, *Prostitution and Prejudice*, pp. 243–8.

'displayed the greatest interest in the Jewish Crêche, of which she was the President' and was a patroness of the City of London Benevolent Society for Assisting Widows of the Jewish Faith. She with others helped to advance the sum of £55,000 for the erection of the Brady Street Dwellings and took a keen interest in the Brady Street Club for Working Boys, subsidizing it by £250 each year which was almost 60 per cent of its income and presiding over its annual meetings. She went on annual visits to the club, sometimes accompanied by her daughter, the Hon. Evelina Rothschild, where she was met with a guard of honour drawn from the Jewish Lads' Brigade and presented with a bouquet before attending a specially arranged concert.[75] Many subsequent stars of the West End stage first honed their talents in the club's concert room.

Aside from her work in education, Lady Rothschild's main concern was rescue work among Jewish women to preserve the honour and good name of the community. For a period of fifty years she served as the president of the Jewish Association for the Protection of Girls and Women (JA). According to Claude Montefiore, a co-worker, 'From the very first she took the deepest interest in all its varied doings, and this interest she maintained uninterruptedly till the end ... each yearly Report was always submitted to her for criticism and approval up till ... 1932.'[76] Under her leadership, the income of the association climbed from £1,188. 3s. 4d in 1899 to £3,301. 7s. 10d in 1913, allowing it to expand its activities in the metropolis.[77] In addition to Charcroft House, the Rescue and Training Home, the Domestic Training Home, and the Lodging House for Respectable Girls, an Industrial School for Girls was opened and three dock agents were employed to meet young, unaccompanied women disembarking at the docks.[78] Apart from Claude Montefiore and his wife, Lady Rothschild was the biggest contributor to the funds of the association, if the legacy of Lady Goldsmid is discounted. Between them, Lord and Lady Rothschild gave £200 towards furnishing the Industrial School in 1905 while, in the following year, she donated

75 *Jewish Chronicle* 11 January 1935, p. 12. Pearman, *Excellent Accommodation*, p. 58. Black, *The Social Politics of Anglo-Jewry 1880–1920*, p. 144. Michael Lazarus, *A Club Called Brady* (London, 1996), pp. 18–19.
76 *Jewish Chronicle* 18 January 1935, p. 10.
77 *JA Reports* 1899 p. 54 and 1913, p. 119.
78 *JA Report* 1913, p. 13.

£400. Through her zeal, an appeal for funds in 1906 met with a generous response with £800 coming from Montefiore, £700 from N. M. Rothschild & Sons and £105 from Baron Armand J. de Rothschild, £600 from Mrs L. Lucas, £500 from Mr and Mrs Bischoffsheim and smaller donations from many others, including the Sassoons.[79] Each year, Lady Rothschild headed the subscription list of the association with £68 plus £10 towards the secretary's salary. When an international Jewish conference was held in 1910 for the suppression of trafficking, Lord and Lady Rothschild held a magnificent reception at their home, with special attention being given to the delegates from abroad, so helping to make the occasion a resounding success.[80]

Paying tribute to Lord Rothschild on his seventieth birthday, Lucien Wolf claimed that 'few people, however, know the scope and range of his private charity. The sum thus distributed in his name and in the names of his brothers by a special secretary at New Court have often been guessed at, but for once guesswork has been very short of the truth.'[81] What was not revealed in Natty's lifetime is now known to historians because a number of charity ledgers dating from 1902 to 1908 survive in the Rothschild Archive. They show that in these years the annual sum distributed in charitable donations fluctuated between £40,001 6s. 8d. for 1903 and £56,466 13s. 2d. for 1905, when it reached its peak.[82]

If the entries in the charity ledger for 1908, which included payments totalling £45,307 4s. 4d. are examined more closely, the pattern and scope of Rothschild largesse emerge more clearly. What soon becomes obvious is that the sums donated to general secular and Christian causes equalled the money gifted to specific Jewish charities. As India was then part of the British Empire, the Indian Relief Fund received £1,000, while Italy, which was in certain ways more remote, had an Earthquake Fund, which was given half this amount. Natty was much influenced by Sir Henry Burdett, thus ensuring that a hefty tranche of his donations went to hospitals. The sum of £1,000 was sent to Guy's and £552 10s to the London Hospital and another £100 to its Poor Fund (23 December), but smaller donations of £262 10s

79 *JA Report* 1905, p. 146, 1906 p. 126, 1912 p. 13, 1907 p. 97.
80 *JA Report* 1907, p. 14.
81 *Daily Graphic* 8 November 1910.
82 RAL VI/16/2 31 December 1903 and 29 December 1905.

and £210 went to the Metropolitan Hospital and Mount Vernon Hospital, while Queen Charlotte's Hospital, St Mary's Hospital and the Royal Dental Hospital each received £105 and University College Hospital and the Throat Hospital £100 each. Just as the Veterans Relief Fund had been granted £1,050 (10 January), so another military hospital charity did well. The King Edward Hospital for Officers received £300 (22 January) and another £500 (23 April). Natty's *alma mater*, Cambridge University, was given £1,500 and King's College gifts of £50 and £300. Charities connected to orphanages also attracted Natty's attention, the Reedham Orphanage (25 March) receiving £200 and the British Orphan Fund and the Orphan Working School equal amounts of cash. The provision of School Meals elicited two gifts of £500 (2 January) and (14 October). Among these charitable donations was a gift of £500 to the Liberal Unionists and £200 to the London Municipal Society (9 May), the political arm of the Conservative party in London. Gifts to rabbis, in many cases for their congregants, were counterbalanced by sums despatched to clergymen, and there were small grants in the hundreds of pounds for group outings and Christmas dinners. The more universally minded Salvation Army was the recipient of larger donations with £52 10s going to it (9 May) and £500 (15 June) and £200 (23 December) being sent to its head, General Booth. Smaller donations were gifted to the Charity Organization Society and its individual branches.

Among Jewish charities, the biggest recipients of assistance from the Rothschilds in 1908 were the Jewish Board of Guardians, the Alliance Israélite Universelle, the Anglo-Jewish Association and the United Synagogue. While the Alliance received two donations of £350 (14 January and 30 December), the United Synagogue Rabbis' Fund was granted £250, £100 went to the Visitation Fund and £200 to Prisoners Care; in addition, £500 went to its Jewish Religious Education Board and £223 12s to the Great Synagogue and £80 6s 6d. to the Central Synagogue. Payments of £476 5s. 0d. (7 July), of £80 and of £450 were made to the AJA. By far the largest recipient of aid was the Jewish Board of Guardians for the Relief of the Jewish Poor, of which Leopold was now treasurer, with gifts of £1,000 (25 June) and £400 (1 September). Other Jewish charities supported by the Rothschilds included the £150 granted to the Home for Aged Jews, £145 5s. (2 April) to the Jews Emigration Society, and the £130 to the Jews Soup Kitchen. Gifts of £100 each were allocated to the Hayes Industrial School

(7 March), the Jews Free School (6 February), the Jews Aged & Needy Society (5 March) and the Education Aid Society (1 June). Jewish charities in Palestine fared less well, the Blind Institute Jerusalem receiving £10 (21 April) and the AJA for the Jaffa Hospital £10 (22 June).[83]

While it is true that Natty kick-started the activity of the Industrial Dwellings Company and retained a supervisory role, the expansion of this philanthropic housing association was due more to the efforts of Nathan Joseph, an architect and key figure in the Russo-Jewish Committee. Lord Rothschild's chief focus of interest remained the Jews' Free School. Large sums of money poured from the Rothschild coffers into the Jewish Board of Guardians and the Jews' Temporary Shelter, but while Natty was involved in key decisions involving these institutions, much of the day-to-day work was delegated to his brother Leo. Outside the Jewish sphere, Natty's main area of interest was the King's Fund and the voluntary London hospitals and Natty devoted considerable time to them and was a heavy contributor to their funds, but whereas he gave the lead for Jewish communal fund-raising he was reluctant to do much arm-twisting elsewhere.

83   RAL VI/16/4 Charity Ledger accounts for 1908.

8

NATTY BECOMES A PUBLIC FIGURE: THE BUDGET CONTROVERSY

Hitherto, Natty had been well-known to a limited audience: the political elite, the City and the Jewish world. As we have seen, Natty, from an early age, imbibed the orthodox Liberal party views on Free Trade and budgetary retrenchment which would result in commerce flourishing between nations, harmonious international relations and general prosperity. After becoming a peer, he later changed his party allegiance and became a Liberal Unionist supporter because of his opposition to Home Rule for Ireland. Once the Liberals had gained a sweeping majority in the 1906 general election, they remained popular, winning two more elections in a row and gradually embarking on a welfare programme, including the provision of free school meals, medical inspection of children and school clinics, old age pensions, health and unemployment insurance and the massive restructuring of the nation's system of taxation.

Since chairing a departmental Committee in 1896–8 which opposed the state-aided provision of old age pensions, Natty had come to regard state-sponsored social services as anathema. To provide the funds for social reform, in 1909, Lloyd George was forced to introduce a radical Budget which tapped new sources of taxation. As the spokesman for City opinion, Natty took the

223

lead in denouncing the licensing fee, supertax and land taxation, inviting the scorn and derision of Lloyd George. It was this combination of social reform and progressive budgets which incensed Natty. From this clash with Lloyd George, he emerged as a public figure but as a political dinosaur with a somewhat damaged reputation.

In July 1896, Lord Rothschild was appointed chairman of a departmental Committee of experts on old age pensions. Under his leadership, the Committee construed its terms of reference as precluding 'consideration of any scheme involving compulsory insurance, or any non-contributory scheme limited to a portion of the working population'. The Committee was strongly opposed to encouraging the formation of a 'compulsory unoccupied class' among the aged, placing more trust in sponsoring 'thrift and self-reliance' among the working class. It concluded that:

> The people thus in a position to require assistance must, in any case, form but a small proportion of the industrial population, and even of this section – which can hardly be estimated at more than a third – only a small proportion of those above 65 years of age who now appear as inmates of the workhouse or infirmary would, in any system of State-aided pensions, be able to support themselves independently. We can hardly, for the benefit of so limited a section of the community, recommend the Government to establish a pension scheme which must be extremely difficult and costly to administer ...

Natty believed in encouraging the affluent to provide private philanthropy for those in need – he was himself a model landowner and generous in his charitable donations – and rejected the expansion of state provision. Not surprisingly, when the Committee reported two years later, it was unable to recommend any scheme of old age pensions as feasible.[1]

In 1906, a new Liberal administration was elected with a sizeable group of members joining with Labour Party M.P.s to espouse a radical social reform agenda, causing Natty to share his concerns with his cousins across the Channel. His opposition to state provision for the poor had hardened and he denounced these schemes as smacking of socialism. On 22 January 1906, Natty wrote to his French cousins that

---

1   Pat Thane, *Old Age in English History: Past Experiences, Present Issues* (Oxford, 2000), pp. 200–4. *Report of the Committee on Old Age Pensions* P. P. XLV (1898), pp. 1–16.

The Elections have all gone one way [against the Conservatives] although the number of Labour members in the new Parliament is small their influence will be great & they ask for a good many things, a large & comprehensive scheme of old age pensions, and a square meal once a day for every child in school, reversal of the Taff Vale decision ... so we shall have a lively time. Their best men say 'We are not Socialists or Anarchists who want to destroy wealth to be used for the benefit of all.'

A couple of months later, he was assuring his cousins that our government has 'given us any amount of Radical measures for Parliament to digest, and I hope for the House of Lords either to alter considerably or to throw out', so that Natty, from the first, had a mindset which contemplated confrontation with the House of Commons.

Early in 1906, the Chancellor of the Exchequer, Herbert Asquith, had appointed a Select Committee under the chairmanship of Sir Charles Dilke M.P. to inquire into the related problems of the differentiation and gradu-ation of the income tax. 'The Chairman of the Inland Revenue [Sir Henry Primrose] gave his evidence yesterday', Natty advised his cousins,

and I expect Ultra Radicals must have been very disappointed. They told him the graduation they would like to impose, and he demonstrated to them ... that this graduation would only bring in about £3,500,000, or about a tenth of the sum the Labour Members want to provide them with Old Age Pensions, and one square meal a day for each of the children; but for all that, I suppose, next year we shall see some form of graduated income tax introduced, if only to satisfy the vanity of the Radical Chancellor of the Exchequer for the time being.[2]

Designating Asquith as a radical was hardly an accurate description, but Natty's analysis of the overall political situation was perceptive and he was right to discern that the Chancellor wanted to increase the taxation of the wealthier classes to pay for old age pensions. When Sir Charles Dilke, its chairman and the leader of a Radical group of M.P.s, drew up a report for the Select Committee on Income Tax advocating the implementation of a graduated tax, his report was rejected in part because two of his supporters on the Committee were absent during the vote. Sir Thomas Whittaker, a

2   RAL X1/130A/O Natty London to his cousins Paris 22 January 1906 and 2 and 22 May 1906.

fellow Liberal M.P. and head of a large insurance company, was persuaded by Reginald McKenna, the Financial Secretary to the Treasury, to draw up an opposing report, presenting the case against the steeper taxation of high incomes. Dilke and his supporters on the Committee, especially Samuel Evans and McCrae, fought back, determined to strengthen the draft report furnished by Whittaker. On some points they were successful, on others they were forced to compromise, on others still the issue was left uncertain.

Consequently, because of the constant cross-voting in the Committee, the report contained a number of startling inconsistencies. Dilke and those members of the Committee who shared his convictions did not object to the statement interpolated in the main body of the report, that a supertax should only be levied in an emergency. Yet the summary of conclusions at the end of the report contained the statement that a supertax was practicable. According to the predilections of the reader, either statement could be taken as the considered opinion of the Committee. Until paragraph 24 was reached, it appeared that the Committee was against calling for the declaration of total incomes, except in the event of a supertax being levied on incomes of over £5,000. Then came confusion: Evans introduced an amendment recommending a universal declaration of total incomes which was carried by the chairman's casting vote. To limit its application, McKenna hastily tacked on a rider, stipulating that the compulsory declaration of income should only apply to the total income on which the recipient himself paid tax; two Liberals, Rose and Trevelyan, now voted for McKenna's proviso and swung the balance of opinion in the Committee on to his side. Just at this point McKenna had to leave the Committee to attend to some business in the Commons; and the words on which a system of graduation and differentiation could be based were added to this qualifying clause. In vain did McKenna and Whittaker urge Dilke to strike out this offending paragraph, so that the report could be interpreted in the sense they wanted. Hence, this crucial passage in the report could be taken as implying that the Committee favoured a scheme for a graduated income tax, together with a compulsory declaration of incomes. On the other hand, when this section put in a final appearance in the summary of conclusions, all reference to this being needed to secure a graduated income tax was omitted, thus favouring McKenna's narrower interpretation.[3] Bernard Mallet of the Board of Inland Revenue admirably summed up the effect of the report in a private letter to Dilke. He declared that, 'on the whole you have gained your points and nothing feasible has been shut out of the of the recommendations of the Select Committee, and nothing too urgently recommended even as regards differentiation, which now stands in the way of the more important object of graduation. Everything now depends on the Chancellor of the Exchequer and the House of Commons. He can do what he likes with the findings of the Committee.'[4]

Natty reported to his French cousins that

the Radicals & Socialists clamour for old age pensions, they affirm that the Chancellor of the Exchequer will increase the death duties by 33%, they now bring in 16 Million £ which would mean an additional £5½ Million and millionaires who now pay 8% would pay 10¼ % and also levy a surtax of 5% on all incomes above a certain amount, which it is calculated will bring in another 3 or 4 Million £. I very much doubt these surmises proving correct as when once socialistic appetite is whetted there is no knowing where they would stop and no one must be better aware of this than the Prime Minister [Sir Henry Campbell-Bannerman] & Mr Asquith.[5]

In fact, Asquith had prepared a rather radical Budget for 1907 but the Cabinet rejected half his scheme, making the Budget appear as a rather innocuous affair. Originally, the Budget consisted of three important features that prepared the way for a wholesale reconstruction of the financial system. There was to be a differentiation of the income tax to help those earning less than £2,000 per annum. If a taxpayer's yearly income fell below this limit, the standard rate of tax was reduced from a shilling in the pound to nine pence. In this way, Asquith distinguished between the tax-paying capacity of a man drawing income from his own labour and those with unearned income derived from land or other investments.

3   Treasury Papers, Reginald McKenna to Herbert Asquith 17 December 1906. BL, Dilke Papers Add. MS. 4391, Thomas Whittaker to Dilke 25 November 1906. Sir Thomas Whittaker M.P., 'The New Income Tax Basis', *Financial Review of Reviews* January 1907, *Daily News* 30 November 1906.
4   BL, Dilke Papers Add. MS.43919, Bernard Mallet to Dilke 1 December 1906.
5   RAL X1/130A/1A Natty London to his cousins Paris 12 April 1907.

Henceforth, it would also be a much simpler matter for a Chancellor to increase the income tax should he need additional revenue. Then there was to be a supertax on all incomes above £4,000 per annum; the supertax would amount to 1d on all incomes from £4,000–7,000, of 2d from £7,000–10,000 and of 3d for incomes above that level.[6] This part of the Budget was dropped after opposition within the Cabinet. Finally, measures were introduced to prevent the interception of imperial taxes by the local authorities. Revenues totalling about £10 million passed straight to the use of the local authorities. Under these conditions, the proceeds of a revision of the licence duties and the taxation of motor cars would have been diverted to local purposes. Asquith resumed Treasury control of these sources of revenue, while ensuring that the local authorities received an equivalent sum from the Exchequer.[7] The 1907 Budget, in its draft form, bore all the indications of a carefully shaped plan to open up additional sources of revenue to the state for financing social reform.

Everything points to the fact that responsibility for rejecting the supertax rested on the Cabinet, and that there was no flinching on Asquith's part. He appears to have rejected the negative opinions of McKenna and Sir Henry Primrose, who pleaded with him to concentrate on the differentiation of the income tax rather than on the imposition of a supertax. Primrose asserted that 'This cod. be an opening of your door by the handle and hinges – To use a supertax cod. be to apply dynamite as a means of opening, with much danger of destruction in various directions.' His close Cabinet colleague, R. B. Haldane, recounted in his autobiography that 'Asquith was doing good work. He had decided, overruling some of his advisers at the Exchequer on the graduation of the income tax and on a better distribution of the burden of taxation, and this was being carried out.' Moreover, the connection between a favourable report from the Select Committee and the rapidity with which a pensions scheme could be introduced was firmly planted in Asquith's mind.[8] Various papers

6   Treasury Papers, undated memorandum on the proposed changes in the 1907 Budget as regards income tax; a Cabinet Paper signed by W. B[lain] 27 February 1907; Stephen Koss, *Asquith* (London, 1976), p. 80.

7   *Daily News* 19 April 1907. Bruce K. Murray, *The People's Budget 1909/10: Lloyd George and Liberal Politics* (Oxford: 1980), pp. 45–6.

8   R. B. Haldane, *Autobiography* (London, 1929), p. 216. Francis Herbert Stead, *How Old Age*

were submitted by Asquith to the Cabinet on the incidence of taxation in the United Kingdom and on the conflicting estimates of the number of taxpayers of different classes and their aggregate incomes, which had been prepared by Sir Henry Primrose and Mr Chiozza Money, the latter a radical Liberal M.P.[9] More importantly, Asquith presented the Cabinet with a cogently argued paper by William Blain, a top Treasury official, summarizing the case for a supertax. There is little doubt that Asquith wanted the Cabinet to reach a favourable decision. The paper opened by stating that the poorest classes contributed an excessive share of revenue to the state, as the indirect taxes, taxes on the articles of consumption, formed such a large proportion of the whole.

> The present Government have recognized the pressing need for social reforms which must entail heavy additional expenditure. No one expects that the reductions of existing expenditure will provide the necessary means. A good deal has already been done, and more perhaps may be possible, in the way of reduction on Army and Navy votes. But the automatic growth of the Civil Services, and the constant extension of their scope are only too likely to absorb the bulk of these savings.

The paper ended by asserting that there was no other country in which so large a proportion of the total national income took the shape of big incomes in the hands of the few. It would take a few years for machinery to be built up for the levying of a supertax. Afterwards, the Department could levy a higher rate of taxation for incomes above £5,000 and for lower incomes as well, if it so wished, so that a scientific graduation throughout the scale of incomes could be imposed.[10]

If anything it was, in fact, Asquith who forced Lloyd George to accept the necessity of a large-scale reconstruction of the national finances. In his 1908 May Budget, which was to be his final one as he had become Prime Minister in April, Asquith reduced the sugar duty from 4/2d. to 1/10d. per

---

Pensions Began To Be (London: n.d.), p. 213.

9   Treasury Papers, Cabinet Papers: memoranda by Chiozza Money M.P on Income Tax with an estimate of the yield graduated from 1d to 1/6d by 1/2d stages together with Notes on the Incidence of Taxation in the United Kingdom, both March 1907; and by Primrose giving an estimate of the number of income tax payers together with their annual incomes arranged in classes March 1907.

10 Treasury Papers, Cabinet Paper signed W. B[lain] 26 February 1907 pp. 1, 2, 5.

hundredweight, thus giving away an annual income of £3.4 million. The money had originally been earmarked for financing part of the cost of old age pensions; only about £1.24 million had been put aside for meeting the cost of old age pensions, and after various concessions had been made in the House, the estimated cost of the scheme had risen from £7–£8 million. Having listened to his criticism of the 1908 Budget, Lloyd George, the new Chancellor of the Exchequer, confessed to Austen Chamberlain: 'I agreed with a good deal of what you said – with more perhaps than you would think and with more than I can say. I wanted to keep the sugar duty on and use it for pensions.'[11] At the same time, the cost of expenditure on battle-ships rose steeply because of the German naval challenge; the worsening of the economic situation at the end of 1907 meant shrinking revenue – all factors that pointed to the necessity for a major reconstruction of the nation's finances in the 1909 Budget.[12] Haldane, a close political ally of Asquith's, assumed that he shared his view that

> In this condition of things, my suggestion is one over which you have already thought much – that we should take our stand on the facts and proclaim a policy of taking, mainly by direct taxation, such toll from the increase and growth of this wealth as will enable us to provide for (1) the increasing cost of Social Reform; (2) National Defence, and also (3) to have a margin in aid of the Sinking Fund.[13]

Whereas the Conservatives were reluctant to reject bills sponsored by the Labour party, such as the Trade Disputes Bill, they were contemptuous of the Liberal administration's measures and tried to emasculate them in the Commons. As George Wyndham told Arthur Balfour, the Tory party leader and a friend of Natty's, 'The root of the matter is that no second Chamber, however composed, would pass the kind of Bill that a modern Liberal Government brings in, i.e. a Bill to please one relatively small minority – e.g. Licensing Bill, which is passed through the House of Commons by other log-rolling minorities expectant of their turn. If the Liberal Party cannot exist without that, then either there can be no Liberal

---

11   Austen Chamberlain, *Politics from Inside* (London, 1936), p. 109.
12   Murray, *The People's Budget*, pp. 48–9.
13   Bod. Lib., Asquith Papers, General Correspondence 1908, memorandum of Haldane to Asquith 9 August 1908 ff.166, 167.

Party, or no Second Chamber; and if the Liberal Party drive the country into that choice, the country will ... prefer a Second Chamber to the Liberal Party.' The more Balfour drastically amended Government measures in the Commons, the bolder the House of Lords became, despatching the Education Bill, the Small Landholders (Scotland) Bill and the Land Values (Scotland) Bill.[14] Despite Natty's friendship with Balfour, he was as yet, in 1906 and 1907, playing a role outside the Opposition's inner counsels.

The response of the Liberal government to this intransigence, under its ailing Prime Minister, Campbell-Bannerman, was feeble. Natty told his cousins on 24 May 1907 that:

> there is no change in the political situation at present and there is a considerable amount of uncertainty about Sir Henry Campbell-Bannerman's future policy. Will he go in for Home Rule pure and simple and alienate a large number of his party and run the chance of losing a good many of his colleagues or is he going to introduce a ... Land Bill which he would force through the House of Commons, if possible and then rely on the Lords throwing it out when he would appeal to the country against the upper Chamber [?]. This political uncertainty hangs like an ugly nightmare over the Stock Exchange ...

A month later, Natty was of the opinion that the government was

> indulging in a platonic discussion this week: the Prime Minister brings in a resolution for limiting the power of the House of Lords. Naturally this resolution is opposed by Mr Balfour and, it will not surprise you to hear, it does not meet with the approval of any portion of the Liberal majority, & there are endless amendments moved from the Liberal & Radical side. The resolution is only firing a blank cartridge & is probably made to influence the next General Election ... but that event is probably a long way further off than most people expect.

This observation was a misreading of the political atmosphere which, in 1908, was growing more acrimonious, as the exchanges on each side intensified when the Licensing Bill was made the central plank of the government's programme. One factor behind Natty's failure to grasp the seriousness of the situation was the ailing Campbell-Bannerman's lacklustre

14 Murray, *The People's Budget*, pp. 56–8.

performance in this debate and for the rest of the 1907 session. 'The long talked of political debate took place in the House of Commons yesterday', Natty declared, 'and it would be difficult to find a just word to describe the Prime Minister's performance, this was a dress rehearsal about a great constitutional question and never, within the memory of living man has a Prime Minister so fumbled and mumbled and ultimately been obliged to read his speech from notes which had got mingled up'. A day later, Leopold advised his cousins that Natty had gone to Tring to speak at a local political demonstration in favour of Walter and that 'the debate on the resolution condemning the House of Lords still goes on, but I cannot say the speeches have been very conclusive on the side of the Government, mostly violent abuse and no logical arguments, now they say there will be no dissolution until 1909, so there will be plenty of time for many things to happen and much to be said before then'.[15]

When the Licensing Bill was introduced by the Liberal administration on 27 February 1908, Natty moved from the periphery to becoming a central player in national politics. Hitherto, he had been known as the pre-eminent spokesman for Anglo-Jewry and as a leader of City opinion, both much more limited roles. The measure was introduced by the government to reduce the excessive drunkenness which was then prevalent. The provisions for a time limit and the transfer of the monopoly value of the public house licence to the state formed the backbone of the Licensing Bill. Under the scheme outlined by Asquith, the number of on-licences were to be reduced on a uniform scale based on the ratio between the number of licences and the density of population over a period of fourteen years; it was the government's intention to reduce the number of such licences by a third by the end of this period; and then to transfer the monopoly value of these licences to the state. During the fourteen-year period, compensation would be payable to former licence-holders from a special fund. Asquith suggested that a difficulty emerged in the case of the

> tied house because ... the rent ... which is exacted by the brewer or distiller from the tenant ... of the tied house, is a rent which in the majority of cases, at any rate, bears no relation whatsoever to the actual value of

15   RAL XI/130A/1A Natty London to his cousins Paris 24 May 1907; same to same 24 and 25 June 1907; and Leo to his cousins 26 June 1907.

the premises. Where the brewer comes in and makes his profit is in his invoicing his goods – the only goods which this tenant, sitting, as it appears, at a very moderate rent, is allowed to dispose of – at a far higher price than the same class of goods ... supplied to the tenant of a free house.

The Kennedy judgment was dismissed as fallacious by Asquith because it added between fifty and one hundred per cent to the compensation payable, by taking into account not the profit made by the trade retailer but the profit made by the brewer in regard to the drink which he supplied to the house. The Bill set out to claw back from the brewers this somewhat over-generous compensation, thus unleashing a political and financial backlash ignited by Natty.[16] To understand Natty's reservations and anxiety about the impact of the Licensing Bill, it is necessary to examine the changes in the economic structure of the brewing industry and assess how far these had repercussions on its organization and political outlook. The period 1880–1914 saw the concentration of the brewing industry in ever larger units, so that, by 1910, 45 per cent of the output was in the hands of 47 companies and the 10 largest accounted for a quarter of the total production. Just as there was a concentration of economic power within the brewing industry, so there was a concentration of power within its attendant organizations, the Burton, London and Country Brewers, who merged to form the Brewers' Society in 1904. The increasing concentration of the industry in turn produced a great competition for retail outlets and a scramble for licensed houses. By the end of the nineteenth century, it was estimated that 75 per cent of the public houses in England and Wales were tied. The London companies, however, entered the market last and between 1895 and 1902 purchased an average of 500 houses per annum. Finally, the rush to buy licensed premises had led to the large-scale flotation of public companies in the brewing industry in the last decades of the nineteenth century and a proliferation in the number of shareholders.[17]

Consequently, far from vertical integration solving the difficulties of the brewing industry, it actually added to them, and if nothing else, the lack of entrepreneurial skill within the industry was starkly exposed. What was

16 Murray, *The People's Budget*, pp. 107–8; *Hansard* 27 February 1908 cols 73–87.
17 John Baxter, *The Organization of the Brewing Industry*, London University PhD Thesis 1945. D. M. Knox, 'The Development of the Tied House System in London', Oxford Economic Papers X 1958 pp. 66–83.

required by an industry with a product which had declining sales was not more integration, but a diversification of production. Competition between the breweries for public houses had forced up their price considerably but by 1903, public house values had fallen heavily and the breweries, especially in London, had to depreciate the value of such property on their books. The London brewers in particular, who were the leaders in their trade, were extremely sensitive to any legislation which threatened to send brewery shares tumbling.[18]

From the first, the Rothschild brothers were extremely hostile to the Licensing Bill, fearing that the implementation of such a measure, which they deemed confiscatory, would cause a collapse in the value of brewery shares with turbulence in the financial markets, and they felt confident that the House of Lords would reject it. Leopold informed his cousins that

> the Government proposal is for all licences to be terminated within a certain number of years after which time the value of the licences will revert to the government, this is virtually nothing but confiscation. The leading Brewery Companies hold most of the public houses and have issued debentures at a comparatively low rate of interest to the public, these have always been considered an excellent security ... Three of the oldest brewery companies in London have a capital of £$1^1/_2$ Million and it is said that their licensed houses stand in their books as being worth £100 Million. Debentures and mortgages on breweries are worth £200 Million. If the Government bill becomes law it would entail a loss from 30 to 50%, they say the Opposition will fight the bill tooth and nail and that the Lords will throw it out.[19]

Natty was equally vehement about the proposed licensing legislation, stating that 'there is a feeling that these confiscatory measures will never pass and the by-elections which have taken place of late must strengthen the hands of the House of Lords, if their Lordships should be called upon to throw out these bills'. Again, a few weeks later, Natty was certain that 'The opposition to the Licensing Bill increases with every day. I think there is no doubt that we shall win [the by-election at] Peckham tomorrow.'[20]

18   Knox, 'The Development of the Tied House System in London'.
19   RAL X1/130A/2 Leo London to cousins Paris 29 January 1908.
20   RAL X1/130A/2 Natty London to his cousins Paris 4 March 1908 and same to same 23 March 1908.

Lord Rothschild opened his campaign against the Bill with a speech delivered to a crowded meeting of brewery debenture-holders in the City on 18 March 1908; a thousand persons at least were unable to gain admission either to this meeting or to an overflow meeting. Natty insisted that the question was a larger one than the interests of the 100,000 debenture-holders, as there was hardly an insurance company which was not a holder of brewery debenture shares and possibly some preference shares. If the Bill were passed, it would not only be the holders of shares in insurance companies who would suffer, but 'the 3,000,000 ordinary policy-holders in those companies, and no doubt ten times as many in the industrial branch ... He believed that if a Bill of this kind were to pass it would be followed by others [cries of hear, hear]. There were various classes of property which were distasteful to the opponents of licensed premises, and the same system adopted in dealing with them might be expected to be adopted in either cases.' Another speaker claimed that they must look to the House of Lords for protection, while, at the same time, they had to convince the Upper House that the country was behind them. A motion was passed condemning the Licensing Bill as confiscating property acquired with the sanction of the state and the protection of the law.[21] So incensed was the normally placid Asquith by this speech that he refused an invitation to Tring from Natty, exclaiming that 'I never allow political differences to interfere with personal & social relations. But ...' On 4 May, Asquith, who had now become Prime Minister, warned that Lloyd George would impose licensing duties if the Bill failed to pass, but his warning seemed to fall on deaf ears.[22]

The National Trade Defence Association directed operations against the Bill in the first phases of the campaign, working in close harmony with the Conservative leaders. The sale of so many retail outlets to the brewery companies had been followed by greater co-ordination between the publicans and brewers through the setting up of this body, though the publicans depended upon brewers for extraordinary expenditure, such as this campaign. Soon after the publication of the legislation, the association announced its strenuous opposition to it, noting that no compromise was possible; moreover,

21 *Brewers Journal* 15 April 1908; *The Times* 19 March 1908.
22 RAL 000/848/37 Herbert Asquith to Natty 20 March 1908; *Daily News* 5 May 1908.

'the Trade' bitterly denounced it as a socialistic measure which, 'if carried out, must eventually affect the whole basis of property holding in this country'.[23] This latter note was kept as a constant refrain in the contest. Without much delay, the brewers' group in the Commons passed similar motions; and when the Conservative party leaders established an Anti-Licensing Committee to watch over the progress of the Bill in the Commons, it followed suit and agreed not to accept the time limit on principle. Of the fifteen brewers sitting as M.P.s in the 1906 Parliament, only one was a Liberal, so that there were not enough individuals to act as a moderating influence.[24] One incident well illustrates the tie-up between 'the Trade' and the Conservative party. When the Brewers' Society booked the Albert Hall for a mass protest meeting against the measure, in order to obtain the services of Balfour as a speaker, it had ostensibly to be organized by the Conservative Central Office; even so, the arrangements for tickets were made jointly by the National Trade Defence Association and Central Office.[25]

Nor should the effectiveness of 'the Trade's' campaign be exaggerated. True, half a million people attended the Hyde Park demonstration against the Bill in September; yet the size of the crowd was not so impressive, as the Suffragettes, with their limited financial resources, had attracted just as large a crowd earlier in the year. In fact, the whole proceedings were elaborately organized, with special trains laid on for demonstrators intending to gather in London, since the leaders of the Licensed Victuallers Association believed that a small turn-out would be disastrous. Despite the employment of canvassers, only 255,000 persons signed the London publicans' petition calling on the Lords to reject the Bill, as the chairman admitted that there was no great eagerness for it on the part of the public.[26]

The primary cause of the Liberal reversals at the by-elections was the advent of a cyclical depression in trade and the activities of 'the Trade'

---

23 *Brewers Journal* 15 March 1908.
24 *Daily News* 5 March, 1, 2 and 30 April 1908; *Brewers Journal* 15 May 1908.
25 *Brewers Journal* 15 March 1908. Licensed Victuallers National Defence League: Minutes of the Council 19 May 1908. Licensed Victuallers Central Protection Society: Minutes of the Council 21 May 1908 and of the Executive, 2 June 1908.
26 *Daily News* 28 September 1908. Sydney O. Nevile, *Seventy Rolling Years* (London, 1958), p. 58; National Victuallers Central Protection Society: minutes of Executive 30 June, 23 September and 28 October 1908.

and a number of other pressure groups, including the Coal Consumers' League. Rejoicing at the Conservatives' sweeping victory at the Peckham by-election, by nearly 2,500 votes, Natty observed that:

> No doubt a combination of circumstances helped to swell the Unionist majority. The Licensing Bill is deservedly most unpopular with all classes; not only will it destroy the Brewing Trade and restrict the comfort and amusements of the public, but it was a measure which threatened all kinds of property and might have inflicted severe harm in banking & financial circles, if the principle embodied in this measure had once been conceded & everything & everybody might be expropriated for the so-called benefit of the State & without any compensation ... there is a large colony of workers in the Gas Co[mpan]y at Peckham & as they all share the profits with the Company, they viewed with dismay any increase in the price of coal. There were subsidiary questions which entered the contest ... [The government] may drop the Bill, & this will not be to their credit. If they elect to go on with the Bill, & force it through the Commons, the Lords will reject it & it will become the most popular & powerful body in the country.[27]

At any rate, the destruction of the Bill in the House of Lords was due not so much to the influence of 'the Trade' as the potency of the City interests which held a large stake in the brewing industry. The floating of public companies by the big breweries transformed their whole ownership structure. The peers were interested in the brewery companies, both as lenders of capital and as ordinary shareholders. Above all, Lord Rothschild and other conservative financiers argued that extreme legislation, such as the Licensing Bill, was one of the factors that had been responsible for depressing of the money market. Indeed, the large institutional investors, the banks and insurance companies, were apprehensive about the way in which the situation was shaping, so that not only did they decline to invest money on the security of licensed property, but they began to call in existing mortgages, pending a settlement on which reliance could be placed.[28] Even if peers were not involved as lenders of capital to breweries on an extensive scale, it was likely that they held some brewery shares. The Home Secretary,

27 RAL XI/130A/2 Natty London to cousins Paris 25 March 1908.
28 *Daily News* 9 October 1907 and 14 November 1908.

Herbert Gladstone, reckoned that there were no less than 600,000 investors in brewery shares, of whom 100,000 were debenture holders.[29] Natty remarked that the new Prime Minister Asquith 'will give way a great deal on the licensing question, but he cannot make sufficient concessions to make the bill acceptable to those who hold brewery debentures and their name is legion'. The widespread ramifications of the ownership of brewery shares can be seen in the conduct of the Representative Church Congress, an Anglican body which, despite the stand of the Bishops in favour of temperance reform, refused to endorse government licensing legislation.[30]

At a meeting in September 1908 to discuss the Conservative peers' tactics in the House of Lords,

> Cromer wanted strong action on Old Age Pensions ... Jem [Salisbury] wanted a guerrilla warfare with H of C by inserting amendments ... though they might be breaches of privilege; the rest of us were for one or two amendments and insisting on them ... Finally, all our amendments were literally kicked out by the Commons ... I say with Jem 'Don't fight at all or stick to it, and above all don't let a lot of weary H of Cmen ... dictate to us.[31]

By 24 June, *The Times* political correspondent predicted that 'when the Licensing Bill is sent to the House of Lords in the autumn, the second reading of the Bill will be rejected, after a full dress debate'. In the autumn of 1908, Natty remarked, in the presence of a journalist, that 150 or 160 peers would vote against the second reading of the Bill, maybe 400. 'Shortly afterwards the statement was published that 150 or 160 peers had intimated that they were in favour of the Bill's rejection, and that the Opposition in the House of Lords would be concentrated under the leadership of Lord Rothschild.' Although Natty denied that a syndicate of financiers had been active behind the scenes, the press picked up the story and claimed that '160 peers had signed a suspiciously secret memorial' to throw out the Bill. Of these pledged peers, 130 were said to be interested in the liquor trade, either as trustees or as part of their property, quite apart from the peers who

29   BL, Viscount Gladstone Papers, Add. MS. 46,092 ff.19. memorandum c. 1907.
30   RAL XI/130A/2 Natty London to cousins Paris 9 April 1908.
31   Andrew Adonis, *Making Aristocracy Work. The Peerage and the Political System in England 1884–1914* (Oxford, 1993), p. 142.

were debenture-holders. Earl Carrington, a member of the government, also gave credence to this rumour in his diary on 13 November 1908. After a groundswell of opinion among the Tory peers against the Bill, Earl Waldegrave, the Conservative whip, issued an agenda in favour of the Bill's rejection.[32] It is interesting to note that after a visit to Natty's country house, Asquith told his chief whip Jack Pease, as early as 16 November 1908, in regard to the Licensing Bill 'Oh they (Peers) will reject it.' A meeting of Conservative peers was called for 24 November at Lansdowne House, when 'with the exception of some 8 or 10 peers, the whole body present agreed to support Lord Lansdowne in refusing to read the Bill a second time', Natty informed his cousins.[33] C. F. G. Masterman told Lloyd George in 1909 that 'I have heard on good authority that when Lord Lansdowne convened that meeting at Lansdowne House he meant to recommend [a] decimating amendment but Lord Rothschild and Co bolted and forced him to rejection.' This is somewhat unlikely, as Lord Lansdowne stated at the meeting that if the House of Lords tried to amend the Bill, it would leave the erroneous assumption that they supported it in principle.

As we have indicated, many influential peers held brewery shares. They included Lord Rothschild with his holdings in Worthington, Watney, Combe Reid, and Truman Hanbury and Buxton. The Marquis of Lansdowne had shares in Bass and Watney which he held as a trustee, and Earl Waldegrave had invested in the Bristol Brewery. On 27 November 1908, the House of Lords refused the Bill a second reading by an overwhelming majority of 272–96.[34] From this welter of rumour and counter-rumour, Natty acquired a reputation in the press, not altogether fairly, as the leader of a cabal of financial purists, who would risk all in challenging government legislation they deemed to be confiscatory.

During the next few months, through the action of the Lords, the government was forced to include land and licence taxation in the Budget

32 *Daily News* 12 and 17 November 1908, and *The Times* 24 June and 26 November 1908. *British Temperance Advocate* December 1908. *Brewers Journal* 15 February 1915. Adonis, *Making Aristocracy Work*, p. 142.
33 Cameron Hazlehurst and Christine Woodland eds., *A Liberal Chronicle* (London, 1994), p. 87. RAL X1/130A/2 Natty London to cousins Paris 24 November 1908.
34 Lucy Masterman, *C. F. G. Masterman* (London, 1939), p. xx. *Alliance News* 26 November 1908. *British Temperance Advocate* January 1909.

to placate their supporters. Harold Spender, a journalist friend of Lloyd George, the new Chancellor of the Exchequer, had remarked before going on a trip to Germany with him in August 1908 to explore how their system of national insurance functioned: 'Driven back by the House of Lords on to the ground of finance, here they [the Liberal party] will accept battle. They will fight this fight through this year and the next.' In early December 1908, Asquith officially opened the campaign at the National Liberal Club. He asked the Liberal party to treat the Lords veto as the dominant issue in politics, exclaiming that Parliament would not be dissolved at the dictates of the Lords.

> One thing is certain, that the Budget of next year will stand on the very centre of our work. By it ... we shall be judged both in the estimation of the present and posterity ... it will and must raise again, in the acutest form, a controversy from which we do not shrink, and which we welcome, namely, whether the admitted and growing needs of a policy of social reform are to be provided by the finance of Free Trade, or by ... returning to the alluring and impoverishing fallacies of Protection?[35]

What we want to stress is that it was the policy of social reform on which the government had decided to embark that made necessary the reconstruction of the financial system; and that the demand for the heavy naval estimates to build more dreadnoughts to overcome the German challenge came after it had been agreed to stand up to the Lords on the issue of finance.[36] Lloyd George and Churchill returned to the theme of Asquith's speech in succeeding weeks when they addressed Liberal party rallies. Churchill advised Asquith confidentially on 26 December 1908 that 'I learn that Lansdowne in private utterly scouts the suggestion that the Lords will reject the Budget Bill.' Likewise, Lloyd George, in conversation with the Liberal journalist Riddell, 'ridiculed the rumour that the Peers would or could interfere with or reject the Budget.'[37]

35 Harold Spender, 'Next Year's Finance', *Contemporary Review* August 1908; *Daily News* 12 December 1908.
36 Murray, *The People's Budget*, pp. 127–30, and Cameron Hazelhurst and Christine Woodland, *A Liberal Chronicle*, pp. 105–6.
37 *Daily News* 22 December 1908 and 14 January 1909. Bod. Lib. Asquith Papers, General Correspondence Winston Churchill to Asquith 26 December 1908 ff.239. Lord Riddell, *More Pages from my Diary, 1909–14* (London, 1934), p. 10.

More pressure was put on the government to proceed with a thorough financial reconstruction when the Lord Mayor called a non-partisan meeting on 31 March 1908 at the Guildhall which was also sponsored by the Navy League to press for the immediate building of four more battleships. The keynote speaker at the meeting was Arthur Balfour, the leader of the Opposition. Lord Rothschild was chosen to move a resolution proclaiming that the City would 'support the Government in any financial arrangements that may be necessary to attain' a heavily augmented naval construction programme, though he qualified this by saying that 'a very strong Navy' did not imply 'an aggressive policy'. By so speaking out, Natty was inviting ridicule, as he did not suggest how the additional funds for such a programme were to be raised in the Budget.[38]

Why did the Lords reverse their position on the Budget? A large part of the answer lies in Natty's ability to mobilize City opinion against the Budget. His first reaction, on 3 May 1909, was measured but – as was to be expected – extremely hostile, as he was strongly opposed to financing social services by raising direct taxation or in principle to their expansion.

> Mr Lloyd George has to budget for a deficit of £16 Millions, so that everyone expected increased taxation of some kind ... provision [has] to be made for old age pensions and for the increased cost of the Navy, both of which two items of expenditure must increase considerably before next year. The fault that is found with the budget and the anger which it has created are due to the fact that the budget is a vindictive one, everyone expected an increase in the Income Tax and perhaps on the whole that increase is not as great as was expected, but the form of the surtax is most objectionable and introduces a dangerous principle of graduation, the alteration in Death Duties is a risky experiment ... One of the most dangerous features of the budget is the abolition of the old Sinking fund ... in future surplus revenue will go to create a fund which may and will be squandered in general benevolence for the benefit of the unemployed and others by the Prime Minister of the day ... there is a terrific outcry against an increase in the Tobacco and Spirit duties, as the prices of the poor man's luxury have immediately risen, but undoubtedly the worst of the budget is the proposed

38   *The Times* 1 April 1908.

taxation in connection with land, the proposals are socialistic and remarkably unfair.[39]

Rivy Grenfell, a scion of another banking family, adopted a contrary view, 'saying they have hit the rich from every corner, and so everyone is crying out. Personally I think there is a great deal to be be said in favour of these socialistic Budgets. Old Rothschild will not eat any less *foie gras* because he has to pay a little more for his motor cars.'[40]

Within a short while, Natty was playing a leading role in organizing a City petition to the government against the Budget. He claimed that

> at all political meetings particularly among agricultural labourers the feeling is as hostile as in Conservative circles ... however Liberals, Radicals and Unionists alike in the City, are unanimous in their condemnation of the budget as it stands and a petition is being drawn up which will require a good deal of skill and attention, a petition which will be largely signed and presented to Parliament. I do not suppose this petition will have much effect in the House of Commons, but it will have a great effect in the country.[41]

Anticipating the government's intention to introduce old age pensions and other benefits for the poor, Natty had long warned that the financial nervousness in markets 'of modern legislative bodies ... is very disagreeable but is perhaps the best cure for the socialistic tendencies.'[42]

Of all the pressure groups connected with the Conservative party, the City was the only one to spring into an immediate denunciation of the whole Budget. The City was overwhelmingly Conservative in opinion, though it contained a small band of government supporters and right wing Liberal Free Traders. The Budget annoyed all sections of the City. Within a week, Sir James MacKay, a Liberal Free Trader, after conferring with Lord Avebury and Sir Felix Schuster, approached the Governor of the Bank of England and asked him to arrange a non-party protest meeting against the Budget. As they were government bankers, the Governor thought that it would not be right *qua* bankers to identify themselves with the

39   RAL X1/130A/3 Natty London to his cousins Paris 3 May 1909.
40   David Kynaston, *The City of London* Vol. 2 (London, 1995), pp. 495–6.
41   RAL X1/130A/3 Natty London to his cousins Paris 10 May 1909.
42   RAL X1/130A/1A Natty London to his cousins Paris 14 March 1907.

movement, though they could take action in an individual capacity.[43] Lord Rothschild, Lord Revelstoke, Lord Avebury and other eminent figures from the banking and financial world, met to decide what form their protest should take. There was a divergence of opinion between those who merely wanted a signed petition against the Budget and those who favoured a public demonstration. For the time being, the Free Traders and Liberals held aloof from the idea of a protest meeting, despite the prompting of the City of London Conservative Association.[44] At any rate, a memorial was drawn up which was presented by Natty to Asquith, the Prime Minister, on 14 May 1909. Ominously, it had been signed by many of the leading Liberals in the City and it attacked the Budget as a whole. 'We view with alarm', it commenced,

> the increasing disproportion of the burden which is being placed on a numerically small class of the community. The great increase and gradu-ation in the death duties and income tax coupled with the new supertax will prove to be seriously injurious to the commerce and industries of the Country ... We feel that the prosperity of all classes has been greatly due to the fact that this country has afforded indisputable safety to Capital, and we should deeply regret if this conviction were in any way weakened.

In conclusion, the new taxes will tend 'to discourage private enterprise and thrift, thus in the long run diminishing employment and reducing wages.'[45]

With anger in the City mounting against the Budget, a large protest meeting was held on 23 June 1909 attended by all shades of opinion in the financial world, particularly those who had previously supported the debenture-holders' gathering. Lord Rothschild was in the chair. In his opening remarks, Natty asserted that:

> All the citizens of London (cheers) – are fully prepared to bear their share in increased taxation (hear, hear) – their full share and more than their share ... To my mind the whole principle [of the Finance Bill] is vicious. (Loud cheers.) Mr Lloyd George and his Majesty's Ministers

43 H. G. Hutchinson, *Life of Sir John Lubbock*, Vol. 2 (London, 1914), p. 255. Birmingham University, Austen Chamberlain Papers, Austen–Mary Chamberlain correspondence 7 May 1909.

44 *Daily Telegraph* 12, 15, 18 and 22 May 1909. *The Times* 11 and 18 May 1909.

45 Kynaston, *The City of London* Vol. II, p. 495. *The Times* 15 May 1909.

wish to establish the principles of Socialism and collectivism; and if they were to succeed in land, there is no reason why they should not succeed in every other kind of property (hear, hear).

He concluded with a warning to the government, telling his audience 'that if you in this hall ... are opposed to this measure, and if your friends in the country are equally opposed to it, if you all take care to make your voices heard, you will not appeal to Parliament in vain (Loud cheers)'.

Every facet of the Budget came under fire, but the speakers still followed the theme of the memorial and the resolution passed at the meeting said nothing fresh: 'this meeting while recognizing the necessity for increased taxation is of the opinion that the cumulative effect of the proposed heavy charges on both capital and income will be to discourage enterprise and thrift, and would prove seriously injurious to the commerce and industries of the country'.[46] Having formed the first branch of the Budget Protest League in any town, the City urged commercial and industrial centres throughout the country to take similar action. At first, it acted independently of the Conservative party in an attempt to capture the support of Liberals and Free Traders.[47] At a speech given the next day to the Land and Housing Reform Joint Committee, Lloyd George replied to the criticisms of the financiers, singling out Lord Rothschild for his choicest barbs. Each retort was a palpable hit on target. What was supposed to be a non-partisan meeting of businessmen and financiers, Lloyd George began, could not come up with one 'sound financial suggestion ... You have simply the same old drivel about Socialism, and, of course, "the thin edge of the wedge" ... which you can find any morning in the columns of the *Daily Mail*.' Then the Chancellor poured his scorn on Lord Rothschild, showing how he was the moving figure behind the opposition to the Licensing Bill and the Budget and how he was trying to set the political agenda on the question of naval re-armament.

> But, really, in all these things I think we are having too much of Lord Rothschild (Cheers). We are not to have temperance reform in this country. Why? Because Lord Rothschild has sent a circular to the Peers to say so (Laughter). We must have more Dreadnoughts. Why?

46 Kynaston, *The City of London* Vol. II, p. 496. *The Times* 24 June 1909.
47 *The Times* 29 June 1909, *Daily Mail* 15 July 1909 and *World* 22 June 1909.

Because Lord Rothschild said so at a meeting in the City (Laughter). We must not pay for them when we have them. Why? Because Lord Rothschild said so at another meeting (Laughter and cheers). You must not have estate duties and a supertax. Why because Lord Rothschild signed a protest on behalf of the bankers to say he would not stand it (Laughter). You must not have a tax on reversions. Why? Because Lord Rothschild, as chairman of an insurance company, has said it would not do (Laughter). You must not have a tax on undeveloped land. Why? Because Lord Rothschild is chairman of an industrial dwellings company (Laughter). You ought not to have Old Age Pensions. Why? Because Lord Rothschild was a member of a Committee that said it could not be done (Laughter). Now, really, I should like to know, is Lord Rothschild the dictator of this country? (Cheers) Are we really to have all ways of reform, financial and social, blocked simply by a notice board? 'No thoroughfare. By order of Nathaniel Rothschild'? (Laughter and cheers). There are countries where they have made it perfectly clear that they are not going to have their policy dictated merely by great financiers, and if this sort of thing goes on this country will join the rest of them. (Cheers)[48]

Natty, in a letter to his cousins, nonchalantly brushed aside these robust criticisms. Lloyd George 'indulged in a violent diatribe against myself which certainly does not hurt me but has made him appear ridiculous in the eyes of the press and has made a great many people very angry'. Rosebery cheered Natty, by writing that 'So violent and vulgar an attack only provokes reaction, more especially when it is levelled at the first of City men, and the most charitable and generous man in England.' But Niall Ferguson conceded that 'Natty's arguments against higher income taxes and death duties have not worn well', particularly when he agreed with the Chancellor that 'the burden of taxation should fall on the shoulders of those best able to bear it'.[49]

On 30 July 1909, Lloyd George, speaking in Limehouse, renewed his attack on the Conservative Party, this time justifying the land taxes and focusing his remarks on the dukes as greedy landlords. He ended his

48 *The Times* 25 June 1909.
49 RAL X1/130A/3 Natty London to his cousins Paris 25 June 1909; RAL 000/848/37 Lord Rosebery to Natty 27 June 1909. Ferguson, *The World's Banker*, p. 956.

oration by stating that 'I made up my mind that, in framing my Budget, no cupboard should be barer, no lot should be harder to bear. By that test, I challenge them to judge the Budget.' Instead of remaining silent, many members of the higher aristocracy unwisely took up Lloyd George's challenge. 'He only wished the Dukes had held their tongues', asserted an exasperated William Joynson-Hicks M.P.,

> every one of them ... It would have been a good deal better for the Conservative Party if, before the Budget was introduced, every Duke had been locked up until the Budget was over ... These men who are going about squealing and say they are going to reduce their subscriptions to charities and football clubs because they were being unduly taxed ought to be ashamed of themselves.

After Lloyd George's Limehouse speech, it was felt that the campaign had turned in favour of the Budget and the Liberal Budget League, guided by the journalistic skills of Sir Henry Norman, proved to be more effective than its Conservative counterpart.[50]

By the autumn of 1909, a consensus had developed in the Unionist party that the House of Lords should reject the Budget and by September Joseph Chamberlain and the Tariff Reformers were also set on this course of action. To unite the party, Balfour had to embrace the cause of Tariff Reform as an alternative to the Liberal Budget and as a means of combating unemployment. Speaking in the debate in the Lords, Natty proclaimed that 'the City fully recognizes that whatever expenditure may have been incurred, and whatever expenditure for whatever purposes may be necessary, it should bear its full share, and more than its full share, towards that expenditure'; and he made the familiar points about the potential damage to commerce and industry flowing from the Budget. He went on to complain that, while it was easy to obtain money for foreign investment because of the outflow of capital, it was 'difficult, if not impossible, to obtain those sums for even the best of English enterprise'. On 30 November 1909, the House of Lords rejected the Budget by 350 votes to 75.[51] Of all the interests attached to the Conservative party, the City pressed from the first for rejection of

---

50 Roy Jenkins, *Mr Balfour's Poodle* (London, 1954), pp. 55–7. Murray, *The People's Budget*, pp. 202–4 and 209.

51 Murray, *The People's Budget*, pp. 209–14 and 232. *The Times* 30 November 1909.

the Budget and Lord Rothschild, as its leading opinion-former, played a prominent role in these deliberations.

It was not until 17 December 1909 that Lloyd George turned his attention again to Lord Rothschild, when speaking at an election meeting in Walworth Hall.

> Who clamoured for additional Dreadnoughts? He remembered a great meeting in the City, presided over by Lord Rothschild (hisses), who demanded that eight Dreadnoughts should be instantly laid down. The Government had ordered four, and Lord Rothschild would not pay (laughter). There was a very cruel King in the past who ordered Lord Rothschild's ancestors to make bricks without straw (loud laughter). That was a much easier job than making Dreadnoughts without money.

To the point about payment for the dreadnoughts, Natty had no effective answer and Lloyd George persisted with his campaign across the country against the noble lord, hurling increasing venom, sometimes tinged with anti-Semitic stereotypes, against his opponent. As Niall Ferguson has claimed, 'Never in the history of the house of Rothschild had a partner put himself in such a politically exposed position.'[52]

To a mainly Jewish audience in Cable Street in the East End, Lord Rothschild claimed that the Jewish refugees who fled from Russia did so 'to escape bureaucracy, and it is a similar bureaucracy that the Liberal Government want to impose upon this country'. He also rounded on Lloyd George, accusing him of stating in a recent speech to Nonconformists, that 'anyone admitted to the Covenant of Abraham, who fought for civil and religious liberty, might be [the first to be] expatriated ... the Jewish electors in every division of the borough of Stepney and their kith and kin throughout England will remember the vista Mr Lloyd has indicated'. His brother Leopold reported that 'the entire audience cheered him vocifer-ously although there was a large proportion of Radicals present who did not agree with all his political utterances'. What Lloyd George said was 'Supposing any statesman should find our land overcrowded, so that, in order to enable us to gain a living at all, it was necessary to expatriate five millions of the population, suppose such a thing was possible, no real

52 *The Times* 18 December 1909. Ferguson, *The World's Banker*, p. 958.

THE UNEXPECTED STORY OF NATHANIEL ROTHSCHILD

statesman would begin with the Nonconformists [honest and industrious workers and capable businessmen]. I do not know what would happen to our friends the peers, for instance. Those Philistines ... who are not all uncircumcised (laughter).' A week later, Natty was forced into an ignominious climb-down, with a public exchange of correspondence with Lloyd George. 'I regret very much that I should have misunderstood your speech ..., and consequently have made a mistake in connexion with it. I hope you will believe that I am very sorry for the incident.' To a Jewish constituent, Lloyd George denied that he had 'ever spoken with disrespect of his [Lord Rothschild's] race ... And certainly the very last race in regard to which I could be guilty of such an offence would be that of the Jews. The Jewish race has provided the world for untold centuries with much of its brains and much of its sense of right.' At the same time, he found room for a jibe against the House of Lords, blaming them for delaying Jewish 'political liberty ... for 25 years after it had been carried by the House of Commons ... It is therefore solely due to the perseverance of the Liberal Party, and the persistence of the House of Commons, in face of the bigotry of the Lords, that Lord Rothschild is able to sit in the British Parliament at all.'[53]

Two days later, Lucien Wolf replied, castigating the Chancellor for claiming that

> the Jews are so deeply indebted to the Liberals for their emancipation that they are precluded from opposing any of the measures of that party or its putative heirs. What adds to the offensiveness of this suggestion is that it is apparently limited to the Jews. Dissenters and Roman Catholics both owed their civil and political rights to the Liberals or Liberalized Tories of their day, and yet I do not find Mr Lloyd George accusing the Unionists of those denominations of ingratitude.[54]

Lloyd George was a tough political street-fighter and his speeches contained numerous innuendoes against Jews, such as 'some of these financiers have brought from Germany their objections to taxation', as well as his 'bricks without straw' speech, and his not-altogether-innocent remarks

53 *The Times* 30 December 1909 and 8 and 12 January 1912. RAL X1/130A/3 Leopold in London to his cousins in Paris 29 December 1909.
54 *The Times* 10 January 1909.

to Nonconformists about Jews; at the same time, he had Jewish political cronies like Sir Henry Norman and Rufus Isaacs but the Riddell diary still shows that he held negative stereotypes about Jews, regarding them as cowards.[55]

Speaking at Liverpool in January 2010, as both parties fought over the key Northern constituencies, Natty declared that

> If credit and confidence were destroyed in this country by a Socialistic Budget or a series of Socialistic Budgets, the number of unemployed in Great Britain and Lancashire would be much greater in proportion than Mr Lloyd George had stated ... Since the introduction of the Budget, there had been a steady flow of capital from this country, and every stockbroker would tell them that his clients had put aside all English securities during the last six months.

In his reply, Lloyd George claimed that

> they heard a good deal about the exportation of capital abroad ... We got the foreigner in four ways. The first we left to Lord Rothschild (laughter and hisses), who knowing this was a Free Trade Country, with plenty of money to spare, garnered his money together, and then lent it to the foreigner. Lord Rothschild had quoted his father ... as having said that there was nothing more fruitful for the trade of a country than the fact that it was able to advance money to foreign lands. He did not know why Lord Rothschild quoted his father, unless it was to prove that wisdom was not always hereditary (Much laughter and cheers).[56]

In his Liverpool speech and in some of his earlier speeches, following the example of his party leader Balfour, Natty had renounced his Free Trade creed. 'He had been brought up as a believer in the principles of Free Trade, but he was convinced that under a wise system of Tariff Reform our statesmen would be able to negotiate with other powers, would be able to break down many of the hostile barriers which now existed, and to unite the Mother Country to her Colonies.'[57] In his address to an East End audience, Natty suggested that 'the great question that would occupy them would be

55 *The Times* 25 June 1909.
56 *The Times* 5 and 10 January 1910.
57 *The Times* 8 December 1909 and 5 and 8 January 1910.

unemployment. He referred to Tariff Reform as a means to alleviate it and said that if he believed that Tariff Reform was likely to increase the cost of living or that the Unionist leaders would sanction such a policy he would not advocate it but would oppose it.'[58]

What Natty thought of Lloyd George was conveyed in a letter to his cousins. 'Lloyd George is irrepressible, whether he is so by chance or on purpose it is difficult to tell, his vulgar abuse of his opponents and of the Peers in particular have however damaged his party far more than anything else and there is no doubt that a great many sober minded Liberals are disgusted with the ... utterances.'[59] Natty's hurt feelings are quite understandable, but his assessment of Lloyd George's political impact during the election campaign was certainly off the mark. On the other hand, Natty quite correctly noted the importance of winning a large number of seats in Lancashire, if the Unionists were to become triumphant in the general election. He stated that

> there are more than 60 seats in Lancashire and 80 if you include Cheshire, a large minority are held by Radicals, but every effort will be made and no stone left unturned to win back the Duchy of Lancashire and the adjoining County to the Unionist Cause which these two counties sustained during the Home Rule campaign. The great cotton spinners are supposed to be Free Traders, but they are strongly anti-socialist, the men owing to unemployment are tariff reformers ...

A few months earlier, in the summer of 1909, before the Tariff Reform machine was thrown into the contest on the Unionist side, support among M.P.s for rejection of the Budget had started to waver. Sir William Bull reported F. E. Smith as saying: 'Look here, the Budget is going like hot cakes in Lancashire. I think the game is up.'[60] Both Natty and Leo continued to relay optimistic reports from Unionist agents about the forthcoming election to his cousins in the closing months of 1909, though they grew more cautious in January 1910 as the election approached. Natty admitted that 'the budget itself is of a socialistic tendency and is the prelude of more

58 *The Times* 29 December 1909.
59 RAL X1/130A/4 Natty London to his cousins Paris 13 January 1913.
60 RAL X1/130A/3 Natty London to his cousins Paris 8 December 1909. Sir William Bull Papers note of 19 August 1909.

socialistic measures. I doubt if the canker of socialism prevails amongst the people ... which will the public prefer, tariff reform or a socialistic budget [?].' As the election drew nearer, he conceded that 'it is difficult to gauge what effect this propaganda may have on the masses who are undoubtedly swayed one way by unemployment but ... are frightened by the bogey of dearer food and tariff reform'.

The result of the election in January 1910 was to give the Liberals 275 seats in the Commons, the Unionists 273, Labour 40, while the Irish Nationalists won 82 seats, making the government dependent on the Irish vote.[61] The ageing Natty was no match on the platform for the highly skilled oratory of Lloyd George, who had transformed him into a bad object, a sinister operator behind the scenes, a hate figure on whom people could discharge all their negative feelings. From being a major player in the City and the Jewish worlds, Natty was reduced in stature to being portrayed as an impotent figure and flawed statesman, who strutted the national stage, even if only in a negative sense. Sensational, yet nevertheless false, rumours about a secret syndicate surrounded his role in the demise of the Licensing Bill, but the bond-holders' meeting was a significant factor in galvanizing elite opinion to press the Lords to give the measure its death warrant. Again, with regard to the throwing out of the Budget by the Lords, Natty played a key role in the City protest and it was the anger of the City, more than that of any other interest, which swept along the Conservative party in its undertow towards the rejection of the Budget. Since its cool initial approach, the Budget Protest League had decided to ignore the Licensed Victuallers National Trade Defence League, while Lord Lansdowne deemed a deputation from the League neither necessary nor desirable.[62] 'From the revenue standpoint', Bruce Murray concluded, 'the "People's Budget", with the exception of the land values duties, proved an unqualified success. No additions to taxation were required until 1914, despite considerable increases in expenditure', while the amended Budget of

61   RAL X1/130A/3 Natty London to his cousins Paris 16 November 1909; Leo to his cousins 18 November and 7 December 1909; Natty to his cousins 8 and 24 December 1909. RAL X1/130A/4 Natty to his cousins 5 January 1910. Murray, *The People's Budget*, pp. 255–6.
62   Licensed Victuallers National Defence League: minutes of the Parliamentary Committee 21 September 1909 and 16 February 1910.

1914–15 'was moving towards a fully graduated income tax.'[63] The success of the Budget was a repudiation of Natty's outmoded fiscal opinions, for which his espousal of tariff reform and his disavowal of Free Trade were a poor substitute. It also allowed the Liberals to win a second general election in December 1910 and to rush through the Parliament Bill in 1911 which curtailed the power of the House of Lords.

63   Murray, *The People's Budget*, pp. 292–5 and 307.

9

Natty and Jewish Intervention in Russia: The Third Phase

A new, more professional approach, to Anglo-Jewry's relations with the Foreign Office on behalf of beleaguered co-religionists overseas was adopted when Lucien Wolf (1857–1930) was given an increasingly executive role from 1908 onwards in the Conjoint Committee of the Board of Deputies of British Jews and the Anglo-Jewish Association.

Educated in Brussels and Paris and fluent in French and German, Wolf evinced an interest in foreign affairs from an early age. His father had fled from Bohemia to Britain after the failure of the 1848 revolution, and the principles of political and economic liberalism shaped Wolf's outlook, so much so that he was convinced that Russia and Romania would one day rapidly pass through this phase of progress. Wolf joined the staff of the *Jewish World* at the age of seventeen, graduating to writing its leaders and subsequently becoming its editor, a post in which he served from 1906 to 1908. In 1890, Wolf was appointed foreign editor of the *Daily Graphic*, a position which he held until 1909, but he continued to write articles for a weekly journal, *The Graphic*, under the title of 'The Foreign Office Bag'. He also wrote a widely noticed commentary on foreign affairs for the *Fortnightly Review* under the pseudonym of 'Diplomaticus'. He was one of the founders of the Jewish Historical Society of England, making significant contributions through papers about the *Marranos* and Menasseh Ben Israel's visit to Oliver Cromwell. With Israel Zangwill, he had founded the Jewish Territorial Organization in a direct challenge to Zionism.[1] He had first come to the attention of Natty in 1896, when he had suggested an international Jewish delegation to visit the Tsar to press for reform. This was vetoed because it would supposedly encourage anti-Semitism in France, but his 1901 memorandum on Romania had left an enduring impression on Natty.[2] While it is true that there was one last memorable intervention in the old *shtadlanut* (intercessor) style by Natty and his brothers before Edward VII visited the Tsar in 1908, the more constrained international situation, with two European power blocs gradually forming, forced Wolf to begin a whole series of foreign policy initiatives in Romania, Russia and Greece on a piecemeal basis, in conjunction with allied Jewish groups in Europe and the United States.[3]

Sir Edward Grey, the Liberal Foreign Secretary, was increasingly guided by the principles of *realpolitik* as regards the advantages of an alliance with Russia. As has been stated, Sir Charles Hardinge returned from St Petersburg in October 1905 to become permanent Under-Secretary at the Foreign Office, where he felt that he would be in a better position to bring about an entente with Russia. A French observer noted that 'In the shadow of the King, and assisted by the permanent Under-Secretary of State, the Minister of Foreign Affairs retains, at the beginning of the twentieth century, the power of an autocrat. Established on the poop, well above the agitation of the democratic mob, the pilot ... steers the ship, lending only an inattentive ear to the distant murmurs of the parliamentary passengers between decks.'[4] In reality, the inexperienced Grey was profoundly influenced by Hardinge and the King, the latter having an extensive but ill-defined input in the formulation of foreign

---

1   'Lucien Wolf: a Memoir', in Cecil Roth, ed., *Essays in Jewish History* (London, 1934), pp. 1–34. Mark Levene, *War, Jews and the New Europe: The Diplomacy of Lucien Wolf 1914–1919* (London, 2009), pp. 12–17. Max Beloff, *Lucien Wolf and the Anglo-Russian Entente – 1914* (London, 1951), p. 11.
2   Yivo, Mowshowitz Collection, reel 4, Natty to Lucien Wolf 10 June 1896.
3   Levene, *War, Jews and the New Europe*, pp. 16–17.
4   Beloff, *Lucien Wolf and the Anglo-Russian Entente 1907–1914*, pp. 10–11.

policy. The Anglo-Russian Convention of 31 August 1907 demarcated the respective spheres of influence of the two powers in Asia, more specifically in Afghanistan, Tibet and Persia, and ushered in an entente between the two powers.[5] When Britain and Russia eventually grew closer together, there was increasing readiness on the part of the British to float state loans for Russia on the London market and to overlook the despotic features of Russian government and the plight of the Jews.

At the beginning of 1907, Lucien Wolf contributed a preface to a book by E. Semenoff entitled *The Russian Government and the Massacres: A Page of the Counter-Revolution*. In it, Wolf lamented that

> The whole moral consciousness of the free nations of the West – and not least of England herself – is being degraded by this officially nurtured apathy ... To me, as an old Liberal born with the echoes of 1848 ringing in his ears, and piously reared on the traditions of England's unswerving and unfaltering championship of oppressed peoples, the policy pursued by Sir Edward Grey in this respect has been profoundly disheartening. I say this without any consciousness, and I believe without any trace, of specifically Jewish feeling, for it was not my co-religionists alone who are being outraged and massacred ... Moreover, the Russian Jews who have taken part in the revolutionary movement are asking nothing for themselves but are fighting solely for the liberation of the whole Russian people, and in harmonious and zealous concert with them. Properly speaking, there are no Jews in this great struggle ... Hence my feeling on this subject is exclusively that of an Englishman and a Liberal.[6]

The English Rothschilds persisted in their policy of a monetary boycott, but now changed their approach by making diplomatic overtures to the Russians in the hope of persuading them to ameliorate the situation of their Jewish subjects, as all other options seemed to be foreclosed. Once Peter Stolypin had been appointed as Prime Minister, the Tsarist autocracy began to recover its nerve and later, a tame Third Duma was elected. Meeting his friend Edward VII at Epsom on 2 June 1908 prior to his visit to Reval, Leo, who was a racing enthusiast, asked the King to intercede with the Tsar on behalf of its persecuted Jewish population, as he knew about the 'warmth'

5   Neilson, *Britain and the Last Tsar*, p. 279.
6   E. Semenoff, *The Russian Government and the Massacres* (London, 1907), pp. xxvii–xxviii.

of the monarch's 'heart'. The three Rothschild brothers drafted a letter to the King, conceding that:

> since the conclusion of the Russo-Japanese War, there has been a considerable revolutionary and anarchical movement in Russia and, were it not for that movement, which was widespread & affected all classes, the Emperor of Russia would not have instituted a certain form of Constitutional Government, and called together the Duma ... the Union of the Russian People and the Octobrists ... were undoubtedly answerable for the outrages on the Jewish population and the horrors which ensued at Kichineff, Kieff, Odessa, and elsewhere ... thousands of innocent people were killed, many women violated, and the property of thousands destroyed ... and the large emigration from Russia was directed at countries where it was hoped the immigrants would not interfere with the existing Labour Market. At that time ... a very small number of the Union of Russian People and the Octobrists were punished but, of late, their punishments have been remitted, those punished have been restored to the favour of the Czar ... The result has been the recrudescence of the persecution of the Jewish population artificially hidden under legal devices. The Jewish population is again terrified, and naturally there are fears both in Russia and elsewhere that emigration may take place on a large and unprecedented scale, which would have the double effect of depriving Russia of industrious and sober workmen, and this extra influx of immigrants would certainly disorganise the position and condition of all workmen in many parts of the world.

This theme had been reiterated by the Jewish elites in Europe since 1880s. They conceded that since the Russo-Japanese War, a certain number of Jews had participated in the revolutionary movement, though the bulk of the Russian Jews remained loyal to the Tsar.[7]

Edward VII replied that it was not constitutionally correct for him to take up the matter with the Tsar, unless so advised by Sir Charles Hardinge and Sir Arthur Nicolson, the British ambassador to Russia, who were accompanying him on the visit to Reval. The question was a delicate one to raise with the Russian Emperor and was 'moreover one of considerable

---

7   RA, VIC/MAIN/W/53/98 Natty, Alfred and Leo to Edward VII 3 June 1908. Rothschild, *Dear Lord Rothschild*, pp. 34–5 and 325 note 56; Davis, *The English Rothschilds*, p. 232.

political importance'.[8] Edward, however, not only insisted on the situation of the Jews being discussed, but wanted to show a memorandum prepared by Cassel about a proposed loan to the Tsar. What Hardinge feared was that the radicals in Parliament would claim that 'The King's visit is intended to "rig the market" and to make a Russian loan in London feasible', something to be avoided. It amused him, 'to see how the Jews, though hating the Russian Govt, are always ready to give them money, if they themselves can "make a bit"'. This was an unfair aspersion on bankers such as the Rothschilds and even Cassel, whose motivation was more complicated.[9] The royal squadron, headed by the royal yacht, steamed into the harbour at Reval on 9 June, enabling the King and his advisers to speak to the Tsar and his ministers for the next two days to pave the way for an entente. A stratagem was devised whereby Nicolson raised the question of the treatment of the Jews while talking to the Prime Minister, Stolypin, about the internal affairs of Russia, as the King was anxious that the matter should be broached; but the Rothschild letter was deliberately suppressed, not being disclosed to anyone.[10] Hardinge sent Lord Rothschild an extract from the reply of Stolypin, when the matter was discussed. Stolypin asserted that he could not break down all the barriers of the Pale to place Jews on an equal footing with Russians. 'Were, however, every Russian Jew permitted to roam and settle freely over the country, he would, by his superior intelligence over the improvident and uneducated peasant rapidly bring nearly every village under his control, and "pogroms" throughout the land would be of daily occurrence which the authorities would be incapable of preventing.' He claimed that because 'the extreme revolutionary movement in Russia had been largely engineered and financed by Jews', he could not move quickly. He hoped next year or in the year after to introduce 'some measure which would at least give some satisfaction to the Jews and improve their position'.[11]

Natty was furious at this dismissive response, letting the King know through Hardinge that he was 'dissatisfied' and that the conversation

8   RA, VIC/MAIN/W/53/99 Lord Knollys to Natty 3 June 1908.
9   RA, VIC,MAIN//W/53/101 Charles Hardinge to Lord Knollys 4 June 1908.
10   RA, VIC/MAIN/W/53/104, 10 June 1908.
11   RAL 000/848/37 Charles Hardinge to Natty 13 June 1908.

would only 'result in further persecutions'.[12] Writing to his French cousins on 15 June 1908, Natty remained unconvinced by Stolypin's assurances of 'very mild legislation', and ridiculed his contention 'that if the Jews had equal rights they would soon hold all the land in Russia and be masters of the country and that the pogroms in fact were risings of unfortunate debtors against modern Shylocks'. The King put a more positive gloss on the Russian assurances, though they amounted, in fact, to a vain diplomatic charade, as innumerable supplicants from Russia had called at the Rothschild offices in the past with similar promises which had never materialized.[13]

Even the closure of the British and American money markets to Russia was breached by the loans of 1906 and 1909 taken up by Barings and Sir Ernest Cassel, who was a cousin of Jacob Schiff. Cassel preferred a policy of 'friendly persuasion' towards the Tsarist regime, extending it loans and hoping for concessions as far as the Jewish population was concerned. In 1909, there is evidence that he wanted to approach the Tsar to discuss Russian policy on this issue, but was rebuffed.[14] Despite the contrary advice from Hardinge, it appears that Edward had asked the Tsar during his Reval visit 'to receive Cassel, if he goes to Russia', emphasizing 'the fact of his being a Privy Councillor'.[15] A new Russian loan for £55 million was floated in January 1909, of which Barings took £6 million; and in which Jewish firms of underwriters, such as Messrs Panmure Gordon & Co., participated, to Natty's annoyance.[16] Because of the Anglo-Russian entente, Lord Rothschild could make little headway through diplomacy, and his policy of excluding Russia from the London money market had collapsed. Yet part of the blame for the failure of British policy must lie with Natty who, in January, 1906 withdrew financial support from Lucien Wolf for the continued publication of the *Russian Correspondence* and was loath publicly to voice criticism of the Tsarist regime's long-term viability. Again, Natty, unlike Lucien Wolf and Nathan Joseph of the Russo-Jewish Committee, was not prepared to countenance the collection of funds for

12   RA, VIC/MAIN/W/53/106 Charles Hardinge to Lord Knollys 16 June 1908.
13   Ferguson, *The World's Banker*, p. 935.
14   Cohen, *Jacob H. Schiff*, pp. 141–3.
15   RA, VIC/MAIN/W/53/104 Charles Hardinge to Lord Knollys 10 June 1908.
16   Kynaston, *The City of London* Vol. 2, pp. 484–5.

use by the anti-Zionist Jewish Bund and Zionist organizations for their self-defence committees and was, in any case, opposed to the Bund because it was a revolutionary party. Jacob Schiff, however, discreetly supported financial aid to Jewish defence groups in Russia.[17]

Once it was clear that the movement for reform in Russia was in retreat and that Jewish emancipation would be deferred yet again, Jacob Schiff took the lead in organizing the flow of Jewish immigrants to the United States. He initiated a scheme known as the Galveston Plan to direct potential Jewish immigrants away from the port of New York, thereby relieving the congestion in the cities of the eastern seaboard. He estimated that the number of refugees seeking a home in the United States and Canada could run into millions. The Texas port of Galveston on the Gulf of Mexico was chosen because railway lines radiated out from there to locations west of the Mississippi and on to the Pacific coast. Schiff pledged the sum of 500,000 dollars for the creation of an organization to assist in the diversion of immigrants. The *Hilfsverein* and the Jewish Territorial Organization (ITO) in Britain were selected by Schiff to publicize the project and to enlist potential immigrants in Europe.[18]

Israel Zangwill, the famous Anglo-Jewish novelist and playwright, had established the ITO in 1905, when the Zionist organization rejected Britain's offer of a territory in East Africa with the aim of founding 'a new Self-governing [Jewish] Colony in the vast lands of the British Empire'. After Zangwill conferred with Lord Rothschild on 13 November 1906, Natty promised him that the Paris and London Rothschild houses would each give £10,000 to an emigration fund, but reiterated that he could have no part in a scheme which would lead to the restoration of 'a Jewish Kingdom with a Hebrew monarch'. As agreed by Natty, his brother Leo became the treasurer of the ITO regulation department's fund, whose executive often met in the Rothschild offices at New Court.[19]

17 Zosa Szajkowski, 'Paul Nathan, Lucien Wolf, Jacob H. Schiff and the Jewish Revolutionary Movements in Eastern Europe', *Jewish Social Studies* XXIX (1967), pp. 13–14 and 18–19.

18 Edward Allan Brawley, 'When the Jews came to Galveston', *Commentary* (April 2009), pp. 31–6. Samuel Joseph, *History of the Baron de Hirsch Fund* (Philadelphia, 1935), pp. 205–10. Cohen, *Jacob H. Schiff*, pp. 160–4.

19 David Vital, *Zionism: The Formative Years* (Oxford, 1982), pp. 437–8; RAL XI/130A/0 Natty to his cousins Paris 13 November 1906.

At the end of 1912, Lord Rothschild refused to subsidize the emigration fund any longer and he influenced Baron Edmond de Rothschild to halt his assistance likewise. Throughout the operation of the Galveston Plan, the Rothschild family had played a subsidiary but helpful role. The scheme was under the overall management of Schiff; even so, Natty continued to believe that the solution to the problems of Russian Jewry lay in Russia and there could not be a massive outflow of migrants. Moreover, 'after seven years of operation, the Galveston movement deflected no more than ten thousand immigrants (about 1.2 per cent) from the ports of the northeast' and in numerical terms was a limited success.[20]

As has been shown, Lucien Wolf's position in the Conjoint Committee shifted from an advisory role to one in which he won executive powers for himself, allowing him to initiate diplomatic interventions on behalf of Jewish communities in Romania in 1908–9; more initiatives followed in 1912 in Russia and Greece concerning the Russian Jewish Passport question and the protection of the Jews of Salonica. Of more significance still was the defence campaign mounted by Wolf in England 1912–13, when Mendel Beilis was charged with ritual murder in Russia. If Wolf's action is contrasted with the communal agitation provoked by a similar charge in Polna, Bohemia in 1899, the shrinking role of the Chief Rabbi and Lord Rothschild in refuting allegations of ritual murder will be apparent.

In the annexation of Bosnia and Herzegovina by Austria in 1908, Wolf saw an opportunity to reopen the issue of Romania's non-compliance with the terms of the Treaty of Berlin as far as its Jewish population was concerned, as a previous attempt made in 1907 had been deemed to be 'inopportune' by the Foreign Office. Due to the annexation of this territory by Austria, a technical infraction of the treaty, a Conference of the Great Powers would be required to grant legality to the incorporation.[21] Under Wolf's direction, in November, 1908, the Conjoint Committee addressed a lengthy memorial on the dire condition of Romanian Jewry to the Foreign Secretary, Sir Edward Grey, on the grounds that other infractions of the

---

20 Central Zionist Archives, Zangwill Papers A120/37, Israel Zangwill to Jacob Schiff 26 December 1912 and 18 January 1913. Szajkowski, 'Paul Nathan, Jacob. H. Schiff, p. 21 and Brawley, 'When the Jews Came to Galveston', p. 35.

21 LMA, ACC3121 C11/2/2 F. A. Campbell to Charles Emanuel 20 April 1907. Wolf, *Notes on the Diplomatic History of the Jewish Question*, p. 45.

Treaty of Berlin should be considered and placed on the agenda of the forthcoming Conference. The memorandum pointed out that, under a 1902 law, foreigners were not permitted to practise a craft unless they could show reciprocity for Romanians in their own country. As Jews were designated as stateless foreigners and thus not under any form of protection, they could not show such reciprocity. Public employment and all the liberal professions were closed to Jews; they could not act as stock or trade brokers; they were excluded from Chambers of Commerce and artisans' guilds. They were even excluded from peddling under an 1884 law, even though there had formerly been 20,000 such peddlers. A heavy fee was imposed on the children of Jews, the majority of whom were classed as foreigners, if they wished to attend school; and they could only be admitted to primary schools when the places available for Christian children were deemed to be sufficient. 'Romania takes her stand on the argument that the Jews have always been aliens in the land, and that the strict letter of the Treaties of 1858 and 1878 did not alter their status', though this construction of international law was highly questionable. In conclusion, the memorandum stated that

> The Treaty of Berlin is, above all, a great charter of emancipation, especially of civil and religious equality ... Hence, to violate this principle is the gravest blow that can be struck at the Treaty, besides being a menace to the peace and social stability of the Near East ... Today this principle has been loyally complied with by all the states of South-Eastern Europe with the single exception of Roumania.[22]

On 4 December 1908, a reply was sent on behalf of the Foreign Secretary to the Conjoint Committee, to the effect that

> As Sir Edward Grey has already stated in the House of Commons, the question of the position of Jews in Roumania would be beyond the scope of the European Conference now in contemplation, whose deliberations are to be confined to dealing with the difficulties arising out of recent events in the Balkan Peninsula. He will, however, forward your memorandum to His Majesty's Minister at Bucharest with instructions to furnish a report on the whole question. If that report confirms

22 LMA, ACC3121 C11/2/2 'Memorandum on the Treaty Rights of the Jews of Roumania' November 1908 pp. 12–16.

> your statements of the disabilities from which the Roumanian Jews are
> alleged to suffer, and proves it to be correct and free from exaggeration,
> His Majesty's Government will be reluctantly compelled to admit that
> the hopes expressed in 1880 ... have not been realised.[23]

After an investigation, the British ambassador conceded that 'however
unfairly the Jew is handicapped in the matter of his civil and political rights
(and this appears to me proved beyond all doubt), he still manages to rub
along somehow or other side by side with the Roumanian, and even to
thrive and multiply at a faster rate than the latter', though this latter point
was disputed by the Conjoint. But 'as regards the urban districts, the Jew
represents one-third of the whole industrial population of the country; and
... as regards the rural population, even if the lot of the Jewish peasant is a
hard one, it is not much, if at all, harder than that of the Roumanian; while,
in respect of the *fermier* [middleman estate manager] class, the Jew is often
an important element in the country ...'[24]

As Wolf explained to Sir Isidore Spielmann, there had been private
negotiations with the Foreign Office with regard to their reply as to the
reopening of the Romanian-Jewish question.

> Of course, we did not expect that the Question would be brought before
> the Conference, but we have been anxious to get a statement from the
> Government agreeing that Roumania is still a defaulter in regard to the
> Treaty of Berlin, and that the Jewish question consequently remains open.
> You will be glad to hear that these negotiations have been very successful,
> and that we have a promise that if the statements in our Memorial are
> borne out by an investigation that has been set on foot in Bucharest, we
> shall get the letter we want. This will be a great gain, for even a Conference
> could not do more.[25]

Wolf afterwards suggested that Sir Edward Grey agreed 'in a letter to the
Conjoint Committee that the charges made in the Memorandum were

23 National Archives, FO 371/511 W. Langley to A. L. Alexander and Claude Montefiore 4
    December 1908.
24 National Archives FO 371/724, Conynham Greene to Edward Grey 18 January 1909 and
    Charles H. L. Emanuel to Edward Grey 29 October 1909.
25 LMA, ACC3121 C11/12/97/1 Lucien Wolf to Sir Charles Hardinge 27 November 1908
    and Sir Isidore Spielmann 10 December 1908.

accurate and that Rumania had not fulfilled her Treaty pledges'. Although this might 'not seem to be a great gain, those who know anything of international politics will be aware that an official statement of this kind has considerable practical importance, and, indeed, it was not lost upon the Cabinet of Bucharest'. Unfortunately, Wolf misjudged the situation because the Foreign Office was opposed to the publication of the correspondence. An attempt at a compromise by including a similar supportive statement in the annual reports of the AJA and Board of Deputies was likewise blocked. Wolf could not conceal his disappointment at the official reply which had 'eviscerated' an essential paragraph of his draft at the request of the Foreign Secretary.[26] An internal Foreign Office minute drew attention 'to the important part which Roumania is likely to play in any future crisis in the Near East, when she may be in a position to turn the scales, it seems most undesirable to give her offence and drive her over to the Austro-German camp', and this was quite apart from the consideration that other signatories to the Treaty of Berlin would not join Britain in demanding that Romania strictly adhere to its provisions as regards its Jewish population.[27] It was pointed out in an earlier occasion that 'The Russians, in particular, in view of their treatment' of 'their own Jews, would lay themselves open to a crushing rejoinder from the Roumanians.'[28] Wolf sadly remarked to David Lindo Alexander that 'owing to some moves on the International Chess Board we are being sacrificed, and all the private protests will be useless'.[29]

On 11 January 1913, Wolf tried again to reopen the Romanian-Jewish question, exploiting the opportunity lent by the Conference of Ambassadors, which met in London, to validate the boundary changes resulting from the First Balkans War. The Conjoint Committee stated in a memorandum that they were opposed to agreeing the border changes for Romania, partly because of Romania's default with regard to the conditions imposed by the Treaty of Berlin, partly because it would enlarge 'the area within which its

26 Wolf, *Notes on the Diplomatic History of the Jewish Question*, p. 46. LMA, ACC3121 C11/12/97/1 Lucien Wolf to Louis Mallet 8 November 1909 and D. L. Alexander 10 November 1909.

27 National Archives, FO 371/724 Conynham Greene to Edward Grey 18 January 1909 and minute by Eyre Crowe 1 November 1909.

28 National Archives, FO 371/511 minute 5 June 1908.

29 LMA, ACC3121 C11/12/97/1 Lucien Wolf to D. L. Alexander 2 December 1909.

Government practises a policy of religious discrimination and intolerance in defiance of the Treaty of Berlin'. Under article XLIV of the treaty, it was required that, for recognition of Romania's independence, 'differences of religious creeds and confessions shall not be alleged against any person as a ground for exclusion or incapacity in matters relating to the enjoyment of civil and political rights'. Nevertheless, Romania's Jewish population of 250,000 were 'denied the elementary rights of citizenship' on grounds that they were aliens, though most of them were descendants of people who had lived in the area for generations. Wolf argued in the memorandum that 'The quality of aliens attributed to them has nothing whatever to do with nationality, in the modern sense of the term, but is a survival of the medieval doctrine that unbelievers have no natural place in the Christian state.' Under the terms agreed by the great powers in 1880, Romania was permitted to emancipate its Jewish population by way of naturalisation though, in the course of thirty-three years, only two hundred Jews had been emancipated, as the means for such a process were "bolted and barred against them". But if the past scandal could not be abated, it should not be condoned which would be the case if the Great Powers agreed to "the present scheme for enlarging the frontiers of Romania"'.[30]

In reply, the Foreign Office prevaricated, declaring that it was still preoccupied with the ongoing Balkans War and was in any case uncertain whether 'any question connected with Roumania will come before the Great Powers ... though the grievances of the Jews will be borne in mind'. Later officials repeated the empty assurances from Romania. On 17 March 1913, the Romanian Minister in London addressed a note to Grey 'referring to the fears which have been expressed in the Parliament and Press of this country lest the Jewish inhabitants of the regions ceded to Rumania, and especially the Jews of Silestria, should lose rights which they had enjoyed as Bulgarian subjects'. He denied that this would be the case.[31] Without coordinating his move with Wolf and the Conjoint Committee, Natty forwarded a letter from his cousin, Edmond, in Paris to Grey about the plight of the Jews in Romania, in which it was noted that Monsieur

---

30 LMA, ACC3121 C11/2/4 Claude Montefiore to Lucien Wolf 6 January 1913 and D. L. Alexander and Claude Montefiore to Edward Grey 11 January 1913.

31 LMA, ACC3121 C11/2/4 Louis Mallet to D. L. Alexander and Claude Montefiore 17 January 1913 and same to same 9 June 1913.

Leven of the Alliance Israélite Universelle had successfully approached the French Foreign Minister on the subject. Grey replied with the soothing words that 'the question is one which I should be delighted to see placed on a satisfactory footing ... at the proper time'.[32] Once the Second Balkan War had broken out on 29 June 1913, Wolf became pessimistic, remarking that 'the wicked are flourishing ... We shall get nothing out of Roumania now that she is cock of the walk'.[33]

Nevertheless, on 13 October 1913, the Conjoint Committee addressed a carefully crafted letter to the Foreign Office, drafted by Wolf, for the protection of the religious and civil rights of minorities in the territories that had recently changed hands in the Balkans under the provisions of the Treaty of Bucharest in August 1913, a treaty that concluded the Second Balkan War. In four of the annexing states, the letter submitted, namely Greece, Bulgaria, Serbia and Montenegro, the constitutions provided equal rights for all religious groups, though Romania constituted a flagrant exception. The attention of the British government was drawn to the position of the Jews in the northern districts of Bulgaria now annexed to Romania, who would be assimilated to the status of

> the oppressed Jewish communities of the annexed State. Moreover, in view of what happened to the Jews of Dobrudja when that province was acquired by Romania in 1878, any unilateral assurances from the cabinet of Bucharest on the subject must fail to inspire confidence ... the Jews of Dobrudja were deprived of their national rights for thirty years after the annexation, and even then they experienced great difficulty in obtaining them.

The Conjoint felt that protection might be attained for minority groups

> by a collective note to the States signatory of the Treaties of London, Bucharest and Constantinople, declaring that the Great Powers regard the Civil and Religious Liberty clauses of the Protocol of 1830 and the Treaty of Berlin as binding upon all of them [the five states concerned] within their new frontiers and throughout all their territories.[34]

32 National Archives, FO 371/1742 Natty to Edward Grey 7 May 1913 with enclosure from Baron Edmond 6 May 1913; and Edward Grey to Natty n.d. mid-May 1913.
33 LMA, ACC3121 C11/2/4 Lucien Wolf to Claude Montefiore 22 July 1913.
34 Wolf, *Notes on the Diplomatic History of the Jewish Question*, pp. 48–51.

Wolf sent a copy of his letter to Lord Rothschild, who would be seeing Sir Edward Grey in the following week and proposed to speak to him about the Balkan question. Natty rang him up, congratulating him on his letter which he 'thoroughly approved of' and 'he has shown it to the Count Mensdorf, the Austrian Ambassador, who also thinks well of it'.[35] Natty met Grey on 15 October 1913 at St James Palace at a royal wedding, that of Prince Arthur of Connaught to the Duchess of Fife, to which they had both been invited, but apart from exchanging pleasantries about how busy he was in the Foreign Office it is not clear whether Grey was able to engage in a substantive way with Natty. It is possible, however, that Natty's conversation with Grey put the Foreign Secretary in a more receptive frame of mind when he received Wolf's proposals.[36] Whereas, in 1902, Natty had taken the lead in demanding better treatment for the Jews of Romania, in some way there had now been a subtle reversal of roles with Natty responding to the initiatives put into motion by Wolf and working closely with him.

Within the Foreign Office, the letter from the Conjoint was well-received, even though the first reaction was somewhat negative. According to Arthur Nicolson,

> there is much sense in this letter for there is no doubt that Roumania, at any rate, will treat the Jews in the territory which she has annexed from Bulgaria as badly as she does the Jews in the rest of her territory. There is no doubt that, if the Powers were unanimous and determined, the necessary guarantees could be obtained and their observance secured but, while we may be able to count on the cooperation of France and Italy (where Jewish influence is strong in governing circles) and, to a less extent, in that of Germany, we should hardly get any help from Austria-Hungary and certainly none from Russia. In any case I do not see why we should take the initiative even if the step were likely to be successful.

The sting was definitely in the tail. On the other hand, Eyre Crowe drafted a reply in a much more positive sense which was preferred by Grey and reworked by him.[37]

35 LMA, ACC3121 C11/2/4 Lucien Wolf to Leo de Rothschild 10 October 1913 and Claude Montefiore 13 October 1913.
36 RAL XI/130A/7 Natty to his cousins Paris 15 October 1913. *The Times* 15 October 1913.
37 National Archives, FO 371/1742 minute of Arthur Nicolson 14 October 1913 and

On 29 October 1913, the Foreign Office replied that 'the Articles of the Treaty of Berlin ... are in no way abrogated by the territorial changes in the Near East, and remain as binding as they have been hitherto'. The government would 'consult with the other Powers as to the policy of reaffirming in some way the provisions of the Treaty of Berlin for the protection of the religious and other liberties of minorities in the territories referred to, when the question of giving formal recognition by the Powers to the recent territorial changes in the Balkan Peninsula is raised'.[38] Wolf decided to give both the letter from the Conjoint and his reply the widest possible coverage in the national press and news agencies to make it difficult for the government to renege on their promises as they had done previously in 1909. Among the dailies selected were *The Times*, *Daily Telegraph* and *The Standard*.[39]

On 17 November 1913, the Conjoint answered that they would put forward 'an amended formula of civil and religious liberty in the Balkans, which they think will clearly express the intentions of the Conference of London and the Congress of Berlin than the provisions on the same subject contained in the Protocol No. 3 of 1830 and the Treaty of 1878'. On 12 March 1914, after protracted correspondence between Wolf and D. L. Alexander and Claude Montefiore, the Conjoint put forward a new formula:

> All persons of whatever religious belief born or residing in the territories annexed to the Kingdom of ------- in virtue of the Treaties of London and Bucharest, and who do not claim a foreign nationality and cannot be shown to be claimed as nationals of a foreign state shall be entitled to full civil and political rights as nationals of the Kingdom of ---------- in accordance with the foregoing stipulations.[40]

To conciliate Sir Edward Grey, the wording of the formula substituted 'all

---

subsequent minutes of Eyre Crowe 19 October 1913 and Edward Grey.

38 Wolf, *Notes on the Diplomatic History of the Jewish Question*, p. 51.

39 LMA, ACC3121 C11/2/4 Charles Emanuel to newspaper editors 25 October and 3 November 1913.

40 Wolf, *Notes on the Diplomatic History of the Jewish Question*, pp. 51–3. LMA ACC3121 C11/2/5 D. L. Alexander to Lucien Wolf 27 January 1914; Wolf to Alexander 19 February 1914; Alexander to Wolf 26 February 1914; Wolf to Alexander 26 February 1914; and same to same 3 March 1914.

persons of whatever religious belief' for 'Jews', as the Foreign Secretary could not be expected to propose a formula that benefited only one group; in addition, the phraseology of the formula was agreed with the Alliance.[41]

Throughout 1913, an international campaign to ameliorate the situation of Romanian Jewry slowly gathered momentum in the United States and France. In March 1913, the American Jewish Committee requested the United States government to make representations to Romania on behalf of its Jews. The Wilson administration instructed its ambassador to contact Sir Edward Grey, chairman of the Ambassadorial Conference in London, to inform him that the ultimate agreement should include 'a provision assuring full civil and religious liberty to the inhabitants ... [of Romania] regardless of race or creed', and the policy was reiterated at the Peace Conference on 5 August 1913.[42] In addition, a American Roumanian Jewish Emancipation Committee was set up in New York with Champ Clark, Speaker of the House of Representatives as President, and Oscar Straus and Dr Max Nordau as Vice-Presidents, with the aim of mustering support for an international conference in Berlin; but Wolf regarded the organization as an interloper and warned that meddling by its executive secretary, Henry Green, would 'prejudice other plans which are now in the course of preparation by the leading Jewish organizations of Europe and America'.[43] Wolf wrote to Mr Archer, Lord Rothschild's secretary, requesting that Natty should not receive him, while he also asked Claude Montefiore to have a word with Leo.[44] At the same time, the French Foreign Minister said that he would act in concert with Britain in the matter and gave instructions in these terms to the French ambassador in London, besides giving assurances to the Alliance. The Chief Rabbi of Bulgaria, Dr M. Ehrenpreis, informed Luigi Luzzatti in October 1913 that the French government had promised their

> energetic cooperation ... on the occasion of the formal ratification of the
> treaty of peace of Bucharest which will be entrusted to the Conference

41 LMA, ACC3121 C11/2/5 Lucien Wolf to Claude Montefiore 10 March 1914.
42 Cyrus Adler, *Jacob H. Schiff. His Life and Letters* vol. 2 (New York, 1928), pp. 155–6.
43 National Archives, FO371/1742 Henry Green to Herbert Asquith 11 August 1913 and Edward Grey 15 October 1913.
44 LMA, ACC3121 C11/2/4 Lucien Wolf to Claude Montefiore 21 December 1913 and Walter H. Page 23 December 1913.

of Ambassadors in London ... Sir Anthony Nicholson [possibly Sir
Arthur Nicolson] has favourably received our petition, but he has not
given me a clear-cut answer about Giolitti's and Pichon's desire that the
British cabinet should take the initiative ... The Jewish circles in London,
including Lord Rothschild, will warmly support our action. You will
soon receive the copy of the very interesting memorandum addressed by
the Jewish Conjoint Committee of London to Sir Edward Grey on the
subject.[45]

It appears that the different Jewish organizations in London, Paris and
New York were working together and coordinating their action with the
encouragement of Wolf, who was in regular contact with the American
ambassador in London.[46]

On the Continent, in November 1913 under the leadership of Dr
Adolphe Stern, who was legal adviser to the British embassy in Romania,
it was decided to set up an International Committee for the Defence of
Religious Liberty with the object of 'chiefly of arousing public opinion
on the Roumanian Jewish question', Wolf explained to Mr Archer, Lord
Rothschild's private secretary. 'Before its programme and other details of its
organization are published', he continued,

> it is proposed to issue a Manifesto on its behalf in the form of a letter to
> the leading newspapers of Europe signed by a few of the most conspicuous
> public men of all countries. Signor Luzzatti, late Prime Minister of Italy,
> the Marquis Visconti-Venosta, an ex-Minister of Foreign Affairs, and M.
> Clemenceau have already agreed to sign the Manifesto, and I understand
> that Mr Roosevelt will do likewise. On behalf of England it is suggested
> by our Continental friends that Lord Rosebery should sign, and at the
> last meeting of the Jewish Conjoint Committee it was resolved that
> either Lord Rothschild or Mr Leopold de Rothschild should be asked to
> approach Lord Rosebery in the matter'.[47]

Reluctantly, Wolf told D. L. Alexander that they would have to co-operate
with Dr Stern's International Committee, despite the fact that it was

45 Luigi Luzzatti, *God in Freedom. Studies in the Relation between Church and State* (New
    York, 1930), pp. 465 and 472–3.
46 LMA, ACC3121 C11/2/4 Wolf to Walter H. Page 4 November and 23 December 1913.
47 LMA, ACC3121 C11/12/103 Lucien Wolf to S. H. Archer 8 April 1914.

blowing their own campaign off course, as it would remain at a standstill until the Manifesto of the International Committee was made public.[48]

In its appeal, the International Committee claimed that

> one might suppose that the condition of the Jews of Russia was worse, but it is not so. If the Russian Jews are more exposed to pogroms, and subject to a great number of restrictions from the legal point of view, they are still better off [than the Romanian Jews]: they are Russian citizens, they can vote and be elected. The Roumanian Jew is considered an alien, a vagrant without shelter in the country where his grandfathers were born.

The appeal was sent to Ion Bratianu, the Prime Minister of Romania, with a covering letter from Luzzatti. On 14 March 1914, Bratianu replied that 'The status of Jews in Roumania is purely an internal problem; and that Jewish "immigrants, addicted for centuries to trade and usury, superimposed themselves on a population which historical circumstances had kept in a primitive economic state". The Romanian nation was determined to maintain its Latin character, an ideal which would only be undermined by the presence of large numbers of Jews who refused to assimilate. Luzzatti replied, 'you claim that "It is a matter of race and not of religion". History has proven that the persecuted isolate themselves, but, once permitted, they fuse with the nation and rejoice in showing their love for the country which had failed to recognize them until then'. To this Bratianu responded by asserting that 'it was impossible for me to join the Jewish question with the present constitutional reform ... When the moment comes Roumania will by herself ... do what others could not impose on her without seriously compromising the process of assimilation of Jews in Roumania.'[49] Because of Bratianu's prevarications, the the International Committee's Manifesto could not be published, and various initiatives on behalf of Romanian Jewry were also stymied.

Wolf had tried to simplify the English wording of the Manifesto, though he could not do so without consulting the other signatories and, as he admitted, to Claude Montefiore and D. L. Alexander, he could 'imagine Lord Rothschild sniffing at it very unsympathetically'. Natty took

48   LMA, ACC3121 C11/2/4 Lucien Wolf to D. L. Alexander 26 November 1913.
49   Luzzatti, *God in Freedom*, pp. 478–83, 489–91 and 493–4.

the French and English versions of the document to 'the country to read and he says he doubts whether Lord Rosebery would sign it, and he does not wish to risk a refusal [on account of the family connection]. He apparently knows all about Mr Balfour [who was equivocating] and this has rendered him the more reluctant to approach Lord Rosebery', but Natty was not adverse to others approaching Rosebery.[50] Despite a request from Lady Constance Battersea, another member of the extended Rothschild family, Rosebery refused to sign the Manifesto, though he concurred with what Balfour said 'about interference with the internal affairs of foreign countries'. Nor did he 'demur to the exception he makes in the case of Roumania ... But, having rightly or wrongly come to this resolution of silence with regard to the affairs of our own country', he decided that, 'I should be justly blamed if I broke that silence to discuss the affairs of a foreign country, in which I must be naturally much less interested than in my own.'[51] Although, in the end, Balfour refused to sign the Manifesto, he did write an appeal on behalf of Romanian Jewry which could be used alongside the Manifesto.[52] Meanwhile, in Britain, Lucien Wolf was preparing to launch a full-scale campaign on behalf of Romanian Jewry in 1914, by publishing a Blue Book incorporating the correspondence between the Conjoint and the Foreign Office. One of the first fruits of this campaign was a significant admission by the Under Secretary of State, Francis Acland, to the Commons on 10 June 1914 that the government

> proposed themselves to inform the Balkan States concerned ... [they] are willing to recognise the recent annexations insofar as such changes constitute a departure from the settlement sanctioned by the Treaty of Berlin and subsequent International agreements between the Powers signatories of the Treaty, provided that the annexing States on their part acknowledge the binding force in respect of the annexed territories of those provisions of the Treaty of Berlin which ensure the equal rights of religious or national minorities.[53]

50 LMA ACC3121 C11/2/5 Lucien Wolf to Claude Montefiore 8 April 1914; S. H. Archer to Wolf 14 April 1914; Wolf to Archer 15 April 1914 and Wolf to Claude Montefiore and D. L. Alexander 15 April 1914.
51 LMA ACC3121 C11/12/103 Lord Rosebery to Lady Battersea 9 June 1914.
52 LMA ACC3121 C11/2/5 Lucien Wolf to Oscar Straus 2 June 1914.
53 Parliamentary Debates, House of Commons Vol. LX111 cols 301 and 302 10 June 1914.

This was followed a month later, on 14 July, by a powerful letter from Wolf to Sir Edward Grey, in which he pointed out that the assurances given as to the early naturalisation of 'the 15,000 Jewish reservists who were "technically foreigners"', had not been honoured. 'However... the fact remains that whereas in 1878 the test of military patriotism sufficed to qualify Roumanian Jews for citizenship, even that has now been denied them.' It had been suggested that the native Jews of Romania could be emancipated 'by the incorporation of Article XLIV of the Treaty of Berlin into the Constitution, and we venture to urge upon His Majesty's Government that a proposal in this sense might well be made at the present moment to the Cabinet of Bucharest'.[54] As Wolf advised Dr Schwartzfeld, he was preparing

> a strong letter to the Foreign Office pointing out that the British Government owe it to themselves and to the public law of Europe that they should ask explanations of the Roumanian Government in regard to the exclusion of the Jewish question from the prospected revision of the Constitution. Besides this, I still think we ought also to proceed with the Parliamentary addresses to the Roumanian Constituante Assembly, but of course it will not be so easy to get signatures as it would have been after the issue of the big Manifesto.[55]

In response to the Conjoint's appeal, Eyre Crowe argued in an internal note that 'We shall surely only burn our fingers by too much meddling with the question. If we were prepared to proceed with the recognition of the annexation in return for the reaffirmation of the clause in the Berlin Act, we could obtain a paper assurance. But as we are not prepared to recognize the annexation, even the paper assurance is out of reach.' Nicolson did not agree, declaring that they should consult the other signatories to the Berlin Treaty.[56] After a discussion with Grey, it was decided to state that only the collective action of the signatories to the Treaty could rectify omissions, but that the suggestions outlined would be borne in mind when

---

54 National Archives, FO 371/1742 D. L. Alexander and Claude Montefiore to Edward Grey 14 July 1914.

55 LMA ACC3121 C11/2/5 Lucien Wolf to Dr Schwartzfeld 8 July 1914.

56 National Archives, FO 371/2089 minutes of Eyre Crowe 22 July 1914, Arthur Nicolson and Edward Grey.

the government came to recognize the annexations of territory by Balkan states.[57]

'Everything is ready for the [Romanian] campaign', Wolf apprised Dr Schwartzfeld,

> and the documents you sent me have all been translated and are ready to be used, but nothing can be done for the moment as we are in doubt whether the Manifesto signed by MM Luzzatti, Clemenceau, Ribot, etc can be published. We have received a letter from M. Luzzatti asking us not to do anything further until the Balkan Questions are settled, and stating that meanwhile he is in correspondence with M. Bratiano. It seems to me that Mr Bratiano has for the second time frightened Mr Luzzatti. You will see if Mr Luzzatti withdraws, we cannot use the Manifesto at all as all the other signatories have been obtained on the strength of his name.[58]

Two weeks later, Wolf told Dr Schwartzfeld that 'in communicating to M. Leven the letter which we have sent to Sir Edward Grey you should suggest to him that representations in the same sense might be made by the Alliance to the French Government. I have urged our friends in Berlin to do this, and I have also written to influential friends in New York asking them to bring the matter under the notice of the United States Government'. Accordingly, Wolf wrote to Louis Marshall enclosing a copy of the letter and begging him to make 'similar representations ... by the American Jewish Committee to Mr Bryan [the Secretary of State]'.[59]

By now, the campaign for Jewish rights in Romania was starting to founder. It had become a victim of the Ulster Crisis which now grabbed public attention as did the impending general European war. While Wolf approved of Dr Nathan's suggestion for a newspaper investigation of the Romanian-Jewish question, he doubted whether at present it would be possible 'for any leading newspaper to give any space to such an investigation' because of the focus of domestic politics on Ulster. He was hopeful,

---

57 National Archives, FO 371/2089 Eyre Crowe to D. L. Alexander and Claude Montefiore 28 July 1914.
58 LMA, ACC3121 C11/2/5 Lucien Wolf to Dr Schwartzfeld 29 June 1914.
59 LMA, ACC3121 C11/12/103 Lucien Wolf to Dr Schwartzfeld 15 July 1914 and Louis Marshall 15 July 1914.

nevertheless, of 'the Ulster question' being 'settled one way or the other within the next few weeks'. At the same time, D. L. Alexander wrote to Wolf that 'in the face of the present European Crisis & the possibility of a general European war the Romanian-Jewish question is not likely to receive attention either here or abroad at the present time'. Wolf replied on 3 August 1914, agreeing that this puts 'an end to our difficulties. We shall not be able to do anything at all now, until the war is over.'[60] A day later, Wolf remarked that the great calamity of a general European war had come to pass and, as he advised Jacques Bigart of the Alliance, 'one of the results will be to stop the [Conjoint's] Roumanian campaign'. Plans for the Parliamentary address to the Romanian Constituent Assembly were put to one side, while the raising of the issue of Romanian Jewry at the Inter-Paliamentary Union in the autumn was shelved, the meeting itself being postponed.[61]

What remained sacrosanct for the British government was the alliance with France and the danger of alienating the Tsarist regime and driving it into the welcoming embrace of the Central Powers, Germany and Austro-Hungary. Human liberty issues in Romania were of secondary importance before 1914. Britain was not prepared to invite a snub from Russia, if she took the risk of inviting the states that had been signatories to the Treaty of Berlin to request Romania to carry out its provisions and emancipate the Jewish population. It was clear that the Tsarist regime would never agree to this, while their own Jewish population was hemmed in by restrictions. All Wolf could extract from Grey was a promise of future action, under which Romania would be compelled to emancipate its Jews in return for recognition of its new borders by the Great Powers after its recent annexation of territory. By invoking these past promises by the British government after World War I, Wolf was able to work in tandem with British diplomats and secure the necessary concessions from the Romanian government for the emancipation of its Jews.[62]

During the First Balkan War which started on 18 October 1912 Greece, among other gains, had conquered the international trading city

60 LMA, ACC3121 C11/2/5 Lucien Wolf to Dr Adolphe Stern 31 July 1914 and D. L. Alexander to Wolf 31 July 1914 and Wolf to Alexander 3 August 1914.
61 LMA ACC3121 C11/2/5 Lucien Wolf to Jacques Bigart 4 August 1914; Wolf to Fred Maddison 29 July 1914 and Wolf to Charles Emanuel 10 August 1914.
62 Mark Levene, *War, Jews and the New Europe*, pp. 249–61 and 354.

of Salonica, wresting it from its Ottoman rulers on 8 November 1912. The war was concluded by the Treaty of London in May 1913. A second round was fought briefly in the summer of 1913 which ended with the signing of the Treaty of Bucharest in August 1913, when Bulgaria recognized Serbian claims to large parts of Macedonia and Romania annexed southern Dobruja. Wolf, as has been seen, exploited the fluid diplomatic situation in order to protect the Jewish population in the Balkans, particularly in localities which were coming under the suzerainty of a new state power.

Salonica was a city with a Jewish population estimated at between 60,000 and 90,000, but it also contained significant Greek and Muslim minorities of 20,000 and 25,000 respectively. Many of these Muslims were Dönmeh, i.e. descended from adherents of Shabbetai Zvi. This supposedly contributed to the Jewish character of the city though, in reality, most were Turkish nationalists. Jews dominated the banks and industry and Jewish dock workers unloaded the many ships in the harbour.[63] Despite protestations from the Greek authorities about their 'liberal and pro-Jewish sentiments', some Greek troops broke into Jewish homes harassing their occupants. 'I gather that the Greek authorities were not to blame [for the recent atrocities]', Lucien Wolf informed Claude Montefiore, 'but the mischief arose from the violent anti-Semitism of the local Greek community – which I have always understood is one of a very low character – and from the want of discipline among the Greek soldiers'.[64] Wolf followed this up by calling at the Foreign Office to discuss the situation with William Tyrell, one of the permanent officials, telling him what the Alliance Israélite Universelle had done and asking him whether the Conjoint could take a similar course of action. Wolf was advised that Britain was content with allowing the Allies to do as they pleased 'so long as there is no differential treatment of the local population or of foreigners'.[65] A scheme proposed by Jewish communal leaders, supported by all the international Jewish

63 Mark Levene, "*Ni grec, ni bulgare, ni turc*": Salonika Jewry and the Balkan Wars, 1912–1913', *Simon Dubnow Yearbook* Vol. 2 (2005), pp. 65–97.
64 LMA, ACC 3121 C11/2/3 Claude Montefiore to Dr Paul Nathan 29 November 1912 and Lucien Wolf to Claude Montefiore 5 December 1912. Mark Mazower, *Salonica City of Ghosts. Christians, Muslims and Jews 1430–1950* (London, 2004), pp. 295, 299 and 300.
65 LMA, ACC3121 C11/2/4 Lucien Wolf to D. L. Alexander and Claude Montefiore 5 February 1912.

organizations and many Zionists, to internationalize the city and grant it protection under the Great Powers angered the Greeks. What is notable is the Zionist orientation of the leading proponents of the scheme for the political and cultural autonomy of the Jewish community of Salonica, who included David Florentin, Dr Max Bodenheimer, Nahum Sokolov, Dr Bernard Fuchs, and Rabbi Dr Marcus Ehrenpreis.[66]

Natty appears to have evinced little interest in the plight of the Jews of Salonica, merely reporting a conversation with John Morley, a Liberal Cabinet minister. He explained that there was no difference between the Sephardi and Ashkenazi communities 'but that the Spanish and Portuguese Jews affirmed that they were the aristocracy of the race having been according to Lord Beaconsfield the last to leave Palestine. His object in asking the question was, he said, because the members of the Sephardian community at Salonika were inclined to give a good deal of trouble to the powers.'[67]

By the time of the Second Balkan War, the Greeks were fearful of losing some of their prized possessions and were anxious to widen their support. This made them willing to make concessions to the Jewish community. Wolf explained to his colleague on the Conjoint, D. L. Alexander, that he wanted 'action to be taken quickly as, at the present moment, the Greeks are sorely in need of sympathy in Western Europe, and they are a little fearful lest Salonika may not after all fall to them. If we wait until their title is definitely recognized we shall probably get nothing out of them, and the whole Jewish community of Salonika will be ruined'. By passing into the Greek orbit, Salonica was cut off from its trading hinterland in the Balkans and this deeply affected its Jewish community. In the same summer month, Wolf urged Ionnis Gennadius, the Greek ambassador to London, 'to get either the Greek Government or the Patriarchate of Constantinople to issue a strong pronouncement on the *Blood Accusation*. I have impressed upon him that nothing will tend more surely to win the confidence of the Jews of Salonika and their coreligionists.'[68]

---

66 Mazower, *Salonica City of Ghosts*, pp. 299–300; Levene, *'Ni grec, ni bulgare, ni turc'*, pp. 84–6. N. M. Gelber, 'An Attempt to Internationalize Salonika 1912–1913', *Jewish Social Studies* (1955), pp. 105–19.

67 RAL XI/130A/7 Natty to his cousins Paris 7 May 1913.

68 LMA, ACC 3121 C11/2/4 Lucien Wolf to D. L. Alexander 4 July and Elkan Adler 8 July 1913.

Despite a rebuff from the communal leaders in Salonica, who highlighted 'the mildest rule of the Greeks' and 'great religious tolerance', Wolf persisted in his efforts to persuade the Greek government to address the real grievances of the Jews in the city. Wolf very much doubted 'the accuracy of this second telegram [from the Jewish community leaders] which put an optimistic gloss on the situation, claiming that the attitude of the Greeks was 'essentially liberal' in view of conflicting information from Salonica.[69] In October 1913, Wolf sent his colleague in Berlin, Dr Paul Nathan, copies of his correspondence with the Greek government, so that the representations which he was making to the German government were consistent with what the Conjoint was demanding. Wolf requested Gennadius to ask his government to issue a statement to allay the 'grievances and apprehensions of the Jews of Salonika'.[70] In December, Wolf informed Gennadius that what Salonica Jewry wanted was a measure of 'economic and municipal autonomy; the right of communal taxation; educational liberty ... the protection of the Sabbath, and hence Sunday trading; and exemption from military service for a number of years'. These demands were rejected by Gennadius, who replied that 'to make special distinctions or grant special privileges would be to upset the very principle of equality which is ... demanded of us'.[71] Wolf continued to press Gennadius, remarking that he was not seeking 'exceptional privileges' for his coreligionists in Salonica, merely fair play. 'Unfortunately so far all the reports I have received from Salonika are of the gloomiest description, and I gather that the hopes which the Jews of the City entertained some months ago ... have almost entirely disappeared.' Venizelos, the Greek Prime Minister, was visiting Salonica, and had expressed his willingness to meet Jewish community leaders to listen to their concerns. Wolf telegraphed the leadership of the Conjoint to advise them of the Greek premier's impending visit. He also coached Samuel Montagu, now ennobled as Lord Swaythling, on the issues

---

69 LMA, ACC 3121 C11/2/4 and 5 Robert Allanti to Lucien Wolf 25 July 1913 and 16 February 1914 with enclosures from Moïse Morpurgo and Wolf to D. L. Alexander 17 February 1914.

70 LMA, ACC 3121 C11/2/4 Lucien Wolf to Claude Montefiore 13 October 1913 and Gennadius 15 January 1914.

71 Levene, *War, Jews and the New Europe*, pp. 171–2. Yivo, Mowschowitch Collection Box 3 Folder 29d Prérogatives dues à la Communauté Israëlite de Salonique.

of concern to Greek Jewry because he was leaving for Athens shortly.[72] As Wolf remarked to Robert Allanti on 16 February 1914,

> The Continental newspapers lately have been full of them, and last week there was an article in the Paris *Temps* ... in which a memorandum of the Chief Rabbi of Salonika is referred to detailing the grievances of the Jews. It is not clear what these grievances are, but they must be serious as the *Temps* admits that a great scheme of emigration of Jews and foreigners is contemplated.[73]

A British diplomat reported that the Jews were concerned by the 'continual spiteful attacks on them in the press and ... the daily requisition of their carts without payment to carry refugees' effects', but dismissed 'such complaints as coming from well-known Turcophiles'.[74] Nevertheless, the Greeks had secured what they wanted in the Peace Treaty and once his bargaining counters had been forfeited, there was little more that Wolf could do.

The American Jewish Committee, of which Jacob Schiff, Louis Marshall and Judge Mayer Sulzberger were the leading spirits, concentrated its energy, from 1908 onwards, on having the 1832 Commercial Treaty with Russia abrogated because of the discrimination practised against American Jews who applied for visas – a situation known as the Russian Passport question; and in December 1911 the Treaty was shelved, much to Russia's displeasure. Ambassador Guild explained frankly to the Russian Foreign Minister that

> the action of the House was unquestionably influenced by a sincere conviction that such action might have far reaching results in inducing Russia to abandon not only restriction of foreign Jews, but restriction on her own Jews and pointed out that from the American point of view, absolute freedom of speech and freedom of movement appeared to be the best cure for treason and conspiracy, by removing any possible grievance.[75]

So too, Wolf, who well understood this, wished to use the issue of the

---

72   LMA, ACC 3121 C11/2/5 Lucien Wolf to Gennadius 12 February 1914 and D. L. Alexander 13 February 1914.
73   LMA, ACC 3121 C11/2/5 Lucien Wolf to Robert Allanti 16 February 1914.
74   National Archives, FO 371/1997 James Morgan to Louis Mallet 20 June 1914.
75   Luzzatti, *God in Freedom*, pp. 711 and 731.

Russian Passports as affecting English Jews who travelled to Russia as a lever with which to open up the whole question of the disabilities under which the Russian Jews languished. He opened his campaign by firing a broadside, a wide-ranging letter to *The Times* in February 1912, covering all aspects of the dispute and freely admitting that since the successful action in the United States 'our co-religionists in France, Germany, and Austria are contemplating like representations to their respective Governments'.[76] In Russia the *Novoe Vremya* newspaper denounced the campaign for the restrictions on Jewish rights of entry into their country to be eased with a threat to exclude all foreign Jews.[77] In the past, the Russian Consul-General in London was easy-going when granting visas, so long as they did not admit to being Jewish, but Baron Heyking, the current holder of this office, was an anti-Semite, making all visitors state their religion on a form and refusing entry visas to any Jews. He confessed to a British diplomat that 'The Jews – we will not have them in Russia – they should be exterminated!'[78] To test opinion, Wolf called at the Foreign Office, advising officials that the Conjoint wished to dispatch a deputation to Sir Edward Grey on the subject, but that, if this were not possible, it would be content with sending a memorial which he was preparing and wondering if these officials had any suggestions to offer him. Arthur Nicolson, the new permanent Under-Secretary, after serving as ambassador at St Petersburg, was hardly a philo-Semite and could see 'no object in Sir E. Grey receiving a deputation', advice which the Foreign Secretary followed. Moreover, Nicolson 'very much doubt[ed] if any representation to the Russian Govt. would have any effect'. Disturbed by Wolf's persistent press attacks on Britain's friendship with Russia, Eyre Crowe minuted that Wolf 'is not to be trusted, and for all we know may wish to use this information [the Foreign Office views on the Russian Passport question] for the purpose of continuing his violent personal attacks on Sir E. Grey'. Sensibly, his colleague, Sir Louis Mallet, responded that Wolf was hardly about to mount an attack on Grey, when he needed his 'help to get the restrictions on the entrance of Jews into Russia removed'.[79]

76 *The Times* 29 February 1912.
77 National Archives, FO 372/381 George Buchanan to Edward Grey 7 March 1912.
78 National Archives, FO 372/381 minute of Mr Norman 11 March 1912.
79 National Archives, FO 372/381 minute of Eyre Crowe 11 March 1912 and Louis Mallet.

Under Wolf's guidance, an exhaustive memorial on the Passport question was sent by the Conjoint Committee to the Foreign Office on 2 August 1912 in the hope of having these visa restrictions on British Jews lifted. Having dealt with the Lewisohn case of 1881 and covered the interpretation of articles I and XI of the Anglo-Russian Treaty of Commerce of 1859, Wolf pinpointed the dilemma facing the government:

> whether Great Britain can be a contracting party to any international instrument opposed to the principle of Religious Liberty and excluding her own nationals from its benefits, and whether in this or any other respect it is competent for any foreign State to question the sovereign right of another State to make its own qualifications for its own citizenship.[80]

Worried by the strength of the arguments advanced by Wolf, Grey decided to take legal advice on the subject from Counsel, William Malkin. He was advised that the construction put on articles I and XI of the 1859 Anglo-Russian Treaty of Commerce and Navigation by the Jews was that 'all British subjects, without distinction of race or creed, have equal rights in regard to entry, residence and trade in the Russian dominions'. The Russian viewpoint was that British Jews were, according to the reservation contained in article I, placed on the same footing as 'Russian subjects, each class or category of British subjects has the same rights, and is subject to the same disabilities, as the corresponding class or category of Russian subjects; consequently British Jews are liable to the same treatment as Russian Jews.' In 1862, the law officers took the view that the emancipation of British Jews in Russia would involve similar treatment for native Jews, thus undermining Russian institutions that was hardly the purpose of a commercial treaty; therefore, they could not dispute the Russian claims. When the issue was re-examined in 1881 by the law officers of the crown following the Lewisohn case, they determined that the construction put on the treaty by the previous set of law officers was incorrect, so that the Jewish interpretation was preferable, but under 'all the [wider] circumstances, we are not prepared

---

80   National Archives, FO 372/381 Memorandum on the grievances of British subjects of the Jewish Faith in regard to the interpretation of Articles I and XI of the Anglo-Russian Treaty of Commerce and Navigation of January 12th, 1859 2 August 1912.

to express a confident dissent from the conclusion at which the Law Officers arrived in their Report of the 6th May 1862'. Malkin concluded that the government could not 'go back [in 1881] on the interpretation of the Treaty which they have accepted for so long'. However, when examining the related issue of entry, he thought that it was doubtful, under the Treaty, whether 'Russia is entitled entirely to exclude British Jews'.[81] What emerges from Malkin's carefully argued legal Opinion was that the construction put on the Treaty by the government was seriously flawed and open to dispute.

In these circumstances, Grey decided to show a draft of the proposed reply to the Conjoint to his Cabinet colleague, the Lord Chancellor, Richard Burdon Haldane, and to obtain a further legal Opinion from him. Haldane stated unequivocally that, in international law, there was a presumption that the scope of a treaty was confined to its political purpose and that its provisions were not to be extended unless the words used were so clear as to leave no reasonable doubt. 'Accordingly, a state is presumed not to have intended to contract itself out of the power which is incidental to its sovereignty of deciding by police regulations what classes of individuals it considers undesirable for admission, either temporarily or permanently, to its territory ... unless its exercise is pushed to great extremes.' He quoted William Edward Hall's *Treatise on International Law* to show that states could ban certain classes of foreigners deemed 'dangerous to its tranquillity' and 'inconvenient to it socially or economically & morally ... Turning to the Treaty now in question ... it is a Treaty of Commerce and Navigation, and its object and scope are therefore *prima facie* restricted to what reciprocal privileges in commerce and navigation imply. Police regulations and the power to make them do not fall within the restrictions in sovereignty which the object and scope of the Treaty contemplate ... A British subject is to be as well off as a Russian subject, or a subject of any other foreign nation in the matters which the Treaty contemplates'. Secondly, he argued that 'the wording of the Treaty is such as [not] to have operated a surrender of the sovereign right of police restrictions on the entry of individuals or classes of individuals unconnected with their nationality. It may be thought narrow minded and oppressive to discriminate against Jews as such', but Russia had

81   National Archives, FO 372/381 Opinion of William Malkin 23 August 1912, pp. 1–18.

not divested itself of this power.[82] All this was disturbing, coming from Haldane, who was a personal friend of and legal adviser to Lord Rothschild and who had been his house guest on frequent occasions, nor were his arguments on the construction of the phraseology of the treaty entirely convincing. For one thing, they clashed with Malkin's opinion and had not recently been tested in a court of law.

Following the advice of his officials, Grey sought the views of the French government on the interpretation of the treaty, discovering that the views of the two governments coincided. He was informed by the French ambassador that Russia had the right to establish distinctions between different categories of foreigners to be admitted, some of whom would be allowed into its territory and others forbidden; and it was also entitled to establish on her territory such police regulation as it judged suitable.[83] So too, the French Foreign Minister, Raymond Poincaré, had affirmed on 5 October 1912 that the Russian Passport question was a matter of Russia's internal affairs, a view that was reiterated by his successor on 3 February 1914; nor was the German government willing to act, when pressed by Berlin's Jewish communal leaders.[84]

Grey, fearful of antagonizing the Russians and jeopardizing the entente with them because of growing suspicions of Germany's intentions, forsook his liberal principles and side-stepped a potential minefield, by refusing to reopen the issue of what construction should be placed on the terms of the Treaty. In his reply, he repeated the argument that this had been carefully considered in 1862 and 1881, declaring that 'an attempt to do so, or to interpret and utilise the Treaty in a sense contrary to the spirit of that decision, would only lead to its termination by formal notice as provided for by the Treaty at the end of twelve months. Such result would in no way advance the interests of those whom you represent, and would in other respects be disadvantageous to British interests.'[85] Happy at the Lord Chancellor's support, Grey minuted that his memorandum

82   National Archives, FO 372/381 Opinion of Richard Burdon Haldane 26 September 1912.
83   National Archives, FO 372/381 Paul Cambon to Edward Grey 27 September 1912; Edward Grey to Paul Cambon 11 October 1912.
84   Soza Szajkowski, 'The European Aspect of the American-Russian Passport Question', *American Jewish Historical Quarterly* XLVI (1956), pp. 86–100.
85   Wolf, *Notes on the Diplomatic History of the Jewish Question*, pp. 82–3.

'will be very useful, if we have to defend the construction placed upon the Treaty hitherto, but the reply as drafted does not invite argument on that point'.[86]

When Mr Phillips, of the American embassy in London, enquired if the British government had taken any action following Jewish representations on the Russian Passport question, they were fobbed off with a non-committal answer and not shown the correspondence with the Conjoint. The Americans were informed that the Foreign Office had 'been in correspondence with the Jewish ass.n with regard to the interpretation of our own Treaty with Russia of 1859, but that we have not addressed any representation recently to the Russian Gov: on the subject of the treatment of British subjects of the Jewish faith.'[87] It was disingenuous for the Foreign Office to pretend that they had gone into the construction of the Treaty with the Conjoint. Wolf did not fully comprehend the strength of the Jewish case, how near he had come to uncovering the flaws in the British government's position, but though he did not persist in his probing, he did try to reopen the issue on a number of other grounds.

During the latter part of 1912, it was arranged that Sergei Sasanov, the Russian Foreign Minister, would be visiting Britain to strengthen relations with Russia; but Wolf deemed it unwise for the Conjoint Committee to

approach the Russian Minister on the Passport question, and I would now add ... that I think it would be unwise to make official representations to him on the general question ... As you know, the Rothschilds have tried the financial screw and have failed. In these circumstances, how can we hope to get a hearing for a repetition of the threat? As long as Russia is content to pay the price of dispensing with Rothschilds' help in the shape of high interest and low price of issue, we are helpless. Nevertheless, I think the matter might be brought unofficially to the notice of the Secretary of State. When I was at the Foreign Office last week I discussed the Passport Question with Mr Tyrell, Sir Edward Grey's private secretary, and told him that Jewish public opinion was getting very impatient, and that I believed it had counted for a good deal in the Manchester election. If you like, I will go to see him again and speak to him about the general

86 National Archives, FO 372/381 Edward Grey minute 1 October 1912.
87 National Archives FO 372/381 minute of William Maycock and Eyre Crowe 14 October 1912.

question. I know that he feels all the embarrassment that the Russian persecutions are causing the Entente.[88]

Wolf confided to Oscar Straus, the American Jewish leader, that he was not unprepared for the rebuff on the Russian Passport question, partly because of the friendship between Britain and Russia. 'We cannot hope to get the Government to denounce the Treaty seeing how large a volume of trade is involved', he admitted, 'but we did hope that they would have adopted our view as set forth in our Memorandum ... and that they would have proposed the reference of the question to the Hague Tribunal. Meanwhile, I have advised that the only thing to be done on the whole Russo-Jewish question is to carry on persistent and implacable war against the Russian Government.'[89] In view of the sympathetic attitude of a number of M.P.s, including Lord Robert Cecil, towards the Jewish aspect of the Passport question, it was decided to approach them on a non-party basis; and, in fact, when the matter was raised in Parliament, the questioning of the Foreign Secretary was left to a non-Jewish member. Despite the passivity of the metropolis, in Leeds and Cardiff deputations of local Jewish leaders lobbied M.P.s, urging action; and Wolf suggested to Mr Burstein in Cardiff that the resignation of all the Jewish M.P.s on Grey's refusal to act might have forced his hand.[90] More realistically, Wolf was proposing to the Foreign Office that Britain 'should open negotiations with the Russian Government for the entire abolition of passports ... it might give the Russian Government ... a golden bridge to retreat over'.[91]

In February 1914, The Jewish Chronicle chided the Anglo-Jewish establishment for its inaction on the Russian Passport question, claiming that when Jacob Schiff was in Britain recently he had told some members of the Conjoint Committee that 'it was largely owing to the *laissez faire* attitude of the leading Jews in England that our American brethren had been unable to push to greater advantage the victory they achieved in obtaining a denunciation of the Russo-American [Commercial] Treaty'.[92] It is notable

88   Yivo, Mowshowitch Collection Box 4 Folder 35 Wolf to Claude Montefiore 9 September 1912.
89   Ibid., reel 4 Wolf to Oscar Straus 11 December 1912.
90   LMA, ACC 3121/A/016 BODs minutes 20 April 1913; *Jewish Chronicle* 14 March 1913, p. 9 and 12 July 1914 p. 9.
91   Yivo, Mowshowitch Collection reel 4, Wolf to Oscar Straus 1 July 1913.
92   *Jewish Chronicle* 6 February 1914 p. 9.

how Lord Rothschild stood outside the campaign on the Russian Passport question in England and only used his political influence occasionally on behalf of Russian Jewry, while all the policy initiatives came from Wolf.

It was only during the visit of Mr Goremykin, the Prime Minister of Russia, to Britain in the summer of 1914 that Wolf saw a new opportunity to press for full civil equality for the Jewish population, thereby exploiting the diplomatic gains secured by the American Jews. On 5 June 1914, the editor of *The Times* ran an editorial defending the right of the government to delay the emancipation of its Jewish population which was highly inaccurate in its presentation of the Jewish position: 'It is impossible for any Russian Government to abrogate, at a stroke of the pen, all the disabilities to which the 5,000,000 of Russian Jews are now legally subject', what many deemed as the semi-official organ of the British government pontificated.

> Russia, is, and will long remain, a State mainly peopled by peasants. To the Government the welfare of the vast peasant population must be an object of vital importance. The Russian peasants are ignorant and needy, and there cannot be much doubt that were the Jews free to move and trade amongst them at pleasure, they would very soon "eat up" the tillers of the soil. Peddling, liquor-dealing and money-lending are the pursuits to which the Oriental Jews naturally take and no Russian statesman can desire to see these industries extended. On the other hand, the attempt to shut out Jewish financiers from the management of joint-stock companies and from the share in legitimate trade and commerce to which their wealth and abilities entitle them is grotesque. Attempts to dictate to her what course she ought to adopt are apt to be resented as impertinent, and so to defeat the very object they have in view.[93]

What rankled with Wolf was that this line of defence had been peddled for a decade or more by the Tsarist autocracy, with no signs of gradual reform but rather a hardening in its stance; and that the editor wanted to cut brutally the length of Wolf's reply. He therefore asked Lord Rothschild to write to Geoffrey Robinson, as Natty had a knack of opening doors that were closed to everyone else. As was usual, the letter drafted by Wolf was signed by David Lindo Alexander and Claude Montefiore, as Presidents of the Board of Deputies of British Jews and the Anglo-Jewish Association.

93 *The Times* 5 June 1914.

Natty told Robinson that the 'letter has all my sympathy and I should have very much liked to see it published in full in *The Times*. In deference to your wishes, however, they have abridged it, though perhaps not as much as the exigencies of your space might require'. He wanted to add his 'petition' to their plea for its publication at an early date.[94] The very next day, the letter was published. Wolf riposted that Jews in Russia did not have a large portion of pedlars and money-lenders, while the state was the only recognized seller of liquor. He added that 'The Jews ... are for the most part artisans and small shopkeepers. They are also, on a very large scale ... workers in the great industries of the Western provinces ...' In addition, the May Laws had resulted in the elimination of Jewish traders as purchasers of agricultural produce over large parts of Russia, so that the trade was concentrated in a small band of dealers, squeezing the price offered for the produce of the peasantry. However, in the Pale of Settlement, where most of the Jews lived, their competition kept credit available at a reasonable rate and the peasantry were better off because of the superior prices paid for their crops. 'In theory the oppression of the Jews is part of the Nationalist and Orthodox conception of the Russian State ... Fundamentally its motive does not differ from that of the exceptional regimes reserved for the Poles, Finns, and other so-called 'heterogeneous nationalities.' In practice it is partly concerned with the tactics of the ultra-Conservative parties against the Liberal movement, and partly with a vested and very remunerative interest of the bureaucracy'. Wolf and the editor of *The Times* were at loggerheads, with the paper reiterating that 'it is a question for Russia, and for Russia only, to decide what degree of emancipation from the fetters which now bind them may safely be given to the different classes of the Jewish community within the Empire'.[95]

Despite the growing shift of power in the Jewish world to the United States and Lord Rothschild's waning influence, he still had an enviable network of contacts, which as yet were inaccessible to the new American Jewish leaders. Thus, in 1899, when the Vatican newspaper the *Osservatore Romano*, in referring to the Polna case, had revived the charge of ritual murder against Jews, Lord Rothschild, at Chief Rabbi Hermann Adler's

94   LMA, ACC 3121 C11/12/103 Natty to Geoffrey Robinson (Dawson) 8 June 1914.
95   *The Times* 9 June 1914.

prompting, had asked the Duke of Norfolk, the premier Catholic layman in Britain, to intervene with the papacy. The Vatican paper had ranted: 'Let certain insatiable people [Jews] be content with Christian money, but let them cease to shed and to suck Christian blood'. The Duke had informed Natty that he had 'written to Cardinal Rampolla strongly in the sense you wish. I sincerely hope the Pope may feel that the circumstances call for a pronouncement'. He added a postscript that 'I know that representations are being made to Rome by others as well as myself'.[96] On 29 November 1899, Nathan Joseph, who was a close adviser to the Chief Rabbi as well as being his brother-in-law, contacted Adler, telling him that 'Mr Leopold [de Rothschild] sent for me y'dy to show me the D. of Norfolk's reply which is encouraging and gracious, and a State paper from the L. C. J. [Lord Chief Justice] Russell, another prominent Catholic layman. You must call at New Court to see both [letters]', while Lord Rothschild instructed his secretary to send the Chief Rabbi the gist of the Duke of Norfolk's reply.[97]

Although the campaign to counter the blood libel accusation was led by the Chief Rabbi, it had a distinctly old-fashioned aspect to it, with heavy reliance on the political clout of Rothschild houses in Vienna, Paris and London and on Rabbi Zadoc Kahn and Rabbi Moritz Gudemann. So alarmed was Chief Rabbi Adler at the situation that he conferred with Cardinal Vaughan, begging him 'to ask the Holy See to issue a pronouncement against the Blood accusation on the lines of the former [Papal] Bulls and Declarations'; and at the same time, apologizing for the absence of Walter Rothschild, Natty's heir, from the deputation.[98] He then embarked on a twofold campaign by drafting a solemn declaration to be signed by outstanding world rabbinic authorities denouncing the ritual murder charge against Jews and by gaining access to the Papal Nuncio in Vienna to ascertain what he had reported to Rome, as a sub-committee of the Holy See had been set up to enquire into the matter. Once it had been

96 *The Tablet* 25 November and 2 December 1899. RAL 000/848/37 Duke of Norfolk to Natty 27 November 1899.

97 LMA, ACC /2805/3/1/3 S. G. Asher to Hermann Adler 28 November 1899, Nathan Joseph to the same 29 November 1899 and Marquis of Ripon to Samuel Montagu 29 November 1899.

98 LMA, Acc/2805/3/1/3 Nathan Joseph to Hermann Adler 20 November 1899; and Memorandum of Adler's interview with Cardinal Vaughan 22 November 1899.

scrutinized in London, the draft declaration was forwarded to the various branches of Rothschild family and the two previously named rabbis, for their approval. On 21 December 1899, Baron Alphonse wrote to Adler acknowledging receipt of the declaration and mentioning that he had had a further conversation with the French Chief Rabbi about its proposed publication. Although willing to do all he could for the protection of the Jewish religion, Zadoc Kahn concurred with him that 'no such step should be taken for the present', even if the subject could be re-opened at a later date.

> But, in the first place, from what I learn from Vienna, it appears that the Rabbis in Austria are quite against the suggested step of publishing a declaration in this connexion, the unfortunate trial [of Dreyfus] now pending having been transferred to the Court of Appeal, and they fear that such a publication, at this juncture, might be maliciously construed as an attempt to influence the minds of the judges. On the other hand, it is very doubtful that such a step would have the contemplated effect in France. The public mind, just now, is engrossed with questions much more important and much more vital. The subject of ritual crime is not one of general interest and the publication of a declaration by the Rabbis, under present circumstances, would either as we say, prove to be *un coup d'épée dans l'eau* ['a blow of the sword in the water', meaning 'a futile gesture'], or might serve as a theme in the anti-Semitic press for giving rise to an agitation in a question which is, at present, practically dormant here.[99]

Overshadowing all the political debate in France was the Dreyfus affair, since Dreyfus had been found guilty at his second court martial at Rennes on 9 September 1899 and only pardoned at the end of the month by President Loubet, but it was not until 12 July 1906 that the Rennes' verdict was finally quashed and the innocence of Dreyfus proclaimed. All communications on the ritual murder allegations in London flowed through New Court with the Lord Chief Justice updating Leo on what was happening in Rome and Sir Horace Rumbold, the British ambassador to Vienna, calling at the bank to give them the latest information on the moves of

99 LMA, ACC/2805/3/1/3 Nathan Joseph to Hermann Adler 1 December 1899; Baron Alphonse de Rothschild to Adler 21 December 1899; Frederick Mocatta to Hermann Adler 4 December 1899; Nathan Joseph to Hermann Adler, 14 December 1899 and 3 January 1900.

the papal nuncio; this was possibly through the intervention of Alfred de Rothschild, who was honorary Austrian Consul and had better access to Rumbold than anyone else.[100] Through the opposition of the Austrian and French Rothschilds and the Chief Rabbis in those countries, nothing came of the declaration against ritual murder. Even here, for reasons that are not altogether clear, Lord Rothschild distanced himself from deep involvement in the campaign, leaving the day-to-day operations to Adler, his own brother Leo and Nathan Joseph.[101]

In 1913, Lord Rothschild was called upon by Lucien Wolf to intervene with the papacy once again in connection with the Beilis case. The European efforts on behalf of Beilis were nevertheless principally the work of Paul Nathan in Berlin, while the direction of the British campaign in defence of Beilis was led by Wolf, with Natty and Chief Rabbi Hertz playing subsidiary roles in the proceedings. In the intermediate years, undertones of the blood libel accusations surfaced in Russia, both during the Kishinev pogrom in 1903 and in the Blondes case in Lithuania in the same year.[102]

There was a fresh upsurge of such accusations in Russia when the murdered body of a youth named Andrei Yushchinsky was found in Kiev on 20 March 1911. A local student leader, Vladimir Golubev, who was a member of the Union of the Russian People and the Double-Headed Eagle, extreme right-wing parties, was convinced that a Jew had committed the crime in order to utilize the victim's blood; frighteningly, this Golubev had important political connections through a demagogic Duma deputy Zamyslovsky to the Minister of Justice, Shcheglovitov, thereby attracting the attention of the Tsar. At Yushchinsky's funeral, leaflets were distributed alleging his killing by the Jews to obtain blood for *matzos*.With influential patrons supporting the accusation of ritual murder, Golubev persuaded the police to concoct a case against a Jew, Mendel Beilis, who was arrested on 22 July 1911 for illegal residence. It was not until 3 August that he was

100 LMA, ACC/2805/3/1/3 Frederick Mocatta to Hermann Adler 4 December 1899 and Horace Rumbold to Lord Rothschild 9 January 1900. *Jewish Chronicle* 31 July 1903, p. 10.

101 LMA, ACC/2805/3/1/3 Lord Russell to Leopold Rothschild 19 December 1899, Leopold Rothschild to Hermann Adler 20 December 1899 and Hermann Adler to Lord Russell 22 December 1899.

102 *Jewish Chronicle* 17 April 1903 p. 8 and 17 July 1903, p. 8. Maurice Samuel, *Blood Accusation: The Strange History of the Beilis Case* (Philadelphia, 1966), pp. 176–7.

charged with the murder of Yushchinsky, and late September before his
defence lawyer suspected that something alarming was about to happen.
A committee of Jewish notables to assist Beilis was quickly formed in
Kiev, though it was not until some time later that he was indicted on a
charge of ritual murder.[103] Not convinced of the guilt of Beilis, a sacked
detective and a newspaper reporter tracked down a gang of thieves led by
Vera Cheberyak, who had committed the crime and stabbed the victim a
number of times so as to make it look like a ritual murder and implicate
Jews. Under pressure from Schiff, the United States cancelled a trade
agreement with Russia to show their displeasure at the discrimination
afforded to American-Jewish passport holders and the framing of Beilis on
a ritual murder charge.[104]

On 11 June 1911, Wolf wrote to *The Times* to voice the apprehensions
of the Russian Jews about the political fall-out from the Beilis case. He cited
a telegram received from St Petersburg stating that

> Anti-Semitic measures of increased severity ... are impending, Object of
> Government to strengthen its position with reactionary elements in view
> of coming elections. The sender of the telegram adds an urgent request
> that I will endeavour to enlist the aid of the British Press in defeating the
> new assault on the scanty liberties of the Russian Jews. I should add that
> the alarm of the Russian Jewries ... [also] arises from a well-grounded
> fear that the intolerant example of the Government may encourage
> the pogrom-mongers to renew the horrors of 1905. From letters which
> have reached me during the last few weeks I know that the apprehen-
> sions of the Jews are profound and widespread. The recent renewal of
> the infamous Blood Accusation and the debate on the subject in the
> Duma have given a powerful stimulus to the inflammatory agitation of
> the hooligans and Black Hundreds of the Nationalist Leagues of the
> Southern and Western provinces.[105]

Previously, such a letter might well have been signed by Lord Rothschild.
Towards the end of the year, Wolf reported to Claude Montefiore that 'The
ITO representative, Dr Jochelmann, told us at a meeting of the Emigration

103 Samuel, *Blood Accusation*, pp. 19 and 62.
104 Samuel, *Blood Accusation*; Cohen, *Jacob H. Schiff*, pp. 144–50.
105 *The Times* 27 June 1911.

Committee at New Court, that the situation was never worse than it is now for the Jews'.[106]

The Beilis case was the catalyst behind Wolf's concern to found a weekly journal called *Darkest Russia*, which he hoped would influence public opinion in Britain. He informed Dr Stephen Wise that

> I keep all our Members of Parliament, University Professors, Newspaper Editors, and in short everybody who has an influence on public opinion, well bombarded with the paper, and I am happy to say that every day I have evidence of its good work. In the present state of political atmosphere, we cannot get up an agitation against Russia, but at any rate we can prevent the national conscience from slumbering. That is to say, that if people will not do anything against Russia, they ... are very chary of doing anything for her.[107]

The publication of *Darkest Russia* was subsidised by a grant from the Jewish Colonization Association (ICA) obtained through the good offices of Claude Montefiore and Leonard Cohen, enabling Wolf to avoid having to appeal to the rather reluctant Rothschilds for funds and allowing him greater editorial freedom. The journal recited the misdeeds of the Tsarist regime from a broad perspective, dealing with such issues as the imprisonment of political prisoners, the plight of the various nationalities subjugated by the autocracy, and the tribulations of the Russian Treasury. He told one contributor that 'What I should like is a letter of about a thousand or twelve hundred words once a fortnight giving an account of the general situation in Poland and the struggle for freedom'. Towards the end of 1912 Wolf was seeking 'some good articles on various aspects of the economic condition of Russia in reply to the Russian Supplement which appeared in *The Times* of last Friday'.[108] The weekly ran from January 1912 until the outbreak of the War in August 1914. In 1913, the annual subsidy amounted to £2,225 for the free printing and circulation of 4,800 copies of the paper, the circulation peaking in 1914 when another thousand copies were printed. The American Jewish Committee provided funds for the

106 School of Slavonic Studies, Wolf Collection, Wolf to Claude Montefiore 7 November 1911.
107 Wolf Collection, Wolf to Stephen Wise 30 September 1913.
108 Wolf Collection, Wolf to Alexander Wronski 11 January 1913 and Wolf to Nadel 19 December 1912.

distribution of the bulk of these thousand additional copies to editors and persons of influence in the United States, the rest were circulated on the Continent.[109] Assessing the impact of his journal, Wolf acknowledged that 'We are quoted occasionally ... but we are used to a very great extent and that I think is far more important than to be quoted. Several of the large newspapers have relied upon us in their efforts to understand certain large political questions in Russia.' In addition, Wolf was confident that his little paper 'had quite a success over the Beilis case, and I have the best reasons for knowing that it is a rankling thorn in the side of Downing Street and of the St. Petersburg Government'.[110]

Through his editorship of *Darkest Russia*, Wolf was in contact in 1912 with the Russian Atrocities Protest Conference, to which twenty-two trade unions, political organizations and educational bodies were affiliated and supplied its secretary with back numbers of his journal for distribution at its meetings. The Conference protested against the treatment meted out to political prisoners in Russia and its repression of the smaller nationalities, including the Jews. 'It also planned to stage a large meeting in Trafalgar Square to condemn the blood accusation and the Lena massacres'.[111] This was the type of working-class audience whom Natty found difficult to reach.

Until a Kievan newspaper claimed in May 1912 that Vera Cheberyak and her gang were behind the crime, the trial date of Beilis had been fixed for 25 May 1912; but now that their case appeared to be collapsing, it was necessary for the prosecution to elaborate the evidence against him and postpone the hearing until the autumn of 1913. Henceforth, it was claimed that Beilis was employed as a dispatcher at a brick factory, where children used to steal a ride on a clay-mixer and it was on one such occasion, when Andrei Yushchinsky was trying to take such a ride, that he was allegedly seized by Beilis and two other Jews.[112] Unfortunately, the brickworks where

109 Wolf Collection, Wolf to Leonard Cohen 18 November 1913, Wolf to Stephen Wise 20 and 24 November 1913 and Wolf to Leonard Cohen 15 January 1914.

110 Wolf Collection, Wolf to Leonard Cohen 28 October 1912 and to Joseph Jacobs 3 December 1913.

111 Wolf Collection, A. Shapiro to Lucien Wolf 26 February 1912, same to same 28 March 1912, and A. Shapiro to Lucien Wolf 21 May 1912.

112 Samuel, *Blood Accusation*, p. 155.

Beilis worked was a short distance from the home of Andrei and his friend Yevegeny, whose mother was Vera Cheberyak.

A new twist was given to the case by linking Beilis to the Hasidic movement through his father, who was a pious Hasid and through a friend, Faivel Schneerson, a rather ignorant hay-and-straw dealer, who by chance bore the same family name as that of the Lubavitcher Rebbe. What was more incriminating was that Beilis had a large black beard, though he was not a regular worshipper at his synagogue. It was further claimed that Beilis had distributed *matzos* for the founder of the brick-works until 1907 and it was a folklore tradition that Christian blood had to be added to them, which was why the young lad was murdered before Passover. Zamyslovsky, the anti-Semitic Duma deputy, had published *The Saratov Affair* in 1911, a fanciful account of a purported murder committed by Jews in the 1850s, in which blood was sent from Saratov to Lubavitch for Rabbi Schneerson to use for ritual purposes. Since then, Zamyslovsky later argued every crime of ritual murder in Russia could be traced back to the Schneerson Lubavitch dynasty.[113]

Although the trial of Beilis did not open until 8 October 1913, steps were taken in England beforehand to assist the defence. In Britain, the campaign on behalf of Beilis started in a lacklustre fashion. 'I am sorry to say that Lord Rothschild will not ask the Lord Mayor [to sign an appeal in support of Beilis]', Wolf informed Claude Montefiore. 'He says that as all the Cabinet Ministers have refused, he does not think it fair to ask people in official positions. I am not sure that he is not right and besides it will be a very good excuse if we are taunted with not having got certain signatures'.[114] Nevertheless, a protest against the blood libel in Kiev, following the lead of Germany, France and Russia was launched by Wolf early in May 1912, and attracted the signatures of leading luminaries from the Church, the medical world, and the legal profession and eminent political and literary figures. Among those who signed were A. J. Balfour, Lord Rosebery, the Archbishops, Thomas Hardy, H. G. Wells and Bernard Shaw. It declared that 'The question is one of humanity, civilization, and truth. The "Blood

113 Eli Rubin, 'The Tsar's Scapegoats: Beilis, the Chassidim and the Jews' (Chabad.org Library); Samuel, *Blood Accusation*, pp. 57–9 and 86.

114 Zosa Szajkowski, 'The Impact of the Beilis Case on Central and Western Europe', *Proceedings of the American Academy for Jewish Research* 31 (1963), p. 204.

Accusation'" is a relic of the days of Witchcraft and Black Magic, a cruel and utterly baseless libel on Judaism, an insult to Western culture and a dishonour to the Churches in whose name it has falsely been formulated by ignorant fanatics.[115] Once again, on 10 May 1912, Wolf had to pen a reply in *The Times* when Baron Heyking, the Russian Consul General, voiced his belief in the Blood Libel in response to the national protest which had appeared in the newspaper a few days earlier, dismissing the authenticity of such claims. Heyking asserted that he was not concerned with 'Judaism and the Jewish people' but with a small 'secret sect carrying the Talmudian teaching to the extreme of ritual murder', an oblique reference to the Hasidim.[116] Wolf reiterated that 'What the blood accusers understood by their accusation is clearly enough stated in the broadsheets and manifestoes with which they have lately littered the Empire'. One such broadsheet tried to rally local opinion by reminding 'Orthodox Russian People remember the name of the youth, Andrei Yushinsky, tortured by the Yids [Zhid]! Christians, watch your children! The Jewish Passover commences on 17 March' ... Wolf added that "the small secret sect" referred to by Baron Heyking is so small and so secret that nobody has ever yet been able to discover a trace of it'.[117] So too, an important group of Hebrew Christians in London concurred that 'There is no Jewish secret sect, and there is no Talmudic teaching, inciting to ritual murder.'[118]

Wolf was in touch with the Reuter's news agency, whose editor was doing his best 'to get our Protest well circulated on the Continent and in America.'[119] In Russia, there was apprehension that a pogrom could arise out of the Blood Libel accusation in Kiev and as a consequence, Vinover, a prominent Duma deputy, tried to secure 'the adhesion of influential Englishmen to a European movement of protest'. On 7 July 1913, Lucien Wolf conferred with Leopold de Rothschild, suggesting to him that 'a formal Memorial to the Pope should be prepared and signed by Lord Rothschild and that Lord Rothschild should ask the Duke of Norfolk to transmit it to Rome'. It was agreed that Wolf would prepare the memorial,

115 *Darkest Russia* 8 May 1912 p. 1; *The Times* 6 May 1912.
116 *The Times* 8 May 1912.
117 *The Times* 12 May 1912.
118 *The Times* 9 May 1912.
119 Yivo, Mowshowitch Collection reel 10, Wolf to Claude Montefiore 1 May 1913.

which would take him a few days, while Leo would sound out Lord
Rothschild to ascertain whether or not he favoured this course of action.
For the time being, at Natty's insistence, the drawing up of a memorial was
shelved.[120] A month later, Baron Alexander Gintsburg travelled to England
to urge Natty to sponsor some initiative. Wolf adamantly 'disapprove[d]
of this fussy piling-up of protests at this stage. It can only make the public
imagine that we have something to be afraid of and that we want to stop
the trial ... Lord R. has summoned me to New Court to consult with him,
but I understand from a message he sent me over the telephone yesterday
that he is in agreement with my view'.[121] Writing to the Chief Rabbi Dr J. H.
Hertz, Natty's private secretary informed him that Baron Gintsburg had
approached Lord Rothschild to take some action on behalf of Beilis prior
to the trial. 'Though Lord Rothschild feels the gravity of the situation he
thinks it would be difficult before the trial actually takes place to stir the
English people, through the newspapers, to a proper appreciation of the
enormity'. He urged the Chief Rabbi to send him a protest note signed
by all the Jewish ministers 'which he will endeavour to send through Sir
Edward Grey to the proper quarter'. Dr Hertz agreed that while the case
was *sub judice* it would be premature to take any action, however guarded.
As the Conjoint Committee of the Anglo-Jewish Association and the
Board of Deputies, of which Wolf was director, had already sent a protest
note to the government, Natty wanted to gather the signatures of all the
Jewish clergy without further consultations. Lord Rothschild was pleased
that the Chief Rabbi's views coincided with his own. 'For the present', his
private secretary explained, 'he will do nothing but he will let you know
when he thinks the time has arrived for further intervention, or action'.[122]
Behind the Chief Rabbi was Lord Rothschild, behind Lord Rothschild was
Wolf, with a more imaginative tactical plan than the persistent negativity
of Natty.

On the Continent, Dr Paul Nathan of the *Hilfsverein* mounted a
strong campaign on behalf of Beilis and was in constant contact with

120 Yivo, Mowshowitch Collection reel 10, Lucien Wolf to Claude Montefiore 7 July 1913.
121 Yivo, Mowshowitch Collection reel 10, Lucien Wolf to Claude Montefiore 7 August 1913;
    Jewish Chronicle 31 October 1913 p. 15.
122 Anglo-Jewish Archives, MS 175/30/6, J. Archer to the Revd J. H. Hertz 6 August 1913,
    Hertz to Natty 8 August 1913 and J. Archer to Hertz 11 August 1913.

Wolf, so that they could coordinate their moves. Under his auspices, a book, *Der Fall Juszczynski* [*The Case of Yushchinsky*] was published in Berlin in 1913 which gathered evidence from doctors in Germany, France, Austria, Switzerland and England undermining the prosecution's medical evidence. These experts maintained that the conclusions drawn from the Obolonsky-Tufanov and the earlier Karpinsky autopsy reports contradicted the facts presented in them. Thus, Professor Halberda of Vienna noted that 'It is not shown [by the description] that the inner organs were sufficiently bloodless to warrant the assumption of death from loss of blood. In the first autopsy the muscles are described as red, the spleen as brown-red; the description of the inner organs as given by the second autopsy similarly does not lead to the conclusion of death by bleeding ... If the killing was committed for the purpose of obtaining and collecting the blood of the boy, the infliction of such a large number of scattered, random, and relatively minor wounds was to little purpose'. Among the testimonies cited in the book was the joint opinion of three senior doctors attached to London University, Charles A. Pepper, A. Mercier and W. H. Wilcox, who had been persuaded by Wolf to comment on the autopsy reports. They submitted that 'It appears to us quite impossible to suppose that the boy was killed for the purpose of collecting his blood ... We entirely and emphatically disagree with the conclusions Professor Sikorsky had arrived at. We hold the strongest opinion that there is nothing in the details of the murder to suggest in any way the race or nationality of the murderer and we are entirely and emphatically opposed to the opinion of Professor Sikorsky that the crime was in any way a ritual murder'.[123] Whereas Wolf felt constrained by what he could say about the impending trial because of British judicial procedure, Nathan had a much freer hand in collecting material for discussion in the German press and had already obtained statements from scholars and clerics disputing the charge of ritual murder.[124]

Again, in 1913, Wolf embarked on a twofold strategy in support of Beilis in an attempt to undermine the prosecution case modelled on Nathan's tactics in Germany. He was not, however, hopeful of inducing

123 Samuel, *Blood Accusation*, pp. 275–7; *The Times* 28 May 1913.
124 Szajkowski, 'The Impact of the Beilis Case', pp. 198–9.

the British press to discuss pro-Beilis expert opinions similar to those gathered by Nathan in Germany. As he explained to Nathan, 'there is a strong prejudice here against saying anything about cases which are *sub judice*'.[125] Nevertheless, Wolf managed to obtain an authoritative pronouncement from Sir James Crichton-Browne, President of the Forensic Medicine section of the International Medical Congress which had recently been held in London, as to what he thought had occurred. In it, Crichton-Browne stated that 'There was no vestige of ground for saying that the murder was a ritual one, but that racial antipathy had conspired to represent it as such'; and his opinion was greeted with acclaim by colleagues. The effect of this was to help undermine the evidence of ritual murder against Beilis, based on a report of Professor Sikorsky, on which the prosecution relied.[126] Secondly, following the German lead, Wolf obtained a declaration from two of the country's leading Hebrew scholars, Dr Driver and Professor Cowley of Oxford, confuting the argument of Father Pranaitis, a key prosecution witness, that Jewish teaching does or can permit ritual murder. Pranaitis had asserted that 'while there is nothing in any Jewish teaching definitely prescribing ritual murder ... the supersession of the Old Testament by the Talmud, the Zohar and the Shulchan Aruch ... renders it quite possible that there is a secret teaching ordering the ritual murder of Christians'. According to Wolf, he then endeavoured 'to show that it is probable by quotations from post-Biblical Jewish authorities which seem to him to illustrate an anti-Christian spirit'. As Wolf made clear to Driver, if Beilis 'is condemned, a massacre might easily follow. Or if not a massacre, further persecutions and cruelties, making the lot of the six million Jews in Russia still more unbearable and agonizing than it even is today'. Wolf appealed to Canon Driver to lend his endorsement to the view that the Old Testament teaching about blood was positive and had never been superseded, while he could point out that other aspects of the ritual murder charges

125 Ibid, pp. 200 and 203–4.
126 Yivo, Mowshowitch Collection reel 10, Sir James Crichton-Browne to Lucien Wolf with enclosure, E. Robbins of the Press Association to Wolf 20 August 1913, Baron Gintsburg to Wolf 30 August 1913, Wolf to Gintsburg 1 September 1913, and Dr James Macdonald to Wolf 22 and 24 September 1913. *Jewish Chronicle* 31 October 1913 p. 15; *The Times* 13 August 1913.

had been 'exhaustively and convincingly dealt with by men like [Franz] Delitzsch and [Hermann L.] Strack'.[127]

Wolf related to Claude Montefiore on 3 September 1913 that he had not proceeded with the suggestion that Lord Rothschild should address a memorial to the Pope, 'partly because I have been occupied with other things and partly because I found that Lord Rothschild was not very enthusiastic about it. But in view of what Dr Yahuda says I think we have now a good peg on which to hang such a memorial and I will proceed with it at once. If the memorial were merely to ask for a pronouncement on the Blood Accusation I agree with Lord Rothschild in thinking that we should get no satisfactory response, but on the question of the authenticity of the Papal Bulls I do not see how in fairness the Pope could refuse to assist us'.[128] Wolf brushed aside Natty's persistent negativity and happily listened to the advice of Professor Yahuda, the distinguished Orientalist. On 7 October 1913, Wolf wrote to his colleague Dr Paul Nathan that 'We have under consideration a proposal to make representations to the Vatican in regard to the Blood Accusation, but I thought and both Lord Rothschild and Mr Montefiore agreed with me, that it would be only a waste of time to ask for a further Papal declaration on the subject. I noticed, however, in the *Gutachen* [report] of Pranaitis a statement that the former Papal Bulls were forgeries. I subsequently suggested that a letter should be addressed to the Cardinal Secretary of State calling his attention to this statement and asking him for a formal testimony of the authenticity of the so-called Bulls. There never were any Bulls, properly so-called and there has only been the Papal Encyclical, that of Innocent 1V, which has dealt directly with the Blood Accusation. The only other Pontifical document of Importance to which we can appeal is the Gutachen of Cardinal Ganganelli [in 1756 when a Blood accusation was made against the Jews in Jampol Poland] and of that there is no record which proves its authenticity. I mention this to warn you and our German friends against repeating the statement that there have been a number of Papal Bulls denouncing the Blood Accusation, as if the

---

127 Yivo, Mowshowitch Collection reel 10, Lucien Wolf to Canon Driver 14 August 1913, same to Claude Montefiore 15 August and 15 and 17 September 1913.
128 Yivo, Mowshowitch Collection reel 10, Wolf to Claude Montefiore 3 September 1913.

truth were known, we might be subjected to a very prejudicial attack by men like Pranaitis. In our letter to Cardinal Merry del Val we have only asked him to authenticate the Encyclical of Pope Innocent IV and the text of Cardinal Ganganelli's *Gutachen* if there is any record of it in the Vatican'.[129]

On 1 October 1913, Wolf informed Leo that 'I enclose a rough draft which I suggest Lord Rothschild should send the Pontifical Secretary of State through the Duke of Norfolk. I am sorry for the delay in preparing [it] ... If Lord Rothschild approves of the draft I will let him have the copies of the two Encyclicals and of the Ganganelli report as soon as I can get them typed'.[130] As noted above, it took another week for Wolf to sort this out and for Natty to sign the letter which had been so carefully crafted for him. Writing to Claude Montefiore on 13 October 1913, Wolf expressed a new confidence in the outcome of the Beilis case. 'The Beilis case is going very well and quite bears out my anticipations. I have always felt that our proper attitude is to give the Russians rope enough and get as much publicity as we can for the embarrassments into which they may get themselves.'[131] Wolf continued to be extremely active in the matter, assuring Alexander on 21 October 1913 that 'Lord Rothschild had received a completely satisfactory reply from Cardinal Merry del Val, and I have sent a notarially and vized copy to Kiew tonight'.[132] By 22 October 1913, 'Dr Nathan was already in possession of a copy of the Vatican's reply certified by the Russian Embassy in London. He immediately sent the copy by special messenger to Kiev, where the document was in the hands of Beilis' lawyers on October 27'. The next day, copies of this correspondence passing between the Cardinal and Lord Rothschild appeared in *The Times*. On 31 October 1913, 'Baron Gunzburg telegraphed to Lord Rothschild from St. Petersburg ... asking him to send the correspondence with the Vatican to the Defence at Kieff. 'I told Lord Rothschild that it had already been sent and acknowledged', wrote Wolf to Dr Nathan. The professional men were asserting their leadership of world Jewry, while the bankers' role was diminishing. Nor was that the end of the matter as far as the Russian judicial system was concerned. On 4 November

129 Yivo, Mowshowitch Collection reel 10, Wolf to Dr Paul Nathan 7 October 1913.
130 Yivo, Lucien Wolf Papers reel 10, Wolf to Leopold de Rothschild 1 October 1913.
131 LMA, ACC 3121 C11/2/4 Wolf to Claude Montefiore 13 October 1913.
132 Yivo, Mowshowitch Collection reel 10, Wolf to D. L. Alexander 21 October 1913.

1913, Wolf let Dr Nathan know that 'The procedure required by the Kiew Court is a very involved one, but Lord Rothschild set to work immediately on Monday morning to get what was wanted. He telegraphed to his agents in Rome to employ an experienced lawyer, obtain the necessary attestations and telegraph to Kiew. At the same time he telegraphed to the Cardinal explaining to him the circumstances which rendered it necessary to trouble him again'.[133] Through Wolf's persistence and the good relations he enjoyed with F. W. Dickinson of Reuter's, the certified copies of the documents passing between Lord Rothschild and the Cardinal were published in *The Times* and in the principal European newspapers. 'I have told Lord Rothschild all about it and he is very pleased', was the message of thanks Wolf passed on to Dickinson. A week later, he told Dickinson that 'I think the result so far as Beilis is concerned is very largely due to the admirable publicity your agency gave to the case. Of course the result otherwise is very unsatisfactory'.[134] Wolf also forwarded the documentation on to the two leading American press agencies to ensure wide distribution in the United States.[135] It seems that the Tsar also read the correspondence; but Nelidov, the Russian ambassador to the Vatican, deliberately held up the passage of the certified copies of the documents to the court, so that they were not placed before the jury. Nevertheless, the widespread publicity given to the papal documents by the European press may have undermined the charge of ritual murder against Beilis in Western Europe. In the United States, the Senate passed a resolution protesting against the 'unjust ritual murder charge against the Jewish people at large, and Mendel Beilis in particular' and asking for it to be withdrawn.[136]

From the United States, Dr Stephen Wise advised Wolf that in his own judgment and 'in the judgment of many who are conversant with the situation, the Associated Press has for years been strongly pro-Russian. Again and again, complaint has been made on this score to Melville Stone, the Manager, and to some Jewish heads of the Press, including Adolph

133 Szajkowski, 'The Impact of the Beilis Case', p. 207. Yivo, Mowshowitch Collection reel 10, Wolf to Paul Nathan 31 October 1913 and 4 November 1913. *The Times* 28 October 1913.
134 Yivo, Mowshowitch Collection reel 10, Dickinson to Wolf 24 October 1913, Wolf to Dickinson 4 November 1913 and 12 November 1913.
135 Yivo, Mowshowitch Collection, reel 10 Wolf to Paul Nathan 18 October 1913.
136 Samuel, *Blood Accusation*, p. 242; *Jewish Chronicle* 7 November 1913, p. 28.

Ochs, but we have never been able to get them to give full and accurate news concerning the Russian situation. The Associated Press is handling the Beilis affair rather better'.[137]

A protest meeting was called at very short notice by the English Zionist Federation for 28 October 1913 at the Memorial Hall, Farringdon Street at which Sir Francis Montefiore presided. None of the Rothschild family attended the meeting, though Lord Rothschild sent a letter which repudiated 'the doctrine of Blood Ritual Murder' and was read to loud applause. Other speakers included the distinguished lawyer A. V. Dicey, George Cave M.P., an Opposition front bench speaker, Father Bampton, Colonel Unsworth of the Salvation Army and the Chief Rabbi Joseph Hertz. The audience included a significant section of Christians, including a group of clerics, but it was hardly a glittering assembly. Dicey, who moved the resolution 'against the baseless and wicked Blood ritual charge against the Jewish people' was disappointed, saying that he wished that 'some one of the numerous Bishops and other orthodox divines who expressed their sympathy could have made an effort to be present'.[138] Compared to the dazzling names who attended the demonstrations to protest at Russian atrocities in the 1880s, the meeting showed a marked falling off in public interest in the Russian persecution of its Jewish population. The reactionary Russian newspaper *Novoe Vremya* gloated that 'the gigantic Jewish meetings of protest which were intended against the trial have not been particularly successful. At the last minute almost all the Christian dignitaries and clergymen refused to be present at the demonstration. Even Lord Rothschild did not attend.'[139] The immediate effect of the meeting, however, was that some London dailies which had hitherto ignored the Beilis case denounced the recrudescence of the Blood libel. Notable among them was the *Daily Mail*, which contended that the press, unlike the government, must be free to denounce the failings, even of its allies.[140] On 2 November 1913, a working-class demonstration organized by the Beilis Protest Committee, an offshoot of the London branch of the Bund, was

137 School of Slavonic Studies, Wolf Collection, Stephen Wise to Wolf 29 October 1913.
138 *Jewish Chronicle* 31 October 1913, pp. 26–31 and *Jewish World* 29 October 1913, p. 18.
   Beloff, *Lucien Wolf and the Anglo-Russian Entente 1907–1914*, p. 6.
139 *Darkest Russia* 12 November 1913, p. 183.
140 *Jewish Chronicle* 31 October 1913, p. 28.

held in Trafalgar Square to denounce 'the charges levelled against the Jews in connexion with the blood ritual trial at Kieff'. About 15,000 people gathered and extra police were summoned to maintain 'order', as some of the crowd were becoming unruly. No support was forthcoming from the Board of Deputies of British Jews.[141]

Natty confided in his cousins that the ritual murder charge against Beilis had 'engaged the assiduous attention of the heads of the Jewish Community for some time past, the Board of Deputies, the Anglo-Jewish Association, the Conjoint Committee, Mr Lucien Wolf and many others besides myself'. But this was slightly disingenuous because the Board and the Anglo-Jewish Association were subservient to the Conjoint Committee as regards the Jewish community's foreign relations, while the Conjoint was under the masterly grip of Lucien Wolf. Even Natty had to place Wolf before himself, when speaking of the leadership of the British campaign on behalf of Beilis in a letter to his cousins. Leopold de Rothschild, who often acted as his brother's spokesman on the Board, strongly supported a new bye-law in 1913 which stated that the chairman shall 'make a confidential statement to the meeting as to the measures dealt with by the Conjoint Foreign Committee, and shall only allow such discussion thereon, as in his opinion shall be consistent with the best interests of the community'. It was a convenient way of covering up the Cousinhood's impotence when it came to acting for beleaguered Jewish communities overseas.[142] Natty further remarked to his French cousins that 'A good many of our Anglican friends were desirous of enlisting a great newspaper campaign, others wanted great protest meetings ... our methods have never had any influence on the Russian Government.' There had been a 'rapprochement' in Britain with Russia 'true or untrue, deep or skin deep'. Nevertheless, the 'graphic resumé of the evidence of that trial prove[s] conclusively that Beilis is innocent, the last few days of the trial will we are told be devoted to historical evidence and romance about the blood ritual ... evidence we wish to contradict'. He praised Wolf for his researches at the British Museum which had resulted in his unearthing of copies of the papal documents denying the validity of

141 *The Times* 3 November 1913 and *Daily Herald* 3 November 1913. Szajkowski, 'The Impact of the Beilis Case', pp. 205–6.
142 *Jewish Chronicle* 31 October 1913, p. 9.

these charges. Through his 'great friend the Duke of Norfolk' Natty had forwarded these documents to the Vatican. He hoped that their impending publication 'will have an enormous influence in Russia, will prevent a renegade Catholic priest from giving false evidence'.[143]

The gravest apprehension was felt by the Jewish community in Russia at an adverse verdict in the Beilis case; and Wolf confided to Dr Nathan that 'whatever the Verdict [it was feared that] the Okhrana & the Black Hundreds have resolved to let lose a great pogrom'.[144] Despite the rigged jury, the prosecution case was starting to come apart in court. Although one of the medical experts, Professor Kosorotov, had been paid a bribe of 4,000 roubles to confirm that the autopsy indicated that this may have been a ritual murder, three other medical witnesses disagreed with him and another remained undecided. Professor Sikorsky, a psychiatrist, but also a pathological anti-Semite, in his rantings and ravings, swore that this type of diabolical crime was 'the racial revenge and vendetta of the Sons of Jacob'.[145] For religious evidence to substantiate their claim of ritual murder, the prosecution relied on a book by the 'Neophyte', supposedly a converted Jew, which overflowed with extravagant calumnies, as well as the evidence of an obscure cleric, Father Pranaitis, languishing in Tashkent. He came unstuck in court when, under cross-examination by the Beilis defence team, he revealed the paucity of his knowledge of Jewish texts, stumbling over a trick question as to when *Baba Bathra* (the name of a Talmudic tractate) had lived and what did she do? He replied that he did not know.[146] Rabbi Mazeh of Moscow addressed the court for eight hours, explaining that the Hasidic movement was not an outlandish sect and that it had reinvigorated Judaism; in fact, it was an integral part of Russian Jewry, thereby demolishing that part of the prosecution case.[147]

Even so, because of the interference of the judge on the side of the prosecution, the worldwide press campaign orchestrated by Wolf was a key factor in persuading the jury to reach a more sensible verdict than might otherwise have been the case. The difficulties the defence had to overcome

143 RAL, X1/130A/7 Natty to his cousins Paris 27 October 1913.
144 Yivo Mowshowitch Collection, reel 10 Wolf to Paul Nathan 18 October 1913.
145 Samuel, *Blood Accusation*, pp. 82, 211–12 and 216–17.
146 Ibid., pp. 87 and 212–16.
147 Rubin, 'The Tsar's Scapegoats'.

were formidable. Vasily Maklakov, one of the leading defence counsels for Beilis, asserted that

> five of the ... [jury] were members of the local branch of the 'Double-headed Eagle' party and that the foreman was a cousin of Poleshchuk, the secret police agent in the case ... there was a stand-up fight among the jury the day before the verdict. This fight was only stopped by the intervention of the police ... he knew that the jury was packed and ... he fully expected an adverse verdict. Five of the jury stood out for a verdict of guilty, and the majority in favour of an acquittal was only one.[148]

Nevertheless, on 8 November 1913, the jury found that it had been proved that the victim, Andrei Yushchinsky, had died in the Jewish surgical hospital with almost total loss of blood, thereby implicating Jews in his ritual murder. As to the second charge of murder against Beilis in collusion with others in a premeditated plan prompted by religious fanaticism, however, he was found not guilty.[149] Wolf sadly summed up the verdict in a letter to Dr Paul Nathan.

> I am afraid that we cannot congratulate ourselves very enthusiastically on the result of the Kiev trial. There can be little doubt that the verdict was engineered by the authorities with the idea of throwing dust into the eyes of foreigners while at the same time reserving the Blood Accusation and even giving it a measure of countenance. Personally I never expected much from the verdict. All that was necessary for us was to obtain the utmost publicity for the trial so as to enlighten public opinion outside Russia as to what is going on in that country. There, I think, we have succeeded. There can be no question that the trial has very seriously shaken Russophile feeling all over the world. Certainly, in this country, and I believe in France, it has made the political friends of Russia very thoughtful and not a little angry. This may be seen in the leading article of *The Times* this morning. For your work in connection with the case everybody who knows about it is extremely grateful, and I am happy to have had a share in collaborating with you.[150]

148 National Archives, FO 371/1747 C, Clive Bayley to Grey 14 November 1913.
149 Samuel, *Blood Accusation*, pp. 248–9.
150 Yivo, Mowshowitch Collection reel 10, Wolf to Paul Nathan 13 November 1913.

A British diplomat agreed that it was 'curious that both Jew and Anti-Semite should find ground for satisfaction in the results of the trial'.[151]

After the trial Charles Emanuel, the secretary of the Board of Deputies of British Jews, forwarded copies of resolutions from Glasgow and Ayr about the validation of the ritual murder charge to the Foreign Office which he wanted forwarded to the Russian ambassador. Eyre Crowe wrote on behalf of Grey, 'that it would be contrary to diplomatic usage for the Secretary of State to forward to the Ambassador of a friendly Power a document recording the criticisms of private individuals upon the internal affairs of that Power, and I accordingly return the resolutions to you herewith' – hardly a heroic answer.[152] Nevertheless, on hearing the result, the Revd J. K. Goldbloom, principal of Redman's Road Talmud Torah and a Zionist leader, gave his charges a day's holiday.[153]

In fact, the British diplomatic response to the prosecution of Beilis was sometimes so even-handed and impartial as to border on the absurd; for British diplomats were not immune to the prejudices that swirled around Russian society and permeated its bureaucracy. Mr Rhode, writing from Odessa, explained that

> Literature shows no clear case for the existence of these [ritual] murders. But amongst nations upon which the Jews have the greatest economic hold, and who fear being gradually strangled out of existence, the belief exists that the blood obtained at these murders is mixed with the unleavened Passover bread called "matsa". This is not supposed to have anything to do with "cannibalism", nor can it be shown that anything in the public Hebrew religion calls for it, but it is thought to be a symbol in a secret and cabalistic operation intended to unite all Jews against all Gentiles and to keep alive in the minds of the Jews the idea that the Jews are the chosen race, that all others are "mere cattle", "mere food" to them and can exist only as far as they can be made to serve and to further the ends of the Jews. This memorandum is not intended to support the whole or any portion of this fearful charge against the Jews; which however is not easily disproved ... It must also be kept in mind

151 National Archives, FO 371/1747 C. A. Smith to Grey 18 November 1913.
152 National Archives, FO 371/1747 Charles Emanuel to Eyre Crowe 19 November and 2 December 1913.
153 A story recounted by my father.

that the Jews are in many respects a strong race. In the same time the Russians double their numbers, the Jews about quadruple them. While the Russian nation doubles its national wealth, the Jews can make their wealth eightfold and all property gradually becomes theirs ... many Russians of all shades of political thought think that millions more Jews must leave Russia, so that all nations should bear a similar burden ... I do not think that in any other country, a case would have been brought against Beilis ... Two things are fairly certain: that the relations between the Jews and Russians will be more strained than before. And that a large number of Jews will leave Russia. This emigration will to a very great measure take place towards Anglo-Saxon countries.[154]

Similarly, Hugh O'Beirne writing from St Petersburg, felt it 'satisfactory to record that the verdict has not been followed by any disorders worth mentioning. I fear however that its effect must be to envenom for the time being the anti-Jewish feeling in the country'.[155]

Most of the British press were on the side of Beilis and it is noteworthy that a venomously anti-Semitic letter which appeared in the *Morning Post*, attacking the Anglican clergy who supported the Beilis protest meeting, was written under the pseudonym of Anglus et Anglicanus and emanated from St Petersburg. It claimed that 'The Talmudist Jews are bred and trained in hatred of all that bears the stamp of Christianity.'[156] So too, American press opinion rejoiced at the verdict, the *New York Tribune* remarking that

The outcome of the trial at Kieff is gratifying. It should have been, and in other country but Russia would have been, a foregone conclusion; if, indeed, the trial itself could have occurred in any other land. There is cause for thankfulness that at last not even in the most conservative corner of Holy Russia can a man surely be made a martyr to a savage superstition lingering from the Dark Ages.[157]

Contemporaries viewed the Beilis case as a titanic struggle for the political soul of Russia, as *The Times* special correspondent reported in

154 National Archives, FO371/1747 memorandum of Mr Rhode 18 November 1913.
155 National Archives, FO371/1747 Hugh O'Beirne to Grey 12 November 1913.
156 *Morning Post* 5 and 11 November 1913. *Daily Telegraph* 12 November 1913. *The Times* 12 November 1913. *Daily Herald* 12 November 1913.
157 *New York Herald Tribune* 11 November 1913.

mid-October. 'It is daily becoming clearer that under the forms of law a momentous political struggle is being fought. This is not the Beilis case. It is possibly a final fight for existence on the part of the innermost powers of reaction – the old unyielding party, the now almost isolated extreme Right – against all the modern forces in Russia.'[158] Hans Rogger summed up the result by stating that

> No one in power who was not stricken with Judeophobia was sufficiently strong, concerned or courageous to prevent or try to prevent it. No one on the anti-Beilis side as yet felt strong or bold enough to prevent or try to attempt to bring a whole nation to his views by force. There had been no grand design; there had not even been a tactical plan. There had been an experiment, conducted by a small band of unsuccessful politicians and honest maniacs to see how far they could go in imposing their cynicism and their madness on the state. They had succeeded beyond all expectation; they found willing allies in two powerful ministers, the approval of the emperor and the silent acquiescence of other members of the government.[159]

According to Albert Lindemann, some officials including the 'Minister of Justice I. G. Shcheglovitov hoped that a highly publicized trial of a Jew for ritual murder would discredit Russia's Jews, weakening the case for lifting their civil disabilities and embarrassing the left more generally.'[160]

From the time of his energetic campaigning on behalf of the Russian and Romanian Jewish population, Wolf envisaged the implementation of a new regime, enforcing their human rights, their civic and religious liberty. Without equal rights for Jews, the rights of every other citizen were at risk. Wolf's American friend, Oscar Straus, explained to him that

> In 1898, during his second mission to Turkey, discrimination was attempted against American Protestant missionaries basing it on Russia's action in making discrimination against American citizens of the Jewish faith. Among these missionaries there were two or three British subjects.

158 *The Times* 18 October 1913.
159 Hans Rogger, *Jewish Policies and Right-Wing Politics in Imperial Russia* (Los Angeles and Berkeley, University of California Press, 1986), p. 55.
160 Albert S. Lindemann, *Esau's Tears: Modern Anti-Semitism and the Rise of the Jews* (Cambridge, 1997), p. 305.

Of course, I would not recognize any such claim, or the validity of any such precedent, and succeeded in preventing the exclusion of the American missionaries as well as that of the British subjects ... if a country permits a discrimination against the class of her citizens upon the basis of a religion, it opens the door for like discrimination to be made in other countries against other classes of citizens.[161]

Wolf pressed Straus for more details of the incident, in the hope of utilizing it as a precedent in his long running dispute with the Foreign Office on the Russian Passport question, though he never appears to have approached them with this precedent in mind.[162] The legal status of Jewish citizens with chequered rights, as in Russia, or no rights at all, as in Romania, who were also categorized as demonic because of the persistence of the Blood Libel and the new paranoid delusions about the Elders of Zion seeking to manipulate mankind when mixed together were potentially an explosive brew.[163] Apart from this, Wolf had been in favour of granting political and cultural autonomy to the Jews of Salonica 'in a free and self-governing port' because they comprised the majority of the population, though these circumstances were exceptional and not of general application.[164] Foreign loans, however, kept Russia afloat, and the efforts of the Rothschilds and Jacob Schiff to place an embargo on them failed. So Wolf used the world's media to challenge the Blood libel utilized by the Tsarist regime against Beilis and, in 1912, launched a new journal entitled *Darkest Russia* in 1912, to hammer away at the autocracy in those places, where it was most vulnerable. Yet, as Wolf observed, Russian financial stability was an illusion. 'A few years ago', he pointed out [in 1912],' many millions were lost by the French and Belgian investors in Russian industrials'. In a subsequent issue of *Darkest Russia*, he observed that 'the huge "free balance", of which the Russian Treasury is continually boasting and which, at the beginning of the present year, was declared to amount to over 42 millions sterling, is composed for the most part of those portions of the loans of 1908 and 1909 which have not been used

161 Yivo, Mowshowitch Collection reel 4 Oscar Straus to Wolf 19 June 1913.
162 Yivo, Mowshowitch Collection reel 4 Wolf to Oscar Straus 1 July 1913.
163 Norman Cohn, *Warrant for Genocide* (Harmondsworth, 1970) and Hadassa Ben-Itto, *The Lie that Wouldn't Die: The Protocols of the Elders of Zion* (London, 2005).
164 Levene, *War, Jews, and the New Europe*, pp. 171–2.

for their earmarked purposes'.[165] He continued to dwell on this theme year
after year; and on 1 July 1914, he wrote prophetically that the

> recent heavy slump in Russians caused by the reckless imposition of
> new company restrictions in pursuit of a narrow Nationalist policy is
> an earnest of still graver catastrophes that may ensue in the near future.
> But, even without any aggravation of the Government's present policy,
> the temper of the people already strained to breaking-point, is a factor
> which the investor in Russian stocks must take seriously into account.
> As we have intimated, there are signs that the popular discontent which
> pervades all sections of Russian society may shortly come to a head.[166]

Writing to Leonard Cohen on 25 March 1914, Wolf was pleased to tell
him that he had 'heard today that Mr Hearst, whose journals as you know
appeal every day to over two million readers, has been very much impressed
by our publications and has written to Mr Mulholland asking him to get
further information from me, so that he may more effectively support our
anti-Russian campaign in the States'. Wolf's press campaign was so effective
that it was reaching an ever-wider international audience.[167]

Since Natty's last grand gesture for Russian Jewry before Edward VII's
trip to Reval to meet the Tsar, Natty's responses on Jewish issues appear to
have become more muted. Moreover, whereas he enjoyed good relations
with Balfour and Lansdowne and they had to pay some attention to his
views, his relationship with Grey was much more distant and he could be
much more easily ignored. Natty refused to utter any complaints about
Russia's chaotic finances; he did nothing to push the Russian Passport
question and he opted out of sponsoring *Darkest Russia*, thus enabling Wolf
to attack the financial competence and viability of the Tsarist regime. Even
where he did lend assistance, as in the Beilis case, he was overshadowed
by the more active organizing role of Lucien Wolf, who led the defence
campaign in Britain and utilized the world's press to undermine the Blood
libel allegations against Beilis. Much of Natty's last minute scramble to
procure documents specially attested by the Cardinal proved in the end

165 *Darkest Russia* 31 January 1912 p. 1 and 7 February 1912, p. 3.
166 *Darkest Russia* 16 April 1913 p. 61, 16 July 1913 p. 118, 24 December 1913, p. 206, and 1
     July 1914, p. 101.
167 Wolf Collection, Wolf to Leonard Cohen 25 March 1914.

to be irrelevant to the findings of the court. Contrast this with the Polna case in 1899, reviving the charges of ritual murder against Jews, when the headquarters of the defence were in New Court under Rothschild auspices.

Apart from forwarding his French cousin's letter to Grey, alerting him to the situation in Romania, Natty did hardly anything throughout Wolf's sustained campaign on behalf of Romanian Jewry, nor did he appear to have any views on whether political and cultural autonomy should be granted to the Jews of Salonica. By concentrating on the big diplomatic issues, the antecedents of the Boer War and taking steps to halt the drift towards War in 1914, Natty allowed his attention to wander from the nitty-gritty of Jewish international diplomacy, thereby providing the space for a new class of Jewish professionals, such as Lucien Wolf and Paul Nathan to take command. Wolf, with his independent stance, challenged not only the dominance of the establishment figures in the Conjoint Committee, but the primacy of Lord Rothschild himself in this sector of Anglo-Jewish affairs.

10

A Good Death

If 1909 had been a bad year for Natty in the national popularity ratings, 1910 ended on a happier note, at least among most sections of Anglo-Jewry, when he celebrated his seventieth birthday on 8 November 1910. His standing among most of the working class and those sections of the middle class enthusiastically supporting social reform had sunk to a new low during the campaigning over the Lloyd George Budget. Even so, 1909 had had its rewarding moments, in particular the communal celebration of the seventieth birthday of Chief Rabbi Hermann Adler, which was marked by a garden party given by the Rothschilds at Gunnersbury on 10 June at which Hermann Adler was presented with an address and his portrait. More than 5,000 Jews travelled to Gunnersbury 'shook hands with the Chief Rabbi and your humble servant [,] walked in the garden and partook of light refreshments; there were a large number of people from the East End of London, a great many working men who all seemed happy and pleased and were well behaved', Natty reported.[1]

An even grander occasion was the celebration of Natty's seventieth birthday. In the morning, he received 'a perfect avalanche of letters, telegrams of congratulation and good wishes from all parts of the world'. For the event, he stayed at Tring Park, where in

1   RAL X1/130A/3 Natty to his cousins Paris 10 and 11 June 1909.

the afternoon, surrounded by his family, he received deputations of well-wishers from his estate staff, the town of Tring led by the vicar and finally separate deputations from the tenant farmers of his Aylesbury and Tring Park estates. 'His Lordship, who was suffering from a cold, which affected his voice, appeared to be otherwise in good health, and manifested the keenest interest in the prosperity or otherwise of the pursuits of those who formed the deputations ...'

The bells of the Parish Church rang out in the early morning and again in the evening in honour of Lord Rothschild's birthday. 'The Tring Brass Band, the Church Lads' Brigade Band, the band of the Salvation Army played outside the Mansion during the evening.'[2] On the following afternoon at New Court at 4.00 p.m., Natty played host to a deputation from the Board of Deputies, who presented him with an album containing a Jewish address of congratulation signed by the Presidents of 148 synagogues and numerous Jewish charitable institutions from the Hayes Industrial School and the Board of Shechita [Ritual Slaughter] to the West Central Jewish Girls Club. Lord Swaythling also presented an address on behalf of the Federation of Synagogues.[3] The next day, Natty reverted to his role of Lord Lieutenant, calling a meeting at Aylesbury to decide on a Bucks memorial for his friend the late King Edward; it was all very exhausting and exhilarating.[4]

Although there was an arrival of a fresh generation of Rothschilds – Walter and Charles, the sons of Natty and Leo's three sons – at New Court, this next generation of Rothschilds failed to rejuvenate the London bank. Walter, Natty's heir, had been a problem child and developed into a problematic adult. He joined the Bank in 1890, but his stay there proved to be so disastrous that he was asked to leave by his father in 1908, when a scandal came to light. All Walter's income was spent on payments for maintaining his natural history museum at Tring and his live animals. Charles Nauheim, the chief clerk in the private department of the Bank, discovered that Walter had made a series of worthless and costly investments and in the end felt the necessity of drawing this to the attention

2   *Jewish Chronicle* 11 November 1910, p. 18; *Bucks Herald* 12 November 1910.
3   *Jewish Chronicle* 11 November 1910, pp. 18–20.
4   *Bucks Herald* 12 November 1910.

of Natty. It also came to light that, for two years, Walter had been hiding the correspondence containing details of his purchases in wicker laundry baskets. It took his younger brother Charles, with the aid of four clerks, six weeks to open all the letters and to compute what was owing in order to put the museum's finances on a sound footing. Natty was incensed, refusing any longer to speak to Walter directly; any conversation between them had to be conveyed through Charles, who acted as an intermediary.[5]

Charles pensioned off Walter's two mistresses, providing each of them with a house and an income of £10,000 per annum with the proviso that they were to keep away from Tring and not contact the Rothschild family. One of the ladies, Marie Fredensen, bore Walter a daughter called Olga.[6] What only surfaced after Walter's death in 1937, due to concealment on his part, was that he had been blackmailed for almost forty years by a peeress, who had once been his mistress, aided and abetted by her equally unscrupulous husband. It was this man who had induced Walter to invest in a number of worthless companies.[7] Society gossips embellished tales of Walter's misdeeds and Lord Balcarres wrote the following distorted account in his diary on 29 January 1908:

> Walter Rothschild is on the verge of bankruptcy. Papa has already paid his debts once or twice: now he has speculated, he has expended huge sums upon a rather indifferent book about extinct birds and they say that a lady friend has absorbed many shekels. Anyhow poor fat Walter has raised money on the post-obits of papa and mama. The former is furious: most of all that, for the first time in history, a Rothschild has speculated unsuccessfully. It is a great blow to the acumen of the family.[8]

Natty's second son, Nathaniel Charles known as Charles, was born in 1877 and was almost ten years younger than his brother, so that it is likely that he joined N. M. Rothschild & Sons around the turn of the century. Like his brother Walter, Charles studied natural science at Cambridge and wanted

5   Rothschild, *Dear Lord Rothschild*, pp. 92 and 229–32.
6   Ibid., pp. 219–22.
7   Ibid., p. 230.
8   John Vincent, ed., *The Crawford Papers: The Journal of David Lindsay Twenty-Seventh Earl of Crawford and Tenth Earl of Balcarres 1871–1940* (Manchester, 1984), p. 105.

to be a naturalist, but unlike his brother was conscientious and dutiful and buckled down to long hours at the Bank. 'By dint of working an eighteen hour day, Charles managed to carry out his duties as a landowner and his scientific studies while also fulfilling his responsibilities at New Court.' However, although brimming with new ideas to invigorate the bank, Charles was not listened to by his father, who wanted to carry on business in the traditional way and was adverse to exposure to risk. After a trip to Japan, Charles became convinced of the opportunities awaiting the Bank in that burgeoning economy, but his insistence on opening an office there was rejected. Nor could he persuade the Rothschild partners to invest in a company making gramophone records.[9]

Natty clung to his preferred business strategy of state loans, participating in a syndicate after the Russo-Japanese War in 1905 to raise £25,000,000 for the Japanese government, by converting their Treasury bonds to a lower rate of interest and issuing an £11 million loan for Brazil in 1913 at five per cent. Alfred was heavily involved in the negotiations with the vice-governor of the Bank of Japan, who was his house-guest at Halton on a number of occasions.[10] In 1910, it was estimated that since Natty had become 'head of the firm in New Court its business in loans and other public issues had reached a total of not less than £450,000,000, and this is in addition to the greatest bill business in the world [somewhat of an exaggeration] and in miscellaneous mercantile transactions on a tremendous scale'.[11] Riskier and more lucrative investment opportunities were left to more enterprising newcomers, such as Sir Ernest Cassel and Sir Edgar Speyer, who master-minded the electrification of the Metropolitan District Railway and funded the building of three London Underground railway lines. Investment in Canada, where there was a capital inflow of £500 million between 1900 and 1914 to spur industrialization, and in petroleum were neglected by the Rothschilds as insufficiently safe areas. Natty informed his French cousins in April 1910 that 'We unfortunately have never had a very great interest in them [oil shares], and I am very much afraid that it is too late to venture

9   Wilson, *Rothschild*, pp. 319–20.
10   Caroline Shaw, *The Necessary Security. An illustrated History of Rothschild Bonds* (London, 2006), pp. 32–4 and Kynaston, *The City of London* Vol. II, p. 372 and 437–8.
11   *Daily Graphic* 8 November 1908.

very largely.'[12] In any case, we have already seen that Natty's knowledge of the American stock market was castigated as poor by advisers to the King's Fund. Third generation firms, such as the London Rothschilds, according to Stanley Chapman stuck 'to safe businesses with modest profit margins'. Nevertheless, acceptances of bills of exchange by N. M. Rothschild & Sons increased from the late 1880s, climbing from £1.4 million in 1890 to £3.2 in 1913, as the expansion in world trade was financed in sterling through the London money market.[13]

Natty left the initiative to developing the oil industry in Baku to his brother-in-law, Baron Alphonse, who formed a company in 1884 to refine crude oil and then market it.[14] Natty brushed aside opportunities to participate in the development of the Middle Eastern oilfields, when the Admiralty wanted to ensure that essential oil supplies were under British control. William Knox D'Arcy secured a valuable oil concession in Southern Persia from the Persian government and arranged for his inter-mediary, Sir Arthur Ellis, to approach Lord Rothschild in December 1903, after Natty had remarked that this was of 'great importance'. But when Ellis stated that a syndicate and an investment of £2 million would be required to develop the potential oilfields, Natty advised him to negotiate with Baron Alphonse. Fearful of foreign involvement, the Admiralty sabotaged these talks, while at the same time arranging for a British company to undertake this investment, and after oil was struck, the Anglo-Persian Oil Company was founded in 1909.[15] A share issue in the Paris market of Royal Dutch having failed, Henry Deterding was determined to launch a London issue, where it was successfully handled by N. M. Rothschild & Sons in 1913.[16] Nevertheless, big opportunities to participate in the burgeoning oil industry were missed by the London house.

Although American trade climbed to record levels, with exports exceeding imports by 61 million dollars in May 1913, Natty's horizons as to the business ventures available in the United States were still constricted

12 Kynaston, *The City of London* Vol. II, pp. 505 and 517.
13 Chapman, *The Rise of Merchant Banking*, pp. 108, 121 and 178.
14 Robert Henriques, *Marcus Samuel* (London, 1960), p. 73.
15 Arthur Cook, *Ace of Spies: The True Story of Sidney Reilly* (Stroud, 2004), pp. 62–8.
16 Joost Jonker and Jan Luiten van Zanden, *From Challenger to Joint Industry Leader, 1890–1939: A History of Royal Dutch Shell* Vol. 1 (Oxford, 2007), pp. 140–1 and 144.

before the First World War.[17] During 1908, the London and Paris houses had seen no other option than to bale out August Belmont for 'old acquaintance and friendship['s] sake', when Belmont's firm was in financial difficulties. In return for a Rothschild loan of £450,000, August Belmont & Co agreed to mortgage properties in the City of New York worth $2,407,750 to the bank in January and within a month, to start repaying the London and Paris houses until the debt was liquidated.[18] Despite the fact that August Belmont rapidly repaid their loan, the Rothschilds were cautious about extending their business in the United States. During 1912, August Belmont received a 'cable on the 5th [January, from the Bank] to sell the rubber held for ... friends as soon as possible. You speak of selling in small parcels, but after consultation with our broker, we are convinced that this would merely result in breaking the market and we recommend that we should sell the amount to be sold in one block'. This was duly done and the proceeds remitted to the Rothschild account.[19] In May, the Rothschild Bank's American agents recommended that the London and Paris Rothschild houses should participate in an issue of bonds by J. P. Morgan & Co in the Interborough Rapid Transit Co. [a forerunner of the New York subway system]. The Rothschild bank cabled back 'that ... [they] would take a participation of $500,000 of the new Interborough Rapid Transit bonds, and yesterday we received your second cable, taking an additional $50,000 of these securities'.[20] In February 1913, August Belmont requested the bank to let them know whether they wished participate in a rights issue of railway company stock 'or sell the 'Rights'. The Rothschilds were advised that

> Besides the shares which are registered in our name, and belonging to you, 500 Union Pacific Railroad Company stock, entitling you to subscribe to 125 shares in Southern Pacific Company stock ... there are 25 shares of Southern Pacific Company stock, registered in our name, entitling you to subscribe to 8 1/3 shares, concerning which we also await your instructions.[21]

17 RAL II 55/22 B August Belmont & Co to N. M. Rothschild & Sons 19 June 1913.
18 RAL XI/III/186/3 N. M. Rothschild & Sons to August Belmont & Co 21 November 1907 and S. Stephany New York to N. M. Rothschild & Sons.
19 RAL II 55/22 August Belmont & Co to N. M. Rothschild & Sons 2 February 1912.
20 Ibid., 31 May and 7 June 1912.
21 Ibid., 17 February 1913.

On the other hand, while their American agents August Belmont wanted to participate in the £21,000,000 Rothschild bonds issue for the Brazilian government in 1914, they were unable to avail themselves of this business because they 'could not take an equal proportion with the other ... [subscribers]'.[22]

From the surviving records it appears that the volume of business between the bank and August Belmont & Co was small. Natty almost seemed more interested in high politics in the United States than in the investment opportunities which were at hand, having the results of the proceedings of the Democratic Convention cabled to him and arranging for his agent to convey to Theodore Roosevelt 'congratulations on his fortunate escape' from assassination.[23]

In addition to his role at the bank, Natty held a number of company directorships. He was chairman of the Alliance Assurance Company, honorary chairman of the Four Per Cent Industrial Dwellings Company, and a director of the Northern France Railway Company and of the South Austrian Railway Company.[24] 'Lord Rothschild was no ordinary chairman [of the Alliance Assurance Company]', claimed Francis Lucas.

> From the foundation of the company his firm had always been in the closest relations with our company. Since the time he had become chairman the connexion had been drawn even closer, and there was not during the whole period of his chairmanship any business proposed of the slightest importance with which he did not make himself thoroughly acquainted. He always found time to attend to any Alliance business and always took the greatest interest in it; in fact, he was very proud of his connexion with the company, and it was ... a source of great satisfaction to him to watch, under his chairmanship and under the able management of Mr Lewis, the steady growth of the company from a position of comparative unimportance to being quite one of the leading British insurance companies.[25]

Just as Natty was a vigorous opponent of state-sponsored social reform, so

22 Ibid., 19 and 26 June 1914.
23 Ibid., 28 June and 18 October 1912.
24 *Financial Times* 1 April 1915.
25 *The Times* 29 April 1915.

his private observations show that he was hardly a champion of limiting the power of the House of Lords. Determined to undermine the veto hitherto exercised by the Upper House, the government introduced the Parliament Bill and threatened to create a large number of new peers, if their lordships baulked at letting it pass. Writing to his French cousins on 9 August 1911, shortly before the decisive vote in the Lords on the Parliament Bill, he turned his attention to Bob Crewe, a newly fledged marquis married to a Rothschild, who was the government spokesman in the upper chamber, and who looked – and was – unwell. Crewe

> acknowledged that our gracious sovereign had been constrained but he expressed at the same time the hope and the belief that the Radical majority having received quite unlimited power would use that power with wisdom and moderation. In strange contrast to this speech was the arrogance of Winston Churchill in the House of Commons, who said this power would be used to carry the most Radical and demagogic measures. Bad as the situation is when the Parliament Bill is passed it is made much worse by the action of the 'Diehards' or 'Ditchers' as they call themselves, who want to defeat the Government in the House of Lords. I should be sorry to say positively they will not do so and if they were victorious there would be a considerable creation of peers, which will enable the Government to pass whatever measures they like. However, as Rosebery says, [we] have a knack in this country of falling on our legs, and it is no use being too pessimistic.[26]

Unwilling to embarrass the new monarch, George V, with whom he enjoyed good relations, Natty, despite his objections to the measure, abstained when, on 10 August 1911, a group of peers tried to carry some wrecking amendments against the Parliament Bill. The government mustered 131 supporters against 114 for the Diehards, their majority being bolstered by the adhesion of 37 Unionist peers and 13 bishops.[27]

In the long, hot summer of 1911 and into the autumn, there were strikes among the dockers, railwaymen and coal miners. Once again, Churchill attracted Natty's anger.

---

26   RAL XI/130A/5 Natty to his cousins Paris 9 August 1911.
27   Jenkins, *Mr Balfour's Poodle*, pp. 167–85; *The Times* 11 August 1911.

Unfortunately, Mr Churchill is at the head of the Home Office and he is always much too much swayed by sentiment. Since he has held the present post strikes have been numerous and the men are beginning to think that they have only to strike to get their way. All the riff-raff of the country find casual labour employment at the Docks and they are the most difficult class to appease, inflamed as they have been during the last few days by the violent speeches of various socialist celebrities. Today they are preventing the carting of goods and London streets are nearly empty under the peaceful picketing methods of the trades unions. We have had to close our refinery owing to the impossibility of obtaining coal or wood ... undoubtedly the greatest hardship will be felt by the poor owing to the great increase in the cost of supplies. Many tons of meat and other provisions are lying waiting in the Thames and it is to be hoped that the ships have enough coal to keep their cold storage machinery going till the strike comes to an end. Otherwise the cost will be enormous.[28]

While sympathizing with Natty's distress at the temporary closure of the firm's refinery, his dismissive assessment of the casual labour situation at the London docks shows a poor grasp of the underlying structural problems which resulted in William Beveridge inserting a clause in the 1913 Insurance Amendment Act to decasualize dock labour at the London Docks.[29]

As a platform speaker, Natty lacked the lightness of touch and the humour of Leo, but his rather hard-line speeches on most issues continued to be fully reported in the national press and this meant that he was still perceived as a polarizing and divisive figure. Speaking on 7 February 1912 at Tring, 'Lord Rothschild said the first duty of the Unionist Party on coming to power would be to repeal the Parliament Act, to reform the House of Lords, and to suspend the action of the Insurance Act until it was moulded more into accordance with the wishes of the people and their customs.'[30]

With his rolling acres and great wealth, Natty was a conscientious landowner and model landlord, who sustained many private schemes for

28 RAL XI/130A/5 Natty to his cousins Paris 10 August 1911.
29 Gordon Phillips and Noel Whiteside, *Casual Labour. The Unemployment Question in the Port Transport Industry 1880–1970* (Oxford, 1985), pp. 103–6. William Beveridge, *Power and Influence* (London, 1953), p. 79.
30 *The Times* 8 February 1912.

the welfare of his tenants and the townspeople of Tring. Perhaps this is why he preferred to rely on the initiatives and charity of landowners and industrialists rather than seek the extension of state-sponsored social services. On 22 March 1909, Lloyd George thanked Lord Rothschild for his 'remarks upon the proposed scheme for a system of contributory insurance against sickness, invalidity etc. I fully recognize the weight of your contention that a scheme of this kind should be considered in conjunction with reform of the existing poor law ...'[31] Yet Natty never really favoured a scheme of compulsory National Health Insurance, calling at first for its suspension; and later in 1913 admitting that 'he could not say that he himself was ever opposed to a contributory scheme of insurance, but thought that a contributory scheme should partake much more of a voluntary than of a compulsory character'.[32] Moreover, in a speech at the Newmarket Town Hall, his brother Leo ridiculed the 1911 Insurance Act. 'There was a horse named "Insurance". It had been trotted out during the past two years and found very groggy.' He did not think it would win a race. 'Look at its pedigree: Insurance by Panel Doctor out of Contribution; Panel doctor, by Underpaid out of Overworked; Contribution by Chancellor out of You must Pay (Loud Laughter). How could a horse with such a pedigree win in any circumstances?'[33] Apart from this, Natty castigated Lloyd George for his plan to raid the Insurance Fund to find the cash to erect what he termed 'jerry-built cottages'; and there was a sharp exchange in correspondence between him and the Chancellor.[34]

Natty forecast that the government 'will have the whole of January [1912] to stump the country and may promise to rob everybody and to confiscate everything as a special ... [concession] to their friends'. Shortly afterwards Natty confided to his cousins that the government was aware of its unpopularity and that ministers were capable 'of initiating still further socialistic legislation and should they do so it is difficult to foretell what may be the result; their last semi-socialistic measure [the Insurance Act 1911] is exciting a great deal of ire and will either become a dead letter or ...

31   Rothschild, *Dear Lord Rothschild*, p. 43.
32   *The Times* 18 November 1913.
33   *The Times* 16 May 1913.
34   *The Times* 18 November 1913. Rothschild, *Dear Lord Rothschild*, pp. 43–4.

be suspended', somewhat wishful thinking on his part but showing his real feelings about the matter.[35]

Yet behind the brusque manner invariably displayed by Natty, there lurked a kind nature, sensitive to the distress and needs of others. Over the years, he had held himself out, with some success, as an honest broker able to mediate in disputes between employers and the working man and woman. In 1889, his services were called upon by Cardinal Manning to help resolve a dock strike, a feat which he accomplished by securing the recognition of the union, decent rates of pay and better working conditions. A surviving but rather illegible notebook of Natty's has a page headed with the words 'Widows and orphans' and 'insist'.[36] Later in the year, three tailoring unions active in the East End called a strike which was supported by leading figures in the English labour movement, including John Burns, Tom Mann and Ben Tillett; it was only ended by the intervention of Natty and Sir Samuel Montagu. Fearful of the association in the public mind of striking Jewish tailors with socialism, on 3 October 1889, Natty's personal representative and Montagu compelled the employers to accede to the strikers' demands for the limitation of hours, while the men agreed to forgo a wage rise for one year. Rothschild contributed £73 to the strike funds and £100 was donated from the unexpended balance of the dockers' strike fund.[37] What appeared to be the assistance of Lord Rothschild in another tailors' strike in the East End in June 1906 was a hoax, a cheque for £1,000 donated to the strike funds turning out to be a fake.[38]

Again, in January 1914 Natty, as a leading Buckinghamshire landowner and Lord Lieutenant of the county, reverted to a rather paternalistic role, offering his services as a mediator in a strike and lock-out of 3,000 chair and furniture makers in High Wycombe and sending £100 to feed the children of necessitous strikers. This was, nevertheless, Natty's first intervention in a major trade dispute for over twenty years.[39] The strike was effectively ended

35 RAL XI/130A/5 and 6A Natty to his cousins Paris 30 November 1911 and 4 January 1912.
36 Rothschild, *Dear Lord Rothschild*, p. 39.
37 Anne J. Kershen, *Uniting the Tailors* (London, 1995), pp. 136–9 and Lloyd P. Gartner, *The Jewish Immigrant in England 1870–1914*, pp. 122–6.
38 William J. Fishman, *East End Jewish Radicals 1875–1914* (London, 1975), p. 283.
39 *The Times* 12 January 1914.

through the negotiating skills of the government arbitrator, Sir George Askwith, who was accepted by both sides as a more neutral figure.

The year 1912 had been a bad one for Leopold, known as Leo. A young Jewish man whom he befriended under the delusion that he had influenced a tutor at King's College to obstruct his studies, jumped on to his carriage and tried to shoot him. Fortunately, Leo escaped unscathed, though a police constable, Charles Berg, was shot in the right side of the throat.[40] The following year was to prove equally difficult for Natty. A young German clerk, Heinrich Kremerskothen, came to London in 1913 and, unable to obtain employment, wrote a threatening letter to Lord Rothschild, demanding the sum of £30,400. After some further letters and threats to other members of the Rothschild family, including Natty's cousin Alice, the blackmailer reduced his demands to £500. The police, as instructed by the blackmailer, placed a package stuffed with banknotes in a hole in a lavatory at Appenrodt's Restaurant in Covent Garden. When Kremerskothen went to the restaurant to collect the package, he was arrested. Natty gave evidence at the committal proceedings that he had received the blackmailing letters. During the trial, at the Central Criminal Court in September, it emerged that Natty 'did not take the threats seriously, and had no personal fear, but he had members of his family staying with him who did not look upon the letter in the same light'. Counsel for the prosecution revealed that earlier, when the accused had written to Lord Rothschild for employment, he had forwarded his letter to a charity but they could not do anything to assist, as the prisoner had relatives who could support him. Counsel added that 'Lord Rothschild did not desire to press the case further than the Recorder thought necessary in the interests of the public generally.' The judge sentenced the prisoner to 15 months imprisonment with hard labour and recommended that he be deported after his sentence.[41] The Rothschilds appeared to act as lightening rods for the discontent pervading the country.

In the last two years before the Great War, Natty continued in his speeches to be a loyal supporter of Conservative policies. His long time political ally, Arthur Balfour, was now the senior member of parliament representing the City of London, allowing the two of them ample

40   *The Times* 5 March and 26 April 1912.
41   *The Times* 4 and 9 August and 4 September 1913.

opportunities for cooperation. When Balfour stepped down as party leader in November 1911, Natty told his cousins that he had known him for 'thirty years so that I can fully appreciate his worth and value, we have always been friends and I hope notwithstanding my age to remain friends for some time to come'.[42]

On 21 January 1913, Balfour addressed a meeting of City men opposed to the Franchise and Registration Bill which extended the electoral base but took the vote away from any bankers and stockbrokers who failed to sleep in the City overnight. Natty railed that

> he would prefer to see them support Mr Asquith in his undisguised hostility to votes for women (Cheers). If by any chance this ill-fated measure, with woman suffrage, became law, the electors of the City of London would be mainly charwomen, who would probably send to Parliament members who were not at all qualified to represent the interests of the finance and commerce of this great Empire.[43]

Natty's principal interest in these years, apart from concerns about Russian Jewry, was the fate of Ireland. In a speech delivered on 17 November 1913 he gloomily predicted that

> The clouds were low on the horizon and there was, he would not say a probability, but a great possibility, of civil war in the kingdom. His own opinion of Home Rule was the same as it had always been; it had been quite unaltered since 1885–6. He could not recognize that Ireland was a distinct nation, and he agreed with Mr Balfour in all that he had to say on the subject. They had a considerable portion of Ireland – Ulster – which used to be Liberal and which was strongly loyal and strongly Protestant, which could not be put under the domination of the rest of the country under a Home Rule scheme.[44]

Since Baron Lionel's friendship with John Delane, the Rothschilds had enjoyed particularly close relations with successive editors of *The Times*. After the death of Lord Rowton, literary executor of the Beaconsfield estate Natty, with the assistance of the other trustees, selected W. F. Monypenny

42   RAL XI/130A/5 Natty to his cousins Paris 8 November 1911.
43   *The Times* 22 January 1913.
44   *The Times* 18 November 1913.

and George Buckle of that newspaper to write the authorised biography of Disraeli. In 1886, Buckle thanked him for a gift of reproductions of his pictures. 'I was particularly pleased to see the "Garrick between Tragedy and Comedy" which I admired so greatly at your house'.[45] When proposals were mooted at the end of 1907 to re-organize *The Times*, Lord Rothschild was consulted by Lord Lansdowne and later by Moberley Bell, Cassel and others, about a scheme for Pearson to purchase the newspaper.[46] On 30 July 1912, Buckle wrote to Natty on the eve of his retirement as editor, saying that 'Your kind words, though they are much too flattering, give me great pleasure; for I know your sincere character, & that you mean them' and introduced his successor.'

> Mr Geoffrey Robinson [was] a man in the prime of young manhood, 37 years old, a Yorkshireman with a small property, who was educated at Eton & Magdalen, Oxford where he got a couple of first classes & was afterwards (like me) a Fellow of All Souls. He was subsequently for a while in the Colonial Office, & was taken to South Africa by Milner as a member of what was colloquially called his *Kindergarten*. Then, after the war, he succeeded Monypenny as editor of the *Star*, and was *The Times*' correspondent in South Africa. He has now been here for a year and a half assisting me most zealously in the office. He is a man of high character & good judgment, alert & keen.

Six months later, Robinson assured Natty that he had wanted to 'come and see ... [him] for several days' because he wished to introduce him to Reginald Nicholson, the new manager at Printing House Square.[47]

In the early months of 1914, Natty thought that the time was ripe for his own intervention to suggest a plan to solve the crisis over Ulster. After speaking with Geoffrey Robinson (later known as Dawson), editor of *The Times*, and Bonar Law, the leader of the Opposition, on 9 February 1914,

---

45   W. F. Monypenny and G. E. Buckle, *The Life of Benjamin Disraeli, Earl of Beaconsfield* (London, 1910–20), Vol. 1 preface p. ix and Vol. 3 preface p. ix. George Buckle to Natty 28 December 1886 and 27 November 1897. *The History of the Times* vol. III, pp. 509–11, 517, 522 and 556.

46   *The History of the Times* (London, 1952), Vol. III, pp. 509–11, 517, 522 and 556.

47   RAL, 000/848/37 George Buckle to Natty 30 July 1912; and Geoffrey Robinson to Natty 2 December 1912 and 8 January 1913.

he approached Lord Stamfordham, King George V's private secretary, telling him that Robinson thought that:

> every endeavour should be made to prevent Civil War and he has always advocated, either a general election or the complete and permanent exclusion of Ulster. Mr Bonar Law was very frank in his conversation with me and I gather at one moment Mr Asquith was prepared to grant nearly the complete exclusion of Ulster ... Mr Bonar Law's view is that to prevent Civil War there must either be a dissolution of Parliament; or else Ulster must remain in its present position, forming an integral part of Great Britain and thereby be quite outside Home Rule ... In adopting this policy, he fully recognises, as I do, that it is a great sacrifice for the Unionist party to make as chance of success at any subsequent election would be much diminished with the Irish question settled. Naturally, Mr Bonar Law is much preoccupied as he thinks Mr Asquith may offer Ulster 'Home Rule within Home Rule'. Mr Bonar Law fancies (although I do not agree with him) this offer might be dust thrown in the eyes of the British Public but such a concession would not remove the chances of Civil War and therefore the only two solutions to be considered at this present moment are *a general election or the complete and permanent exclusion of Ulster from the Home Rule scheme.*[48]

Lord Stamfordham thanked Natty warmly for his

> Memorandum which I will show to the King. Personally, ever since last summer I have ventured to say that the total exclusion of Ulster with the right to "come in" to be decided by a referendum of the people of Ulster was the only chance of a peaceful settlement – But the opposition & 'The Times' preferred 'a general election' – The latter they will not get unless the Government is beaten on some side issue – the Government will not now, look at the exclusion of Ulster ... The whole situation is full of anxiety. Many thanks for saying you will be ready to come and see me – Meanwhile we will await the events of the next few days.[49]

In February 1914 Balfour, with Sir Edward Carson, spoke to a meeting of City men on the subject of Ireland, warning the government that 'when

---

48 RA, PS/PSO/GV/C/K/2553/3/84 Memorandum from Lord Rothschild 9 February 1914.

49 RAL 000/848/37 Lord Stamfordham to Natty 9 February 1914.

their modifications in the [Home Rule] Bill were offered, half-measures would be useless, and he declared that the Government were already in the rapids leading to civil war'. Natty, in moving the main resolution, noted that the financial clauses of the measure would have to be altered, and asked that if there were safeguards for Ulster, how were the rights of the loyal minority in the rest of Ireland to be protected?[50] Natty had immense sympathy for the hardliners in the Conservative party on the Home Rule Bill, so much so that he pledged £10,000 to a secret fund being organized by Milner to 'succour the Provisional Government of Ulster' should such an eventuality become necessary.[51] Slowly but inevitably the government and the Unionists were drifting, however, towards a compromise. As Andrew Adonis has pointed out, 'In particular, the two-year veto on Home Rule [under the Parliament Act] gave the Ulstermen and their Unionist allies both the opportunity and a timetable to mobilize Ulster resistance, such that by the summer of 1914 Asquith conceded that the 1912 bill could only be complemented with special provisions for Ulster.'[52] King George V, working for conciliation between the parties, was assured by Redmond that, once the Home Rule Bill had been enacted, 'the Nationalist Party would be able to do many things to meet the views of Ulster which at present were impossible'.[53]

Over the years, the Rothschilds had tried to preserve peaceful relations between the major European powers and Alfred had worked constantly for an alliance with Germany in the hope that if the strongest military and naval powers were allies, European peace would be ensured for generations to come. In 1897, Natty confessed to Schomberg McDonnell that 'I am in no sense a Philo-German nor do I believe in the divine right of Kings but I am sure that the right thing now would be to settle the Greek things as soon as possible and to come to terms with old Hartzfeld [the German ambassador].'[54] A year later, Alfred arranged for Joseph Chamberlain, the

---

50 *The Times* 19 February 1914.

51 A. M. Gollin, *Proconsul in Politics: A Study of Lord Milner in Opposition and Power* (London, 1964), pp. 187–8.

52 Adonis, *Making Aristocracy Work*, p. 159.

53 Harold Nicholson, *King George V: His Life and Reign* (London, 1953), p. 243.

54 Hatfield House, 3 Marquess, Rothschild file, Natty to Schomberg McDonnell 7 September 1897.

most powerful member of the Cabinet, to have private discussions at his home in Seamore Place with the German ambassador on how to cooperate over China. When a dispute erupted between British and German financial groups as to railway concessions in China, Alfred and his clerk, Joseph Nauheim, intervened and produced an acceptable compromise solution. In September 1898, a secret treaty was signed between the British and German governments for the division of the Portuguese colonies in Africa, in case Portugal required a foreign loan and sought to dispose of them. Through Alfred's goodwill. these negotiations were brought to a successful conclusion. Shortly before the Boer War, a dispute broke out between Britain and Germany over Samoa. An agreement was reached in November 1899 under which Samoa became a German colony while, in return, Britain received the German Solomon Islands in the Pacific, with the exception of Bougainville, as compensation. Again, Alfred played a prominent role in the positive outcome of these negotiations, enhanced by his close friendship with Baron von Eckardstein, the *chargé d'affaires* at the German embassy in London. At the end of January 1900, during the Boer War, Eckardstein, with the assistance of Alfred, negotiated the release of a German steamer which had been seized as a prize by the Royal Navy because it was believed to be carrying arms for the Boers, thereby averting German intervention on the side of Kruger.[55]

Eckardstein blamed the interference of senior German politicians for the collapse of negotiations with Lansdowne and Chamberlain for an Anglo-German alliance in the opening months of 1901. Chamberlain told him, in January 1901, during a stay at the Duke of Devonshire's country house, that he favoured 'a combination with Germany and an association with the Triple Alliance'. On 18 March, Lansdowne, the Foreign Secretary, took soundings for a defensive alliance between Britain and Germany, but Germany proposed too high a price for such an agreement. 'Thus Alfred Rothschild and his brother Lord Rothschild, had told me ...', declared Eckardstein, 'that some of the Ministers, and among them Arthur Balfour, had said that no dependence could be placed on the Kaiser and von Bülow, because they kept falling back into their old flirtations with Russia'. A deal was proposed with Germany, whereby Britain was to occupy Tangier and

55   RAL 000/150 Memorandum possibly by Baron von Eckardstein undated.

the whole of the Mediterranean coast of Morocco, excepting the Spanish portions, while Germany was to be given a number of coaling stations there. Following the termination of these talks, Alfred wrote to Eckardstein on 14 June 1901 that 'Your negotiations in March and April were *ta'khles* (Yiddish for 'practicality'); but what is going on now is *sohabheshmus* (Yiddish for 'blether'). Nobody in England has any more use for the fine empty phrases of Bülow ... Joe [Chamberlain], who dined with me, is quite disheartened. He will have nothing more to do with the people in Berlin. If they are so short-sighted, says he, as not to be able to see the whole new world system depends upon it [an Anglo-German alliance], then there is nothing to be done for them'.[56] Apart from this, so long as Salisbury stayed on as Prime Minister, he remained suspicious of Germany's intentions and would not countenance an alliance. Holstein advised von Bülow that 'Since Salisbury's departure Rothschild can once again be used in political matters. He is on good terms with Balfour and Chamberlain; Salisbury used to cut him'. In the summer of 1902, Holstein wanted to use Alfred as an intermediary to bring 'the continuing newspaper war ... to an end'.[57]

The suddenness of the growing Balkan crisis towards the end of July 1914, which resulted in a general European conflagration, took even the most perceptive observers by surprise. When Natty wrote to his cousins on 23 July 1914, he was mainly concerned with news about Ulster, having been 'told on very good authority that the Conference [to settle the dispute] failed to arrive at a satisfactory conclusion ... Although it was supposed that there was a deadlock at the Conference yesterday we may hope that something satisfactory may have been settled in the early hours of the morning between Lord Lansdowne and Mr Asquith behind the Speaker's chair.' As an afterthought he added, 'We have nothing new and definite about Austria and Servia but there is a general idea that the various matters in dispute will be arranged without an appeal to arms.'[58] By 27 July, Natty was becoming increasingly concerned by the imbroglio, telling

56 Baron von Eckardstein, *Ten Years at the Court of St. James* (London, 1921), pp. 184–5, 215–16 and 221–2. A. J. P. Taylor, *The Struggle for Mastery in Europe 1848–1918* (Oxford, 1954), pp. 396–7.

57 Ferguson, *The World's Banker*, p. 920; Roberts, *Salisbury* p. 801; Norman Rich and M. H. Fisher, eds, *The Holstein Papers* (Cambridge, 1965), vol. IV p. 116.

58 RAL X1/130A/8 Natty to his cousins Paris 23 July 1914.

his relatives that '[N]o one thinks and talks about anything else but the European situation and the consequences which might arise if serious steps were not taken to prevent a European conflagration'. Nevertheless, it was 'the universal opinion that Austria was quite justified in the demands she made on Servia and it would ill-become the great Powers if by a hasty and ill-conceived action they did anything which might be viewed as condoning brutal murder', though Austria had not 'acted with diplomatic skill'. He felt certain that the British government would leave 'no stone ... unturned in the attempts which will be made to preserve the peace of Europe and in this policy, although the ... two rival parties in the state are more sharply divided than they have ever been, Mr Asquith will have the entire country at his back'.[59]

Two days later, Natty appeared to reprimand his cousins with the circuitous phrase that 'I think I may say we believe you to be wrong, not you personally, but French opinion, in attributing sinister motives and underhand dealings to the German Emperor, he is bound by certain treaties and engage-ments to come to the assistance of Austria if she is attacked by Russia but that is the last thing he wishes to do.' A semi-official communiqué published in the German press indicated that negotiations were proceeding directly between St Petersburg and Berlin with 'a desire on both sides to build a golden bridge, this may be perhaps slightly humiliating to the other Chancelleries. I do not know that it is, but it would be the greatest blessing for the world if the war is localized'.[60] A day later, he confided that 'I wish I could send you something accurate or rather encouraging about the situation ... the Powers are still talking and negotiating between themselves and endeavouring to localize the bloodshed and misery'. He was growing increasingly despondent about the aggressive tone of some of the British press, particularly *The Times*. It had noted on 27 July that there was a possibility of having to '"vindicate" our international friendships with the whole strength of our Empire'. On 28 July, it called on the hostile political parties – Germans looked for civil war in Ireland—to 'close ranks'. On 30 July, it harked back to memories of the great French Wars.'[61]

59   Ibid., 27 July 1914.
60   Ibid., 29 July 1914.
61   'Sir John Clapham's account of the financial crisis in August 1914' in R. S. Sayers, *The Bank of England 1891–1944* (Cambridge, 1976), Vol.3, Appendix 3 p. 32.

Personally, I am of opinion that little or no good is done by the ultra blood-thirsty articles which appear in some portions of our Press, they only inflame the already very excitable feeling in Russia and, clumsy as Austria may have been, it would be ultra-criminal if millions of lives were sacrificed in order to sanctify the theory of murder, a brutal murder which the Servians have committed.[62]

Meanwhile on 28 July 1914 Austria-Hungary partially mobilized and declared war on Serbia. Two days later, in response as protector of the Slavs, Russia mobilized. Natty prayed that France would exert its financial leverage on Russia to avoid a general European war in ignorance of the bellicosity of some German ministers and generals and the Kaiser's unpredictability, given his obsession about a British conspiracy inspired by his uncle, the late King Edward VII, to encircle Germany. On 31 July, Natty stated that:

there are persistent rumours in the City that the German Emperor is using all of his influence at both St. Petersburg & Vienna to find a solution which would not be distasteful either to Austria or Russia. I am convinced also that this very laudatory example is being strenuously followed here. Now I venture to ask you what the French govt is doing at the present moment and what is their policy? I hope and trust M. Poincaré who is undoubtedly a "persona gratiosus" with the Czar is not only pointing out to but also impressing upon the Russian Govt 1) that the result of a war, however powerful a country their ally may be, is doubtful, but whatever the result may be, the sacrifices and misery attendant upon it are stupendous & untold. In this case the calamity would be greater than anything ever seen or known before. 2) France is Russia's greatest creditor, in fact the financial and economic conditions of the two countries are intimately connected & we hope that you will do your best to bring any influence you may have, to bear upon your statesman even at the last moment, to prevent the hideous struggle from taking place, and to point out to Russia that she owes this to France.[63]

With the drift towards war, the international financial crisis predicted by Bloch and Angell gathered momentum, causing the stock exchanges in

---

62   RAL X1/130A/8 Natty to his cousins Paris 30 July 1914.
63   Ibid. 31 July 1914.

Vienna and Hungary to close on 27 July. On the same day, Natty informed the Paris house that 'All the foreign Banks and particularly the German ones took a very large amount of money out of the Stock Exchange today, and although the brokers found most of the money they wanted, if not all, the markets were at one time quite demoralized, a good many weak speculators selling at nil prix and all the foreign speculators selling Consols.'[64] A day later, among the items of political gossip which Asquith imparted to Venetia Stanley, was the news that 'Lord Rothschild [came] to tell me that he had received an order from the Paris house to sell a vast quantity of Consols here for the French Gov & Savings Banks, which he has refused to do. It looks ominous.' Natty was obdurate, partly because he wanted to stem the outflow of funds from London, partly because he wished to impede any French preparations for war.[65] By 31 July 1914, the London Stock Exchange was closed and remained shut until 4 January 1915, while the bank rate was raised to eight per cent, followed by a further rate increase of two per cent, a day later.[66]

Norman Angell in *The Great Illusion* (1909) argued that 'war would bring economic disaster to victor and vanquished alike, the capitalist has no country, that arms and conquests and jugglery with frontiers serve no ends of his, and may well defeat them'. It was the Jewish capitalists, notably Lord Rothschild and Albert Ballin, the German shipping magnate, who most exemplified these characteristics in their efforts to halt the drift towards war. Through his friendship with Asquith and Haldane, Natty was able to influence Grey, the Foreign Secretary, who, on 31 July 1914, still hesitated about advocating British intervention because he was convinced that 'the commercial and financial situation was extremely serious', and that 'there was a danger of a complete collapse that would involve everyone in ruin'.[67] Where could these thoughts have come from that were a crystallization of City opinion but from Natty? In an interview with Hugh Chisholm, the financial editor of *The Times*, Natty explained that he had written to the

64 Ibid. 27 July 1914. Niall Ferguson, *The War of the World. History's Age of Hatred* (London, 2006), pp. 837.

65 Michael and Eleanor Brock, eds, *H. H. Asquith: Letters to Venetia Stanley* (Oxford, 1982), pp. 131–2.

66 Ferguson, *The World's Banker*, p. 963 and *The War of the World*, p. 87.

67 James Joll, *The Origins of the First World War* (London, 1984), pp. 136–7.

head of his family in France that 'a terrible financial crisis was impending, that the writer had only £1,000,000 in the Bank of England and £800,000 in the Union of London and Smith's Bank – barely enough to meet his engagements, and that his Paris relatives should draw no more cheques or bills upon him since he could not pay them'.[68]

To avert Britain joining in a large-scale European war was Natty's desperate wish, and there still seemed to be time. Natty enjoyed cordial relations with Geoffrey Robinson (later Dawson), who was appointed editor of Britain's most influential journal in 1912, but his relations with other members of the staff were more tense.[69] At the editorial conference held in the office of *The Times* on Friday 31 July, Hugh Chisholm, the financial editor, reported to Northcliffe that 'Lord Rothschild and ... Leopold Rothschild, convinced that ... [it] was doing the greatest possible harm by its leading articles that were "hounding the country into war" had urged him to do all he could to secure the reversal of the whole tendency'. Chisholm was against a policy of neutrality, however, and the rest of the editorial team agreed with him. Wickham Steed, the foreign editor, denounced Lord Rothschild's plea as 'a dirty German-Jewish international financial attempt to bully us into advocating neutrality'. On Saturday 1 August 1914, *The Times* gave its answer, in the form of an even stiffer editorial.[70] Asquith, the Prime Minister, it opened, announced that

> the Government had just heard – not from St. Petersburg, but from Germany – that Russia has proclaimed a general mobilization of her Army and Fleet, and that in consequence martial law was proclaimed in Germany. It was understood ... that mobilization would follow in Germany if the Russian mobilization continued ... we believe that large bodies of German troops are already massed on the French frontier. Substantial rumours from Paris indicate that there will probably be a general mobilization in France today ... The conflict which seems to be at hand must have world-wide results, and cannot, in any sense, be regarded as affecting the Continent of Europe alone. Such a vast and overwhelming struggle will directly affect our overseas communications,

68 Henry Wickham Steed, *Through Thirty Years 1892–1922* (London, 1924), Vol. 2 p. 8.
69 RAL 000/848/37 George Buckle to Natty 30 July 1912 and Geoffrey Robinson to Natty 2 December 1912.
70 *The History of The Times* Vol. IV pp. 207–8. Steed, *Through Thirty Years 1892–1922*, p. 9.

more especially the route to India, the safety of our food supplies, the security of our seaborne trade, perhaps, most of all, the maritime supremacy which is the cardinal condition of our independent national existence ... We have nothing to avenge and nothing to acquire. In this vital issue we can only be guided by two considerations – the duty we owe to our friends and the instinct of self-preservation ... We dare not stand aside with folded arms and placidly watch our friends placed in peril of destruction.[71]

Paul Schwabach, the head of the Bleichroder Bank, admitted to Alfred on Saturday 1 August that British intervention seemed inevitable, but that they could console themselves that they had 'tried, with all their might, to improve relations between our countries'.[72] Wickham Steed remembered that Saturday 'as the most terrible day of my life. It was known that Germany was about to declare war on Russia, and that war between Germany and France would follow immediately. The one question was whether England would stand firm'. On the same day, there was another editorial conference at *The Times* with Northcliffe stating the case for Britain to go to war. During the conference, Natty telephoned Northcliffe and asked him to visit him and his younger brother Leopold, when they begged him to realign the paper's policy for Britain to follow the path of neutrality. According to Steed 'they assured Northcliffe that they had received such information of the overwhelming military and naval strength of Germany that, if England went to war, "the British Empire would be swept off the face of the earth in a few weeks" ... They had made similar representations to the Chancellor of the Exchequer Mr Lloyd George, who appreciated the situation.'[73] Wickham Steed's anti-Semitic bias is well-known, so that this garbled account of a conversation at which he was not present should be discounted, and all agree that it was Natty's disquiet at the financial implications of the prospect of a major European war that influenced him to urge that Britain should keep out of the conflict. The Rothschilds were such supreme patriots that they would never have indulged in defeatist talk, whatever German messages they were relaying in the hope of keeping

71   *The Times* 1 August 1914.
72   Ferguson, *The World's Banker*, pp. 963–4.
73   Steed, *Through Thirty Years 1892–1922*, Vol. 2, pp. 10–12. *The History of the Times* Vol. IV, p. 210.

Britain neutral. Not content with this action, on 1 August Lord Rothschild, in addition, addressed a personal appeal to the Kaiser for peace.[74]

The next day, Sunday 2 August 1914, there were two inconclusive Cabinet meetings, at the second of which Lloyd George threatened to resign. According to Paul Cambon, the French ambassador in London, 'The late Lord Rothschild told me that he was called to ... 10 Downing Street while the Cabinet was sitting on the morning of the 2nd. He told me afterwards that he had worked for intervention, but I was not quite reassured' in view of his previous strong support for Britain's neutrality.[75] On Monday 3 August, Lloyd George reversed his position when news came that Belgium had rejected an ultimatum 'for free passage through their territory and had appealed for British support'. Natty shared the viewpoint of the British government, informing his cousins that the infringement of Belgian sovereignty was 'an act which England could never tolerate'.[76]

Albert Ballin, owner of the Hamburg-Amerika steamship line, came to Britain in July 1914 on a semi-official mission to promote peace, talking to Grey, Haldane and Churchill. After his return to Germany, he sent a message on 1 August 1914 drafted by officials on behalf of the Kaiser to the manager of his London office for Mr Walter, the second-largest proprietor of *The Times*, which he wanted printed in the newspaper. It ran as follows:

> I hear with astonishment that, in France and elsewhere in the world, it is imagined that Germany wants to carry on an aggressive war, and that she has with this aim brought about the present situation. It is said that the Emperor was of the opinion that the moment had come to have a final reckoning with His enemies; but what a terrible error that is! Whoever knows the Emperor as I do, whoever knows how very seriously He takes the responsibility of the Crown, how His moral ideas are rooted in true religious feeling, must be astonished that anyone could attribute such motives to him ... He has worked unswervingly to keep the peace, and has together with England thrown His whole influence into the scales to find a peaceful solution in order to save his people from the horrors of war ... Now Germany's frontiers are menaced by Russia which drags

74 Joll, *The Origins of the First World War*, p. 30.
75 Steed, *Through Thirty Years 1892–1922*, Vol. 2 p. 16.
76 Stephen Koss, *Asquith* (London, 1976), pp. 157–60. RAL XI/130A/8 Natty to his cousins Paris 4 August 1914.

her Allies into the war, now Germany's honour is at stake ... Russia alone forces the war upon Europe. Russia must carry the full weight of responsibility.[77]

Looking back in 1915, he regretted that he had not told the Kaiser 'emphatically' that his fleet was not in need of protection and that the huge battleship construction programme was unnecessary. 'But I could never summon the courage to do so ... We were all too weak towards the Kaiser'.[78]

All these well-intentioned efforts for peace by Natty and Ballin were fruitless once Germany had violated Belgium's neutrality by invading her territory on 3 August 1914 and declaring war on France. The very next day, Britain declared war on Germany in support of her French ally.[79] Suspicious of a carefully planned German propaganda campaign in which Ballin was being used, Steed blocked the printing of the appeal. Yet as Sebastian Faulkes, who was serving on the centenary committee to plan the commemoration of the outbreak of the war, remarked '1914 was a political and diplomatic failure at a high level and that has to be recognised. So in 2014 there has to be a degree of breast-beating, a sense of mea culpa and an acknowledgment that this was avoidable', echoing the views of Christopher Clark in *The Sleepwalkers*.[80] More recently, Richard Evans argued that Fritz

> Fischer showed that official German policy in September 1914 did indeed aim at subjugating a large part of Europe to the political and economic domination of the Reich. But nobody has ever been able to demonstrate convincingly that the German government went to war in August 1914 with these aims in mind ... Far from being a ruthless dictator, the Kaiser, who changed his mind on an almost hourly basis in the run-up to the war, was a flighty, indecisive leader ... Nobody can say with any certainty what would have happened had the Germans won the war, but it is safe to say that the rigid imposition of a monolithic dictatorship on Germany and the rest of Europe by the Kaiser would not have been on the cards.[81]

77 Steed, *Through Thirty Years 1892–1922*, Vol. 2 pp. 17–18.
78 Lamar Cecil, *Albert Ballin* (Princeton, 1967), p. 212.
79 Stead, *Through Thirty Years 1892–1922*, pp. 17–18.
80 *The Times* 27 April 2013. Christopher Clark, *The Sleepwalkers: How Europe went to War in 1914* (London, 2013), pp. 555–62. Ferguson, *The Pity of War* (London, 1998).
81 *Guardian* 13 July 2013.

Seen from this vantage point, Natty and Ballin's efforts to keep the peace had much to commend them: both men were a step in advance of the bellicose thinking of most of their contemporary politicians and diplomats; they were true Europeans.

R. S. Sayers explained that

> The [financial] crisis began in the European stock exchanges, where fear of war – well ahead of London – caused heavy sales of internationally traded securities and the threatened or actual closure of one market after another. This partial breakdown of long-term capital markets preceded and – by placing impossible burdens of excess positions on the foreign exchange markets – largely caused the breakdown of short-term international credit. The collapse of international stock exchanges of course had immediate effect on the London Stock Exchange ... More certainly destructive was the implication of the foreign exchange crisis for the bill market, as it became apparent that foreign borrowers were not able to remit in good time to the London accepting houses funds for paying bills falling due in the next week or two.[82]

Swift action put an end to the immediate crisis. As has been stated, the Stock Exchange was closed on 31 July, while the regular Bank Holiday on 3 August was extended until 7 August to allow the banks to remain shut for an extended period of time. A month's moratorium – the word was not used – for bills of exchange was imposed. The bank rate was increased to 10 per cent, then rapidly lowered to 5 per cent by 8 August at the insistence of the bankers. To increase liquidity, government-backed Treasury notes for 10s and £1 were issued.[83]

Natty cooperated with the government to help rush the emergency measures into place, by participating in some of the sessions of the Treasury War Conference chaired by Lloyd George between 4 and 6 August 1914.[84] As he informed his French cousins on 5 August 1914, 'The Banking Community has had several interviews with the Chancellor of the Exchequer, and as far as one can judge everything will be done to satisfy their wishes,

---

82   Sayers, *The Bank of England 1891–1944*, Vol. 1 p. 70.
83   Sir John Clapham in ibid., Vol. 3 p. 34. R. Sayers, *The Bank of England 1891–1944* Vol. 1 pp. 74–5.
84   Richard Roberts, *Saving the City. The Great Financial Crisis of 1914* (Oxford, 2013), p. 117.

in fact in circumstances like the present ones the Governor, the Bank of England and the Bankers in general must work harmoniously together, other[wise] the position of the financial Community might become very serious and unpleasant.'[85] A couple of days later he admitted that

> We have had rather a rough time, the moratorium apparently has had a very good effect, naturally business will be dislocated for some time and it seems to be universal opinion that no one should attempt to earn kudos, by separating himself from the general action of the business community, we and all other accepting houses have instructed our bankers to refuse payment of our acceptances falling due & refer the same to us for re-acceptance for one calendar month under the terms of the proclamation.

A week later, Natty remained sanguine.

> You ask us my dear Edouard about the money situation here, the transactions are so vast and so complicated in the London money market that it was quite natural there should have been a good deal of disturbance at first. I should not like to say that all the difficulties have been got over but I can [say] this that for the present very efficient measures have been taken to bring back as far as possible a normal state of affairs, naturally there are continually points cropping up but as I venture to tell some of the highest authorities, it is best to deal with them when they crop up and not raise spectres in advance.[86]

What had Natty contributed in the negotiations to alleviate the crisis? Summing up, Marcello de Cecco claimed that Natty had warned Lloyd George's advisers of the immense disruptive power of the joint stock banks unless they were sufficiently appeased. 'They can play you a nasty trick, they are very powerful', he bluntly told the Chancellor. 'Second, he backed with his eloquent silence the Chancellor's proposal which the banks were finally persuaded to approve.'[87]

In addition, Natty was very helpful as regards the moratorium for payments of bills of exchange by the accepting houses. On 14 August

---

85 RAL XI/130A/8 Natty to his cousins Paris 5 August 1914.
86 RAL XI/130A/8 Natty to his cousins Paris 7 and 14 August 1914.
87 Marcello de Cecco, *The International Gold Standard: Money and Empire* (London, 1984), pp. 163–6.

1914, he informed Lloyd George that 'My time is your time, and whenever you wish to see me, I am at your service, and whatever I can do you may be sure I will do.'[88] When the government sent a questionnaire to bankers and business leaders as to whether the moratorium should be continued after 4 September 1914, the overwhelming majority of provincial manufacturers opposed its prolongation. City opinion, however, was strongly in favour of its continuance. On 28 August, Natty pressed the City view on the Chancellor of the Exchequer. Hence 'emphatically it is absolutely necessary that the moratorium should be renewed for at least one month. Were it not renewed the effect would be disastrous ... the oversea[s] trade and commerce would immediately cease. No one would care to accept fresh bills or undertake fresh liabilities. I cannot too strongly urge this point on you as I feel convinced were the moratorium suspended we might be appalled by the consequences.' 'When your letter arrived I was sitting in a Cabinet Committee which was considering the question', Lloyd George advised him, 'we took the view which you put so forcefully in your letter' and extended 'the general Moratorium for a month with an intimation that it would probably have to be extended considerably longer for Bills.'[89]

Towards the end of September, Leo informed his cousin that

> The moratorium which has been prolonged to 4th of October is coming to an end as far as acceptances are concerned on that day and in order to enable the accepting houses to honour their signature, the Bank of England is going to make advances to approved firms. As regards the Stock Exchange it has not been possible to open it ... proposals have been submitted to the Joint Stock Banks as to how their loans would be prolonged and asking them if they would agree to some suggestions which will be ultimately submitted to the Government, it is difficult to know if the Government can accept the plan *in extenso*, but there is no doubt that the Chancellor of the Exchequer will do his best to help also in this.[90]

---

88 National Archives, T 170/25 Natty to Lloyd George 14 August 1914.
89 Roberts, *Saving the City*, p. 185. National Archives, T170/25 Natty to Lloyd George and same to same 28 August 1914.
90 RAL X1/130A/8 Leo to Edouard in Paris, 25 September 1914.

While it was true that the acceptance market was stabilized, N. M. Rothschild & Sons lost almost £1.5 million in 1914 or about 23 per cent of its capital, an enormous sum and a heavy blow to its standing.[91]

'The financial crisis of 1914 was the most severe systemic crisis London has ever experienced – even worse than 1866 or 2007–2008 – featuring the comprehensive breakdown of its financial markets.' It was only due to the brilliant inventiveness of Lloyd George and his team of advisers that it was surmounted.[92] As Mervyn King has pointed out 'Over the next five months [after 7 August when the banks re-opened], the Chancellor, Lloyd George, and Treasury Officials essentially recapitalised the City. The Bank of England purchased a large volume of bills held in bank and other financial balance sheets in London with all potential losses indemnified by the Government on behalf of the taxpayer. The Bank bought one third of the entire discount market, some 5.3 per cent of GDP.'[93]

The goodwill which the Rothschilds now showed to Lloyd George was fully reciprocated on his part, as can be seen from the following passage from his *War Memoirs*:

> Amongst those whose advice I sought was Lord Rothschild. My previous contact with him was not of a propitiatory character. He had led the opposition in the City to my scheme for Old Age Pensions and to my Budget proposals in 1909, and I had assailed him in phrases which were not of the kind to which the head of the great house of Rothschild had hitherto been subjected ... However, this was no time to allow political quarrels to intrude into our counsel. The nation was in peril. I invited him to the Treasury for a talk. He came promptly. We shook hands. I said, 'Lord Rothschild, we have had some political unpleasantness.' He interrupted me: 'Mr Lloyd George, this is no time to recall those things. What can I do to help?' I told him. He undertook to do it at once. It was done.[94]

In a tribute to Lord Rothschild published in the *Reynold's Newspaper* after his death, Lloyd George extolled him as a person with

91   Ferguson, The *World's Banker*, p. 967.
92   Roberts, *Saving the City*, pp. 5 and 98–9.
93   Ibid., foreword p. ix.
94   David Lloyd George, *War Memoirs* (London, 1938), vol. 1 p. 70.

a high sense of duty to the State and ... [who] gave me the benefit of his wide experience and knowledge of finance; but he never confined help merely to good advice. He was prepared to make sacrifices for what he genuinely believed in. It will therefore surprise no one who knew him to learn that he was one of those who recommended the double income-tax, with a heavier supertax, for the war expenditure. He was essentially public-spirited. We need such men in this crisis, especially when they are men who have won dominating influence.[95]

In November 1914, the Chancellor of the Exchequer, in a supplementary budget with Natty's support, doubled the income tax, raising it from 1s 4d to 2s 8d and in turn increasing the supertax for 'incomes exceeding £3,000 to a maximum of 1s 4d on income in excess of £11,000'. Now that Natty helped rally City opinion behind Lloyd George, it was a far cry from the political dissent and turmoil of Edwardian England. After attending his funeral, Lloyd George remarked that Lord Rothschild was 'a nice old boy' who 'required time to think, but in due course usually came forward with some sagacious proposal. He gathered opinions from other people, and mostly made a wise selection'. His praise was sincere and heartfelt.[96]

So too, Lord Parmoor extolled Natty in his role of Lord Lieutenant of Buckinghamshire

for the splendid support he has made as regards the organisation of our Territorial Force [introduced by the Haldane reforms] and our military resources in this country since the commencement of the war. He has spared himself in no way, and he has done a good deal to arouse the enthusiasm and to develop the resources of our county. It is largely due to his influence ... that our county in proportion to its numbers has recruited ... the third best of any county in the United Kingdom.[97]

Like other members of the landed class, Natty was much involved with the army and in 1884 had risen to the rank of captain in the Bucks Yeomanry, a feat surpassed by Walter, who became a major in the same regiment.[98] On the occasion of Queen Victoria's jubilee in 1897, the Queen was received

95   *The Times* 5 April 1915.
96   Lloyd George, *War Memoirs*, pp. 71–2. Lord Riddell, *War Diary* (London, 1933), p. 72.
97   *Bucks Herald* 10 April 1915.
98   Rothschild, *Dear Lord Rothschild*, pp. 80–1.

at Slough by Natty as Lord Lieutenant and went in procession to Windsor Castle being accompanied by an advance 'escort of the Royal Bucks Yeomanry, and an escort of Household Cavalry'. In 1911, on the occasion of King George V's coronation, Natty, as Lord Lieutenant, presided over similar ceremonies in which the Territorial Force was given a significant role.[99] Various members of the family also helped sustain the war effort. By August 1915, Natty's nephew, Major Lionel de Rothschild, from his office at New Court, had recruited over forty young Jewish men from the East End and surrounding districts for the Royal Bucks Yeomanry, the Oxford and Bucks Light Infantry and the Bucks Royal Army Medical Corps to replace mounting casualties.[100]

During the First World War, Natty sent additional supplies of food on a regular basis and other items at his own expense to local commanders for their men.[101] Thus, on one occasion, he was thanked 'heartily for a consignment of 10 cases ... with all kinds of good things in them. The chickens are better than any chickens I have ever eaten, & I expect when I try the grouse, partridge and pheasants, &c, we shall find them equally good'.[102] On another occasion, Brigadier General Jackson remarked that 'I have only today learnt that the 5 telescopes which were handed to me some fortnight or so ago for the use of the artillery of this Division were a gift from you.'[103] So too, Lieutenant Colonel E. W. Wall wrote to Natty 'to acknowledge receipt with many thanks of 39 Balaclava helmets for the use of my regiment'.[104]

Natty also received reports from Winston Churchill's brother John, an officer in a cavalry regiment, about what was happening to his Rothschild relatives and labourers from nearby estates at the front. Their father Lord Randolph Churchill had been a close political friend.' I saw Jimmy

99 RA/PSO/GV/PS/MAIN/4179/1-2,5,34-7. Natty to Arthur Bigge 15 December 1910; Bigge to Natty 16 December 1910 and 20 March 1911; Tonman Mosley to Natty 27 May 1911; and Natty to Bigge 30 May and telegrams 7 June 1911.

100 Harold Pollins, 'Hellfire Corner: Jewish Soldiers in the First World War', *Bulletin of the Military Historical Society* (May, 1999).

101 RAL 000/848/37 Col. J. A. Tyler to Natty 14 January and 18 March 1915 and Cyril M. Hamil to Natty circa March 1915.

102 RAL 000/848/37 Col. J. A. Tyler to Natty 23 February 1915.

103 Ibid. Brigadier General H. K. Jackson to Natty 3 December 1914.

104 Ibid. E. W. Wall to Natty 11 January 1915.

Rothschild [Natty's cousin] the other day dash by in a large motor', John remarked. 'He is doing very well & is attached to one of the English armies. He was in a house ... when an enormous shell – nicknamed "Black Maria" landed on the roof. The whole house crumbled to bits and out of the debris emerged Jimmy untouched. I hear he behaved with great *sang froid* ... No one here dare conjecture when the war will be over. Shall we see next year's Derby?'[105] Whereas the Boer War enabled a gentleman to develop his military skills, the Great War was nastier and bloodier. 'I remember our fury in 1900 to find our field guns could not fire well over 4000 yards – but they use [them] in action at 2500 yards & even closer. The German fire is nerve wracking. They fire all day and most of the night ... The regulars of course do not think much of the territorials, and I have heard "Save us from Kitchener's army", very often said ...', John wrote a week later.

> Of course Yeomanry cannot compete with our marvellous cavalry – but I believe these young healthy country fellows will be of very great use and will help to take the strain off the regulars ... They [the deadly Maxim guns] are always right up in the firing line and the continuous rattle is disconcerting. It is all very horrible and I think everyone hates it. There is no enjoyment in this war – but it is better to be here than in London.[106]

When Natty sent Winston Churchill one of John's notes from the front in January 1915, he thanked him, adding that 'The waiting is dull, but time is on our side'.[107]

Colonel J. A. Tyler also kept Natty well informed about the ebb and flow of the battles along the Front. At the beginning of 1915, he reported that 'The rain has produced a curious state of affairs on some parts of our line. The Germans have been driven back by the trenches being full of water, & the Allies also, so that in places the combatants are 1000 yards apart instead of 100, & a kind of mutual understanding has caused them to stop firing at one another ...'[108] A month later, in February, he claimed that 'Close up to the trenches we observe & direct our gunfire from roofs of shell & bullet pierced houses, going to & fro among the ruins by curious ways through

105 RAL 000/848/37 John Churchill to Natty 29 October 1914.
106 Ibid. 5 November 1914.
107 Ibid. Winston Churchill to Natty 13 January 1915.
108 000/848/37 Col. Tyler to Natty 14 January 1915.

old partially demolished walls & outbuildings, with barricades erected with sandbags to screen from view ... & to protect from chance shrapnel or rifle bullets'. A week later, Tyler admitted that 'So little of importance has taken place along our front during the last two months, that the army feels that people are saying they are doing nothing ... A few unlucky shells bring up the numbers killed. I hear a big shell fell in a farm in which the Life Guards were resting. Seven were killed and many wounded ... The changes that have taken place in the staff, have I think, pleased the army. Sir William Robertson, who has become the Chief of staff is considered a very powerful man and there is no doubt he is infusing fresh vigour into everyone'.[109] The last letter received by Natty, despatched on 18 March 1915, ended on an optimistic note. After earlier describing a massive Allied bombardment 'with 4 to 5 tons of shells' being poured on the Germans during the first hour, Colonel Tyler noted that it was 'evident that the Germans are weakening ... since we took 2 or 3 units of Trenches from them ... they have only on one day made a serious counter-attack, & then resigned themselves to the loss of ground'.[110]

In September 1914 Natty told his French cousins that 'No one can foresee the duration of this horrid War, and whether it be long or short, here we are straining every nerve to carry the contest to a successful conclusion'. A month later, he was commending 'the endurance of the troops and the strategy and tactics of the generals which have enabled the Allies to drive the Germans back from the gates of Paris to the Belgian frontier ... the times are trying ... however we must not complain when one thinks of the many good and brave men who are fighting for their Country, suffering at all times, too many will never come home again, and we can only be grateful and proud that on the anniversary of the battle of Trafalgar ... [when] England expects every man to do his duty ... they are doing it'. By December, Natty apologized for a lack of information of substance, saying 'I have no news and only wish I could see the end of the war, we are raising a large number of troops here'.[111]

Having covered in an earlier chapter Natty's long-standing interest in public health reform and his service as Treasurer of the Prince of Wales

109 Ibid. Col. Tyler to Natty 8 and 14 February 1915.
110 Ibid. 12 and 18 March 1915.
111 RAL X1/130A/8 Natty to Edouard 15 September, 21 October and 17 December 1914.

Hospital Fund from its inception in 1897, it was not altogether surprising to find him, in 1914, in the position of Chairman of the Council of the British Red Cross. On 13 August 1914, Natty wrote a letter to *The Times*, pleading for a concentration of effort to avoid 'the same confusion that so crippled Red Cross effort in the South African War, with the same evils of overlapping, of uncoordinated and disunited work'.[112] At the end of the month, Northcliffe advised Natty, that he

> 'had just seen Mr Hedley Le Bas, who has kindly approached *The Times* on behalf of the Red Cross Fund, and I have undertaken to do that which *The Times* has only done on two previous occasions in its history – open a fund'.[113] Writing to the newspaper two months later, Natty acknowledged that 'At the outset we appealed for money for the general needs of the British Red Cross Society. Of late we have asked specially for 500 contributions, each of £400, wherewith to purchase motor ambulances. Today we are proud to record that our General Fund has reached half a million and that the 500 motor ambulances have been provided ... Our ambulances, swelled probably to 700 in number by the yet unrecorded offers of private cars suitable for conversion into ambulances and now being so converted, will probably cost an immense sum per week if they are to be maintained on the Continent in the high efficiency proper for their work'.

To perfect their organization, the British Red Cross Society and the St. John Ambulance Association formed a Joint Committee to coordinate their efforts.[114] Nor was this the end of Natty's campaigning, for he induced the Church leaders to issue an appeal for a service of intercession on Sunday 3 January 1915, when all the money collected would go to the fund. Similar arrangements were made with the Chief Rabbi, who undertook to pass on the offerings promised on Saturday 2 January to the fund.[115] Sir Robert Arundell Hudson, Chairman of the Finance Committee of the two organizations, wrote to Natty, warning him that a letter was on its way from the King expressing satisfaction at their work and asking him to approve their

112 *The Times* 15 August 1914.
113 RAL 000/848/37 Northcliffe to Natty 28 August 1914.
114 *The Times* 23 October 1914.
115 *Ibid.* 9 December 1914.

draft reply. He continued that 'I have spoken to Charles on the telephone, & he says I have his permission to disturb you this evening by sending a messenger down to Tring. The bearer will bring back your answer which I can thus get when I reach the office at 9 in the morning'. On 19 February 1915, King George wrote a letter to Natty asking him to pass on to the Joint Committee of the two societies his thanks for collecting one million pounds. He added that 'The Queen and I congratulate you personally in achieving the great results already obtained, and I wish you all success in the work which still lies before you and those who are associated with you'.[116] Although not a close friend of Natty like his father, the King had entertained Natty and Emma as his guests at Windsor Castle a year earlier for a brief stay.[117] Hence, although he had been a divisive political figure since 1908 and 1909, and a robust opponent of state-sponsored welfare for the masses, shortly before his death, Natty enjoyed great prestige as a national unifier in his role as Chairman of the Council of the British Red Cross and as a supporter of high taxation for all classes of society to prosecute the war to a successful conclusion.

Was Sir Robert Hudson's above letter merely couched in polite language or was it indicating that all was not well with Natty, who was convalescing at Tring? Lord Haldane, in his memoirs, reported that when he visited Lord Rothschild in his Piccadilly home in 1915, he 'found him lying down and obviously very ill. But he stretched out his hand before I could speak, and said, "Haldane, I do not know what you had come for except to see me, but I have said to myself that if Haldane asks me to write a cheque for him for £25,000 and to ask no questions, I will do it on the spot". I told him that it was not for a cheque, but only to get a ship stopped that I was come. He sent a message to stop the ship at once'.[118]

Without warning, a medical bulletin appeared in *The Times*, signed by three eminent doctors, stating that Lord Rothschild had undergone 'a serious operation' at 148 Piccadilly on Saturday 27 March 1915 and that he had 'made satisfactory progress'. He 'had been in indifferent health for some weeks, but it was thought that he was suffering from nothing more

116 RAL 000/848/37 R. A. Hudson to Natty 18 February 1914, King George to Natty and Queen Alexandra to Natty, both 19 February 1915.
117 *The Times* 30 January and 2 February 1914.
118 Haldane, *An Autobiography*, pp. 162–3.

severe than gout', reported the *Bucks Herald*. On Tuesday, it was still being reported that 'Lord Rothschild continues to make favourable progress' and 'on Wednesday morning, although the bulletin stated that he had passed a restless night and was not so well, the seriousness of his condition was not realised except by those in immediate attendance upon him. The end came with much more suddenness than was expected, for as late as three o'clock in the afternoon inquiries elicited the reply that danger was not apprehended. He passed peacefully away at half-past four' on 31 March 1915.[119] The surgery had been performed by Sir J. W. Thomson Walker F. R. C. S., who had been educated in Edinburgh, London and Vienna, and was a specialist in prostate and renal problems; Natty's death probably followed complications following prostate surgery.[120]

Natty was buried in the United Synagogue's Willesden Cemetery in the small enclosure reserved for his family. From 148 Piccadilly, the hearse, 'followed by two carriages with the chief mourners, left at noon' on Good Friday. 'Despite the short notice of the ceremony, thousands of people witnessed the last journey of a great man. Even in Park-lane and Edgware-road, there were miniature crowds, but the length of Willesden-lane for two miles was lined with silent mourners'. Among those who attended the simple burial service were Lloyd George, Lord Haldane, Herbert Samuel, Lord Reading, Lord Annaly representing the King, A. J. Balfour, Viscount Milner, and Lord Rosebery. Among the absentees was Alfred, a valetudinarian, who feigned illness and did not attend his brother's funeral. Natty's sons, Walter, who succeeded to the title, and Charles recited *kaddish*, the mourners' prayer.[121]

By 18 August 1915, probate had been granted of the will of Lord Rothschild. His estate was provisionally valued at £2,500,000 in net personality, that is, on all Natty's property except land and any interests in land passing to his heirs. Because of wartime conditions, it was also impossible to secure a valuation of some foreign interests; and, therefore, the value of his total assets was considerably higher than that disclosed in the first instance for probate purposes. Walter was not named among the executors

---

119 *Bucks Herald* 3 April 1915 and *The Times* 29 and 31 March 1915.
120 *Medical Directory* (London, 1914), p. 367.
121 *Bucks Herald* 10 April 1915.

of his father's will because of his erratic behaviour and his father's lack of
confidence in him. Instead he was granted a life annuity of £5,000 which
was in addition to two annual amounts settled on him under the will of
the testator's great-uncle, Baron Amschel Mayer Rothschild, and under the
will of the testator's uncle, Sir Anthony de Rothschild. To his wife Emma,
Natty left a life interest in his town house at 148 Piccadilly and £100,000
plus his jewellery. The residue of his estate and the major portion of his art
collection were bequeathed to Charles with a request that 'he will keep up
Tring Park as a residence for his mother during her life'. All Natty's capital
and any interest accruing on it in N. M. Rothschild & Sons was left to the
reliable and hard-working Charles and he had every confidence that his
brothers would admit Charles as a partner.[122]

Charles worked an eighteen-hour day, combining his duties at the
bank with some hastily snatched leisure hours devoted to his zoological
research; when he was made a partner and then quickly promoted to the
position of senior partner at the bank, overcoming his uncles' opposition to
this move, he even increased this frenzied pace of activity. That is because,
in addition to his other responsibilities, he became Financial Adviser to
the Ministry of Munitions. He also had to administer his father's estate
and raise the necessary cash to pay the death duties, in part achieved by
selling all the pedigree livestock at Tring Park. But despite the assistance
of Lionel, Leo's eldest son, who remained at the Bank for the duration of
the War, the manifold demands made on him were too severe for him to
cope with, resulting in him falling victim to the influenza pandemic of
1918 and succumbing to *encephalitis lethargica*. He travelled to Switzerland
once again to recuperate from the side effects of this debilitating disease,
acute depression. Charles committed suicide in 1923. Like his father,
he left an estate of more than £2 million, though in his case a slightly
smaller amount of £2.25 million and burdened his trustees with death
duties of at least £915,000.[123] To maintain Tring Park, his wife Rozsika
economized and Emma sold the dower house which Natty had provided
for her at Champneys on Wigginton Hill. Even so, Emma was still able to
maintain a staff of fourteen to assist her, while Rozsika struggled to sort

122 *The Times* 17 April 1915.
123 *The Times* 29 November 1923.

out the financial problems. Walter stayed on at Tring Park, living in his old bedroom .[124] Emma died on 8 January 1935, her son Walter, the second Lord Rothschild on 27 August 1937. It is noteworthy that the Dowager Countess of Gosford attended the memorial service for Emma, hinting perhaps at a reconciliation between them or was it that they were united in cherishing Natty's memory?[125]

Before her marriage, Emma had 'studied mathematics and science, and it was probably through her [influence]that her two sons [Walter and Charles] acquired their great interest in these subjects'.[126] Torn as he was between his love of science and his deep attachment to his father, Charles sacrificed his career as a scientist for years of service at the family bank. Emma, however, in certain respects, won a posthumous victory, for she was indeed also a lover of the countryside. When Charles' son Victor, her grandson, inherited Tring Park, he was pursuing the career of a research scientist at Cambridge and he decided to remain at Cambridge rather than become a country landowner with a town house in London. Thus, it was in her grandchildren, Victor and his sister Miriam, the latter a world-renowned expert on fleas, that Emma's ambitions were rekindled; both became Fellows of the Royal Society, the nation's premier scientific institution and remain the only brother and sister to do so. Tring Park and the Piccadilly house were unwelcome encumbrances. Forthwith, in April 1937, Victor put the art treasures of 148 Piccadilly, mainly assembled by Baron Lionel, up for auction, raising, to his amazement, £125,262. Away went the paintings by Dutch and Flemish masters; away went the fine pieces of French furniture 'by famous makers such as Boulle, C. Wolff, M. Carlin and G. Landrin'; away went the three Gobelins tapestries and the Sèvres porcelain, 'among them ... a superb apple-green *garniture de cheminée* of three vases and a dinner and dessert service of 225 pieces, many painted by Le Bel'; away went the eighteenth-century heavy English silver ornaments. His uncle Walter, who died on 27 August 1937, intended that his Tring Zoological Museum and its contents should be left to the nation. Victor generously offered the trustees, in addition, the house at Tring Park and

124 Wilson, *Rothschild*, pp. 328–30. Rothschild, *Dear Lord Rothschild*, pp. 287–8.
125 *The Times* 15 January 1935.
126 *The Times* 11 January 1935.

300 acres of parkland around it for the relocation of their natural history collection, an offer that, through timidity, the trustees turned down. Still feeling burdened, Victor wanted to rid himself of the 'grandiose' family estate and in October 1938, he disposed of nearly 2,000 acres of the land at Tring Park, consisting of eleven farms, smallholdings, cottages and shops, plus a stud farm.[127] For the duration of the Second World War the grand house itself was retained by the family, but a few years later it was sold for more mundane use as a school.

127 *The Times* 2 March and 29 April 1937 and 27 September 1938. Kenneth Rose, *Elusive Rothschild: The Life of Victor, Third Baron* (London, 2003), pp. 57–8.

Sources and Bibliography

PRINCIPAL ARCHIVES, LIBRARIES AND MANUSCRIPT COLLECTIONS

Alliance Israelite Archive, Paris
Birmingham University Library
Bodleian Libraries, Oxford
British Library, London
Central Archives for the History of the Jewish People, Jerusalem, Israel
Central Zionist Archives, Jerusalem, Israel
Hatfield House, Hatfield, 3rd Marquess, Series E Rothschild
Industrial Dwellings Society, London
Licensed Victuallers' National Defence League, London
London Metropolitan Archives
National Maritime Museum, Greenwich
National Archives, London
Rothschild Archive, London
Royal Archives, Windsor
School of Slavonic and East European Studies, London University
Southampton University, Anglo-Jewish Archives
Yivo Archives, Lucien Wolf-David Mowshowitch Collection, Record Group 348

UK PARLIAMENTARY PAPERS

Parliamentary Select Committee on Foreign Loans PP. XLIX 1875

Report of the Committee on Old Age Pensions PP. XLV 1898
Royal Commission on Alien Immigration PP.IX 1903
Russia No.2 (1882) Correspondence Respecting the Treatment of Jews in Russia PP.LXXXI 1882

NEWSPAPERS AND PERIODICALS

Brewers Journal
British Temperance Advocate
Bucks Herald
Daily Herald
Daily News
Daily Telegraph
Darkest Russia
Jewish Chronicle
Jewish World
Morning Post
New York Herald Tribune
The Tablet
The Times
The Times Literary Supplement

BIBLIOGRAPHY

Adler, Cyrus, *Jacob H. Schiff: His Life and Letters* (New York, 1928) vols 1 and 2.

Adonis, Andrew, *Making Aristocracy Work: The Peerage and the Political System in England 1884–1914* (Oxford, 1993).

Alderman, Geoffrey, *Modern British Jewry* (Oxford, 1998).

Allett, John, 'New Liberalism, Old Prejudices: J. A. Hobson and the "Jewish Question"', *Jewish Social Studies* 49:2 (Spring 1987): 99–114.

Allfrey, Alfred, *Edward VII and his Jewish Court* (London, 1991).

Alsberg, Paul A., 'Documents on the Brussels Conference of 1906', *Michael* 2 (1973): 145–53.

Bahlman, Dudley W. R., *The Diary of Sir Edward Hamilton* (Oxford, 1993).

Baron, Salo W., *The Russian Jews Under the Tsars and Soviets* (New York, 1987).

Battersea, Constance, *Reminiscences of Lady Battersea* (London,1922).

Baxter, John, *The Organization of the Brewing Industry*, London University PhD 1945.

Bayme, Steven Gilbert, *Jewish Leadership and Anti-Semitism in Britain, 1898–1918*, Columbia University PhD 1977.

Bein, Alexander, *Theodore Herzl* (Philadelphia, 1945).

Ben-Itto, Hadassah, *The Lie That Wouldn't Die, The Protocols of the Elders of Zion* (London, 2005).

Beloff, Max, *Lucien Wolf and the Anglo-Russian Entente 1907–1914* (London, 1951).

Bermant, Chaim, *The Cousinhood* (London, 1971).

Best, Gary Dean, *To Free a People. American Jewish Leaders and the Jewish Problem in Eastern Europe* (Westport, CT, 1982).

Beveridge, William, *Power and Influence* (London, 1953).

Black, Eugene C., *The Social Politics of Anglo-Jewry 1880–1920* (Oxford, 1988).

Black, Gerry, *J. F. S. The History of the Jews' Free School since 1732* (London, 1998).

—*Lord Rothschild and the Barber* (London, 2000).

Bloom, Cecil, 'Samuel Montagu and Zionism', *Transactions of the Jewish Historical Society* XXXIV (1994–6): 17–41.

Blunt, Wilfred Scawen, *Secret History of the British Occupation of Egypt* (London, 1907).

Boodry, Kathryn, 'August Belmont and the Atlantic Trade in Cotton 1837–1865', *The Rothschild Archive Review* (2009–10): 8–19.

Brawley, Edward Allan, 'When Jews came to Galveston', *Commentary* (April 2009): 31–6.

Bristow, Edward J., *Prostitution and Prejudice: The Jewish Fight Against White Slavery 1870–1939* (Oxford, 1982).

Brock, Michael and Eleanor, eds, *H. H. Asquith: Letters to Venetia Stanley* (Oxford, 1982).

Cain, P. J. and A. G. Hopkins, *British Imperialism: Innovation and Expansion 1688–1914* (London, 1993).

Cannadine, David, *The Decline and Fall of the British Aristocracy* (London, 1992).

—'The Empire Strikes Back', *Past and Present* 147 (May 1995): 180–94.

Carr, Raymond, *Spain 1808–1939* (Oxford, 1966).

Chamberlain, Austen, *Politics from the Inside* (London, 1936).

Chapman, Stanley, *The Rise of Merchant Banking* (London, 1984).

—'Rhodes and the City of London: Another View of Imperialism', *Historical Journal* 28:3 (1985): 647–66.

Clark, Christopher, *The Sleepwalkers: How Europe Went to War in 1914* (London, 2013).

Chernow, Ron, *The Warburgs: A Family Saga* (London, 1995).

Cohen, Lucy, *Lady de Rothschild and her Daughters 1821–1931*(London, 1935).

Cohen, Naomi W., *Jacob Schiff: A Study in Jewish Leadership* (Hanover, NH, 1999).

Cohn, Norman, *Warrant for Genocide* (Harmondsworth, 1970).

Conlin, Jonathan, 'Butlers and Boardrooms: Alfred de Rothschild as a Collector and Connoisseur', *The Rothschild Archive Review* (2005–6): 26–33.

Cook, Arthur, *Ace of Spies: The True Story of Sidney Reilly* (Stroud, 2004).

Cross, William, *The Life and Secrets of Almina Carnarvon* (Newport, 2011).

Davis, Richard, *Political Change and Continuity: A Buckinghamshire Study* (Newton Abbot, 1972).

—*The English Rothschilds* (London, 1983).

Dumett, Raymond E., ed., *Gentlemanly Capitalism and British Imperialism: The New Debate on Empire* (London, 1999).

Eckardstein, Baron von, *Ten Years at the Court of St. James 1895–1905* (London, 1921).

Endelman, Todd, *Broadening Jewish History: Towards a Social History of the Jews* (Oxford, 2011).

Dubnov, S. M., *History of the Jews in Russia and Poland* (Philadelphia, 1946), vol. 2.

Elon, Amos, *Herzl* (New York, 1986).

Emden, Paul H., *The Randlords* (London, 1935).

Feder, Ernest, 'Paul Nathan and his work for East European and Palestinian Jewry', *Historia Judaica* 14 (April 1952): 3–26.

Feldman, David, *Englishmen and Jews. Social Relations and Political Culture 1840–1914* (New Haven, 1994).

Feldman, Eliyahu, 'British Diplomats and British Diplomacy and the 1905 Pogroms in Russia', *Slavonic and East European History Review* 65:4 (1987): 579–608.

—'The French Rothschilds and the Russian Loan of April 1891', *Zion* 56:2 (1991): 162–72.

—'The Rothschilds and the Russian Loans: High Finance and Jewish Solidarity' in *Reshaping the Past: Jewish History and the Historians. Studies in Contemporary Jewry* vol. 10 (Jerusalem, 1994), pp. 231–56.

Ferguson, Niall, *The Pity of War* (London, 1998).

—*The World's Banker. The History of the House of Rothschild* (London, 1998).

—*The War of the World: History's Age of Hatred* (London, 2006).

Fishman, William J., *East End Jewish Radicals 1875–1914* (London, 1975).

Foster, R. F., *Lord Randolph Churchill: A Political Life* (Oxford, 1981).

Fraenkel, Josef, 'Herzl and the Rothschild Family', *Herzl Year Book* III (1960): 217–36.

Frankel, Jonathan, *Prophecy and Politics, Socialism, Nationalism & the Russian Jews 1862–1917* (Cambridge, 1981).

Friedman, Isaiah, *The Question of Palestine: British–Jewish–Arab Relations* (London, 1973).

Gainer, Bernard, *The Alien Invasion: The Origins of the Aliens Act of 1905* (London, 1972).

Garrad, John A., *The English and Immigration* (London, 1971).

Gartner, Lloyd P., *The Jewish Immigrant in England 1870–1914* (London, 1960).

—'Anglo-Jewry and the Jewish International Traffic in Prostitution', *AJS Review* (1982–3): 129–78.

George, David Lloyd, *War Memoirs* (London, 1938), vol. 1.

Gollin, A. M., *Proconsul in Politics: A Study of Lord Milner in Opposition and Power* (London, 1964).

Green, Abigail, 'The British Empire and the Jews: An Imperialism of Human Rights?', *Past and Present* (May 2008): 175–205.

—*Moses Montefiore: Jewish Liberator, Imperial Hero* (Cambridge, MA, 2010).

Gutwein, David, *The Divided Elite: Economics, Politics and Anglo-Jewry 1882–1917* (Leiden, 1992).

Haldane, Richard Burdon, *An Autobiography* (London, 1929).

Hall, Michael, *Waddesdon Manor* (New York, 2002).

Harris, Jose and Pat Thane, 'British and European Bankers 1880–1914: An "Aristocratic Bourgeoisie"?' in Pat Thane et al., eds, *Essays for Eric Hobsbawm* (Cambridge, 1984), pp. 215–34.

Hazlehurst, Cameron and Christene Woodlands, *A Liberal Chronicle* (London, 1994).

Henriques, Robert, *Marcus Samuel* (London, 1960).

Hirshfield, Claire, 'The Anglo-Boer War and the Issue of Jewish Culpability', *Journal of Contemporary History* 15:4 (October 1980): 619–31.

Hopkins, H. G., 'The Victorians and Africa: A Reconsideration of Egypt, 1882', *Journal of African History* 27:2 (1986): 363–91.

Hutchinson, H. G., *Life of Sir John Lubbock* (London, 1914), vol. 2.

Ireland, George, *Plutocrats: A Rothschild Inheritance* (London, 2007).

Jenkins, Roy, *Mr Balfour's Poodle* (London, 1954).

Jenkins, T. A., 'The Funding of the Liberal Unionist Party and the Honours System', *English Historical Review* 105 (1990): 920–38.

Joll, James, *The Origins of the First World War* (London, 1984).

Joseph, Samuel, *History of the Baron de Hirsch Fund* (Philadelphia, 1935).

Judge, Edward H., *Easter in Kishinev. Anatomy of a Pogrom* (New York, 1992).

Jonker, Jost and Jan Luiten van Zaden, *From Challenger to Joint Industry Leader, 1890–1939: A History of Royal Dutch Shell* (Oxford, 2007), vol. 1.

Kershen, Anne J., *Uniting the Tailors* (London, 1995).

Kessler, David, 'The Rothschilds and Disraeli in Buckinghamshire', *Transactions of the Jewish Historical Society of England* XXIX (1982–6): 231–52.

King, Frank H., 'One Letter and a New Understanding: The Rothschild Archive and the Story of the Pekin Syndicate', *The Rothschild Archive Review* (2006–7): 41–7.

Klier, John Doyle, *Russians, Jews and the Pogroms 1881–1882* (Cambridge, 2011).

Knox, D. M., 'The Development of the Tied House System in London', *Oxford Economic Papers* X (1958): 66–83.

Koss, Stephen, *Asquith* (London, 1976).

Kubicek, Robert V., *Economic Imperialism in Theory and Practice: The Case of South African Gold Mining Finance 1886–1914* (Durham, NC, 1979).

Kynaston, David, *The City of London: A World of its Own, 1815–90* (London, 1994), vol. 1.

—*The City of London: Golden Years, 1890–1914* (London, 1996), vol. 2.

—*The City of London: Illusions of Gold 1914–1945* (London, 1999), vol. 3.

Langham, Raphael, *250 Years of Convention and Contention: A History of the Board of Deputies of British Jews, 1760–2010* (London, 2010).

Landes, David, *Dynasties* (London, 2008).

Lazarus, Michael, *A Club Called Brady* (London, 1996).

Lee, Sidney, *King Edward VII: A Biography* (London, 1925), vol. 1.

Leslie, Anita, *Edwardians in Love* (London, 1972).

Levene, Mark, '"*Ni grec, ni bulgare, ni turc*": Salonika Jewry and the Balkan Wars 1912–1913', *Simon Dubnow Yearbook* 2 (2005): 65–97.

—*War, Jews and the New Europe: The Diplomacy of Lucien Wolf 1914–1919* (London, 2009).

Lindemann, Albert S., *Esau's Tears, Modern Anti-Semitism and the Rise of the Jews* (Cambridge, 1997).

Lipman, Vivian, *Social History of the Jews in England 1850–1950* (London, 1954).

—*A Century of Social Service: The History of the Jewish Board of Guardians* (London, 1959).

Levin, Vladimir, 'Preventing Pogroms: Patterns in Jewish Politics in Early Twentieth-Century Russia' in Jonathan Dekel Chen et al., eds, *Anti-Jewish Violence: Rethinking the Pogroms in East European History* (Bloomington, IN, 2011).

Loewe, Louis, ed., *Diaries of Sir Moses and Lady Montefiore* (London, 1983).

López-Morrell, Miguel A., *The House of Rothschild in Spain 1812–1941* (Farnham, 2013).

Luzzatti, Luigi, *God in Freedom: Studies in the Relation between Church and State* (New York, 1930).

Masterman, Lucy, *C. F. G. Masterman* (London, 1939).

Matthew, H. C. G., ed., *The Gladstone Diaries* (Oxford, 1990), vol. X.

Mazower, Mark, *Salonica City of Ghosts: Christians, Muslims and Jews 1430–1950* (London, 2004).

Mendelsohn, Richard, *Sammy Marks: The Uncrowned King of the Transvaal* (Athens, OH, 1991).

—and Milton Shain, *The Jews in South Africa* (Johannesburg, 2008).

Milner, Alfred, *England in Egypt* (London, 1894).

Monypenny, W. F. and G. E. Buckle, *The Life of Benjamin Disraeli, Earl of Beaconsfield* (London, 1910), vol. 1.

Morley, John, *Life of Gladstone* (London, 1903), vol. 2.

Morris, Sussanah, 'Market Solutions for Social Problems: Working-class Housing in Nineteenth-century London', *Economic History Review* LIV:3 (2001): 525–45.

Murray, Bruce K., *The People's Budget 1909/10: Lloyd George and Liberal Politics* (Oxford, 1980).

Nelson, Keith, *Britain and the Last Tsar: British Policy and Russia 1894–1917* (Oxford, 1995).

Nevile, Sydney O., *Seventy Rolling Years* (London, 1958).

Newman, Aubrey, *The United Synagogue 1870–1970* (London, 1976).

Nicholson, Harold, *King George V: His Life and Reign* (London, 1953).

Norman, Theodore, *An Outstretched Arm: A History of the Jewish Colonization Association* (London: 1985).

Oppenheim, Israel, 'The Kovno Circle of Rabbi Yitzhak Elhanan Spektor' in Selwyn Troen and Benjamin Pinkus, eds, *Organizing Rescue* (London, 1992).

Patai, Raphael, ed., *The Complete Diaries of Theodore Herzl* (New York, 1960), vol. IV.

Pearman, Hugh, *Excellent Accommodation: The First Hundred Years of the Industrial Dwellings Society* (London, 1985).

Penslar, Derek J., *Zionism and Technocracy* (Bloomington, IN, 1996).

Phillips, Gordon and Noel Whiteside, *Casual Labour: The Unemployment Question in the Port Transport Industry 1880–1970* (Oxford, 1985).

Platt, D. C. M., *Finance, Trade, and Politics in British Foreign Policy* (Oxford, 1968).

Pollins, Harold, 'Hellfire Corner: Jewish Soldiers in the First World War', *Bulletin of the Military Historical Society* 63 (May 1999): 169–224.

Porter, Andrew, '"Gentlemanly Capitalism" and Empire: The British

Experience since 1750?' in *Journal of Imperial & Commonwealth History* 18:3 (1990): 265–95.

Prochaska, F. K., *Philanthropy and the Hospitals of London: The King's Fund 1897–1990* (Oxford, 1992).

Ramm, Agatha, *Gladstone–Granville Correspondence 1876–1886* (Oxford, 1962), vol. 1.

Reinharz, Jehuda, *Chaim Weizmann: The Making of a Zionist Leader* (New York, 1985).

Rich, Norman and M. H. Fisher, *The Holstein Papers* (Cambridge, 1955), vol. 1.

Richardson, J. Hall, *From the City to Fleet Street* (London, 1927).

Riddell, Lord, *More Pages from My Diary, 1909–14* (London, 1934).

Ridley, Jane, *Bertie: A Life of Edward VII* (London, 2012).

Roberts, Andrew, *Salisbury, Victorian Titan* (London, 2000).

Roberts, Richard, *Saving the City: The Great Financial Crisis of 1914* (Oxford, 2013).

Robinson, Roland and John Gallagher, *Africa and the Victorians: The Official Mind of Imperialism* (London, 1981).

Rogger, Hans, *Jewish Policies and Right-wing Politics in Imperial Russia* (Los Angeles and Berkeley, 1986).

Rose, Kenneth, *Elusive Rothschild: The Life of Victor, Third Baron* (London, 2003).

Roth, Cecil, *The Magnificent Rothschilds* (London, 1927).

Rothschild, Miriam, *Dear Lord Rothschild: Birds, Butterflies and History* (London, 1983).

Rovner, Adam, 'A Portuguese Palestine', *History Today* (December 2012): 29–35.

Rubens, K. D., 'The 4% Industrial Dwellings Company Ltd: Its Formation and East End Developments, 1885–1901' in Aubrey Newman, ed., *The Jewish East End* (London, 1981).

Sachar, Howard M., *A History of Israel* (Oxford, 1976).

Sack, Benjamin Gutelius, *History of the Jews in Canada* (Montreal, 1945), vol. 1.

Samuel, Maurice, *The Strange History of the Beiliss Case* (Philadelphia, 1966).

Sayers, R. S., *The Bank of England 1891–1944* (Cambridge, 1976).

Schama, Simon, *Two Rothschilds and the Land of Israel* (London, 1978).

Schwarz, Daniel R., '"*Mene, Meme, Tekel, Upharsin*": Jewish Perspectives on Disraeli's Fiction', in Todd Endelman and Tony Kushner, eds, *Disraeli's Jewishness* (London, 2002).

Semenoff, E., *The Russian Government and the Massacres* (London, 1907).

Shaftesley, John M., 'Nineteenth-Century Jewish Colonies in Cyprus', *Transactions of the Jewish Historical Society of England* XXII (1970): 88–107.

Shaw, Caroline, 'Egyptian Finances in the Nineteenth Century: A Rothschild Perspective', *The Rothschild Archive Review* (2005–6): 34–8.

—*The Necessary Security: An Illustrated History of Rothschild Bonds* (London, 2006).

Sherman, A. J., 'German Jewish Bankers in World Politics: The Financing of the Russo-Japanese War', *Leo Baeck Year Book* XXVIII (1983): 59–73.

Soroka, Marina, *Britain, Russia and the Road to the First World War* (Surrey, 2012).

Slïozberg, Henri, *Baron Horace O. De Gunzbourg: Sa Vie, Son Oeuvre* (Paris, 1933).

Smith, Paul, *Disraeli* (Cambridge, 1999).

Southgate, Donald, *The Passing of the Whigs* (London, 1965).

Stanislawski, Michael, *Zionism and the Fin de Siècle* (Berkeley, 2001).

Szajkowski, Zosa, 'The Impact of the Beilis Case in Central and Western Europe', *Proceedings of the American Academy for Jewish Research* 31 (1963): 197–218.

—'Paul Nathan, Lucien Wolf, Jacob H. Schiff and the Jewish Revolutionary Movements in Eastern Europe 1903–1917', *Jewish Social Studies* XXIX (1967): 3–26 and 75–91.

Stead, Francis Herbert, *How Old Age Pensions Began to Be* (London, 1909).

Steed, Henry Wickham, *Through Thirty Years 1892–1922* (London, 1924), vol. 2.

Stern, Fritz, *Gold and Iron: Bismarck, Bleichroder and the Building of the German Empire* (London, 1982).

Supplementary Statement Issued by the Russo-Jewish Committee in Confirmation of 'The Times' Narrative (London, 1982).

Taylor, A. J. P., *The Struggle for the Mastery of Europe 1848–1918* (Oxford, 1954).

Thane, Pat, 'Financiers and the British State: The Case of Sir Ernest Cassel', *Business History* (1986): 35–61.

—*Old Age in English History, Past Experiences, Present Issues* (Oxford, 2000).

The Times, *The History of The Times: The Twentieth Century Test, 1884–1912* (London, 1947), vol. 3.

—*The History of The Times: The 150ᵗʰ Anniversary and Beyond 1912–1948* (London, 1952), vol. IV.

Thorold, Algar Labouchere, *The Life of Henry Labouchere* (London, 1913).

Tulchinsky, Gerald, *Taking Root. The Origins of the Canadian Jewish Community* (Hanover, NH, 1993).

Turrell, Robert Vicar, 'Rhodes, De Beers and Monopoly', *Journal of Imperial and Commonwealth History* (May 1982): 311–43.

—and Jean-Jacques van Helten, 'The Rothschilds, the Exploration Company and Mining Finance', *Business History* 28:2 (April 1986): 181–205.

Vincent, John, ed., *The Crawford Papers: The Journal of David Lindsey, Twenty-Seventh Earl of Crawford and Tenth Earl of Balcarres 1871–1940* (Manchester, 1984).

Vital, David, *The Origins of Zionism* (Oxford, 1975).

—*Zionism: The Formative Years* (Oxford, 1988).

—*A People Apart: The Jews in Europe 1789–1939* (Oxford, 1999).

Warnke-Dakers, Kerstin, 'Lord Rothschild and his Poor Brethren: East European Jews in London 1880–1906' in Georg Heuberger, ed., *The Rothschilds. Essays in the History of a European Jewish Family* (Sigmaringen, 1994), pp. 113–28.

Weintraub, Stanley, *Disraeli. A Biography* (New York, 1993).

—*Charlotte and Lionel: A Rothschild Love Story* (New York, 2003).

Weisbord, Robert G., *African Zion* (Philadelphia, 1968).

Weisgal, Meyer W., ed., *Letters and Papers of Chaim Weizmann* (Oxford, 1968–72), vol. 3.

Weizmann, Chaim, *Trial and Error* (London, 1949).

White, Jerry, *Rothschild Buildings: Life in an East End Tenement Block 1887–1920* (London, 1980).

Whyte, Frederic, *The Life of W. T. Stead* (London, 1925), vol. 2.

Wilburn, Kenneth, 'The Nature of the Rothschild Loan, International Capital and South African Railway Diplomacy, Politics and Construction

1891–2', *South African Journal of Economic History* 3:1 (March 1988): 4–19.

Wilson, Derek, *Rothschild: A Story of Wealth and Power* (London, 1989).

Wolf, Lucien, *Notes on the Diplomatic History of the Jewish Question* (London, 1919).

—*Essays in Jewish History*, Cecil Roth, ed. (London, 1934).

Zeldin, Theodore, *France 1848–1945* (Oxford, 1977), vol. 2.

Ziegler, Philip, *The Sixth Great Power: Barings 1762–1929* (London, 1988).

—*Legacy: Cecil Rhodes, the Rhodes Trust, and Rhodes Scholarships* (New Haven, 2008).

INDEX